1000 Recipes Cupcakes

1000 Recipes Cupcakes

igloobooks

Published in 2013
by Igloo Books Ltd
Cottage Farm
Sywell
Northants
NN6 0BJ
www.igloobooks.com

Food photography and recipe development: PhotoCuisine UK
Front and back cover images © PhotoCuisine UK

LEO002 0813
2 4 6 8 10 9 7 5 3 1
ISBN: 978-1-78197-440-7

Printed and manufactured in China

CONTENTS

SECTION	PAGE
POPULAR EVERYDAY	6
CELEBRATION AND PARTY	104
UNIQUE AND NOVELTY	202

POPULAR EVERYDAY

1

MAKES 18

Caramel Cupcakes

PREPARATION TIME 15 MINUTES

COOKING TIME 3 HOURS 20 MINUTES

COOLING TIME 1 - 2 HOURS

INGREDIENTS

400 g / 14 oz can of condensed milk
175 g / 6 oz / 1 ¼ cups self-raising flour, sifted
175 g / 6 oz / 3/4 cup light muscovado sugar
175 g / 6 oz / 3/4 cup butter, softened
3 large eggs
1 tsp vanilla extract

- Put the unopened can of condensed milk in a saucepan of water and simmer for 3 hours, ensuring it doesn't boil dry. Leave to cool completely.
- Preheat the oven to 190°C (170° fan) / 375F / gas 5 and line an 18-hole cupcake tin with silicone cases.
- Combine the flour, sugar, butter, eggs and vanilla extract in a bowl and whisk together for 2 minutes or until smooth.
- Divide the mixture between the cases, then bake for 15 – 20 minutes.
- Test with a wooden toothpick, if it comes out clean, the cakes are done.
- Transfer the cakes to a wire rack and leave to cool completely.
- Open the can of condensed milk and beat the caramel until smooth.
- Spread each cupcake liberally with the caramel, swirling with the back of the spoon.

Banoffee Cupcakes

2

- Add a chopped banana to the cake mixture and top the caramel layer with sliced banana and a dollop of whipped cream.

3

MAKES 12

Ice Mint Rose Cupcakes

PREPARATION TIME 35 MINUTES

COOKING TIME 15 - 20 MINUTES

INGREDIENTS

110 g / 4 oz / ⅔ cup self-raising flour, sifted
110 g / 4 oz / ½ cup caster (superfine) sugar
110 g / 4 oz / ½ cup butter, softened
2 large eggs
a few drops of peppermint extract

TO DECORATE:
150 g / 5 ½ oz fondant icing
12 sugar paste roses
white ribbon bows to decorate

- Preheat the oven to 190°C (170° fan) / 375F / gas 5 and line a 12-hole cupcake tin with paper cases.
- Combine the flour, sugar, butter, eggs and peppermint extract in a bowl and whisk together for 2 minutes or until smooth.
- Divide the mixture between the cases, then transfer the tin to the oven and bake for 15 – 20 minutes.
- Test with a wooden toothpick, if it comes out clean, the cakes are done.
- Transfer the cakes to a wire rack and leave to cool completely.
- Roll out the fondant icing between 2 sheets of grease proof paper and cut out 12 circles the same diameter as the top of the cupcakes.
- Wet the back of the icing circles and attach them to the top of the cakes, then top with the sugar paste roses.
- Glue a ribbon bow onto the front of each paper case.

Peppermint Rose Cupcakes

4

- Use a few drops of green food colouring to colour the icing pale green, kneading in a few drops of peppermint extract at the same time.

5

MAKES 12

Chocolate and Strawberry Muffin Cupcakes

- Preheat the oven to 180°C (160° fan) / 350F / gas 4 and line a 12-hole cupcake tin with paper cases.
- Beat the egg in a jug with the oil and milk until well mixed.
- Mix the flour, cocoa, baking powder and sugar in a bowl, then pour in the egg mixture and strawberry pieces and stir just enough to combine.
- Divide the mixture between the cases, then bake in the oven for 20 – 25 minutes.
- Test with a wooden toothpick, if it comes out clean, the cakes are done.
- Transfer the cakes to a wire rack and leave to cool completely.
- Whip the cream with the icing sugar and vanilla until it holds its shape, then spoon it into a piping bag, fitted with a large star nozzle.
- Pipe a big swirl on top of the cakes and top each one with half a strawberry.

Chocolate and Pear Muffin Cupcakes

6

- Replace the chopped strawberries with a peeled, chopped pear and decorate each cupcake with a thin slice of pear.

PREPARATION TIME 15 MINUTES

COOKING TIME 20 – 25 MINUTES

INGREDIENTS

1 large egg
125 ml / 4 ½ fl. oz / ½ cup sunflower oil
125 ml / 4 ½ fl. oz / ½ cup milk
350 g / 12 ½ oz / 2 ⅓ cups self-raising flour, sifted
50 g / 1 ¾ oz / ½ cup unsweetened cocoa powder, sifted
1 tsp baking powder
200 g / 7 oz / ¾ cup caster (superfine) sugar
150 g / 5 ½ oz strawberries, chopped

TO DECORATE:

300 ml / 10 ½ fl. oz / 1 ¼ cups double (heavy) cream
2 tbsp icing (confectioners') sugar
1 tsp vanilla extract
6 strawberries, halved

7

MAKES 12

Raspberry Cream Cheese Cupcakes

- Preheat the oven to 190°C (170° fan) / 375F / gas 5 and line a 12-hole cupcake tin with paper cases.
- Combine the flour, sugar, butter and eggs in a bowl and whisk together for 2 minutes or until smooth.
- Divide the mixture between the cases, then transfer the tin to the oven and bake for 15 – 20 minutes.
- Transfer the cakes to a wire rack and leave to cool.
- Beat the cream cheese and butter together until light and fluffy then beat in the icing sugar a quarter at a time.
- Add the vanilla extract then whip the mixture for 2 minutes or until smooth and light.
- Spoon the icing into a piping bag, fitted with a large plain nozzle, and pipe a swirl of icing on top of each cake, then top each one with a raspberry.

Raspberry and Orange Cream Cheese Cupcakes

8

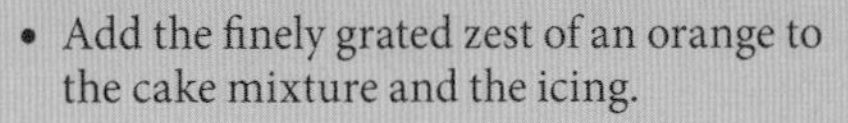

- Add the finely grated zest of an orange to the cake mixture and the icing.

PREPARATION TIME 30 MINUTES

COOKING TIME 15 - 20 MINUTES

INGREDIENTS

110 g / 4 oz / ⅔ cup self-raising flour, sifted
110 g / 4 oz / ½ cup caster (superfine) sugar
110 g / 4 oz / ½ cup butter, softened
2 large eggs
75 g / 2 ½ oz / ½ cup raspberries

TO DECORATE:

110 g / 4 oz / ½ cup cream cheese
55 g / 2 oz / ¼ cup butter, softened
110 g / 4 oz / 1 cup icing (confectioners') sugar
1 tsp vanilla extract
12 raspberries

9

MAKES 18

Flower Garland Cupcakes

Flower Spiral Cupcakes

10

- Arrange the flowers in a spiral on top of each cake.

Violet Garland Cupcakes

11

- Replace the flower waters with a few drops of violet extract and arrange crystallised violets in a garland on top of each cake.

PREPARATION TIME 15 MINUTES

COOKING TIME 15 - 20 MINUTES

INGREDIENTS

110 g / 4 oz / ⅔ cup self-raising flour, sifted
110 g / 4 oz / ½ cup caster (superfine) sugar
110 g / 4 oz / ½ cup butter, softened
2 large eggs
1 tsp orange flower water
a few drops of lavender extract

TO DECORATE:
200 g / 7 oz / 2 cups icing (confectioners') sugar
1 – 2 tsp rose water
multi-coloured sugar flowers to decorate

- Preheat the oven to 190°C (170° fan) / 375F / gas 5 and line a 12-hole cupcake tin with paper cases.
- Combine the flour, sugar, butter, eggs, orange flower water and lavender extract in a bowl and whisk together for 2 minutes or until smooth.
- Divide the mixture between the cases, then transfer the tin to the oven and bake for 15 – 20 minutes.
- Test with a wooden toothpick, if it comes out clean, the cakes are done.
- Transfer the cakes to a wire rack and leave to cool completely.
- Sieve the icing sugar into a bowl and add just enough rose water to make a thick, pourable icing.
- Spoon it on top of the cupcakes then arrange the sugar flowers in garlands before leaving the icing to set.

12

MAKES 12

Apple Crumble Muffin Cupcakes

- Preheat the oven to 180°C (160° fan) / 350F / gas 4 and oil a 12-hole silicone cupcake mould.
- Beat the egg in a jug with the lemon zest, oil and milk until well mixed.
- Mix the flour, baking powder and sugar in a bowl, then pour in the egg mixture and grated apple, and stir just enough to combine.
- To make the crumble layer, rub the butter into the flour and stir in the ground almonds, chopped almonds and brown sugar.
- Spoon the cake mixture into the mould and top with the crumble mixture, then bake in the oven for 20 – 25 minutes.
- Test with a wooden toothpick, if it comes out clean, the cakes are done.
- Transfer the cakes to a wire rack and leave to cool completely.

PREPARATION TIME 25 MINUTES

COOKING TIME 20 – 25 MINUTES

INGREDIENTS

1 large egg
1 lemon, zest finely grated
125 ml / 4 ½ fl. oz / ½ cup sunflower oil
125 ml / 4 ½ fl. oz / ½ cup milk
375 g / 13 oz / 2 ½ cups self-raising flour, sifted
1 tsp baking powder
200 g / 7 oz / ¾ cup caster (superfine) sugar
1 eating apple, peeled and grated

FOR THE CRUMBLE:
75 g / 2 ½ oz butter
50 g / 1 ¾ oz plain (all purpose) flour
30 g / 1 oz ground almonds
30 g / 1 oz blanched almonds, chopped
40 g / 1 ½ oz light brown sugar

13

Rhubarb Crumble Muffin Cupcakes

- Swap the grated apple for 2 sticks of rhubarb, cut into small cubes.

14

MAKES 12

Raspberry and Ginger Cupcakes

- Preheat the oven to 190°C (170° fan) / 375F / gas 5 and line a 12-hole cupcake tin with paper cases.
- Combine the flour, sugar, butter, eggs and ground ginger in a bowl and whisk together for 2 minutes or until smooth.
- Fold in the raspberries and divide the mixture between the cases, then transfer the tin to the oven and bake for 15 – 20 minutes.
- Test with a wooden toothpick, if it comes out clean, the cakes are done.
- Transfer the cakes to a wire rack and leave to cool completely.
- Beat the butter until smooth, then gradually whisk in the icing sugar.
- Spoon the mixture into a piping bag, fitted with a large star nozzle, and pipe a swirl of icing on top of each cake, then top with the raspberries.

PREPARATION TIME 30 MINUTES

COOKING TIME 15 - 20 MINUTES

INGREDIENTS

110 g / 4 oz / ⅔ cup self-raising flour, sifted
110 g / 4 oz / ½ cup caster (superfine) sugar
110 g / 4 oz / ½ cup butter, softened
2 large eggs
1 tsp ground ginger
75 g / 2 ½ oz / ½ cup raspberries

TO DECORATE:
100 g / 3 ½ oz / ½ cup butter, softened
200 g / 7 oz / 2 cups icing (confectioners') sugar
2 tbsp ginger syrup
12 raspberries

15

Redcurrant and Ginger Cupcakes

- Replace the raspberries with redcurrants.

16

MAKES 12

Lemon and Lime Cupcakes

PREPARATION TIME 30 MINUTES

COOKING TIME 15 - 20 MINUTES

INGREDIENTS

110 g / 4 oz / ⅔ cup self-raising flour, sifted
110 g / 4 oz / ½ cup caster (superfine) sugar
110 g / 4 oz / ½ cup butter, softened
2 large eggs
1 lemon, zest finely grated
1 lime, zest finely grated

TO DECORATE:
100 g / 3 ½ oz / ½ cup butter, softened
200 g / 7 oz / 2 cups icing (confectioners') sugar
1 tsp lemon juice
1 tsp lime juice
a few drops of green food colouring
lemon zest for sprinkling

- Preheat the oven to 190°C (170° fan) / 375F / gas 5 and line a 12-hole cupcake tin with paper cases.
- Combine the flour, sugar, butter, eggs and zests in a bowl and whisk together for 2 minutes or until smooth.
- Divide the mixture between the cases, then transfer the tin to the oven and bake for 15 – 20 minutes.
- Test with a wooden toothpick, if it comes out clean, the cakes are done.
- Transfer the cakes to a wire rack and leave to cool completely.
- Beat the butter until smooth, then gradually whisk in the icing sugar, citrus juices and food colouring.
- Spoon the mixture into a piping bag, fitted with a large star nozzle, and pipe a swirl of icing on top of each cake, then sprinkle with lemon zest.

17

Lemon, Lime and Orange Cupcakes

- Add the grated zest of an orange to the cake mixture and top the cakes with lemon, lime and orange zest.

18

MAKES 12

Chocolate-Chip Muffin Cupcakes

PREPARATION TIME 35 MINUTES

COOKING TIME 20 – 25 MINUTES

INGREDIENTS

1 large egg
125 ml / 4 ½ fl. oz / ½ cup sunflower oil
125 ml / 4 ½ fl. oz / ½ cup milk
375 g / 13 oz / 2 ½ cups self-raising flour, sifted
1 tsp baking powder
200 g / 7 oz / ¾ cup caster (superfine) sugar
100 g / 3 ½ oz dark chocolate chips (minimum 60% cocoa solids)

- Preheat the oven to 180°C (160° fan) / 350F / gas 4 and line a 12-hole cupcake tin with paper cases.
- Beat the egg in a jug with the oil and milk until well mixed.
- Mix the flour, baking powder and sugar in a bowl, then pour in the egg mixture and chocolate chips and stir just enough to combine.
- Divide the mixture between the cases and bake for 20 – 25 minutes.
- Test with a wooden toothpick, if it comes out clean, the cakes are done.
- Transfer the cakes to a wire rack and leave to cool completely.

19

White Chocolate Chip Muffin Cupcakes

- Use white chocolate chips in place of the dark chocolate chips.

MAKES 12

Chocolate Muffin Cupcakes

PREPARATION TIME 15 MINUTES

COOKING TIME 20 – 25 MINUTES

INGREDIENTS

1 large egg
125 ml / 4 ½ fl. oz / ½ cup sunflower oil
125 ml / 4 ½ fl. oz / ½ cup milk
350 g / 12 ½ oz / 2 ⅓ cups self-raising flour, sifted
50 g / 1 ¾ oz / ½ cup unsweetened cocoa powder, sifted
1 tsp baking powder
200 g / 7 oz / ¾ cup caster (superfine) sugar

- Preheat the oven to 180°C (160° fan) / 350F / gas 4 and line a 12-hole cupcake tin with silicone cases.
- Beat the egg in a jug with the oil and milk until well mixed.
- Mix the flour, cocoa, baking powder and sugar in a bowl, then pour in the egg mixture and stir just enough to combine.
- Divide the mixture between the cases, then bake in the oven for 20 – 25 minutes.
- Test with a wooden toothpick, if it comes out clean, the cakes are done.
- Serve warm or leave to cool on a wire rack.

21

Coffee Muffin Cupcakes

- Replace the cocoa powder with 1 tbsp of instant espresso powder.

22

Chocolate Orange Muffin Cupcakes

- Add the grated zest of an orange and 2 tbsp of chopped candied orange peel to the cake mixture.

23

MAKES 12

Strawberry and Lime Cupcakes

PREPARATION TIME 30 MINUTES

COOKING TIME 15 - 20 MINUTES

INGREDIENTS

110 g / 4 oz / ⅔ cup self-raising flour, sifted
110 g / 4 oz / ½ cup caster (superfine) sugar
110 g / 4 oz / ½ cup butter, softened
2 large eggs
1 lime, zest finely grated

TO DECORATE:
100 g / 3 ½ oz / ½ cup butter, softened
200 g / 7 oz / 2 cups icing (confectioners') sugar
2 tsp lime juice
a few drops of green food colouring
12 strawberries, hulled

- Preheat the oven to 190°C (170° fan) / 375F / gas 5 and line a 12-hole cupcake tin with paper cases.
- Combine the flour, sugar, butter, eggs and lime zest in a bowl and whisk together for 2 minutes or until smooth.
- Divide the mixture between the cases, then transfer the tin to the oven and bake for 15 – 20 minutes.
- Test with a wooden toothpick, if it comes out clean, the cakes are done.
- Transfer the cakes to a wire rack and leave to cool completely.
- Beat the butter until smooth, then gradually whisk in the icing sugar, lime juice and food colouring.
- Spoon the mixture into a piping bag, fitted with a large star nozzle, and pipe a swirl of icing on top of each cake, then finish with the strawberries.

Raspberry and Lime Cupcakes

24

- Replace the strawberries with 3 raspberries per cake.

25

MAKES 12

Chocolate Orange Marbled Cupcakes

PREPARATION TIME 15 MINUTES

COOKING TIME 20 – 25 MINUTES

INGREDIENTS

1 large egg
125 ml / 4 ½ fl. oz / ½ cup sunflower oil
125 ml / 4 ½ fl. oz / ½ cup milk
375 g / 13 oz / 2 ½ cups self-raising flour, sifted
1 tsp baking powder
200 g / 7 oz / ¾ cup caster (superfine) sugar
1 orange, zest finely grated
2 tbsp unsweetened cocoa powder

- Preheat the oven to 180°C (160° fan) / 350F / gas 4 and line a 12-hole cupcake tin with silicone cases.
- Beat the egg in a jug with the oil and milk until well mixed.
- Mix the flour, baking powder and sugar in a bowl, then pour in the egg mixture.
- Stir everything together just enough to combine then divide between 2 bowls. Stir the orange zest into one bowl and the cocoa into the other, then spoon alternate spoonfuls into the cases and marble together with a skewer.
- Bake the cakes for 20 – 25 minutes.
- Test with a wooden toothpick, if it comes out clean, the cakes are done.
- Transfer the cakes to a wire rack and leave to cool completely.

White and Dark Marbled Muffin Cupcakes

- Omit the orange zest and add 75 g of finely chopped white chocolate to the non-cocoa bowl.

27

MAKES 12

Chocolate Smarties Cupcakes

- Preheat the oven to 190°C (170° fan) / 375F / gas 5 and line a 12-hole cupcake tin with paper cases.
- Combine the flour, sugar, butter, eggs and cocoa in a bowl and whisk together for 2 minutes or until smooth.
- Divide the mixture between the cases, then transfer the tin to the oven and bake for 15 – 20 minutes.
- Test with a wooden toothpick, if it comes out clean, the cakes are done.
- Transfer the cakes to a wire rack and leave to cool completely.
- Beat the butter until smooth, then gradually whisk in the icing sugar and cocoa powder.
- Spoon the mixture into a piping bag, fitted with a large star nozzle, and pipe a swirl of icing on top of each cake, then decorate with the Smarties.

Chocolate Rainbow Cupcakes

28

- Add 75 g of Smarties to the cake mixture before baking.

PREPARATION TIME 30 MINUTES

COOKING TIME 15 - 20 MINUTES

INGREDIENTS

110 g / 4 oz / ⅔ cup self-raising flour, sifted
110 g / 4 oz / ½ cup caster (superfine) sugar
110 g / 4 oz / ½ cup butter, softened
2 large eggs
2 tbsp unsweetened cocoa powder

TO DECORATE:
100 g / 3 ½ oz / ½ cup butter, softened
200 g / 7 oz / 2 cups icing (confectioners') sugar
1 tbsp cocoa powder
Smarties to decorate

29

MAKES 12

Chocolate Peanut Cupcakes

- Preheat the oven to 190°C (170° fan) / 375F / gas 5 and line a 12-hole cupcake tin with paper cases.
- Combine the flour, sugar, butter, eggs, cocoa and peanut butter in a bowl and whisk together for 2 minutes or until smooth.
- Divide the mixture between the cases, then transfer the tin to the oven and bake for 15 – 20 minutes.
- Test with a wooden toothpick, if it comes out clean, the cakes are done.
- Transfer the cakes to a wire rack and leave to cool completely.
- Beat the butter until smooth, then gradually whisk in the icing sugar, cocoa powder and peanut butter.
- Spoon the mixture into a piping bag, fitted with a large star nozzle, and pipe a swirl of icing on top of each cake, then decorate with the peanut M&Ms.

Chocolate Reese's Cupcakes

30

- Top the cakes with mini Reese's cups instead of the M&Ms.

PREPARATION TIME 30 MINUTES

COOKING TIME 15 - 20 MINUTES

INGREDIENTS

110 g / 4 oz / ⅔ cup self-raising flour, sifted
110 g / 4 oz / ½ cup caster (superfine) sugar
110 g / 4 oz / ½ cup butter, softened
2 large eggs
2 tbsp unsweetened cocoa powder
2 tbsp smooth peanut butter

TO DECORATE:
100 g / 3 ½ oz / ½ cup butter, softened
200 g / 7 oz / 2 cups icing (confectioners') sugar
1 tbsp cocoa powder
1 tbsp smooth peanut butter
peanut M&Ms to decorate

31

MAKES 12

Rainbow Sprinkle Muffin Cupcakes

PREPARATION TIME 25 MINUTES

COOKING TIME 20 – 25 MINUTES

INGREDIENTS

1 large egg
125 ml / 4 ½ fl. oz / ½ cup sunflower oil
125 ml / 4 ½ fl. oz / ½ cup milk
375 g / 13 oz / 2 ½ cups self-raising flour, sifted
1 tsp baking powder
200 g / 7 oz / ¾ cup caster (superfine) sugar
3 tbsp multi-coloured sugar strands, plus extra for sprinkling
icing (confectioners') sugar for dusting

- Preheat the oven to 180°C (160° fan) / 350F / gas 4 and line a 12-hole cupcake tin with paper cases.
- Beat the egg in a jug with the oil and milk until well mixed.
- Mix the flour, baking powder, sugar and sugar strands in a bowl, then pour in the egg mixture and stir just enough to combine.
- Spoon the mixture into the cases, then bake in the oven for 20 – 25 minutes.
- Test with a wooden toothpick, if it comes out clean, the cakes are done.
- Transfer the cakes to a wire rack and leave to cool completely, then sprinkle with icing sugar and extra sugar strands.

32

Rainbow Nut Muffin Cupcakes

- Add 75 g of chopped mixed nuts to the cake mixture.

33

Rainbow Raisin Muffin Cupcakes

- Add 75 g of raisins to the cake mixture.

34

MAKES 12

Chocolate and Banana Cupcakes

- Preheat the oven to 190°C (170° fan) / 375F / gas 5 and line a 12-hole cupcake tin with paper cases.
- Combine the flour, sugar, butter and eggs in a bowl and whisk together for 2 minutes or until smooth.
- Fold in the banana and chocolate chips then divide the mixture between the cases and bake for 15 – 20 minutes.
- Test with a wooden toothpick, if it comes out clean, the cakes are done.
- Transfer the cakes to a wire rack and leave to cool completely.
- Beat the butter until smooth, then gradually whisk in the icing sugar and cocoa powder.
- Spoon the mixture into a piping bag, fitted with a large star nozzle, and pipe a swirl of icing on top of each cake. Top each one with a slice of banana and serve immediately.

PREPARATION TIME 30 MINUTES

COOKING TIME 15 - 20 MINUTES

INGREDIENTS

110 g / 4 oz / ⅔ cup self-raising flour, sifted
110 g / 4 oz / ½ cup caster (superfine) sugar
110 g / 4 oz / ½ cup butter, softened
2 large eggs
1 banana, chopped
50 g / 1 ¾ oz / ⅓ cup chocolate chips

TO DECORATE:
100 g / 3 ½ oz / ½ cup butter, softened
200 g / 7 oz / 2 cups icing (confectioners') sugar
1 tbsp cocoa powder
1 banana, sliced

Double Chocolate and Banana Cupcakes

35

- Add 2 tbsp of cocoa powder to the cake ingredients before whisking.

36

MAKES 12

Chocolate Mirabelle Cupcakes

- Preheat the oven to 190°C (170° fan) / 375F / gas 5 and line a 12-hole cupcake tin with paper cases.
- Combine the flour, sugar, butter, eggs and cocoa in a bowl and whisk together for 2 minutes or until smooth.
- Divide the mixture between the cases, then transfer the tin to the oven and bake for 15 – 20 minutes.
- Test with a wooden toothpick, if it comes out clean, the cakes are done.
- Transfer the cakes to a wire rack and leave to cool completely.
- Heat the cream until it starts to simmer, then pour it over the chopped chocolate and stir until smooth.
- Top each cake with a mirabelle, then spoon over the warm chocolate ganache and leave to cool.

PREPARATION TIME 30 MINUTES

COOKING TIME 15 - 20 MINUTES

INGREDIENTS

110 g / 4 oz / ⅔ cup self-raising flour, sifted
110 g / 4 oz / ½ cup caster (superfine) sugar
110 g / 4 oz / ½ cup butter, softened
2 large eggs
2 tbsp unsweetened cocoa powder

TO DECORATE:
200 ml / 7 fl. oz / 3/4 cup double (heavy) cream
200 g / 7 oz dark chocolate, minimum 60% cocoa solids, chopped
12 mirabelles preserved in syrup, drained

Chocolate Greengage Cupcakes

37

- Replace the mirabelles with preserved greengages in syrup.

38

MAKES 12

Cherry and Chestnut Cream Cupcakes

PREPARATION TIME 30 MINUTES

COOKING TIME 15 – 20 MINUTES

INGREDIENTS

110 g / 4 oz / 1 cup self-raising flour, sifted
110 g / 4 oz / ½ cup caster (superfine) sugar
110 g / 4 oz / ½ cup butter, softened
2 large eggs
50 g / 1 ¾ oz / ⅓ cup glace cherries, chopped

TO DECORATE:
225 ml / 8 fl. oz / 3/4 cup double (heavy) cream
200 g / 7 oz / 3/4 cup sweetened chestnut puree
12 glace cherries

- Preheat the oven to 190°C (170° fan) / 375F / gas 5 and line a 12-hole cupcake tin with paper cases.
- Combine the flour, sugar, butter, eggs and cherries in a bowl and whisk together for 2 minutes or until smooth.
- Divide the mixture between the paper cases, then transfer the tin to the oven and bake for 15 – 20 minutes.
- Test with a wooden toothpick, if it comes out clean, the cakes are done.
- Transfer the cakes to a wire rack and leave to cool completely.
- To make the topping, whisk the cream until it holds its shape, then fold in the chestnut puree.
- Spoon the chestnut cream into a piping bag fitted with a large star nozzle and pipe a swirl on top of each cake, then top with the glace cherries.

Orange and Chestnut Cream Cupcakes

39

- Replace the cherries with finely chopped candied orange peel and add the grated zest of an orange to the cake mixture.

40

MAKES 12

Lemon and Blue Sweetie Cupcakes

PREPARATION TIME 30 MINUTES

COOKING TIME 15 - 20 MINUTES

INGREDIENTS

110 g / 4 oz / ⅔ cup self-raising flour, sifted
110 g / 4 oz / ½ cup caster (superfine) sugar
110 g / 4 oz / ½ cup butter, softened
2 large eggs
1 lemon, zest finely grated

TO DECORATE:
100 g / 3 ½ oz / ½ cup butter, softened
200 g / 7 oz / 2 cups icing (confectioners') sugar
1 tbsp lemon juice
blue sweets to decorate

- Preheat the oven to 190°C (170° fan) / 375F / gas 5 and line a 12-hole cupcake tin with paper cases.
- Combine the flour, sugar, butter, eggs and lemon zest in a bowl and whisk together for 2 minutes or until smooth.
- Divide the mixture between the cases, then transfer the tin to the oven and bake for 15 – 20 minutes.
- Test with a wooden toothpick, if it comes out clean, the cakes are done.
- Transfer the cakes to a wire rack and leave to cool completely.
- Beat the butter until smooth, then gradually whisk in the icing sugar and lemon juice.
- Spoon the mixture into a piping bag, fitted with a large star nozzle, and pipe a swirl of icing on top of each cake, then finish with the blue sweets.

Lemon Jelly Bean Cupcakes

41

- Replace the blue sweets with lemon flavour jelly beans.

42

MAKES 12

Strawberry Sweetie Cupcakes

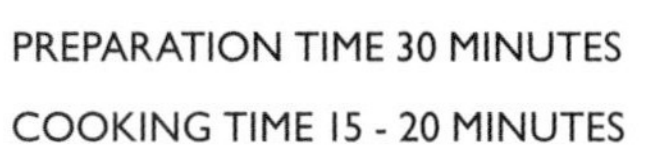

PREPARATION TIME 30 MINUTES

COOKING TIME 15 - 20 MINUTES

INGREDIENTS

110 g / 4 oz / ⅔ cup self-raising flour, sifted
110 g / 4 oz / ½ cup caster (superfine) sugar
110 g / 4 oz / ½ cup butter, softened
2 large eggs

TO DECORATE:
100 g / 3 ½ oz / ½ cup butter, softened
200 g / 7 oz / 2 cups icing (confectioners') sugar
2 tbsp strawberry syrup
12 strawberries, hulled
strawberry flavoured sweets to decorate

- Preheat the oven to 190°C (170° fan) / 375F / gas 5 and line a 12-hole cupcake tin with paper cases.
- Combine the flour, sugar, butter and eggs in a bowl and whisk together for 2 minutes or until smooth.
- Divide the mixture between the cases, then transfer the tin to the oven and bake for 15 – 20 minutes.
- Test with a wooden toothpick, if it comes out clean, the cakes are done.
- Transfer the cakes to a wire rack and leave to cool completely.
- Beat the butter until smooth, then gradually whisk in the icing sugar and strawberry syrup.
- Spoon the mixture into a piping bag, fitted with a large star nozzle, and pipe a swirl of icing on top of each cake, then finish with the strawberries and sweets.

Blackcurrant Sweetie Cupcakes

43

- Replace the strawberries and strawberry sweets with blackcurrants and blackcurrant sweets. Use blackcurrant syrup instead of strawberry syrup in the icing.

Orange Sweetie Cupcakes

44

- Add the grated zest of an orange to the cake mixture and icing. Decorate the cakes with orange slice jelly sweets.

45

MAKES 18

Chocolate and Pecan Buttercream Cupcake

PREPARATION TIME 10 MINUTES

COOKING TIME 45 MINUTES

INGREDIENTS

1 large egg
125 ml / 4 ½ fl. oz / ½ cup sunflower oil
125 ml / 4 ½ fl. oz / ½ cup milk
350 g / 12 ½ oz / 2 ⅓ cups self-raising flour, sifted
50 g / 1 ¾ oz / ½ cup unsweetened cocoa powder, sifted
1 tsp baking powder
200 g / 7 oz / ¾ cup caster (superfine) sugar
150 g / 5 ½ oz dark chocolate chunks (minimum 60% cocoa solids)
50 g / 1 ¾ oz / ½ cup pecan nuts, chopped

TO DECORATE:
100 g / 3 ½ oz / ½ cup butter, softened
200 g / 7 oz / 2 cups icing (confectioners') sugar
1 tsp vanilla extract
12 pecan nuts

- Preheat the oven to 180°C (160° fan) / 350F / gas 4 and line a 12-hole cupcake tin with paper cases.
- Beat the egg in a jug with the oil and milk until well mixed.
- Mix the flour, cocoa, baking powder and sugar in a bowl, then pour in the egg mixture, chocolate chunks and chopped pecans and stir just enough to combine.
- Divide the mixture between the cases, then bake in the oven for 20 – 25 minutes.
- Test with a wooden toothpick, if it comes out clean, the cakes are done. Transfer the cakes to a wire rack and leave to cool completely.
- Beat the butter with the icing sugar and vanilla until smooth and well whipped.
- Pipe the icing on top of the cakes, then top each one with a pecan.

Chocolate, Orange and Pecan Buttercream Cupcakes

46

- Replace the vanilla extract in the buttercream with the zest and juice of half an orange and add the grated zest of an orange to the cake mixture.

47

MAKES 24

Chocolate and Almond Mini Cupcakes

PREPARATION TIME: 25 MINUTES

COOKING TIME: 15 – 20 MINUTES

INGREDIENTS

1 large egg
½ tsp almond extract
125 ml / 4 ½ fl. oz / ½ cup sunflower oil
125 ml / 4 ½ fl. oz / ½ cup milk
375 g / 13 oz / 2 ½ cups self-raising flour, sifted
1 tsp baking powder
1 tbsp unsweetened cocoa powder
2 tbsp ground almonds
200 g / 7 oz / ¾ cup caster (superfine) sugar

- Preheat the oven to 180°C (160° fan) / 350F / gas 4 and line a 24-hole mini cupcake tin with paper cases.
- Beat the egg in a jug with the almond extract, oil and milk until well mixed.
- Mix the flour, baking powder, cocoa, ground almonds and sugar in a bowl, then pour in the egg mixture and stir just enough to combine.
- Divide the mixture between the cases and bake for 15 – 20 minutes.
- Test with a wooden toothpick, if it comes out clean, the cakes are done.
- Transfer the cakes to a wire rack and leave to cool completely.

Chocolate and Pistachio Mini Muffin Cupcakes

48

- Replace the ground almonds with ground pistachios and add 2 tbsp of chopped pistachios to the cake mixture.

49

MAKES 12

Glace Cherry Star Cupcakes

- Preheat the oven to 190°C (170° fan) / 375F / gas 5 and line a 12-hole cupcake tin with paper cases.
- Combine the flour, sugar, butter, eggs and cherries in a bowl and whisk together for 2 minutes or until smooth.
- Divide the mixture between the cases, then transfer the tin to the oven and bake for 15 – 20 minutes.
- Test with a wooden toothpick, if it comes out clean, the cakes are done. Transfer the cakes to a wire rack and leave to cool completely.
- Sieve the icing sugar into a bowl and add just enough water to make a thick, spreadable icing.
- Colour the icing with a few drops of pink food colouring then spoon it on top of the cupcakes.
- Press half a glace cherry into the centre of each cake and decorate with sugar stars then tie a ribbon round the paper cases.

PREPARATION TIME: 15 MINUTES

COOKING TIME: 15 - 20 MINUTES

INGREDIENTS

110 g / 4 oz / ⅔ cup self-raising flour, sifted
110 g / 4 oz / ½ cup caster (superfine) sugar
110 g / 4 oz / ½ cup butter, softened
2 large eggs
75 g / 2 ½ oz / ½ cup glace cherries, quartered

TO DECORATE:

100 g / 3 ½ oz / 1 cup icing (confectioners') sugar
a few drops of pink food colouring
6 glace cherries, halved
sugar stars and pink ribbons to decorate

Angelica Star Cupcakes

50

- Replace the cherries with glace angelica and colour the icing pale green.

51

MAKES 12

Simple Chocolate Cupcakes

- Preheat the oven to 190°C (170° fan) / 375F / gas 5 and line a 12-hole cupcake tin with paper cases.
- Combine the flour, sugar, butter, eggs and cocoa in a bowl and whisk together for 2 minutes or until smooth.
- Divide the mixture between the cases, then transfer the tin to the oven and bake for 15 – 20 minutes.
- Test with a wooden toothpick, if it comes out clean, the cakes are done.
- Transfer the cakes to a wire rack and leave to cool completely.

PREPARATION TIME 15 MINUTES

COOKING TIME 15 - 20 MINUTES

INGREDIENTS

110 g / 4 oz / ⅔ cup self-raising flour, sifted
110 g / 4 oz / ½ cup caster (superfine) sugar
110 g / 4 oz / ½ cup butter, softened
2 large eggs
2 tbsp unsweetened cocoa powder

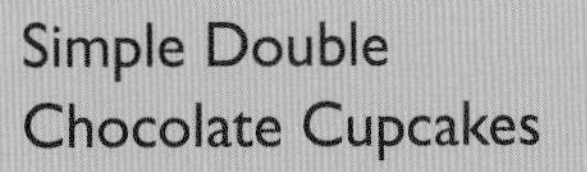

Simple Double Chocolate Cupcakes

52

- Add 75 g of chocolate chips to the cake mixture before baking.

53

MAKES 12

Glace-Iced Lemon Cupcakes

PREPARATION TIME 30 MINUTES

COOKING TIME 15 - 20 MINUTES

INGREDIENTS

110 g / 4 oz / ⅔ cup self-raising flour, sifted
110 g / 4 oz / ½ cup caster (superfine) sugar
110 g / 4 oz / ½ cup butter, softened
2 large eggs
1 lemon, zest finely grated

TO DECORATE:
200 g / 7 oz / 2 cups icing (confectioners') sugar
1 – 2 tsp lemon juice
purple sugar sprinkles to decorate

- Preheat the oven to 190°C (170° fan) / 375F / gas 5 and line a 12-hole cupcake tin with paper cases.
- Combine the flour, sugar, butter, eggs and lemon zest in a bowl and whisk together for 2 minutes or until smooth.
- Divide the mixture between the cases, then transfer the tin to the oven and bake for 15 – 20 minutes.
- Test with a wooden toothpick, if it comes out clean, the cakes are done.
- Transfer the cakes to a wire rack and leave to cool completely.
- Sieve the icing sugar into a bowl and add just enough lemon juice to make a thick, spreadable icing.
- Spoon the icing onto the cakes and sprinkle with purple sugar sprinkles.

54

Chocolate Glace-Iced Lemon Cupcakes

- Add 2 tsp of cocoa powder to the icing sugar before adding the lemon juice.

55

Lemon Curd-Iced Lemon Cupcakes

- Spread the cakes with lemon curd instead of the glace icing.

56

MAKES 12

Coconut Buttercream Cupcakes

- Preheat the oven to 190°C (170° fan) / 375F / gas 5 and line a 12-hole cupcake tin with paper cases.
- Combine the flour, sugar, butter, eggs and coconut in a bowl and whisk together for 2 minutes or until smooth.
- Divide the mixture between the cases, then transfer the tin to the oven and bake for 15 – 20 minutes.
- Test with a wooden toothpick, if it comes out clean, the cakes are done.
- Transfer the cakes to a wire rack and leave to cool completely.
- Beat the butter until smooth, then gradually whisk in the icing sugar and coconut syrup.
- Spoon the mixture into a piping bag, fitted with a large star nozzle, and pipe a swirl of icing on top of each cake.
- Sprinkle with chocolate vermicelli.

PREPARATION TIME 30 MINUTES

COOKING TIME 15 - 20 MINUTES

INGREDIENTS

110 g / 4 oz / ⅔ cup self-raising flour, sifted
110 g / 4 oz / ½ cup dark brown sugar
110 g / 4 oz / ½ cup butter, softened
2 large eggs
2 tbsp desiccated coconut

TO DECORATE:
100 g / 3 ½ oz / ½ cup butter, softened
200 g / 7 oz / 2 cups icing (confectioners') sugar
2 tbsp coconut syrup
chocolate vermicelli for sprinkling

Coconut and Orange Buttercream Cupcakes

57

- Add the grated zest of an orange to the cake mixture and icing.

58

MAKES 12

Dulce de Leche Cupcakes

- Preheat the oven to 190°C (170° fan) / 375F / gas 5 and line a 12-hole cupcake tin with paper cases.
- Combine the flour, sugar, butter, eggs and vanilla extract in a bowl and whisk together for 2 minutes or until smooth.
- Divide the mixture between the cases, then transfer the tin to the oven and bake for 15 – 20 minutes.
- Test with a wooden toothpick, if it comes out clean, the cakes are done.
- Transfer the cakes to a wire rack and leave to cool completely, then spread each cupcake liberally with dulce de leche and swirl with the back of the spoon.

PREPARATION TIME 20 MINUTES

COOKING TIME 15 - 20 MINUTES

INGREDIENTS

110 g / 4 oz / ⅔ cup self-raising flour, sifted
110 g / 4 oz / ½ cup caster (superfine) sugar
110 g / 4 oz / ½ cup butter, softened
2 large eggs
1 tsp vanilla extract
450 g / 1 lb jar of dulce de leche

Lime and Dulce de Leche Cupcakes

59

- Add the finely grated zest and juice of a lime to the cake ingredients before whisking.

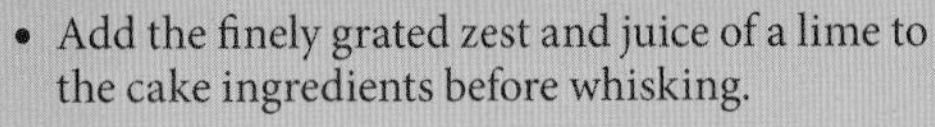

60

Candied Lemon Cream Cheese Cupcakes

MAKES 12

PREPARATION TIME 30 MINUTES

COOKING TIME 15 - 20 MINUTES

INGREDIENTS

110 g / 4 oz / ⅔ cup self-raising flour, sifted
110 g / 4 oz / ½ cup caster (superfine) sugar
110 g / 4 oz / ½ cup butter, softened
2 large eggs
75 g / 2 ½ oz / ½ cup candied lemon peel, finely chopped

TO DECORATE:
110 g / 4 oz / ½ cup cream cheese
55 g / 2 oz / ¼ cup butter, softened
110 g / 4 oz / 1 cup icing (confectioners') sugar
1 tsp vanilla extract
3 tbsp candied lemon peel, finely chopped
2 tsp demerara sugar

- Preheat the oven to 190°C (170° fan) / 375F / gas 5 and line a 12-hole cupcake tin with paper cases.
- Combine the flour, sugar, butter and eggs in a bowl and whisk together for 2 minutes or until smooth.
- Fold in the candied peel and divide the mixture between the cases, then bake for 15 – 20 minutes.
- Test with a wooden toothpick, if it comes out clean, the cakes are done. Transfer the cakes to a wire rack and leave to cool completely.
- Beat the cream cheese and butter together until light and fluffy then beat in the icing sugar and vanilla extract. Whip the mixture for 2 minutes or until smooth and light.
- Spoon the icing onto the cakes then sprinkle with candied peel and demerara sugar.

61

Candied Orange Cream Cheese Cupcakes

- Replace the candied lemon peel with candied orange peel.

62

White Chocolate Puddle Cupcakes

MAKES 12

PREPARATION TIME 15 MINUTES

COOKING TIME 15 - 20 MINUTES

INGREDIENTS

110 g / 4 oz / ⅔ cup self-raising flour, sifted
110 g / 4 oz / ½ cup caster (superfine) sugar
110 g / 4 oz / ½ cup butter, softened
2 large eggs
75 g / 2 ½ oz / ½ cup white chocolate chips

TO DECORATE:
100 g / 3 ½ oz white chocolate, chopped
sugar cake sprinkles

- Preheat the oven to 190°C (170° fan) / 375F / gas 5 and line a 12-hole cupcake tin with paper cases.
- Combine the flour, sugar, butter and eggs in a bowl and whisk together for 2 minutes or until smooth.
- Fold in the chocolate chips then divide the mixture between the cases and bake for 15 – 20 minutes.
- Test with a wooden toothpick, if it comes out clean, the cakes are done.
- Transfer the cakes to a wire rack and leave to cool completely.
- Melt the chocolate in a microwave or bain marie and spoon some on top of each cake.
- Sprinkle with cake sprinkles and serve while the chocolate is still liquid.

63

White Chocolate and Orange Puddle Cupcakes

- Add the finely grated zest of an orange to the cake mixture.

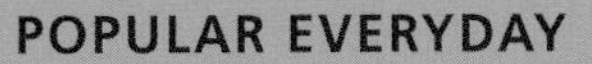

64

MAKES 12

Banana Cupcakes

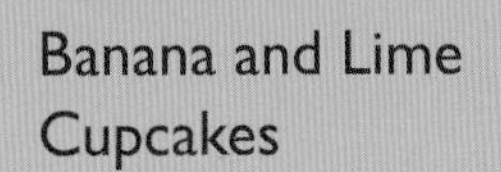

Banana and Lime Cupcakes

65

- Add the finely grated zest and juice of a lime to the cake mixture when you add the oil.

Banana and Mango Cupcakes

66

- Add 50 g of chopped dried mango to the cake mixture and decorate the cakes with dried mango and banana slices.

PREPARATION TIME 15 MINUTES

COOKING TIME 15 - 20 MINUTES

INGREDIENTS

3 very ripe bananas
100 g / 3 ½ oz / ½ cup soft light brown sugar
2 large eggs
125 ml / 4 ½ fl. oz / ½ cup sunflower oil
225 g / 8 oz / 1 ½ cups plain (all-purpose) flour
1 tsp bicarbonate of (baking) soda
dried banana chips to decorate

- Preheat the oven to 200°C (180° fan) / 400F / gas 6 and line a 12-hole cupcake tin with paper cases.
- Mash the bananas with a fork then whisk in the sugar, eggs and oil.
- Sieve the flour and bicarbonate of soda into the bowl and stir just enough to evenly mix all the ingredients together.
- Divide the mixture between the paper cases, then transfer the tin to the oven and bake for 15 – 20 minutes.
- Test with a wooden toothpick, if it comes out clean, the cakes are done.
- Transfer the cakes to a wire rack and leave to cool completely before topping with dried banana chips.

67

MAKES 12

Orange Cream Cheese Cupcakes

PREPARATION TIME 30 MINUTES

COOKING TIME 15 - 20 MINUTES

INGREDIENTS

110 g / 4 oz / ⅔ cup self-raising flour, sifted
110 g / 4 oz / ½ cup caster (superfine) sugar
110 g / 4 oz / ½ cup butter, softened
2 large eggs
1 orange, zest finely grated

TO DECORATE:
110 g / 4 oz / ½ cup cream cheese
55 g / 2 oz / ¼ cup butter, softened
110 g / 4 oz / 1 cup icing (confectioners') sugar
1 tbsp orange juice

- Preheat the oven to 190°C (170° fan) / 375F / gas 5 and line a 12-hole cupcake tin with thick paper cases.
- Combine the flour, sugar, butter, eggs and orange zest in a bowl and whisk together for 2 minutes or until smooth.
- Divide the mixture between the cases, then transfer the tin to the oven and bake for 15 – 20 minutes.
- Test with a wooden toothpick, if it comes out clean, the cakes are done.
- Transfer the cakes to a wire rack and leave to cool.
- Beat the cream cheese and butter together until light then beat in the icing sugar and orange juice. Whip the mixture for 2 minutes.
- Add the orange juice then whip the mixture for 2 minutes or until smooth and light.
- Spoon the icing into a piping bag fitted with a star nozzle and pipe a small rosette onto each cake.

Lemon Cream Cheese Cupcakes

68

- Replace the orange juice and zest with lemon juice and zest.

69

MAKES 12

Orange and Cranberry Muffin Cupcakes

PREPARATION TIME 12 MINUTES

COOKING TIME 20 – 25 MINUTES

INGREDIENTS

1 large egg
1 orange, zest finely grated
125 ml / 4 ½ fl. oz / ½ cup sunflower oil
125 ml / 4 ½ fl. oz / ½ cup milk
375 g / 13 oz / 2 ½ cups self-raising flour, sifted
1 tsp baking powder
200 g / 7 oz / ¾ cup caster (superfine) sugar
75 g / 2 ½ oz / ⅓ cup dried cranberries
icing (confectioners') sugar for dusting

- Preheat the oven to 180°C (160° fan) / 350F / gas 4 and line a deep 12-hole cupcake tin with strips of greaseproof paper.
- Beat the egg in a jug with the orange zest, oil and milk until well mixed.
- Mix the flour, baking powder and sugar in a bowl, then pour in the egg mixture and dried cranberries and stir just enough to combine.
- Spoon the mixture into the tin, then bake in the oven for 20 – 25 minutes.
- Test with a wooden toothpick, if it comes out clean, the cakes are done.
- Transfer the cakes to a wire rack and leave to cool completely before dusting lightly with icing sugar.

Orange and Sultana Muffin Cupcakes

70

- Replace the cranberries with sultanas.

71

MAKES 12

Oat Cupcakes with Choc-Chip Buttercream

- Preheat the oven to 190°C (170° fan) / 375F / gas 5 and line a 12-hole cupcake tin with paper cases.
- Combine the flour, sugar, butter, eggs and oats in a bowl and whisk together for 2 minutes or until smooth.
- Divide the mixture between the cases, then transfer the tin to the oven and bake for 15 – 20 minutes.
- Test with a wooden toothpick, if it comes out clean, the cakes are done.
- Transfer the cakes to a wire rack and leave to cool completely.
- Beat the butter until smooth, then gradually whisk in the icing sugar and vanilla extract.
- Spoon the mixture into a piping bag, fitted with a large star nozzle, and pipe a swirl of icing on top of each cake. Sprinkle with chocolate chips.

PREPARATION TIME 30 MINUTES

COOKING TIME 15 - 20 MINUTES

INGREDIENTS

110 g / 4 oz / ⅔ cup self-raising flour, sifted
110 g / 4 oz / ½ cup caster (superfine) sugar
110 g / 4 oz / ½ cup butter, softened
2 large eggs
50 g / 1 ¾ oz / ½ cup rolled porridge oats

TO DECORATE:
100 g / 3 ½ oz / ½ cup butter, softened
200 g / 7 oz / 2 cups icing (confectioners') sugar
1 tsp vanilla extract
3 tbsp dark chocolate chips

72

Oat Cupcakes with Granola Buttercream

- Use 4 tbsp of granola to decorate the cakes instead of the chocolate chips.

73

MAKES 12

Lime Curd Cupcakes

- Preheat the oven to 190°C (170° fan) / 375F / gas 5 and line a 12-hole cupcake tin with paper cases.
- Combine the flour, sugar, butter, eggs and lime zest in a bowl and whisk together for 2 minutes or until smooth.
- Divide the mixture between the cases, then transfer the tin to the oven and bake for 15 – 20 minutes.
- Transfer the cakes to a wire rack and leave to cool.
- Dissolve the cornflour in the lime juice and put it in a saucepan with the rest of the ingredients.
- Stir constantly over a medium heat to melt the butter and dissolve the sugar.
- After 6 or 7 minutes the mixture should thicken. Continue to stir until it starts to bubble then leave to cool to room temperature.
- Spoon the lime curd on top of the cakes and sprinkle with lime zest.

PREPARATION TIME 30 MINUTES

COOKING TIME 15 - 20 MINUTES

INGREDIENTS

110 g / 4 oz / ⅔ cup self-raising flour, sifted
110 g / 4 oz / ½ cup caster (superfine) sugar
110 g / 4 oz / ½ cup butter, softened
2 large eggs
1 lime, zest finely grated

TO DECORATE:
1 tsp cornflour (cornstarch)
3 limes, juiced
2 large eggs, beaten
110 g / 4 oz / 1 cup butter
85 g / 3 oz / ⅓ cup caster (superfine) sugar
finely pared lime zest for sprinkling

74

Grapefruit Curd Cupcakes

- Replace the lime juice with 100 ml of freshly squeezed grapefruit juice.

75

MAKES 12

Vanilla Cupcakes with Glace Icing

Sultana Cupcakes with Glace Icing

76

- Add 75 g of sultanas to the cake mixture.

Nutty Cupcakes with Glace Icing

77

- Add 75 g of chopped mixed nuts to the cake mixture.

PREPARATION TIME 30 MINUTES

COOKING TIME 15 - 20 MINUTES

INGREDIENTS

110 g / 4 oz / ⅔ cup self-raising flour, sifted
110 g / 4 oz / ½ cup caster (superfine) sugar
110 g / 4 oz / ½ cup butter, softened
2 large eggs
1 tsp vanilla extract

TO DECORATE:
200 g / 7 oz / 2 cups icing (confectioners') sugar
edible metallic balls to decorate

- Preheat the oven to 190°C (170° fan) / 375F / gas 5 and line a 12-hole cupcake tin with paper cases.
- Combine the flour, sugar, butter, eggs and vanilla in a bowl and whisk together for 2 minutes or until smooth.
- Divide the mixture between the cases, then transfer the tin to the oven and bake for 15 – 20 minutes.
- Test with a wooden toothpick, if it comes out clean, the cakes are done.
- Transfer the cakes to a wire rack and leave to cool completely.
- Sieve the icing sugar into a bowl and add just enough water to make a thick, pourable icing.
- Spoon the icing onto the cakes and decorate with edible metallic balls.

78

MAKES 12

Chocolate Chip Buttercream Cupcakes

- Preheat the oven to 190°C (170° fan) / 375F / gas 5 and line a 12-hole cupcake tin with paper cases.
- Combine the flour, sugar, butter, eggs, cocoa powder and chocolate chips in a bowl and whisk together for 2 minutes or until smooth.
- Divide the mixture between the cases, then transfer the tin to the oven and bake for 15 – 20 minutes.
- Test with a wooden toothpick, if it comes out clean, the cakes are done.
- Transfer the cakes to a wire rack and leave to cool completely.
- Beat the butter until smooth, then gradually whisk in the icing sugar and cocoa powder.
- Spoon the mixture into a piping bag, fitted with a small star nozzle, and pipe rosettes of the icing on top.

PREPARATION TIME 30 MINUTES

COOKING TIME 15 - 20 MINUTES

INGREDIENTS

110 g / 4 oz / ⅔ cup self-raising flour, sifted
110 g / 4 oz / ½ cup caster (superfine) sugar
110 g / 4 oz / ½ cup butter, softened
2 large eggs
2 tbsp unsweetened cocoa powder
100 g / 3 ½ oz / ⅔ cup dark chocolate chips

TO DECORATE:
100 g / 3 ½ oz / ½ cup butter, softened
200 g / 7 oz / 2 cups icing (confectioners') sugar
1 tbsp unsweetened cocoa powder

Spotty Chocolate Buttercream Cupcakes

79

- Add 75 g of white chocolate chips to the cake mixture and top the buttercream with more white chocolate chips.

80

MAKES 12

Gold Nugget Buttercream Cupcakes

- Preheat the oven to 190°C (170° fan) / 375F / gas 5 and line a 12-hole cupcake tin with paper cases.
- Combine the flour, sugar, butter, eggs and ground ginger in a bowl and whisk together for 2 minutes or until smooth.
- Fold in the stem ginger then divide the mixture between the cases and bake for 15 – 20 minutes.
- Transfer the cakes to a wire rack and leave to cool.
- Beat the butter until smooth, then gradually whisk in the icing sugar until smooth.
- Spoon the icing into a piping bag and pipe a big swirl on top of each cake.
- Lay the yellow Smarties out on a sheet of newspaper and spray them lightly with edible gold spray. Leave them to dry for a few minutes, then arrange them on top of the cakes.

PREPARATION TIME 40 MINUTES

COOKING TIME 15 - 20 MINUTES

INGREDIENTS

110 g / 4 oz / ⅔ cup self-raising flour, sifted
110 g / 4 oz / ½ cup caster (superfine) sugar
110 g / 4 oz / ½ cup butter, softened
2 large eggs
1 tsp ground ginger
3 pieces of stem ginger, roughly chopped

TO DECORATE:
100 g / 3 ½ oz / ½ cup butter, softened
200 g / 7 oz / 2 cups icing (confectioners') sugar
yellow Smarties and edible gold spray to decorate

Silver Nugget Buttercream Cupcakes

- Use purple Smarties and spray them silver.

82

MAKES 12

Carrot and Lemon Cupcakes

PREPARATION TIME 35 MINUTES

COOKING TIME 20 – 25 MINUTES

INGREDIENTS

175 g / 6 oz / 1 cup soft brown sugar
2 large eggs
150 ml / 5 fl. oz / ⅔ cup sunflower oil
175 g / 6 oz / 1 ¼ cups wholemeal flour
3 tsp baking powder
1 lemon, zest finely grated
200 g / 7 oz / 1 ⅔ cups carrots, peeled and coarsely grated

TO DECORATE:

110 g / 4 oz / ½ cup cream cheese
55 g / 2 oz / ¼ cup butter, softened
110 g / 4 oz / 1 cup icing (confectioners') sugar
1 lemon, juiced and zest finely grated

- Preheat the oven to 190°C (170° fan) / 375F / gas 5 and line a 12-hole cupcake tin with paper cases.
- Whisk the sugar, eggs and oil together for 3 minutes.
- Fold in the flour, baking powder and lemon zest, followed by the grated carrots.
- Divide the mixture between the paper cases, and bake for 20 - 25 minutes.
- Test with a wooden toothpick, if it comes out clean, the cakes are done. Transfer the cakes to a wire rack and leave to cool completely.
- Beat the cream cheese and butter together until light and fluffy then beat in the icing sugar a quarter at a time. Add 1 tbsp of the lemon juice and whip for 2 minutes.
- Spoon the icing onto the cakes and sprinkle with a little lemon zest.

Courgette and Lemon Cupcakes

83

- Grate 200 g of courgette into a clean tea towel, then wrap up and squeeze out all the liquid. Use in place of the carrots.

84

MAKES 12

Chestnut Muffin Cupcakes

PREPARATION TIME 30 MINUTES

COOKING TIME 15 – 20 MINUTES

INGREDIENTS

1 large egg
125 ml / 4 ½ fl. oz / ½ cup sunflower oil
125 ml / 4 ½ fl. oz / ½ cup milk
375 g / 13 oz / 2 ½ cups self-raising flour, sifted
1 tsp baking powder
200 g / 7 oz / ¾ cup caster (superfine) sugar
50 g / 1 ¾ oz / ½ cup canned chestnuts, chopped

TO DECORATE:

225 ml / 8 fl. oz / 3/4 cup double (heavy) cream
200 g / 7 oz / 3/4 cup sweetened chestnut puree
chocolate vermicelli for sprinkling

- Preheat the oven to 180°C (160° fan) / 350F / gas 4 and line a deep 12-hole cupcake tin with paper cases.
- Beat the egg in a jug with the oil and milk until well mixed.
- Mix the flour, baking powder, sugar and chopped chestnuts in a bowl, then pour in the egg mixture and stir just enough to combine.
- Spoon the mixture into the cases, then bake in the oven for 20 – 25 minutes.
- Transfer the cakes to a wire rack and leave to cool completely.
- To make the topping, whisk the cream until it holds its shape, then fold in the chestnut puree.
- Spoon the chestnut cream into a piping bag fitted with a large star nozzle and pipe a swirl on top of each cake, then sprinkle with chocolate vermicelli.

Chestnut and Chocolate Chunk Muffin Cupcakes

85

- Add 100 g of dark chocolate chunks to the cake mixture.

86

MAKES 12

Orange Jelly Sweet Cupcakes

PREPARATION TIME 1 HOUR

COOKING TIME 15 - 20 MINUTES

INGREDIENTS

110 g / 4 oz / ⅔ cup self-raising flour, sifted
110 g / 4 oz / ½ cup caster (superfine) sugar
110 g / 4 oz / ½ cup butter, softened
2 large eggs
1 orange, juiced and zest finely grated

TO DECORATE:
200 g / 7 oz / 2 cups icing (confectioners') sugar
1 – 2 tsp orange juice
a few drops of dark pink food colouring
36 orange jelly sweets

- Preheat the oven to 190°C (170° fan) / 375F / gas 5 and line a 12-hole cupcake tin with paper cases.
- Combine the flour, sugar, butter, eggs and orange juice and zest in a bowl and whisk together for 2 minutes or until smooth.
- Divide the mixture between the cases, then transfer the tin to the oven and bake for 15 – 20 minutes.
- Test with a wooden toothpick, if it comes out clean, the cakes are done.
- Transfer the cakes to a wire rack and leave to cool completely.
- Sieve the icing sugar into a bowl and add just enough orange juice to make a thick spreadable icing.
- Add a few drops of food colouring and streak it through, then spoon the icing onto the cakes and top each one with 3 orange jelly sweets.

87

Wine Gum Cupcakes

- Replace the orange jelly sweets with wine gums.

88

Lemon Bonbon Cupcakes

- Replace the orange juice and zest with lemon juice and zest and top the cakes with lemon bonbons.

89

Vanilla Cupcakes with Chocolate Caramel

MAKES 18

PREPARATION TIME 15 MINUTES

COOKING TIME 3 HOURS
20 MINUTES

INGREDIENTS

175 g / 6 oz / 1 ¼ cups self-raising flour, sifted
175 g / 6 oz / 3/4 cup caster (superfine) sugar
175 g / 6 oz / 3/4 cup butter, softened
3 large eggs
1 tsp vanilla extract

FOR THE TOPPING:
400 g / 14 oz can of condensed milk
200 g / 7 oz dark chocolate, finely chopped

- Make the caramel topping in advance. Put the unopened can of condensed milk in a saucepan of water and simmer for 3 hours, adding more water as necessary to ensure it doesn't boil dry. Leave the can to cool a little.
- When the can is just cool enough to handle, open it and scoop half of the caramel into a bowl. Stir in the chocolate until melted and smoothly combined.
- Store the other half of the caramel in the fridge for future recipes.
- Preheat the oven to 190°C (170° fan) / 375F / gas 5 and line an 18-hole cupcake tin with paper cases.
- Combine the flour, sugar, butter, eggs and vanilla extract in a bowl and whisk together for 2 minutes or until smooth.
- Divide the mixture between the cases, then transfer the tin to the oven and bake for 15 – 20 minutes.
- Test with a wooden toothpick, if it comes out clean, the cakes are done.
- Transfer the cakes to a wire rack and leave to cool completely before icing with the chocolate caramel.

90

Orange and Violet Cupcakes

MAKES 12

PREPARATION TIME 30 MINUTES

COOKING TIME 15 - 20 MINUTES

INGREDIENTS

110 g / 4 oz / ⅔ cup self-raising flour, sifted
110 g / 4 oz / ½ cup caster (superfine) sugar
110 g / 4 oz / ½ cup butter, softened
2 large eggs
1 orange, zest finely grated

TO DECORATE:
200 g / 7 oz / 2 cups icing (confectioners') sugar
1 orange, juiced and zest finely grated
crystallised violets for sprinkling

- Preheat the oven to 190°C (170° fan) / 375F / gas 5 and line a 12-hole cupcake tin with paper cases.
- Combine the flour, sugar, butter, eggs and orange zest in a bowl and whisk together for 2 minutes or until smooth.
- Divide the mixture between the cases, then transfer the tin to the oven and bake for 15 – 20 minutes.
- Test with a wooden toothpick, if it comes out clean, the cakes are done.
- Transfer the cakes to a wire rack and leave to cool completely.
- Sieve the icing sugar into a bowl and add just enough orange juice to make a thick, pourable icing.
- Stir in half of the orange zest, then spoon it onto the cakes and sprinkle with the violets and the rest of the zest.

91

MAKES 12

Chocolate and Orange Cupcakes

- Preheat the oven to 190°C (170° fan) / 375F / gas 5 and line a 12-hole cupcake tin with paper cases.
- Combine the flour, sugar, butter, eggs, cocoa and grated orange zest in a bowl and whisk together for 2 minutes or until smooth.
- Divide the mixture between the cases, then transfer the tin to the oven and bake for 15 – 20 minutes.
- Test with a wooden toothpick, if it comes out clean, the cakes are done.
- Transfer the cakes to a wire rack and leave to cool completely before removing the paper cases and sprinkling with finely pared orange zest.

PREPARATION TIME 15 MINUTES

COOKING TIME 15 - 20 MINUTES

INGREDIENTS

110 g / 4 oz / ⅔ cup self-raising flour, sifted
110 g / 4 oz / ½ cup caster (superfine) sugar
110 g / 4 oz / ½ cup butter, softened
2 large eggs
2 tbsp unsweetened cocoa powder
1 orange, zest finely grated
finely pared orange zest for sprinkling

92

Crème de Cacao Cupcakes

MAKES 12

PREPARATION TIME 30 MINUTES

COOKING TIME 15 - 20 MINUTES

INGREDIENTS

110 g / 4 oz / ⅔ cup self-raising flour, sifted
110 g / 4 oz / ½ cup caster (superfine) sugar
110 g / 4 oz / ½ cup butter, softened
2 large eggs
1 tbsp clear crème de cacao

TO DECORATE:
200 g / 7 oz / 2 cups icing (confectioners') sugar
1 – 2 tsp clear crème de cacao
chocolate curls to decorate

- Preheat the oven to 190°C (170° fan) / 375F / gas 5 and line a 12-hole cupcake tin with paper cases.
- Combine the flour, sugar, butter, eggs and crème de cacao in a bowl and whisk together for 2 minutes or until smooth.
- Divide the mixture between the cases, then transfer the tin to the oven and bake for 15 – 20 minutes.
- Test with a wooden toothpick, if it comes out clean, the cakes are done.
- Transfer the cakes to a wire rack and leave to cool completely.
- Sieve the icing sugar into a bowl and add just enough crème de cacao to make a thick, pourable icing.
- Spoon the icing onto the cakes and decorate with chocolate curls.

93

Simple Vanilla Cupcakes

MAKES 12

PREPARATION TIME 15 MINUTES

COOKING TIME 15 - 20 MINUTES

INGREDIENTS

110 g / 4 oz / ⅔ cup self-raising flour, sifted
110 g / 4 oz / ½ cup caster (superfine) sugar
110 g / 4 oz / ½ cup butter, softened
2 large eggs
1 tsp vanilla extract

- Preheat the oven to 190°C (170° fan) / 375F / gas 5 and line a 12-hole cupcake tin with paper cases.
- Combine the flour, sugar, butter, eggs and vanilla extract in a bowl and whisk together for 2 minutes or until smooth.
- Divide the mixture between the cases, then transfer the tin to the oven and bake for 15 – 20 minutes.
- Test with a wooden toothpick, if it comes out clean, the cakes are done.
- Transfer the cakes to a wire rack and leave to cool completely.

94

MAKES 12

Vanilla Cupcakes with Chocolate Ganache

PREPARATION TIME 30 MINUTES

COOKING TIME 15 - 20 MINUTES

INGREDIENTS

110 g / 4 oz / ⅔ cup self-raising flour, sifted
110 g / 4 oz / ½ cup caster (superfine) sugar
110 g / 4 oz / ½ cup butter, softened
2 large eggs
1 tsp vanilla extract

TO DECORATE:
200 ml / 7 fl. oz / 3/4 cup double (heavy) cream
200 g / 7 oz dark chocolate, minimum 60% cocoa solids, chopped

- Preheat the oven to 190°C (170° fan) / 375F / gas 5 and line a 12-hole cupcake tin with paper cases.
- Combine the flour, sugar, butter, eggs and vanilla in a bowl and whisk together for 2 minutes or until smooth.
- Divide the mixture between the cases, then transfer the tin to the oven and bake for 15 – 20 minutes.
- Test with a wooden toothpick, if it comes out clean, the cakes are done.
- Transfer the cakes to a wire rack and leave to cool completely.
- Heat the cream until it starts to simmer, then pour it over the chopped chocolate and stir until smooth.
- Leave to cool and thicken to a pipable consistency, then spoon it into a piping bag fitted with a large star nozzle. Pipe a big swirl of ganache onto each cake.

Vanilla Cupcakes with White Chocolate Ganache

95

- Use white chocolate in place of the dark chocolate.

96

MAKES 12

Cappuccino Cupcakes

PREPARATION TIME 30 MINUTES

COOKING TIME 15 - 20 MINUTES

INGREDIENTS

110 g / 4 oz / ⅔ cup self-raising flour, sifted
110 g / 4 oz / ½ cup caster (superfine) sugar
110 g / 4 oz / ½ cup butter, softened
2 large eggs
1 tbsp instant espresso powder

TO DECORATE:
150 ml / 5 ½ fl. oz / ⅔ cup double (heavy) cream
2 tbsp icing (confectioners') sugar
1 tbsp drinking chocolate powder

- Preheat the oven to 190°C (170° fan) / 375F / gas 5 and line a 12-hole cupcake tin with paper cases.
- Combine the flour, sugar, butter, eggs and espresso powder in a bowl and whisk together for 2 minutes or until smooth.
- Divide the mixture between the cases, then transfer the tin to the oven and bake for 15 – 20 minutes.
- Test with a wooden toothpick, if it comes out clean, the cakes are done.
- Transfer the cakes to a wire rack and leave to cool completely.
- Whip the cream with the icing sugar until it holds its shape, then spread a thin layer over the cakes and sprinkle with the chocolate powder.

Hot Chocolate Powder Cupcakes

97

- Replace the espresso powder with 2 tbsp of hot chocolate powder. Top the cream with mini marshmallows.

98

MAKES 12

Vanilla Cupcakes with Meringue Icing

- Preheat the oven to 190°C (170° fan) / 375F / gas 5 and line a 12-hole cupcake tin with paper cases.
- Combine the flour, sugar, butter, eggs and vanilla in a bowl and whisk together for 2 minutes or until smooth.
- Divide the mixture between the cases, then transfer the tin to the oven and bake for 15 – 20 minutes.
- Test with a wooden toothpick, if it comes out clean, the cakes are done.
- To make the meringue topping, whisk the egg whites until stiff, then gradually whisk in half the sugar until the mixture is very shiny. Fold in the remaining sugar then spoon the mixture into a large piping bag fitted with a plain nozzle.
- Pipe a swirl of meringue on top of each cake and return to the oven for 10 minutes or until the topping is golden brown.

PREPARATION TIME 30 MINUTES

COOKING TIME 15 - 20 MINUTES

INGREDIENTS

110 g / 4 oz / ⅔ cup self-raising flour, sifted
110 g / 4 oz / ½ cup caster (superfine) sugar
110 g / 4 oz / ½ cup butter, softened
2 large eggs
1 tsp vanilla extract

TO DECORATE:
4 large egg whites
110 g / 4 oz / ½ cup caster (superfine) sugar

Coffee Cupcakes with Meringue Icing

99

- Add 1 tbsp of instant espresso powder to the cake mixture.

100

MAKES 12

Blackcurrant Cupcakes

- Preheat the oven to 190°C (170° fan) / 375F / gas 5 and line a 12-hole cupcake tin with strips of greaseproof paper.
- Combine the flour, sugar, butter, eggs and vanilla extract in a bowl and whisk together for 2 minutes or until smooth.
- Fold in the blackcurrants then divide the mixture between the cases and bake for 15 – 20 minutes.
- Test with a wooden toothpick, if it comes out clean, the cakes are done.
- Transfer the cakes to a wire rack and leave to cool completely.

PREPARATION TIME 15 MINUTES

COOKING TIME 15 - 20 MINUTES

INGREDIENTS

110 g / 4 oz / ⅔ cup self-raising flour, sifted
110 g / 4 oz / ½ cup caster (superfine) sugar
110 g / 4 oz / ½ cup butter, softened
2 large eggs
1 tsp vanilla extract
75 g / 2 ½ oz / ½ cup blackcurrants

Blackcurrant and Apple Cupcakes

101

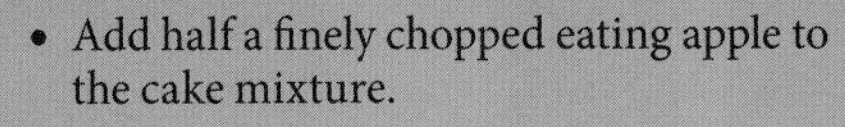

- Add half a finely chopped eating apple to the cake mixture.

102

MAKES 18

Vanilla Cream Cheese Cupcakes

PREPARATION TIME 10 MINUTES

COOKING TIME 45 MINUTES

INGREDIENTS

110 g / 4 oz / ⅔ cup self-raising flour, sifted
110 g / 4 oz / ½ cup caster (superfine) sugar
110 g / 4 oz / ½ cup butter, softened
2 large eggs
1 tsp vanilla extract

TO DECORATE:

110 g / 4 oz / ½ cup cream cheese
55 g / 2 oz / ¼ cup butter, softened
110 g / 4 oz / 1 cup icing (confectioners') sugar
1 tsp vanilla extract
colourful cake sprinkles to decorate

- Preheat the oven to 190°C (170° fan) / 375F / gas 5 and double line a 12-hole cupcake tin with paper cases.
- Combine the flour, sugar, butter, eggs and vanilla extract in a bowl and whisk together for 2 minutes or until smooth.
- Divide the mixture between the cases, then transfer the tin to the oven and bake for 15 – 20 minutes.
- Test with a wooden toothpick, if it comes out clean, the cakes are done.
- Transfer the cakes to a wire rack and leave to cool completely.
- Beat the cream cheese and butter together until light and fluffy then beat in the icing sugar a quarter at a time.
- Add the vanilla extract then whip the mixture for 2 minutes or until smooth and light.
- Spread the icing onto the cakes, swirling with the back of the spoon, then scatter over the cake sprinkles.

103

Peppermint Cream Cheese Cupcakes

- Replace the vanilla extract in the cake mixture and icing with a few drops of peppermint extract.

104

Vanilla Goat's Curd Cupcakes

- Replace the cream cheese with a mild fresh goat's curd cheese.

105

MAKES 12 Chocolate-Glazed Chocolate Cupcakes

- Preheat the oven to 190°C (170° fan) / 375F / gas 5 and line a 12-hole cupcake tin with paper cases.
- Combine the flour, sugar, butter, eggs and cocoa in a bowl and whisk together for 2 minutes or until smooth.
- Divide the mixture between the cases, then transfer the tin to the oven and bake for 15 – 20 minutes.
- Test with a wooden toothpick, if it comes out clean, the cakes are done.
- Transfer the cakes to a wire rack and leave to cool completely.
- Stir the chocolate, butter and honey together over a low heat until it forms a smooth glaze.
- Leave the mixture to cool to body temperature, then spoon it over the cakes.

PREPARATION TIME 30 MINUTES

COOKING TIME 20 – 25 MINUTES

INGREDIENTS

110 g / 4 oz / ⅔ cup self-raising flour, sifted
110 g / 4 oz / ½ cup caster (superfine) sugar
110 g / 4 oz / ½ cup butter, softened
2 large eggs
2 tbsp unsweetened cocoa powder

TO DECORATE:
200 g / 7 oz dark chocolate (minimum 60% cocoa solids), chopped
50 g / 1 ¾ oz / ¼ cup butter
4 tbsp runny honey

106

Chocolate-Glazed Orange Cupcakes

- Omit the cocoa powder from the cake mixture and replace with the finely grated zest of an orange.

107

MAKES 12 Vanilla Cupcakes with Chocolate Topping

- Preheat the oven to 190°C (170° fan) / 375F / gas 5 and line a 12-hole cupcake tin with paper cases.
- Combine the flour, sugar, butter, eggs and vanilla extract in a bowl and whisk together for 2 minutes or until smooth.
- Divide the mixture between the cases, then transfer the tin to the oven and bake for 15 – 20 minutes.
- Test with a wooden toothpick, if it comes out clean, the cakes are done.
- Transfer the cakes to a wire rack and leave to cool completely.
- Beat the butter until smooth, then gradually whisk in the icing sugar and cocoa powder.
- Spoon the mixture into a piping bag, fitted with a small star nozzle, and pipe rosettes of the icing in concentric circles on top.

PREPARATION TIME 30 MINUTES

COOKING TIME 15 - 20 MINUTES

INGREDIENTS

110 g / 4 oz / ⅔ cup self-raising flour, sifted
110 g / 4 oz / ½ cup caster (superfine) sugar
110 g / 4 oz / ½ cup butter, softened
2 large eggs
1 tsp vanilla extract

TO DECORATE:
100 g / 3 ½ oz / ½ cup butter, softened
200 g / 7 oz / 2 cups icing (confectioners') sugar
1 tbsp unsweetened cocoa powder

108

Cinnamon Cupcakes with Chocolate Buttercream

- Replace the vanilla extract with 2 tsp ground cinnamon.

109

Mini Vanilla Muffin Cupcakes

MAKES 24

PREPARATION TIME 25 MINUTES

COOKING TIME 20 – 25 MINUTES

INGREDIENTS

1 large egg
1 tsp vanilla extract
125 ml / 4 ½ fl. oz / ½ cup sunflower oil
125 ml / 4 ½ fl. oz / ½ cup milk
375 g / 13 oz / 2 ½ cups self-raising flour, sifted
1 tsp baking powder
200 g / 7 oz / ¾ cup caster (superfine) sugar

- Preheat the oven to 160°C (140° fan) / 325F / gas 3 and line a 24-hole mini cupcake tin with paper cases.
- Beat the egg in a jug with the vanilla extract, oil and milk until well mixed.
- Mix the flour, baking powder and sugar in a bowl, then pour in the egg mixture and stir just enough to combine.
- Divide the mixture between the cases then bake for 20 – 25 minutes.
- Test with a wooden toothpick, if it comes out clean, the cakes are done.
- Transfer the cakes to a wire rack and leave to cool completely.

Mini Raisin Muffin Cupcakes

110

- Add 75 g of raisins to the cake mixture when you add the eggs.

111

Prune and Hazelnut Cupcakes

MAKES 12

PREPARATION TIME 15 MINUTES

COOKING TIME 15 - 20 MINUTES

INGREDIENTS

110 g / 4 oz / ⅔ cup self-raising flour, sifted
110 g / 4 oz / ½ cup caster (superfine) sugar
110 g / 4 oz / ½ cup butter, softened
2 large eggs
2 tbsp ground hazelnuts (cobnuts)
24 prunes

- Preheat the oven to 190°C (170° fan) / 375F / gas 5 and line a 12-hole cupcake tin with foil cases.
- Combine the flour, sugar, butter, eggs and ground hazelnuts in a bowl and whisk together for 2 minutes or until smooth.
- Divide the mixture between the cases and top each cake with 2 prunes.
- Transfer the tin to the oven and bake for 15 – 20 minutes.
- Test with a wooden toothpick, if it comes out clean, the cakes are done.
- Transfer the cakes to a wire rack and leave to cool completely.

Apricot and Pistachio Cupcakes

112

- Replace the prunes with dried apricots and use ground pistachio nuts instead of hazelnuts.

MAKES 24

Mini Wholemeal Cupcakes

Spiced Mini Wholemeal Cupcakes

114

- Add 1 tsp of mixed spice to the cake mixture.

Mini Wholemeal Raisin Cupcakes

115

- Add 75 g of raisins to the cake mixture.

PREPARATION TIME 15 MINUTES

COOKING TIME 12 - 15 MINUTES

INGREDIENTS

55 g / 2 oz / ⅓ cup self-raising flour, sifted
55 g / 2 oz / ⅓ cup stoneground wholemeal flour
110 g / 4 oz / ½ cup caster (superfine) sugar
110 g / 4 oz / ½ cup butter, softened
2 large eggs
1 tsp vanilla extract

- Preheat the oven to 190°C (170° fan) / 375F / gas 5 and oil a 24-hole silicone cupcake mould.
- Combine the flours, sugar, butter, eggs and vanilla extract in a bowl and whisk together for 2 minutes or until smooth.
- Divide the mixture between the cases and bake for 12 - 15 minutes.
- Test with a wooden toothpick, if it comes out clean, the cakes are done.
- Turn out the cakes onto a wire rack and leave to cool completely.

116

MAKES 24 Almond and Chocolate Mini Cupcakes

PREPARATION TIME 15 MINUTES

COOKING TIME 12 - 15 MINUTES

INGREDIENTS

110 g / 4 oz / ⅔ cup self-raising flour, sifted
110 g / 4 oz / ½ cup caster (superfine) sugar
110 g / 4 oz / ½ cup butter, softened
2 large eggs
2 tbsp unsweetened cocoa powder
2 tbsp ground almonds
24 whole almonds

- Preheat the oven to 190°C (170° fan) / 375F / gas 5 and line a 24-hole mini cupcake tin with paper cases.
- Combine the flour, sugar, butter, eggs, cocoa powder and ground almonds in a bowl and whisk together for 2 minutes or until smooth.
- Divide the mixture between the cases, then press a whole almond into the top of each one.
- Transfer the tin to the oven and bake for 12 - 15 minutes. Test with a wooden toothpick, if it comes out clean, the cakes are done.
- Transfer the cakes to a wire rack and leave to cool completely before peeling off the paper cases.

Chocolate and Walnut Mini Cupcakes

- Replace the ground almonds with finely chopped walnuts and decorate each cake with a walnut half.

118

MAKES 12 Chocolate-Glazed Mocha Cupcakes

PREPARATION TIME 30 MINUTES

COOKING TIME 20 – 25 MINUTES

INGREDIENTS

110 g / 4 oz / ⅔ cup self-raising flour, sifted
110 g / 4 oz / ½ cup caster (superfine) sugar
110 g / 4 oz / ½ cup butter, softened
2 large eggs
2 tbsp unsweetened cocoa powder
1 tbsp instant espresso powder

TO DECORATE:
200 g / 7 oz dark chocolate (minimum 60% cocoa solids), chopped
50 g / 1 ¾ oz / ¼ cup butter
4 tbsp runny honey

- Preheat the oven to 190°C (170° fan) / 375F / gas 5 and line a 12-hole cupcake tin with paper cases.
- Combine the flour, sugar, butter, eggs, cocoa and espresso powder in a bowl and whisk together for 2 minutes or until smooth.
- Divide the mixture between the cases, then transfer the tin to the oven and bake for 15 – 20 minutes.
- Test with a wooden toothpick, if it comes out clean, the cakes are done.
- Transfer the cakes to a wire rack and leave to cool completely.
- Stir the chocolate, butter and honey together over a low heat until it forms a smooth glaze.
- Leave the mixture to cool to body temperature, then spoon it over the cakes.

Chocolate-Glazed Coffee Cupcakes

119

- Omit the cocoa powder from the cake mixture.

120

MAKES 12

Glace-Iced Walnut Cupcakes

- Preheat the oven to 190°C (170° fan) / 375F / gas 5 and line a 12-hole cupcake tin with paper cases.
- Combine the flour, sugar, butter, eggs and ground walnuts in a bowl and whisk together for 2 minutes or until smooth.
- Divide the mixture between the cases, then transfer the tin to the oven and bake for 15 – 20 minutes.
- Test with a wooden toothpick, if it comes out clean, the cakes are done.
- Transfer the cakes to a wire rack and leave to cool completely.
- Sieve the icing sugar into a bowl and add just enough water to make a thick, spreadable icing.
- Spoon the icing onto the cakes and top each one with a walnut half.

PREPARATION TIME 30 MINUTES

COOKING TIME 15 - 20 MINUTES

INGREDIENTS

110 g / 4 oz / ⅔ cup self-raising flour, sifted
110 g / 4 oz / ½ cup caster (superfine) sugar
110 g / 4 oz / ½ cup butter, softened
2 large eggs
2 tbsp finely ground walnuts

TO DECORATE:
200 g / 7 oz / 2 cups icing (confectioners') sugar
12 walnut halves

Glace-Iced Pecan Cupcakes

121

- Replace the ground walnuts with ground pecans and top the cakes with pecan halves.

122

MAKES 12

Chocolate Button Cupcakes

- Preheat the oven to 190°C (170° fan) / 375F / gas 5 and line a 12-hole cupcake tin with paper cases.
- Combine the flour, sugar, butter and eggs in a bowl and whisk together for 2 minutes or until smooth.
- Fold in the chocolate buttons then divide the mixture between the cases and bake for 15 – 20 minutes.
- Test with a wooden toothpick, if it comes out clean, the cakes are done.
- Transfer the cakes to a wire rack and leave to cool completely.
- Beat the cream cheese and butter together until light and fluffy then beat in the icing sugar a quarter at a time.
- Add the vanilla extract then whip the mixture for 2 minutes or until smooth and light.
- Spread the icing onto the cakes and top each one with a giant chocolate button.

PREPARATION TIME 30 MINUTES

COOKING TIME 15 - 20 MINUTES

INGREDIENTS

110 g / 4 oz / ⅔ cup self-raising flour, sifted
110 g / 4 oz / ½ cup light muscovado sugar
110 g / 4 oz / ½ cup butter, softened
2 large eggs
75 g / 2 ½ oz / ⅔ cup chocolate buttons, chopped

TO DECORATE:
110 g / 4 oz / ½ cup cream cheese
55 g / 2 oz / ¼ cup butter, softened
110 g / 4 oz / 1 cup icing (confectioners') sugar
1 tsp vanilla extract
12 giant chocolate buttons

Chocolate Smarties Cream Cheese Cupcakes

123

- Use Smarties in the cake mixture instead of buttons and decorate the top of the cakes with Smarties.

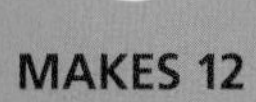
124

MAKES 12

Chocolate Chunk Muffin Cupcakes

White Chocolate Chunk Muffin Cupcakes

125

- Use white chocolate chunks instead of dark chocolate chunks.

Chocolate Orange Chunk Muffin Cupcakes

126

- Add the grated zest of an orange to the cake mixture and use orange-flavoured chocolate chunks.

PREPARATION TIME 15 MINUTES

COOKING TIME 20 – 25 MINUTES

INGREDIENTS

1 large egg
125 ml / 4 ½ fl. oz / ½ cup sunflower oil
125 ml / 4 ½ fl. oz / ½ cup milk
375 g / 13 oz / 2 ½ cups self-raising flour, sifted
1 tsp baking powder
200 g / 7 oz / ¾ cup caster (superfine) sugar
150 g / 5 ½ oz dark chocolate chunks (minimum 60% cocoa solids)

- Preheat the oven to 180°C (160° fan) / 350F / gas 4 and line a 12-hole cupcake tin with paper cases.
- Beat the egg in a jug with the oil and milk until well mixed.
- Mix the flour, baking powder and sugar in a bowl, then pour in the egg mixture and chocolate chunks and stir just enough to combine.
- Divide the mixture between the cases, then bake in the oven for 20 – 25 minutes.
- Test with a wooden toothpick, if it comes out clean, the cakes are done.
- Serve the cakes warm from the oven while the chocolate is still molten.

127

MAKES 12

Banana and Ginger Cupcakes

- Preheat the oven to 200°C (180° fan) / 400F / gas 6 and line a 12-hole cupcake tin with foil cases.
- Mash the bananas with a fork then whisk in the sugar, eggs, oil and stem ginger.
- Sieve the flour and bicarbonate of soda into the bowl and stir just enough to evenly mix all the ingredients together.
- Divide the mixture between the cases, then transfer the tin to the oven and bake for 15 – 20 minutes.
- Test with a wooden toothpick, if it comes out clean, the cakes are done.
- Transfer the cakes to a wire rack and leave to cool completely before topping with dried banana chips.

PREPARATION TIME 15 MINUTES

COOKING TIME 15 - 20 MINUTES

INGREDIENTS

3 very ripe bananas
100 g / 3 ½ oz / ½ cup soft light brown sugar
2 large eggs
125 ml / 4 ½ fl. oz / ½ cup sunflower oil
3 pieces of stem ginger, chopped
225 g / 8 oz / 1 ½ cups plain (all-purpose) flour
1 tsp bicarbonate of (baking) soda
dried banana chips to decorate

Banana and Cardamom Cupcakes

128

- Omit the stem ginger and add ½ tsp ground cardamom.

129

MAKES 24

Hot Toddy Mini Muffin Cupcakes

- Preheat the oven to 160°C (140° fan) / 325F / gas 3 and line a 24-hole mini cupcake tin with paper cases.
- Beat the egg in a jug with the honey, whisky, oil and milk until well mixed.
- Mix the flour, baking powder, spices, lemon zest and sugar in a bowl, then pour in the egg mixture and candied peel and stir just enough to combine.
- Divide the mixture between the cases then bake for 20 – 25 minutes.
- Test with a wooden toothpick, if it comes out clean, the cakes are done.
- Transfer the cakes to a wire rack to cool for a few minutes then serve warm.

PREPARATION TIME 25 MINUTES

COOKING TIME 20 – 25 MINUTES

INGREDIENTS

1 large egg
50 ml / 1 ¾ oz / ¼ cup runny honey
2 tbsp whisky
125 ml / 4 ½ fl. oz / ½ cup sunflower oil
125 ml / 4 ½ fl. oz / ½ cup milk
375 g / 13 oz / 2 ½ cups self-raising flour, sifted
1 tsp baking powder
¼ tsp ground star anise
¼ tsp ground cinnamon
½ tsp ground ginger
1 lemon, zest finely grated
150 g / 5 ½ oz / ⅔ cup caster (superfine) sugar
75 g / 2 ½ oz / ⅓ cup candied orange peel, roughly chopped

Hot Toddy Muffin Cupcakes

130

- Use the mixture to make 12 full sized cupcakes and increase the cooking time to 30 minutes.

131

MAKES 12

Hot Chocolate and Almond Cupcakes

PREPARATION TIME 30 MINUTES

COOKING TIME 15 - 20 MINUTES

INGREDIENTS

110 g / 4 oz / ⅔ cup self-raising flour, sifted
25 g / 1 oz / ¼ cup ground almonds
110 g / 4 oz / ½ cup caster (superfine) sugar
110 g / 4 oz / ½ cup butter, softened
2 large eggs
2 tbsp unsweetened cocoa powder
½ tsp almond extract

- Preheat the oven to 190°C (170° fan) / 375F / gas 5 and line 12 individual cake tins with greaseproof paper.
- Combine the flour, ground almonds, sugar, butter, eggs, cocoa and almond extract in a bowl and whisk together for 2 minutes or until smooth.
- Spoon the mixture into the tins and bake for 15 – 20 minutes.
- Test with a wooden toothpick, if it comes out clean, the cakes are done.
- Serve the cakes hot from the oven.

132

Hot Orange and Almond Cupcakes

- Replace the cocoa powder with the grated zest of an orange.

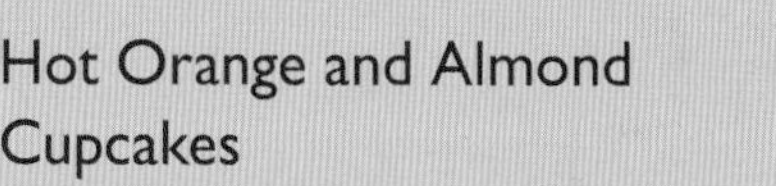

133

MAKES 12

Blueberry and Fig Muffin Cupcakes

PREPARATION TIME 25 MINUTES

COOKING TIME 20 – 25 MINUTES

INGREDIENTS

1 large egg
1 orange, zest finely grated
125 ml / 4 ½ fl. oz / ½ cup sunflower oil
125 ml / 4 ½ fl. oz / ½ cup milk
375 g / 13 oz / 2 ½ cups self-raising flour, sifted
1 tsp baking powder
200 g / 7 oz / ¾ cup caster (superfine) sugar
75 g / 2 ½ oz / ½ cup blueberries
75 g / 2 ½ oz / ½ cup fresh figs, chopped

- Preheat the oven to 180°C (160° fan) / 350F / gas 4 and line a 12-hole cupcake tin with paper cases.
- Beat the egg in a jug with the orange zest, oil and milk until well mixed.
- Mix the flour, baking powder and sugar in a bowl, then pour in the egg mixture, blueberries and figs and stir just enough to combine.
- Divide the mixture between the cases, then bake in the oven for 20 – 25 minutes.
- Test with a wooden toothpick, if it comes out clean, the cakes are done.
- Transfer the cakes to a wire rack and leave to cool completely.

134

Raspberry and Fig Muffin Cupcakes

- Replace the blueberries with raspberries.

MAKES 12

Glace-Iced Lemon and Ginger Cupcakes

Glace-Iced Lime and Ginger Cupcakes

136

- Replace the lemon juice and zest with lime juice and zest and top the cakes with finely chopped stem ginger.

Glace-Iced Orange and Ginger Cupcakes

137

- Replace the lemon juice and zest with orange juice and zest.

PREPARATION TIME 30 MINUTES

COOKING TIME 15 - 20 MINUTES

INGREDIENTS

110 g / 4 oz / ⅔ cup self-raising flour, sifted
110 g / 4 oz / ½ cup caster (superfine) sugar
110 g / 4 oz / ½ cup butter, softened
2 large eggs
1 lemon, zest finely grated
1 tsp ground ginger

TO DECORATE:
200 g / 7 oz / 2 cups icing (confectioners') sugar
1 – 2 tsp lemon juice
multi-coloured sugar sprinkles to decorate

- Preheat the oven to 190°C (170° fan) / 375F / gas 5 and line a 12-hole cupcake tin with paper cases.
- Combine the flour, sugar, butter, eggs, lemon zest and ground ginger in a bowl and whisk together for 2 minutes or until smooth.
- Divide the mixture between the cases, then transfer the tin to the oven and bake for 15 – 20 minutes.
- Test with a wooden toothpick, if it comes out clean, the cakes are done.
- Transfer the cakes to a wire rack and leave to cool completely.
- Sieve the icing sugar into a bowl and add just enough lemon juice to make a thick, spreadable icing.
- Spoon the icing onto the cakes and sprinkle with sugar sprinkles.

138

MAKES 12

Oat and Cream Cheese Cupcakes

PREPARATION TIME 30 MINUTES

COOKING TIME 15 - 20 MINUTES

INGREDIENTS

110 g / 4 oz / ⅔ cup self-raising flour, sifted
110 g / 4 oz / ½ cup caster (superfine) sugar
110 g / 4 oz / ½ cup butter, softened
2 large eggs
50 g / 1 ¾ oz / ½ cup rolled porridge oats

TO DECORATE:

110 g / 4 oz / ½ cup cream cheese
55 g / 2 oz / ¼ cup butter, softened
110 g / 4 oz / 1 cup icing (confectioners') sugar
1 tsp vanilla extract
sugar cake sprinkles to decorate

- Preheat the oven to 190°C (170° fan) / 375F / gas 5 and line a 12-hole cupcake tin with paper cases.
- Combine the flour, sugar, butter, eggs and oats in a bowl and whisk together for 2 minutes or until smooth.
- Divide the mixture between the cases, then transfer the tin to the oven and bake for 15 – 20 minutes.
- Test with a wooden toothpick, if it comes out clean, the cakes are done.
- Transfer the cakes to a wire rack and leave to cool completely.
- Beat the cream cheese and butter together until light and fluffy then beat in the icing sugar a quarter at a time.
- Add the vanilla extract then whip the mixture for 2 minutes or until smooth and light.
- Spoon the icing onto the cakes and scatter over the cake sprinkles.

Oat and Honey Cream Cheese Cupcakes

139

- Omit the cake sprinkles. Drizzle the cakes with honey and top the cream cheese frosting with toasted oats.

140

MAKES 12

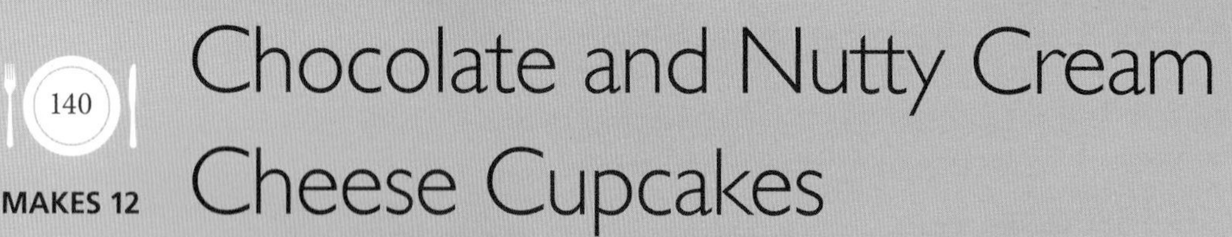

Chocolate and Nutty Cream Cheese Cupcakes

PREPARATION TIME 30 MINUTES

COOKING TIME 15 - 20 MINUTES

INGREDIENTS

110 g / 4 oz / ⅔ cup self-raising flour, sifted
110 g / 4 oz / ½ cup caster (superfine) sugar
110 g / 4 oz / ½ cup butter, softened
2 large eggs
2 tbsp hazelnut (cob nut) syrup
2 tbsp unsweetened cocoa powder

TO DECORATE:

110 g / 4 oz / ½ cup cream cheese
55 g / 2 oz / ¼ cup butter, softened
110 g / 4 oz / 1 cup icing (confectioners') sugar
2 tbsp hazelnut (cob nut) syrup
12 dark chocolate shards

- Preheat the oven to 190°C (170° fan) / 375F / gas 5 and line a 12-hole cupcake tin with paper cases.
- Combine the flour, sugar, butter, eggs, hazelnut syrup and cocoa powder in a bowl and whisk together for 2 minutes or until smooth.
- Divide the mixture between the cases, then transfer the tin to the oven and bake for 15 – 20 minutes.
- Test with a wooden toothpick, if it comes out clean, the cakes are done.
- Transfer the cakes to a wire rack and leave to cool completely.
- Beat the cream cheese and butter together until light and fluffy then beat in the icing sugar a quarter at a time.
- Add the hazelnut syrup then whip the mixture for 2 minutes or until smooth and light.
- Spoon the icing onto the cakes and top each one with a chocolate shard.

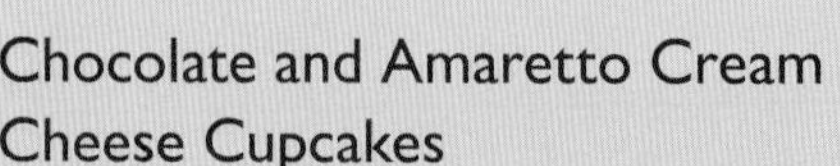

Chocolate and Amaretto Cream Cheese Cupcakes

141

- Replace the hazelnut syrup in the cake mixture and icing with amaretto.

142

MAKES 12

Nutella Layer Cupcakes

- Preheat the oven to 190°C (170° fan) / 375F / gas 5 and line a 12-hole cupcake tin with paper cases.
- Combine the flour, sugar, butter, eggs and vanilla extract in a bowl and whisk together for 2 minutes or until smooth.
- Divide two thirds of the mixture between the cases, then stir the Nutella into the rest of the cake batter.
- Divide the Nutella mixture between the cases, then transfer the tin to the oven and bake for 15 – 20 minutes.
- Test with a wooden toothpick, if it comes out clean, the cakes are done.
- Transfer the cakes to a wire rack and leave to cool completely.

PREPARATION TIME 15 MINUTES

COOKING TIME 15 - 20 MINUTES

INGREDIENTS

110 g / 4 oz / ⅔ cup self-raising flour, sifted
110 g / 4 oz / ½ cup caster (superfine) sugar
110 g / 4 oz / ½ cup butter, softened
2 large eggs
1 tsp vanilla extract
100 g / 3 ½ oz / ½ cup Nutella

Orange and Nutella Layer Cupcakes

143

- Add the finely grated zest of an orange to the cake mixture.

144

MAKES 24

Mini Almond Muffin Cupcakes

- Preheat the oven to 180°C (160° fan) / 350F / gas 4 and line a 24-hole mini cupcake tin with paper cases.
- Beat the egg in a jug with the almond extract, oil and milk until well mixed.
- Mix the flour, baking powder and sugar in a bowl, then pour in the egg mixture, and half of the flaked almonds and stir just enough to combine.
- Divide the mixture between the cases and sprinkle with the rest of the flaked almonds, then bake for 20 – 25 minutes.
- Test with a wooden toothpick, if it comes out clean, the cakes are done.
- Transfer the cakes to a wire rack and leave to cool completely.

PREPARATION TIME 25 MINUTES

COOKING TIME 20 - 25 MINUTES

INGREDIENTS

1 large egg
½ tsp almond extract
125 ml / 4 ½ fl. oz / ½ cup sunflower oil
125 ml / 4 ½ fl. oz / ½ cup milk
375 g / 13 oz / 2 ½ cups self-raising flour, sifted
1 tsp baking powder
200 g / 7 oz / ¾ cup caster (superfine) sugar
75 g / 2 ½ oz / 1 cup flaked (slivered) almonds

Iced Mini Almond Muffin Cupcakes

145

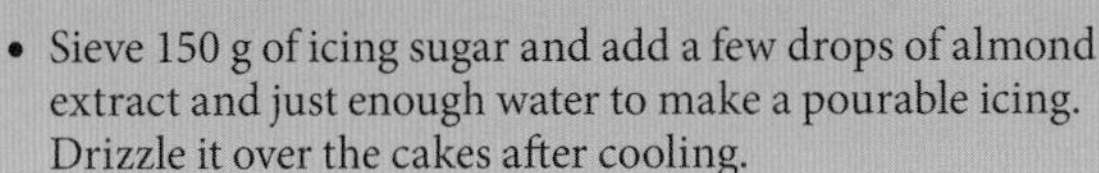

- Sieve 150 g of icing sugar and add a few drops of almond extract and just enough water to make a pourable icing. Drizzle it over the cakes after cooling.

146

MAKES 12

Cherry Bakewell Cupcakes

PREPARATION TIME 30 MINUTES

COOKING TIME 15 - 20 MINUTES

INGREDIENTS

75 g / 2 ½ oz / ½ cup self-raising flour, sifted
55 g / 1 ¾ oz / ½ cup ground almonds
110 g / 4 oz / ½ cup caster (superfine) sugar
110 g / 4 oz / ½ cup butter, softened
2 large eggs
½ tsp almond extract
200 g / 7 oz / ⅔ cup cherry jam

TO DECORATE:
200 g / 7 oz / 2 cups icing (confectioners') sugar
6 glace cherries, halved

- Preheat the oven to 190°C (170° fan) / 375F / gas 5 and line a 12-hole cupcake tin with foil cases.
- Combine the flour, ground almonds, sugar, butter, eggs and almond extract in a bowl and whisk together for 2 minutes or until smooth.
- Divide half of the mixture between the cases and top each one with a spoonful of jam.
- Top with the rest of the cake mixture, then transfer the tin to the oven and bake for 15 – 20 minutes.
- Test with a wooden toothpick, if it comes out clean, the cakes are done.
- Turn out the cakes onto a wire rack and leave to cool completely.
- Sieve the icing sugar into a bowl and add just enough water to make a thick, spreadable icing.
- Spoon the icing onto the cakes and top each one with half a glace cherry.

147

Almond Bakewell Cupcakes

- Use apricot jam instead of cherry jam and replace the glace cherries with a scattering of toasted flaked almonds.

148

Marmalade Bakewell Cupcakes

- Replace the cherry jam with marmalade and top the icing with finely pared orange zest.

149

MAKES 12

Chocolate and Grenadine Cupcakes

- Preheat the oven to 190°C (170° fan) / 375F / gas 5 and line a 12-hole cupcake tin with paper cases.
- Combine the flour, sugar, butter, eggs, cocoa and grenadine in a bowl and whisk together for 2 minutes or until smooth.
- Divide the mixture between the cases, then transfer the tin to the oven and bake for 15 – 20 minutes.
- Test with a wooden toothpick, if it comes out clean, the cakes are done.
- Transfer the cakes to a wire rack and leave to cool completely.
- Pipe a flower on top of each cake with the glitter gel and top each one with a mini chocolate button.

PREPARATION TIME 20 MINUTES

COOKING TIME 15 - 20 MINUTES

INGREDIENTS

110 g / 4 oz / ⅔ cup self-raising flour, sifted
110 g / 4 oz / ½ cup caster (superfine) sugar
110 g / 4 oz / ½ cup butter, softened
2 large eggs
2 tbsp unsweetened cocoa powder
2 tbsp grenadine

TO DECORATE:
edible pink glitter piping gel
12 mini chocolate buttons

Chocolate and Blackcurrant Cupcakes

150

- Replace the grenadine with blackcurrant cordial.

151

MAKES 12

Prune and Walnut Cupcakes

- Preheat the oven to 190°C (170° fan) / 375F / gas 5 and line a 12-hole cupcake tin with foil cases.
- Combine the flour, sugar, butter, eggs and ground walnuts in a bowl and whisk together for 2 minutes or until smooth.
- Divide the mixture between the cases and top each cake with 2 prunes.
- Transfer the tin to the oven and bake for 15 – 20 minutes.
- Test with a wooden toothpick, if it comes out clean, the cakes are done.
- Transfer the cakes to a wire rack and leave to cool completely before dusting with icing sugar.

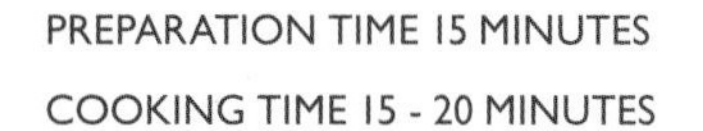
PREPARATION TIME 15 MINUTES

COOKING TIME 15 - 20 MINUTES

INGREDIENTS

110 g / 4 oz / ⅔ cup self-raising flour, sifted
110 g / 4 oz / ½ cup caster (superfine) sugar
110 g / 4 oz / ½ cup butter, softened
2 large eggs
2 tbsp ground walnuts
24 prunes
icing (confectioners') sugar for dusting

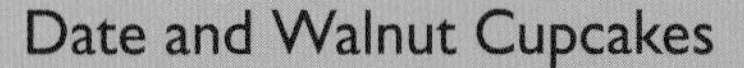

Date and Walnut Cupcakes

- Replace the prunes with stoned medjool dates.

153

Glace-Iced Vanilla Cupcakes

MAKES 12

PREPARATION TIME 30 MINUTES

COOKING TIME 15 - 20 MINUTES

INGREDIENTS

110 g / 4 oz / ⅔ cup self-raising flour, sifted
110 g / 4 oz / ½ cup caster (superfine) sugar
110 g / 4 oz / ½ cup butter, softened
2 large eggs
1 tsp vanilla extract

TO DECORATE:
200 g / 7 oz / 2 cups icing (confectioners') sugar
chocolate vermicelli for sprinkling

- Preheat the oven to 190°C (170° fan) / 375F / gas 5 and line a 12-hole cupcake tin with paper cases.
- Combine the flour, sugar, butter, eggs and vanilla in a bowl and whisk together for 2 minutes or until smooth.
- Divide the mixture between the cases, then transfer the tin to the oven and bake for 15 – 20 minutes.
- Test with a wooden toothpick, if it comes out clean, the cakes are done.
- Transfer the cakes to a wire rack and leave to cool completely.
- Sieve the icing sugar into a bowl and add just enough water to make a thick, pourable icing.
- Spoon the icing onto the cakes and sprinkle with chocolate vermicelli.

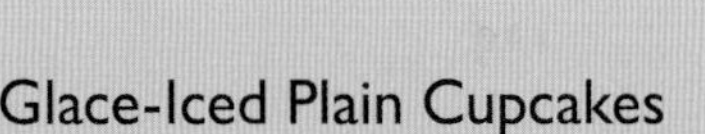

Glace-Iced Plain Cupcakes

154

- Omit the vanilla extract when making the cake mixture.

155

Mini No-Bake Pomegranate Cheesecakes

MAKES 24

PREPARATION TIME 40 MINUTES

COOKING TIME 5 MINUTES

INGREDIENTS

50 g / 1 ¾ oz / ¼ cup butter
200 g / 7 oz digestive biscuits, crushed
150 g / 5 ½ oz / ⅔ cup cream cheese
150 g / 5 ½ oz / ⅔ cup condensed milk
2 lemons, juiced
75 g / 2 ½ oz / ⅓ cup pomegranate seeds

- Melt the butter and stir in the crushed biscuits then divide between 2 x 12-hole loose-bottomed mini sandwich tins and press down well.
- Beat the cream cheese with an electric whisk until smooth then whisk in the condensed milk.
- Whisk in the lemon juice until the mixture starts to thicken, then spoon onto the biscuit bases.
- Leave to chill in the fridge for 1 hour.
- When the cheesecakes have set, carefully push each one up and out of the tin, remove the tin bottoms and arrange on a serving plate.
- Sprinkle with pomegranate seeds.

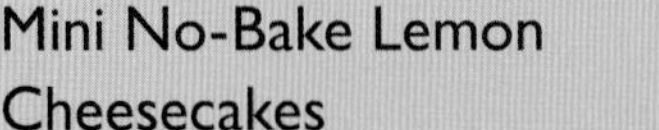

Mini No-Bake Lemon Cheesecakes

156

- Top each cheesecake with a sprinkling of finely pared lemon zest.

157

MAKES 6

Molten Centre Chocolate Cherry Cupcakes

Molten Centre Chocolate Marmalade Cupcakes

158

- Replace the cherry jam with shredless marmalade.

Molten Centre White Chocolate and Apricot Cupcakes

159

- Replace the milk chocolate with white chocolate and use apricot jam instead of cherry jam.

PREPARATION TIME 50 MINUTES

COOKING TIME 8 MINUTES

INGREDIENTS

150 g / 5 ½ oz milk chocolate, chopped
150 g / 5 ½ oz / ⅔ cup butter, chopped
100 g / 3 ½ oz / ⅓ cup cherry jam (jelly)
3 large eggs, plus 3 egg yolks
1 tbsp plain (all-purpose) flour

- Line a 6-hole cupcake tray with silicone cases.
- Melt the chocolate, butter and jam together in a saucepan.
- Leave to cool a little then beat in the eggs and egg yolks and fold in the flour.
- Divide the mixture between the cases, then chill for 30 minutes.
- Preheat the oven to 180°C (160° fan) / 350F / gas 4.
- Bake the cakes for 8 minutes, then leave to cool for 10 minutes before serving warm.

160

MAKES 6

Melting Centre Chocolate Cupcakes

PREPARATION TIME 50 MINUTES

COOKING TIME 8 MINUTES

INGREDIENTS

150 g / 5 ½ oz dark chocolate, minimum 60% cocoa solids, chopped
150 g / 5 ½ oz / ⅔ cup butter, chopped
85 g / 3 oz / ⅓ cup caster (superfine) sugar
3 large eggs, plus 3 egg yolks
1 tbsp plain (all-purpose) flour

- Line a 6-hole cupcake tray with paper cases.
- Melt the chocolate, butter and sugar together in a saucepan, stirring to dissolve the sugar.
- Leave to cool a little then beat in the eggs and egg yolks and fold in the flour.
- Divide the mixture between the cases, then chill for 30 minutes.
- Preheat the oven to 180°C (160° fan) / 350F / gas 4.
- Bake the cakes for 8 minutes, then leave to cool for 10 minutes before serving warm.

161

Melting Centre Chocolate Orange Cupcakes

- Stir the finely grated zest of an orange into the chocolate mixture before adding the eggs.

162

MAKES 12

Dried Cranberry and Almond Cupcakes

PREPARATION TIME 15 MINUTES

COOKING TIME 15 - 20 MINUTES

INGREDIENTS

110 g / 4 oz / ⅔ cup self-raising flour, sifted
110 g / 4 oz / ½ cup caster (superfine) sugar
110 g / 4 oz / ½ cup butter, softened
2 large eggs
2 tbsp ground almonds
75 g / 2 ½ oz / ⅓ cup dried cranberries
icing (confectioners') sugar for dusting

- Preheat the oven to 190°C (170° fan) / 375F / gas 5 and line a 12-hole cupcake tin with foil cases.
- Combine the flour, sugar, butter, eggs and ground almonds in a bowl and whisk together for 2 minutes or until smooth.
- Divide the mixture between the cases and bake for 15 – 20 minutes.
- Test with a wooden toothpick, if it comes out clean, the cakes are done.
- Transfer the cakes to a wire rack and leave to cool completely then top with the dried cranberries and sprinkle with icing sugar.

163

Dried Sour Cherry and Almond Cupcakes

- Replace the dried cranberries with dried sour cherries and flavour the cake mixture with ½ tsp of almond extract. Sprinkle with flaked (slivered) almonds.

164

MAKES 12

Dried Fruit-Topped Cupcakes

- Preheat the oven to 190°C (170° fan) / 375F / gas 5 and line a 12-hole cupcake tin with foil cases.
- Combine the flour, sugar, butter, eggs and vanilla extract in a bowl and whisk together for 2 minutes or until smooth.
- Divide the mixture between the cases and top with the dried fruits of your choice.
- Transfer the tin to the oven and bake for 15 – 20 minutes.
- Test with a wooden toothpick, if it comes out clean, the cakes are done.
- Transfer the cakes to a wire rack and leave to cool completely.

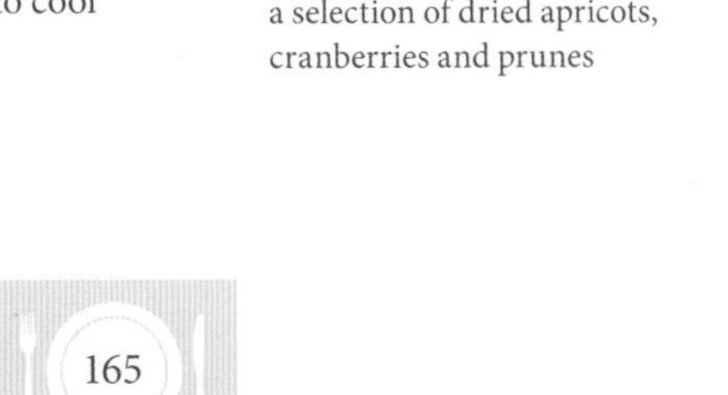

PREPARATION TIME 15 MINUTES

COOKING TIME 15 - 20 MINUTES

INGREDIENTS

110 g / 4 oz / ⅔ cup self-raising flour, sifted
110 g / 4 oz / ½ cup caster (superfine) sugar
110 g / 4 oz / ½ cup butter, softened
2 large eggs
1 tsp vanilla extract
a selection of dried apricots, cranberries and prunes

Nut-Topped Cupcakes

165

- Replace the dried fruits with a selection of peanuts, Brazil nuts and desiccated coconut.

166

MAKES 24

Marsala Sultana Mini Cupcakes

- Pour the Marsala over the sultanas and leave to macerate for 3 hours.
- Preheat the oven to 190°C (170° fan) / 375F / gas 5 and oil a 24-hole silicone mini cupcake mould.
- Combine the flour, sugar, butter, eggs and Marsala sultanas in a bowl and whisk together for 2 minutes or until smooth.
- Spoon the mixture into the mould then bake for 12 - 15 minutes.
- Test with a wooden toothpick, if it comes out clean, the cakes are done.
- Transfer the cakes to a wire rack and leave to cool completely then dust lightly with icing sugar.

PREPARATION TIME 3 HOURS 15 MINUTES

COOKING TIME 12 - 15 MINUTES

INGREDIENTS

3 tbsp Marsala
75 g / 2 ½ oz / ½ cup sultanas
110 g / 4 oz / ⅔ cup self-raising flour, sifted
110 g / 4 oz / ½ cup caster (superfine) sugar
110 g / 4 oz / ½ cup butter, softened
2 large eggs
icing (confectioners') sugar for dusting

Rum and Raisin Mini Cupcakes

167

- Replace the sultanas with raisins and the Marsala with dark rum.

168

MAKES 12

Poppy Seed Cream Cheese Cupcakes

PREPARATION TIME 30 MINUTES

COOKING TIME 15 - 20 MINUTES

INGREDIENTS

110 g / 4 oz / ⅔ cup self-raising flour, sifted
110 g / 4 oz / ½ cup caster (superfine) sugar
110 g / 4 oz / ½ cup butter, softened
2 large eggs
1 tbsp poppy seeds

TO DECORATE:
110 g / 4 oz / ½ cup cream cheese
55 g / 2 oz / ¼ cup butter, softened
110 g / 4 oz / 1 cup icing (confectioners') sugar
1 tbsp lemon juice
poppy seeds for sprinkling

- Preheat the oven to 190°C (170° fan) / 375F / gas 5 and line a 12-hole cupcake tin with thick paper cases.
- Combine the flour, sugar, butter, eggs and poppy seeds in a bowl and whisk together for 2 minutes or until smooth.
- Divide the mixture between the cases, then transfer the tin to the oven and bake for 15 – 20 minutes.
- Test with a wooden toothpick, if it comes out clean, the cakes are done.
- Transfer the cakes to a wire rack and leave to cool completely.
- Beat the cream cheese and butter together until light and fluffy then beat in the icing sugar a quarter at a time.
- Add the lemon juice then whip the mixture for 2 minutes or until smooth and light.
- Spoon the icing onto the cakes and sprinkle with poppy seeds.

169

Sesame Cream Cheese Cupcakes

- Replace the poppy seeds with sesame seeds and add 1 tsp of sesame oil to the cake mixture.

170

Sunflower Seed Cream Cheese Cupcakes

- Replace the poppy seeds with roasted sunflower seeds.

171

MAKES 24

Mini Peanut Butter Muffin Cupcakes

- Preheat the oven to 180°C (160° fan) / 350F / gas 4 and line a 24-hole mini cupcake tin with paper cases.
- Beat the egg in a jug with the peanut butter, oil and milk until well mixed.
- Mix the flour, baking powder and sugar in a bowl, then pour in the egg mixture and stir just enough to combine.
- Divide the mixture between the cases then bake for 20 – 25 minutes.
- Test with a wooden toothpick, if it comes out clean, the cakes are done.
- Transfer the cakes to a wire rack and leave to cool completely.

PREPARATION TIME 25 MINUTES

COOKING TIME 20 – 25 MINUTES

INGREDIENTS

1 large egg
4 tbsp crunchy peanut butter
125 ml / 4 ½ fl. oz / ½ cup sunflower oil
125 ml / 4 ½ fl. oz / ½ cup milk
375 g / 13 oz / 2 ½ cups self-raising flour, sifted
1 tsp baking powder
200 g / 7 oz / ¾ cup caster (superfine) sugar

Double Peanut Butter Mini Cupcakes

172

- Ice the cupcakes with smooth peanut butter.

173

MAKES 12

Gluten-Free Chocolate Cupcakes

- Preheat the oven to 190°C (170° fan) / 375F / gas 5 and line a 12-hole cupcake tin with paper cases.
- Combine the flour, cocoa, baking powder, sugar and eggs in a bowl and whisk together for 2 minutes or until smooth.
- Divide the mixture between the cases, then transfer the tin to the oven and bake for 15 – 20 minutes.
- Test with a wooden toothpick, if it comes out clean, the cakes are done.

PREPARATION TIME 15 MINUTES

COOKING TIME 15 - 20 MINUTES

INGREDIENTS

110 g / 4 oz / ⅔ cup gluten-free plain (all purpose) flour, sifted
1 tbsp unsweetened cocoa powder
2 tsp baking powder
110 g / 4 oz / ½ cup caster (superfine) sugar
110 g / 4 oz / ½ cup butter, softened
2 large eggs

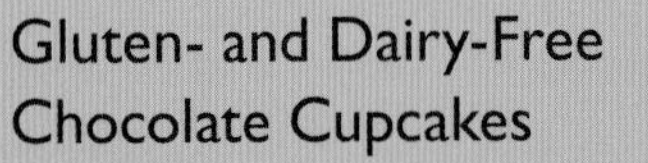

Gluten- and Dairy-Free Chocolate Cupcakes

174

- Replace the butter with dairy-free baking spread.

175

MAKES 12

Raspberry Muffin Cupcakes

PREPARATION TIME 25 MINUTES

COOKING TIME 20 – 25 MINUTES

INGREDIENTS

1 large egg
1 orange, zest finely grated
125 ml / 4 ½ fl. oz / ½ cup sunflower oil
125 ml / 4 ½ fl. oz / ½ cup milk
375 g / 13 oz / 2 ½ cups self-raising flour, sifted
1 tsp baking powder
200 g / 7 oz / ¾ cup caster (superfine) sugar
75 g / 2 ½ oz / ½ cup raspberries

- Preheat the oven to 180°C (160° fan) / 350F / gas 4 and line a deep 12-hole cupcake tin with greaseproof paper.
- Beat the egg in a jug with the orange zest, oil and milk until well mixed.
- Mix the flour, baking powder and sugar in a bowl, then pour in the egg mixture and raspberries, and stir just enough to combine.
- Spoon the mixture into the tin, then bake in the oven for 20 – 25 minutes.
- Test with a wooden toothpick, if it comes out clean, the cakes are done.
- Transfer the cakes to a wire rack and leave to cool completely.

Wholemeal Raspberry Muffin Cupcakes

176

- Replace half of the flour with stoneground wholemeal flour and add an extra teaspoon of baking powder.

177

MAKES 12

Rice Flour Muffin Cupcakes

PREPARATION TIME 20 MINUTES

COOKING TIME 20 – 25 MINUTES

INGREDIENTS

1 large egg
125 ml / 4 ½ fl. oz / ½ cup sunflower oil
125 ml / 4 ½ fl. oz / ½ cup milk
375 g / 13 oz / 2 ½ cups rice flour, sifted
2 tsp baking powder
200 g / 7 oz / ¾ cup caster (superfine) sugar

- Preheat the oven to 180°C (160° fan) / 350F / gas 4 and grease a 12-hole silicone mini bundt mould.
- Beat the egg in a jug with the oil and milk until well mixed.
- Mix the flour, baking powder and sugar in a bowl, then pour in the egg mixture and stir just enough to combine.
- Spoon the mixture into the mould, then bake in the oven for 20 – 25 minutes.
- Test with a wooden toothpick, if it comes out clean, the cakes are done.
- Transfer the cakes to a wire rack and leave to cool completely.

Lime and Rice Flour Muffin Cupcakes

178

- Add the grated zest of 2 limes to the cake mixture.

MAKES 12

Chocolate-Glazed Brownie Cupcakes

Chilli Chocolate Brownie Cupcakes

180

- Add a large pinch of chilli (chili) powder to the chocolate and butter mixture in the saucepan.

Chocolate Cherry Brownie Cupcakes

181

- Add 75 g of chopped glace cherries to the cake mixture.

PREPARATION TIME 25 MINUTES

COOKING TIME 30 – 35 MINUTES

INGREDIENTS

100 g / 3 ½ oz dark chocolate (minimum 60 % cocoa solids), chopped
75 g / 2 ½ oz / 3/4 cup unsweetened cocoa powder, sifted
225 g / 8 oz / 1 cup butter
450 g / 1 lb / 2 ½ cups light brown sugar
4 large eggs
100 g / 3 ½ oz / ⅔ cup self-raising flour

TO DECORATE:
100 g / 3 ½ oz dark chocolate (minimum 60 % cocoa solids), chopped
edible silver balls

- Preheat the oven to 160°C (140° fan) / 325F / gas 3 and line a 12-hole cupcake tin with paper cases.
- Melt the chocolate, cocoa and butter together in a saucepan, then leave to cool a little.
- Whisk the sugar and eggs together with an electric whisk for 3 minutes or until very light and creamy.
- Pour in the chocolate mixture and sieve over the flour, then fold everything together until evenly mixed.
- Divide the mixture between the cases and bake for 30 – 35 minutes or until they are just set in the centre.
- Transfer the cakes to a wire rack and leave to cool completely.
- Melt the chocolate in a microwave or bain marie, then leave to cool until it starts to thicken.
- Dip the top of each cake in the chocolate and decorate with the silver balls.

182

MAKES 12

Chocolate Brownie Cupcakes

PREPARATION TIME 25 MINUTES

COOKING TIME 30 – 35 MINUTES

INGREDIENTS

100 g / 3 ½ oz dark chocolate (minimum 60 % cocoa solids), chopped
75 g / 2 ½ oz / 3/4 cup unsweetened cocoa powder, sifted
225 g / 8 oz / 1 cup butter
450 g / 1 lb / 2 ½ cups light brown sugar
4 large eggs
100 g / 3 ½ oz / ⅔ cup self-raising flour
Smarties to decorate

- Preheat the oven to 160°C (140° fan) / 325F / gas 3 and oil and line a 12-hole silicone cupcake mould.
- Melt the chocolate, cocoa and butter together in a saucepan, then leave to cool a little.
- Whisk the sugar and eggs together with an electric whisk for 3 minutes or until very light and creamy.
- Pour in the chocolate mixture and sieve over the flour, then fold everything together until evenly mixed.
- Divide the mixture between the moulds and bake for 30 – 35 minutes or until they are just set in the centre.
- Leave the cakes to cool completely before unmoulding. Wrap each cake in tissue paper and top with the Smarties.

183

MAKES 12

Peanut Cupcakes

PREPARATION TIME 15 MINUTES

COOKING TIME 15 - 20 MINUTES

INGREDIENTS

110 g / 4 oz / ⅔ cup self-raising flour, sifted
110 g / 4 oz / ½ cup caster (superfine) sugar
110 g / 4 oz / ½ cup butter, softened
2 large eggs
2 tbsp ground peanuts
75 g / 2 ½ oz / ⅔ cup roasted peanuts

- Preheat the oven to 190°C (170° fan) / 375F / gas 5 and line a 12-hole cupcake tin with foil cases.
- Combine the flour, sugar, butter, eggs and ground peanuts in a bowl and whisk together for 2 minutes or until smooth.
- Divide the mixture between the cases and bake for 15 – 20 minutes.
- Test with a wooden toothpick, if it comes out clean, the cakes are done.
- Transfer the cakes to a wire rack and leave to cool completely before topping with the roasted peanuts.

184

MAKES 12

White Chocolate Cupcakes

- Preheat the oven to 190°C (170° fan) / 375F / gas 5 and line a 12-hole cupcake tin with silicone cases.
- Combine the flour, sugar, butter and eggs in a bowl and whisk together for 2 minutes or until smooth.
- Melt the chocolate in a microwave or bain marie then fold it into the cake mixture.
- Divide the mixture between the cases, then transfer the tin to the oven and bake for 15 – 20 minutes.
- Test with a wooden toothpick, if it comes out clean, the cakes are done.
- Transfer the cakes to a wire rack and leave to cool completely before sprinkling with white chocolate flakes.

PREPARATION TIME 15 MINUTES

COOKING TIME 15 - 20 MINUTES

INGREDIENTS

110 g / 4 oz / ⅔ cup self-raising flour, sifted
110 g / 4 oz / ½ cup caster (superfine) sugar
110 g / 4 oz / ½ cup butter, softened
2 large eggs
75 g / 2 ½ oz white chocolate
white chocolate flakes to decorate

185

Strawberry Cupcakes

MAKES 12

PREPARATION TIME 10 MINUTES

COOKING TIME 45 MINUTES

INGREDIENTS

110 g / 4 oz / ⅔ cup self-raising flour, sifted
110 g / 4 oz / ½ cup caster (superfine) sugar
110 g / 4 oz / ½ cup butter, softened
2 large eggs
100 g / 3 ½ oz strawberries, halved

- Preheat the oven to 190°C (170° fan) / 375F / gas 5 and line a 12-hole cupcake tin with thick paper cases.
- Combine the flour, sugar, butter and eggs in a bowl and whisk together for 2 minutes or until smooth.
- Fold in the strawberries and divide the mixture between the cases, then bake for 15 – 20 minutes.
- Test with a wooden toothpick, if it comes out clean, the cakes are done.
- Transfer the cakes to a wire rack and leave to cool completely.

186

MAKES 8

Bundt Cupcakes

PREPARATION TIME: 15 MINUTES

COOKING TIME: 25 MINUTES

INGREDIENTS

225 g / 8 oz / 1 cup butter, softened
225 g / 8 oz / 1 cup caster (superfine) sugar
4 large eggs, beaten
150 g / 5 ½ oz / 1 cup self-raising flour

TO DECORATE:

200 g / 7 oz / 2 cups icing (confectioners') sugar

- Preheat the oven to 180°C (160° fan) / 350F / gas 4 and butter 8 mini bundt tins.
- Cream the butter and sugar together until well whipped then whisk in the eggs in 4 stages, beating well after each addition.
- Fold in the flour then divide the mixture between the tins.
- Bake the cakes for 25 minutes or until a skewer inserted in the centre comes out clean.
- Turn the cakes out onto a wire rack and leave to cool completely.
- Sieve the icing sugar into a bowl and add just enough water to make a thick, pourable icing.
- Spoon the icing over the cakes and leave to set for 1 hour.

187

MAKES 12

Blackberry Muffin Cupcakes

PREPARATION TIME 25 MINUTES

COOKING TIME 20 – 25 MINUTES

INGREDIENTS

1 large egg
1 lemon, zest finely grated
125 ml / 4 ½ fl. oz / ½ cup sunflower oil
125 ml / 4 ½ fl. oz / ½ cup milk
375 g / 13 oz / 2 ½ cups self-raising flour, sifted
1 tsp baking powder
200 g / 7 oz / ¾ cup caster (superfine) sugar
75 g / 2 ½ oz / ½ cup blackberries

- Preheat the oven to 180°C (160° fan) / 350F / gas 4 and line a 12-hole cupcake tin with paper cases.
- Beat the egg in a jug with the lemon zest, oil and milk until well mixed.
- Mix the flour, baking powder and sugar in a bowl, then pour in the egg mixture and blackberries, and stir just enough to combine.
- Spoon the mixture into the tin, then bake in the oven for 20 – 25 minutes.
- Test with a wooden toothpick, if it comes out clean, the cakes are done.
- Transfer the cakes to a wire rack and leave to cool completely.

188

Blackberry and Apple Muffin Cupcakes

- Add half a finely chopped eating apple to the cake mixture and sprinkle the tops with demerara sugar before baking.

189

MAKES 12

Dried Apricot and Almond Cupcakes

PREPARATION TIME 15 MINUTES

COOKING TIME 15 - 20 MINUTES

INGREDIENTS

110 g / 4 oz / ⅔ cup self-raising flour, sifted
110 g / 4 oz / ½ cup caster (superfine) sugar
110 g / 4 oz / ½ cup butter, softened
2 large eggs
2 tbsp ground almonds
½ tsp almond extract
24 dried apricots

- Preheat the oven to 190°C (170° fan) / 375F / gas 5 and line a 12-hole cupcake tin with foil cases.
- Combine the flour, sugar, butter, eggs, ground almonds and almond extract in a bowl and whisk together for 2 minutes or until smooth.
- Spoon the mixture into the cases and press 2 dried almonds into the top of each one, then bake for 15 – 20 minutes.
- Test with a wooden toothpick, if it comes out clean, the cakes are done.
- Turn out the cakes onto a wire rack and leave to cool completely.

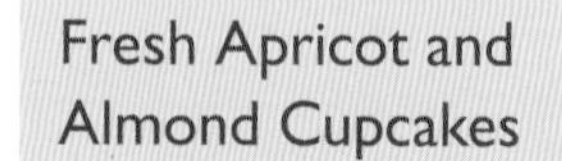

190

Fresh Apricot and Almond Cupcakes

- Replace the dried apricots with half a fresh apricot on top of each cupcake.

191

ENOUGH TO ICE 12

Chantilly Cream for Cupcakes

- Put the cream, sugar and vanilla extract in a bowl.
- Use an electric whisk to whip the cream until it starts to thicken. Reduce the speed of the whisk and continue to whip the cream until it holds its shape. Keep stopping and checking to avoid over-whipping.
- Spread or pipe the cream onto the cupcakes and top with the decorations of your choice.
- Keep the cakes in the fridge until you are ready to serve them.

PREPARATION TIME 10 MINUTES

INGREDIENTS

300 ml / 10 ½ fl. oz / 1 ¼ cups double (heavy) cream
2 tbsp icing (confectioners') sugar
1 tsp vanilla extract

Lemon Curd Cream for Cupcakes

192

- Replace the icing sugar and vanilla extract with 4 tbsp of lemon curd.

193

MAKES 12

Low-Fat Chocolate Cupcakes

- Preheat the oven to 180°C (160° fan) / 350F / gas 4 and line a 12-hole Yorkshire pudding tin with shallow paper cases.
- Whisk the egg yolks and caster sugar together for 4 minutes or until pale and thick.
- Sieve the flour, baking powder and cocoa together then fold it into the bowl.
- Whip the egg whites to stiff peaks in a very clean bowl, then fold them into the cake mixture in two stages.
- Spoon the mixture into the cases, being careful to retain as many air bubbles as possible, and bake for 10 – 15 minutes or until a skewer inserted comes out clean.
- Leave to cool in the tin for 10 minutes before transferring to a wire rack to cool completely.

PREPARATION TIME 15 MINUTES

COOKING TIME 10 – 15 MINUTES

INGREDIENTS

4 large eggs, separated
175 g / 6 oz / 3/4 cup caster (superfine) sugar
75 g / 2 ½ oz / ½ cup self-raising flour
1 tsp baking powder
25 g / 1 oz / ¼ cup unsweetened cocoa powder
icing (confectioners') sugar to dust

Fatless Cupcakes

194

- Omit the cocoa powder and extra tsp of baking powder.

Rhubarb Jam Muffin Cupcakes

MAKES 12

Greengage Jam Muffin Cupcakes

- Replace the rhubarb jam with greengage jam.

Gooseberry Jam Muffin Cupcakes

197

- Replace the rhubarb jam with gooseberry jam.

PREPARATION TIME 25 MINUTES

COOKING TIME 20 – 25 MINUTES

INGREDIENTS

1 large egg
1 orange, zest finely grated
125 ml / 4 ½ fl. oz / ½ cup sunflower oil
125 ml / 4 ½ fl. oz / ½ cup milk
375 g / 13 oz / 2 ½ cups self-raising flour, sifted
1 tsp baking powder
200 g / 7 oz / ¾ cup caster (superfine) sugar
75 g / 2 ½ oz / ¼ cup rhubarb jam

- Preheat the oven to 180°C (160° fan) / 350F / gas 4 and line a 12-hole cupcake tin with thick paper cases.
- Beat the egg in a jug with the orange zest, oil and milk until well mixed.
- Mix the flour, baking powder and sugar in a bowl, then pour in the egg mixture and rhubarb jam, and stir just enough to combine.
- Spoon the mixture into the cases, then bake in the oven for 20 – 25 minutes.
- Test with a wooden toothpick, if it comes out clean, the cakes are done.
- Transfer the cakes to a wire rack and leave to cool completely.

198

MAKES 12

Orange Muffin Cupcakes

- Preheat the oven to 180°C (160° fan) / 350F / gas 4 and line a deep 12-hole cupcake tin with paper cases.
- Beat the egg in a jug with the orange zest, oil and milk until well mixed.
- Mix the flour, baking powder and sugar in a bowl, then pour in the egg mixture and stir just enough to combine.
- Spoon the mixture into the tin, then bake in the oven for 20 – 25 minutes.
- Test with a wooden toothpick, if it comes out clean, the cakes are done.
- Transfer the cakes to a wire rack and leave to cool completely.

PREPARATION TIME 25 MINUTES

COOKING TIME 20 – 25 MINUTES

INGREDIENTS

1 large egg
1 orange, zest finely grated
125 ml / 4 ½ fl. oz / ½ cup sunflower oil
125 ml / 4 ½ fl. oz / ½ cup milk
375 g / 13 oz / 2 ½ cups self-raising flour, sifted
1 tsp baking powder
200 g / 7 oz / ¾ cup caster (superfine) sugar

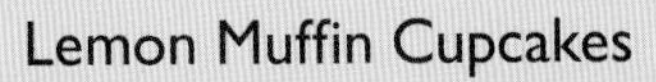

Lemon Muffin Cupcakes

199

- Replace the orange zest with lemon zest.

200

MAKES 12

Squidgy Chocolate Mini Cupcakes

- Line a 12-hole mini cupcake tray with paper cases.
- Melt the chocolate, butter and sugar together in a saucepan, stirring to dissolve the sugar.
- Leave to cool a little then beat in the eggs and egg yolks and fold in the flour.
- Divide the mixture between the cases, then chill for 30 minutes.
- Preheat the oven to 180°C (160° fan) / 350F / gas 4.
- Bake the cakes for 6 minutes, then transfer to a wire rack and leave to cool completely.

PREPARATION TIME 50 MINUTES

COOKING TIME 8 MINUTES

INGREDIENTS

150 g / 5 ½ oz dark chocolate, minimum 60% cocoa solids, chopped
150 g / 5 ½ oz / ⅔ cup butter, chopped
85 g / 3 oz / ⅓ cup caster (superfine) sugar
3 large eggs, plus 3 egg yolks
1 tbsp plain (all-purpose) flour

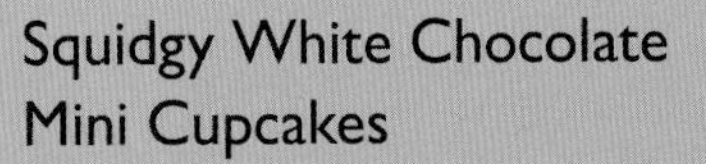

Squidgy White Chocolate Mini Cupcakes

201

- Replace the dark chocolate with good quality white chocolate.

202

MAKES 12

Violet and Lemon Cream Cheese Cupcakes

PREPARATION TIME 30 MINUTES

COOKING TIME 15 - 20 MINUTES

INGREDIENTS

110 g / 4 oz / ⅔ cup self-raising flour, sifted
110 g / 4 oz / ½ cup caster (superfine) sugar
110 g / 4 oz / ½ cup butter, softened
2 large eggs
1 lemon, zest finely grated
1 tbsp violet syrup

TO DECORATE:
110 g / 4 oz / ½ cup cream cheese
55 g / 2 oz / ¼ cup butter, softened
110 g / 4 oz / 1 cup icing (confectioners') sugar
1 tbsp lemon juice
12 crystallised violets

- Preheat the oven to 190°C (170° fan) / 375F / gas 5 and line a 12-hole cupcake tin with foil cases.
- Whisk all of the cake ingredients together for 2 minutes or until smooth.
- Divide the mixture between the cases, then bake for 15 – 20 minutes.
- Test with a wooden toothpick, if it comes out clean, the cakes are done. Transfer the cakes to a wire rack and leave to cool completely.
- Beat the cream cheese and butter together until light and fluffy then beat in the icing sugar and lemon juice whip the mixture for 2 minutes or until smooth and light.
- Spoon the icing onto the cakes and top each one with a crystallised violet.

203

Violet and Orange Cream Cheese Cupcakes

- Replace the lemon zest and juice with orange zest and juice.

204

MAKES 12

Chocolate and Cinnamon Cupcakes

PREPARATION TIME 30 MINUTES

COOKING TIME 15 - 20 MINUTES

INGREDIENTS

110 g / 4 oz / ⅔ cup self-raising flour, sifted
110 g / 4 oz / ½ cup light muscovado sugar
110 g / 4 oz / ½ cup butter, softened
2 large eggs
2 tbsp unsweetened cocoa powder
1 ½ tsp ground cinnamon
100 g / 3 ½ oz dark chocolate (minimum 60 % cocoa solids), chopped

TO DECORATE:
110 g / 4 oz / ½ cup cream cheese
55 g / 2 oz / ¼ cup butter, softened
110 g / 4 oz / 1 cup icing (confectioners') sugar
1 tsp vanilla extract
ground cinnamon for sprinkling

- Preheat the oven to 190°C (170° fan) / 375F / gas 5 and line a 12-hole cupcake tin with paper cases.
- Combine all of the cake ingredients in a bowl and whisk together for 2 minutes or until smooth.
- Divide the mixture between the cases and bake for 15 – 20 minutes.
- Transfer the cakes to a wire rack and leave to cool.
- Beat the cream cheese and butter together until light and fluffy then beat in the icing sugar a quarter at a time.
- Add the vanilla extract then whip the mixture for 2 minutes or until smooth and light.
- Spoon the icing into a piping bag fitted with a star nozzle and pipe it onto the cakes.
- Sprinkle with cinnamon.

205

Chocolate Chilli Cream Cheese Cupcakes

- Omit the cinnamon and use ½ tsp of chilli (chili) powder instead.

MAKES 12

Blackberry and Cinnamon Muffin Cupcakes

Blackberry and Clove Muffin Cupcakes

207

- Replace the ground cinnamon with ½ tsp of ground cloves.

Blackberry and Cardamom Muffin Cupcakes

208

- Replace the cinnamon with ¼ tsp of ground cardamom seeds.

PREPARATION TIME 20 MINUTES

COOKING TIME 20 – 25 MINUTES

INGREDIENTS

1 large egg
125 ml / 4 ½ fl. oz / ½ cup sunflower oil
125 ml / 4 ½ fl. oz / ½ cup milk
375 g / 13 oz / 2 ½ cups self-raising flour, sifted
1 tsp baking powder
1 tsp ground cinnamon
200 g / 7 oz / ¾ cup caster (superfine) sugar
75 g / 2 ½ oz / ½ cup blackberries

- Preheat the oven to 180°C (160° fan) / 350F / gas 4 and line a 12-hole cupcake tin with paper cases.
- Beat the egg in a jug with the oil and milk until well mixed.
- Mix the flour, baking powder, cinnamon and sugar in a bowl, then pour in the egg mixture and blackberries, and stir just enough to combine.
- Spoon the mixture into the tin, then bake in the oven for 20 – 25 minutes.
- Test with a wooden toothpick, if it comes out clean, the cakes are done.
- Transfer the cakes to a wire rack and leave to cool completely.

209

MAKES 24

Glace-Iced Almond Mini Cupcakes

PREPARATION TIME 25 MINUTES

COOKING TIME 12 - 15 MINUTES

INGREDIENTS

110 g / 4 oz / ⅔ cup self-raising flour, sifted
110 g / 4 oz / ½ cup caster (superfine) sugar
110 g / 4 oz / ½ cup butter, softened
2 large eggs
2 tbsp ground almonds
½ tsp almond extract

TO DECORATE:
200 g / 7 oz / 2 cups icing (confectioners') sugar
a few drops of almond essence
pastel coloured sweets to decorate

- Preheat the oven to 180°C (160° fan) / 350F / gas 4 and line a 24-hole mini cupcake tin with paper cases.
- Combine the flour, sugar, butter, eggs, ground almonds and almond extract in a bowl and whisk together for 2 minutes or until smooth.
- Divide the mixture between the cases and bake for 12 - 15 minutes.
- Test with a wooden toothpick, if it comes out clean, the cakes are done.
- Transfer the cakes to a wire rack and leave to cool completely.
- Sieve the icing sugar into a bowl and add the almond extract and just enough water to make a thick, spreadable icing.
- Spoon the icing onto the cakes and top each one with a sweet.

Glace-Iced Pistachio Mini Cupcakes

- Replace the ground almonds with ground pistachios and sprinkle the icing with chopped pistachio nuts.

211

MAKES 12

Chocolate Malteser Cupcakes

PREPARATION TIME 30 MINUTES

COOKING TIME 15 - 20 MINUTES

INGREDIENTS

110 g / 4 oz / ⅔ cup self-raising flour, sifted
110 g / 4 oz / ½ cup caster (superfine) sugar
110 g / 4 oz / ½ cup butter, softened
2 large eggs
2 tbsp malt extract
2 tbsp unsweetened cocoa powder

TO DECORATE:
200 g / 7 oz / 2 cups icing (confectioners') sugar
12 Maltesers

- Preheat the oven to 190°C (170° fan) / 375F / gas 5 and line a 12-hole cupcake tin with paper cases.
- Combine the flour, sugar, butter, eggs, malt extract and cocoa in a bowl and whisk together for 2 minutes or until smooth.
- Divide the mixture between the cases, then transfer the tin to the oven and bake for 15 – 20 minutes.
- Test with a wooden toothpick, if it comes out clean, the cakes are done.
- Transfer the cakes to a wire rack and leave to cool completely.
- Sieve the icing sugar into a bowl and add just enough water to make a thick, spreadable icing.
- Spoon the icing onto the cakes and top each one with a Malteser.

Chocolate Malteser Buttercream Cupcakes

212

- Spread the cakes with chocolate buttercream instead of the glace icing before topping with the Maltesers.

213

MAKES 12

Blueberry and Lemon Cupcakes

- Preheat the oven to 190°C (170° fan) / 375F / gas 5 and line a 12-hole cupcake tin with paper cases.
- Combine the flour, sugar, butter, eggs and lemon zest in a bowl and whisk together for 2 minutes or until smooth.
- Divide the mixture between the cases, then transfer the tin to the oven and bake for 15 – 20 minutes.
- Test with a wooden toothpick, if it comes out clean, the cakes are done.
- Transfer the cakes to a wire rack and leave to cool completely.
- Sieve the icing sugar into a bowl and add just enough lemon juice to make a thick, spreadable icing.
- Spoon the icing onto the cakes and top with the blueberries.

PREPARATION TIME 30 MINUTES

COOKING TIME 15 - 20 MINUTES

INGREDIENTS

110 g / 4 oz / ⅔ cup self-raising flour, sifted
110 g / 4 oz / ½ cup caster (superfine) sugar
110 g / 4 oz / ½ cup butter, softened
2 large eggs
1 lemon, zest finely grated

TO DECORATE:
200 g / 7 oz / 2 cups icing (confectioners') sugar
1 – 2 tsp lemon juice
100 g / 3 ½ oz / ⅔ cup blueberries

214

Raspberry and Lemon Cupcakes

- Replace the blueberries with raspberries.

215

MAKES 12

Double Chocolate Muffin Cupcakes

- Preheat the oven to 180°C (160° fan) / 350F / gas 4 and line a 12-hole cupcake tin with paper cases.
- Beat the egg in a jug with the oil and milk until well mixed.
- Mix the flour, cocoa, baking powder and sugar in a bowl, then pour in the egg mixture and chocolate chunks and stir just enough to combine.
- Divide the mixture between the cases, then bake in the oven for 20 – 25 minutes.
- Test with a wooden toothpick, if it comes out clean, the cakes are done.
- Serve warm or leave to cool on a wire rack.

PREPARATION TIME 15 MINUTES

COOKING TIME 20 – 25 MINUTES

INGREDIENTS

1 large egg
125 ml / 4 ½ fl. oz / ½ cup sunflower oil
125 ml / 4 ½ fl. oz / ½ cup milk
350 g / 12 ½ oz / 2 ⅓ cups self-raising flour, sifted
50 g / 1 ¾ oz / ½ cup unsweetened cocoa powder, sifted
1 tsp baking powder
200 g / 7 oz / ¾ cup caster (superfine) sugar
150 g / 5 ½ oz dark chocolate chunks (minimum 60% cocoa solids)

216

Triple Chocolate Muffin Cupcakes

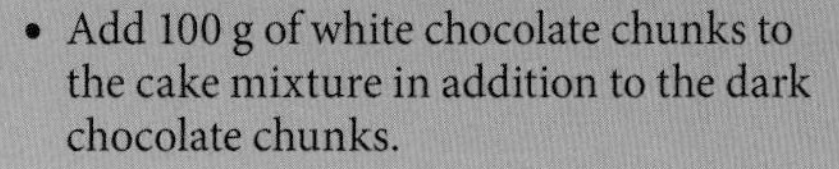

- Add 100 g of white chocolate chunks to the cake mixture in addition to the dark chocolate chunks.

217

MAKES 12

Sweet Dreams Cupcakes

PREPARATION TIME 20 MINUTES

COOKING TIME 20 – 25 MINUTES

INGREDIENTS

1 large egg
125 ml / 4 ½ fl. oz / ½ cup sunflower oil
125 ml / 4 ½ fl. oz / ½ cup milk
375 g / 13 oz / 2 ½ cups self-raising flour, sifted
1 tsp baking powder
200 g / 7 oz / ¾ cup caster (superfine) sugar
75 g / 2 ½ oz / 1 ¼ cups mini marshmallows

TO DECORATE:
100 g / 3 ½ oz / ½ cup butter, softened
200 g / 7 oz / 2 cups icing (confectioners') sugar
1 tsp vanilla extract
150 g / 5 ½ oz / 2 ½ cups mini marshmallows

- Preheat the oven to 180°C (160° fan) / 350F / gas 4 and line a deep 12-hole cupcake tin with paper cases.
- Beat the egg in a jug with the oil and milk until well mixed.
- Mix the flour, baking powder, sugar and marshmallows in a bowl, then pour in the egg mixture and stir just enough to combine.
- Spoon the mixture into the cases, then bake in the oven for 20 – 25 minutes.
- Test with a wooden toothpick, if it comes out clean, the cakes are done. Transfer the cakes to a wire rack and leave to cool completely.
- Beat the butter until smooth, then gradually whisk in the icing sugar and vanilla extract.
- Pipe the buttercream onto the cakes and top with the mini marshmallows.

218

Chocolate Marshmallow Dreams

- Sprinkle some grated chocolate over the cupcakes for an indulgent finish.

219

Marshmallow and Orange Cupcakes

- Add the grated zest of an orange to the cake mixture and 1 tbsp of orange juice to the buttercream.

220

MAKES 12

Jasmine Cupcakes

- Preheat the oven to 190°C (170° fan) / 375F / gas 5 and line a 12-hole cupcake tin with paper cases.
- Combine the flour, sugar, butter, eggs and jasmine syrup in a bowl and whisk together for 2 minutes or until smooth.
- Divide the mixture between the cases, then transfer the tin to the oven and bake for 15 – 20 minutes.
- Test with a wooden toothpick, if it comes out clean, the cakes are done.
- Transfer the cakes to a wire rack and leave to cool completely, then sit each cake in an espresso cup.
- Sieve the icing sugar into a bowl and add just enough jasmine syrup to make a thick, spreadable icing.
- Spread the icing onto the cakes and decorate with sugar flowers.

PREPARATION TIME 30 MINUTES

COOKING TIME 15 - 20 MINUTES

INGREDIENTS

110 g / 4 oz / ⅔ cup self-raising flour, sifted
110 g / 4 oz / ½ cup caster (superfine) sugar
110 g / 4 oz / ½ cup butter, softened
2 large eggs
1 tbsp jasmine syrup

TO DECORATE:
200 g / 7 oz / 2 cups icing (confectioners') sugar
1 - 2 tsp jasmine syrup
sugar flowers to decorate

Earl Grey Cupcakes

221

- Replace the jasmine syrup with earl grey tea syrup.

222

MAKES 24

Mini Coconut Cupcakes

- Preheat the oven to 180°C (160° fan) / 350F / gas 4 and line a 24-hole mini cupcake tin with paper cases.
- Combine the flour, sugar, butter, eggs and desiccated coconut in a bowl and whisk together for 2 minutes or until smooth.
- Divide the mixture between the cases and bake for 12 - 15 minutes.
- Test with a wooden toothpick, if it comes out clean, the cakes are done.
- Transfer the cakes to a wire rack and sprinkle with more desiccated coconut before leaving them to cool completely.

PREPARATION TIME 15 MINUTES

COOKING TIME 12 - 15 MINUTES

INGREDIENTS

110 g / 4 oz / ⅔ cup self-raising flour, sifted
110 g / 4 oz / ½ cup caster (superfine) sugar
110 g / 4 oz / ½ cup butter, softened
2 large eggs
2 tbsp desiccated coconut, plus extra for sprinkling

Mini Coconut Buttercream Cupcakes

223

- Top the cakes with buttercream made from 200 g of icing sugar, 100 g of softened butter and 2 tbsp of desiccated coconut.

224

MAKES 24

Chocolate and Hazelnut Mini Cupcakes

PREPARATION TIME 15 MINUTES

COOKING TIME 12 - 15 MINUTES

INGREDIENTS

110 g / 4 oz / ⅔ cup self-raising flour, sifted
110 g / 4 oz / ½ cup caster (superfine) sugar
110 g / 4 oz / ½ cup butter, softened
2 large eggs
2 tbsp unsweetened cocoa powder
2 tbsp ground hazelnuts (cob nuts)
200 g / 7 oz / 3/4 cup Nutella

- Preheat the oven to 190°C (170° fan) / 375F / gas 5 and line a 24-hole mini cupcake tin with paper cases.
- Combine the flour, sugar, butter, eggs, cocoa powder and ground hazelnuts in a bowl and whisk together for 2 minutes or until smooth.
- Divide the mixture between the cases and bake for 12 - 15 minutes.
- Test with a wooden toothpick, if it comes out clean, the cakes are done.
- Transfer the cakes to a wire rack and cool for 10 minutes, then spread with Nutella and leave to cool completely.

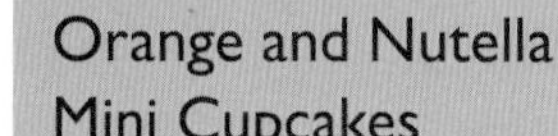

Orange and Nutella Mini Cupcakes

225

- Replace the cocoa powder with the finely grated zest of an orange and top the Nutella with chopped candied orange peel.

226

MAKES 12

Malted Cupcakes

PREPARATION TIME 30 MINUTES

COOKING TIME 15 - 20 MINUTES

INGREDIENTS

110 g / 4 oz / ⅔ cup self-raising flour, sifted
110 g / 4 oz / ½ cup caster (superfine) sugar
110 g / 4 oz / ½ cup butter, softened
2 large eggs
2 tbsp malt extract

TO DECORATE:
300 ml / 10 ½ fl. oz / 1 ¼ cups double (heavy) cream
2 tbsp malt extract
48 Maltesers

- Preheat the oven to 190°C (170° fan) / 375F / gas 5 and line a 12-hole cupcake tin with paper cases.
- Combine the flour, sugar, butter, eggs and malt extract in a bowl and whisk together for 2 minutes or until smooth.
- Divide the mixture between the cases, then transfer the tin to the oven and bake for 15 – 20 minutes.
- Test with a wooden toothpick, if it comes out clean, the cakes are done.
- Transfer the cakes to a wire rack and leave to cool completely.
- Whip the cream with the malt extract until it holds its shape, then spoon it into a piping bag fitted with a large star nozzle.
- Pipe a big swirl of cream onto the cupcakes and top each one with 4 Maltesers.

Horlicks Cupcakes

227

- Replace the malt extract in the cakes and cream with Horlicks malted milk powder. Decorate with Maltesers as before.

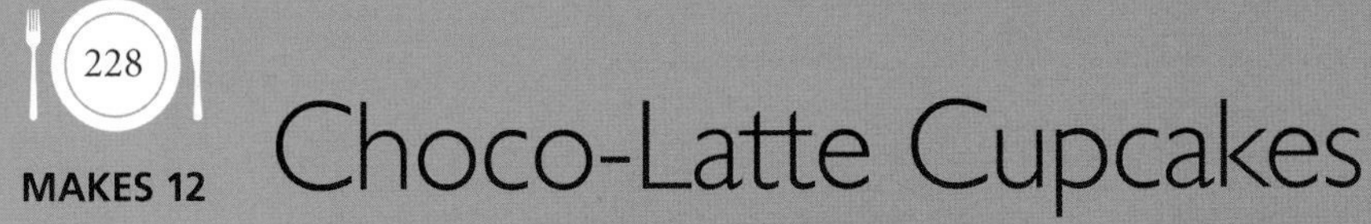

228

MAKES 12

Choco-Latte Cupcakes

PREPARATION TIME 45 MINUTES

COOKING TIME 15 - 18 MINUTES

INGREDIENTS

FOR THE BATTER

110 g / 4 oz / ⅔ cup self-raising flour, sifted
110 g / 4 oz / ½ cup margarine, softened
110 g / 4 oz / ½ cup caster (superfine) sugar
1 tsp vanilla extract
2 large eggs
a pinch of salt

FOR THE BUTTERCREAM

100 g / 3 ½ oz / ½ cup butter, softened
200 g / 7 oz / 2 cups icing(confectioners') sugar
30 g / 1 oz / 2 tbsp cocoa powder
1 tbsp whole milk

TO GARNISH

100 g / 3 ½ oz / ⅔ cup milk chocolate, chopped
1 tsp coffee granules

- Preheat the oven to 180°C (160° fan) / 350F / gas 4.
- Line a 12-hole cupcake tin with 12 cupcake cases.
- Beat together all the ingredients for the batter in a mixing bowl for 2 minutes until smooth and creamy.
- Divide evenly between the paper cases before rapping the tin on a work surface to help settle the batter.
- Bake for 15-18 minutes until risen; test with a wooden toothpick, if it comes out clean, the cakes are done.
- Remove to a wire rack to cool as you prepare the buttercream.
- Beat the softened butter with the cocoa powder, icing sugar and milk in a mixing bowl until smooth and creamy.
- Spoon into a piping bag fitted with a straight-sided nozzle and pipe buttercream onto the cupcakes.
- Melt the chopped chocolate in a heatproof bowl set atop a saucepan of simmering water, stirring occasionally.
- Remove from the heat and drizzle in pretzel-like shapes onto a greaseproof-lined baking tray.
- Let the shapes chill for 15 minutes before removing and peeling away from the greaseproof paper.
- Garnish the cupcakes with the chocolate shapes and a sprinkle of coffee granules before serving.

229

White and Milk Chocolate Cupcakes

- Substitute the milk chocolate for the garnish with white chocolate.

230

Chocolate Butterfly Cupcakes

- Pipe the melted chocolate into individual butterfly wings on the greaseproof paper. Peel off and arrange 2 wings on top of each cake.

231

Squidgy Milk Chocolate Mini Cupcakes

MAKES 12

PREPARATION TIME 50 MINUTES

COOKING TIME 8 MINUTES

INGREDIENTS

150 g / 5 ½ oz dark chocolate, minimum 60% cocoa solids, chopped
150 g / 5 ½ oz / ⅔ cup butter, chopped
85 g / 3 oz / ⅓ cup caster (superfine) sugar
3 large eggs, plus 3 egg yolks
1 tbsp plain (all-purpose) flour

- Line a 12-hole mini cupcake tray with paper cases.
- Melt the chocolate, butter and sugar together in a saucepan, stirring to dissolve the sugar.
- Leave to cool a little then beat in the eggs and egg yolks and fold in the flour.
- Divide the mixture between the cases, then chill for 30 minutes.
- Preheat the oven to 180°C (160° fan) / 350F / gas 4.
- Bake the cakes for 6 minutes, then transfer to a wire rack and leave to cool completely.

232

Squidgy Chocolate Orange Mini Cupcakes

- Replace the milk chocolate with orange-flavoured chocolate.

233

Blue Pearl Cupcakes

MAKES 24

PREPARATION TIME 30 MINUTES

COOKING TIME 25 MINUTES

INGREDIENTS

250 g / 9 oz / 2 cups plain (all purpose) flour
1 tsp bicarbonate of (baking) soda
1 tsp salt
½ tsp ground cinnamon
½ tsp ground nutmeg
140 g / 5 oz / 1 ¼ cup butter, softened
200 g / 7 oz / 1 cup caster (superfine) sugar
2 eggs
1 tsp vanilla extract
4 tbsp buttermilk
225 g / 8 oz / 2 cups ripe bananas, mashed
2 apples, peeled, cored and grated

TO DECORATE

125 g / 4 ½ oz / ½ cup butter, unsalted, softened
300 g / 10 ½ oz / 2 ½ cups icing (confectioners') sugar
½ tsp vanilla extract
½ tbsp milk
blue sugar pearls

- Preheat the oven to 190°C (170° fan) / 375F / gas 5 and line a cupcake tin with paper cases.
- Sift together the flour, bicarbonate of soda, salt, cinnamon and nutmeg.
- In separate bowl cream butter and sugar.
- Mix in the egg, buttermilk and vanilla extract.
- Gently mix in the flour. Fold in mashed banana and apple.
- Spoon cupcake mix into each paper case.
- Bake, for 20 - 25 minutes.
- Place on wire rack to cool.
- To make the buttercream, beat the butter with a whisk until soft then gradually beat in the icing sugar, vanilla and milk.
- Pipe buttercream swirls. Add pearls.

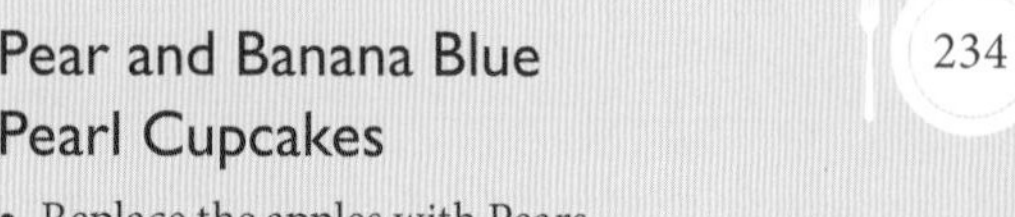

234

Pear and Banana Blue Pearl Cupcakes

- Replace the apples with Pears.

235

MAKES 12

Almond Muffin Cupcakes

- Preheat the oven to 180°C (160° fan) / 350F / gas 4 and line a deep 12-hole cupcake tin with paper cases.
- Beat the egg in a jug with the almond essence, oil and milk until well mixed.
- Mix the flour, baking powder, sugar and ground almonds in a bowl, then pour in the egg mixture and stir just enough to combine.
- Spoon the mixture into the cases, then bake in the oven for 20 – 25 minutes.
- Test with a wooden toothpick, if it comes out clean, the cakes are done.
- Transfer the cakes to a wire rack and leave to cool completely before arranging the flaked almonds on top.

PREPARATION TIME 20 MINUTES

COOKING TIME 20 – 25 MINUTES

INGREDIENTS

1 large egg
½ tsp almond essence
125 ml / 4 ½ fl. oz / ½ cup sunflower oil
125 ml / 4 ½ fl. oz / ½ cup milk
375 g / 13 oz / 2 ½ cups self-raising flour, sifted
1 tsp baking powder
200 g / 7 oz / ¾ cup caster (superfine) sugar
50 g / 1 ¾ oz / ½ cup ground almonds
50 g / 1 ¾ oz / ⅔ cup flaked (slivered) almonds

236

Almond and Apricot Muffin Cupcakes

- Add 75 g of chopped dried apricots to the cake mixture. Spread the cakes with warm apricot jam before topping with the flaked almonds.

237

MAKES 12

Pink-Iced Orange Cupcakes

- Preheat the oven to 190°C (170° fan) / 375F / gas 5 and line a 12-hole cupcake tin with paper cases.
- Combine the flour, sugar, butter, eggs and orange zest in a bowl and whisk together for 2 minutes or until smooth.
- Divide the mixture between the cases and bake for 15 – 20 minutes.
- Test with a wooden toothpick, if it comes out clean, the cakes are done. Transfer the cakes to a wire rack and leave to cool completely.
- Whisk the royal icing powder with 25 ml of cold water for 5 minutes with an electric whisk until smooth and thick. Colour the icing pale pink.
- Spoon half of the icing into a piping bag fitted with a plain nozzle and pipe a dome on top of each cake.
- Spoon the rest of the icing into a piping bag fitted with a star nozzle and pipe a star in the centre of each icing dome.

PREPARATION TIME 30 MINUTES

COOKING TIME 15 - 20 MINUTES

INGREDIENTS

110 g / 4 oz / ⅔ cup self-raising flour, sifted
110 g / 4 oz / ½ cup caster (superfine) sugar
110 g / 4 oz / ½ cup butter, softened
2 large eggs
1 orange, zest finely grated

TO DECORATE:

150 g / 5 ½ oz / 1 ½ cups royal icing powder
a few drops of pink food colouring

238

Blue-Iced Lemon Cupcakes

- Replace the orange zest with lemon zest and colour the icing blue instead of pink.

239

Mini Chocolate and Blackberry Cupcakes

MAKES 24

240

Mini Chocolate and Raspberry Cream Cupcakes

- Replace the blackberries with raspberries.

241

Mini Orange and Blackberry Cream Cupcakes

- Replace the cocoa in the cake mixture with the grated zest of an orange. Add 1 tbsp of orange juice to the cream.

PREPARATION TIME 30 MINUTES

COOKING TIME 12 - 15 MINUTES

INGREDIENTS

110 g / 4 oz / ⅔ cup self-raising flour, sifted
110 g / 4 oz / ½ cup caster (superfine) sugar
110 g / 4 oz / ½ cup butter, softened
2 large eggs
2 tbsp unsweetened cocoa powder

To decorate:
300 ml / 10 ½ fl. oz / 1 ¼ cups double (heavy) cream
2 tbsp icing (confectioners') sugar
½ tsp vanilla extract
24 blackberries

- Preheat the oven to 190°C (170° fan) / 375F / gas 5 and line a 24-hole mini cupcake tin with paper cases.
- Combine the flour, sugar, butter, eggs and cocoa in a bowl and whisk together for 2 minutes or until smooth.
- Divide the mixture between the cases and bake for 12 - 15 minutes.
- Test with a wooden toothpick, if it comes out clean, the cakes are done.
- Transfer the cakes to a wire rack and leave to cool completely.
- Whip the cream with the icing sugar and vanilla extract until it holds its shape, then spoon it into a piping bag, fitted with a large star nozzle.
- Pipe a swirl on top of the cakes then top each one with a blackberry.

242

MAKES 12

Marmalade Cream Cupcakes

- Preheat the oven to 190°C (170° fan) / 375F / gas 5 and line a 12-hole cupcake tin with paper cases.
- Whisk all of the cake ingredients together until smooth.
- Divide the mixture between the paper cases and bake for 15 – 20 minutes.
- Test with a wooden toothpick, if it comes out clean, the cakes are done. Transfer the cakes to a wire rack and leave to cool completely.
- To make the topping, whisk the cream with the icing sugar until it forms soft peaks.
- Spoon the whipped cream into a piping bag fitted with a large star nozzle and pipe a swirl on top of each cake.
- Top each cake with 1 tsp of marmalade and a sprinkle of orange zest.

PREPARATION TIME 30 MINUTES

COOKING TIME 15 – 20 MINUTES

INGREDIENTS

110 g / 4 oz / 1 cup self-raising flour, sifted
110 g / 4 oz / ½ cup caster (superfine) sugar
110 g / 4 oz / ½ cup butter, softened
2 large eggs
3 tbsp Seville orange marmalade

TO DECORATE:
225 ml / 8 fl. oz / 3/4 cup double (heavy) cream
2 tbsp icing (confectioners') sugar
4 tbsp Seville orange marmalade
1 orange, zest finely pared

Lime Marmalade Cream Cupcakes

243

- Replace the Seville orange marmalade with lime marmalade and sprinkle with finely pared lime zest.

244

MAKES 12

Banana and Poppy Seed Cupcakes

- Preheat the oven to 200°C (180° fan) / 400F / gas 6 and line a 12-hole cupcake tin with paper cases.
- Mash the bananas with a fork then whisk in the sugar, eggs, oil and poppy seeds.
- Sieve the flour and bicarbonate of soda into the bowl and stir just enough to evenly mix all the ingredients together.
- Divide the mixture between the paper cases, then transfer the tin to the oven and bake for 15 – 20 minutes.
- Test with a wooden toothpick, if it comes out clean, the cakes are done.
- Transfer the cakes to a wire rack and leave to cool completely.

PREPARATION TIME 15 MINUTES

COOKING TIME 15 - 20 MINUTES

INGREDIENTS

3 very ripe bananas
100 g / 3 ½ oz / ½ cup soft light brown sugar
2 large eggs
125 ml / 4 ½ fl. oz / ½ cup sunflower oil
2 tbsp poppy seeds
225 g / 8 oz / 1 ½ cups plain (all-purpose) flour
1 tsp bicarbonate of (baking) soda

Banana and Cinnamon Cupcakes

245

- Omit the poppy seeds and add 1 tsp of ground cinnamon to the cake mixture with the flour.

246

MAKES 8

Ginger Nut Cupcakes

PREPARATION TIME 30 MINUTES

COOKING TIME 15 - 20 MINUTES

INGREDIENTS

4 ginger nut biscuits, crushed
110 g / 4 oz / ⅔ cup self-raising flour, sifted
110 g / 4 oz / ½ cup caster (superfine) sugar
110 g / 4 oz / ½ cup butter, softened
2 large eggs
1 tsp ground ginger

TO DECORATE:
200 ml / 7 fl. oz / 3/4 cup double (heavy) cream
2 tbsp icing (confectioners') sugar

- Preheat the oven to 190°C (170° fan) / 375F / gas 5. Oil 8 ramekins, then sprinkle with the crushed ginger nuts and shake to coat.
- Combine the flour, sugar, butter, eggs and ground ginger in a bowl and whisk together for 2 minutes or until smooth.
- Divide the mixture between the ramekins, then bake for 15 – 20 minutes.
- Test with a wooden toothpick, if it comes out clean, the cakes are done.
- Transfer the cakes to a wire rack and leave to cool completely.
- Whip the cream with the icing sugar until it holds its shape, then spoon it into a piping bag fitted with a large star nozzle.
- Pipe a rosette of cream on top of each cake.

Rusk Cupcakes

247

- Replace the ginger nut biscuits with rusk biscuits.

248

MAKES 24

Glazed Fresh Cherry Mini Cupcakes

PREPARATION TIME 15 MINUTES

COOKING TIME 12 - 15 MINUTES

INGREDIENTS

110 g / 4 oz / ⅔ cup self-raising flour, sifted
110 g / 4 oz / ½ cup caster (superfine) sugar
110 g / 4 oz / ½ cup butter, softened
2 large eggs
1 tsp vanilla extract
75 g / 2 ½ oz / ½ cup cherries, stoned and chopped

TO DECORATE:
100 g / 3 ½ oz / 1 cup icing (confectioners') sugar
a few drops of almond extract
a few drops of pink food colouring
24 black cherries, stoned

- Preheat the oven to 190°C (170° fan) / 375F / gas 5 and line a 24-hole mini cupcake tin with paper cases.
- Combine the flour, sugar, butter, eggs, vanilla extract and cherries in a bowl and whisk together for 2 minutes or until smooth.
- Divide the mixture between the cases, then transfer the tin to the oven and bake for 12 - 15 minutes.
- Test with a wooden toothpick, if it comes out clean, the cakes are done.
- Transfer the cakes to a wire rack and leave to cool completely.
- Sieve the icing sugar into a bowl and add the almond extract and just enough water to make a thin pourable glaze.
- Colour the icing with a few drops of pink food colouring then spoon it on top of the cupcakes and top with the cherries.

Glazed Preserved Cherry Mini Cupcakes

249

- When fresh cherries aren't in season, replace them with preserved black cherries in syrup. Drain well before chopping.

MAKES 12

Chocolate Brownie Cupcakes with Chantilly

Chocolate Orange Brownie Cream Cupcakes

- Add the grated zest of an orange to the cake mixture and Chantilly.

Mint Choc Brownie Cream Cupcakes

252

- Add a few drops of peppermint essence to the cake mixture and cream.

PREPARATION TIME 35 MINUTES

COOKING TIME 30 – 35 MINUTES

INGREDIENTS

100 g / 3 ½ oz dark chocolate (minimum 60 % cocoa solids), chopped
75 g / 2 ½ oz / 3/4 cup unsweetened cocoa powder, sifted
225 g / 8 oz / 1 cup butter
450 g / 1 lb / 2 ½ cups light brown sugar
4 large eggs
100 g / 3 ½ oz / ⅔ cup self-raising flour

TO DECORATE:
300 ml / 10 ½ fl. oz / 1 ¼ cups double (heavy) cream
2 tbsp icing (confectioners') sugar
1 tsp vanilla extract

- Preheat the oven to 160°C (140° fan) / 325F / gas 3 and line a 12-hole cupcake tin with paper cases.
- Melt the chocolate, cocoa and butter together in a saucepan, then leave to cool a little.
- Whisk the sugar and eggs together with an electric whisk for 3 minutes or until very light and creamy.
- Pour in the chocolate mixture and sieve over the flour, then fold everything together until evenly mixed.
- Divide the mixture between the cases and bake for 30 – 35 minutes or until they are just set in the centre.
- Transfer the cakes to a wire rack and leave to cool completely.
- Whip the cream with the sugar and vanilla extract until it holds its shape, then spoon it into a piping bag fitted with a large star nozzle.
- Pipe a big swirl on top of each cake and chill until ready to serve.

253

MAKES 24

Glitter Magic Cupcakes

PREPARATION TIME 30 MINUTES

COOKING TIME 18 - 20 MINUTES

INGREDIENTS

225 g / 8 oz / 1 cup butter, softened
250 g / 9 oz / 1 ¼ cups caster (superfine) sugar
3 eggs
1 tsp vanilla extract
300 g / 11 oz / 2 ½ cups plain (all-purpose) flour
1 ½ tsp baking powder
¼ tsp bicarbonate of (baking) soda
¼ tsp salt
240 ml / 8 ½ fl. oz / 1 cup buttermilk
125 g / 4 ½ oz / ½ cup butter, unsalted, softened
300 g / 10 ½ oz / 2 ½ cups icing (confectioners') sugar
½ tsp vanilla extract
½ tbsp milk
edible glitter
pink pearls

- Preheat the oven to 180°C (160° fan) / 350F / gas 4 and line a cupcake tin with paper cases.
- Cream butter and sugar until light and fluffy.
- Gradually beat in eggs and vanilla.
- Combine the flour, baking powder, baking soda and salt; add to creamed mixture alternately with buttermilk, beating well after each addition.
- Spoon cupcake mix into each paper case.
- Bake, for 18-20 minutes. Test with a wooden toothpick, if it comes out clean, the cake is done.
- Place on wire rack to cool.
- To make the buttercream, beat the butter with a whisk until soft then gradually beat in the icing sugar, vanilla and milk.
- Pipe buttercream swirls. Sprinkle with edible glitter and place pink pearls on top.

Pink Glitter Magic Cupcakes

254

- Add a few drops of pink food colouring to the cupcake mixture.

255

MAKES 12

White Choc Chip Dream Cupcakes

PREPARATION TIME 30 MINUTES

COOKING TIME 20 - 25 MINUTES

INGREDIENTS

2 eggs
250 ml / 9 fl. oz / 1 cup milk
100 g / 3 ½ oz / ½ cup granulated sugar
100 g / 3 ½ oz / ½ cup brown sugar
1 tsp vanilla extract
400 g / 7 oz / 3 cups plain (all purpose) flour
4 tsp baking powder
1 tsp salt
150 g / 5 ½ oz white chocolate

TO DECORATE

125 g / 4 ½ oz / ½ cup unsalted butter, softened
300 g / 10 ½ oz / 2 ½ cups icing (confectioners') sugar
½ tsp vanilla extract
½ tbsp milk
white chocolate drops

- Preheat the oven to 200°C (180° fan) / 400F / gas 6 and line a cupcake tin with paper cases.
- Place the eggs, oil, vanilla extract, sugars and milk in a large mixing bowl and beat together.
- In another bowl place the flour, salt and baking powder and mix thoroughly.
- Chop the chocolate into small pieces and stir into the flour. Pour in the liquid, and mix together until just blended.
- Spoon the cake mixture into the paper cases.
- Bake, for 20-25 minutes. Test with a wooden toothpick, if it comes out clean, the cake is done.
- Place on a wire rack to cool.
- To make the buttercream, whisk the butter until soft then gradually beat in the icing sugar, vanilla and milk.
- Pipe on buttercream swirls and then place a chocolate drop on top.

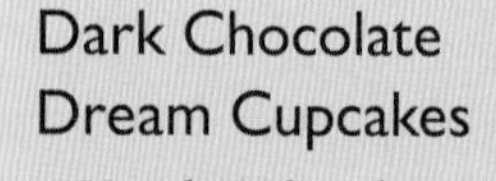

Dark Chocolate Dream Cupcakes

256

- Use plain chocolate instead of white.

257

MAKES 18

Choco-Vanilla Teaser Cupcakes

- Preheat the oven to 180°C (160° fan) / 350F / gas 4 and line a cupcake tin with paper cases.
- Cream butter and sugar until pale and fluffy with an electric whisk.
- Gradually mix in the egg and vanilla extract.
- Gently mix in the flour and cocoa, adding the milk.
- Spoon cupcake mix into each paper case.
- Bake, for 18-20 minutes. Test with a wooden toothpick, if it comes out clean, the cake is done.
- Place on a wire rack to cool.
- To make the buttercream beat butter with a whisk until soft then gradually beat in icing sugar, vanilla and milk.
- Pipe on the buttercream. Top with a malteser.

PREPARATION TIME 10 MINUTES

COOKING TIME 45 MINUTES

INGREDIENTS

125 g / 4 ½ oz / ½ cup butter unsalted, softened
125 g / 4 ½ oz / ½ cup caster (superfine) sugar
2 medium eggs, room temperature
½ tsp vanilla extract
125 g / 4 ½ oz / 1 cup self-raising flour
2 tbsp cocoa
45 ml / 1 ½ fl. oz / ¼ cup milk

TO DECORATE

125 g / 4 ½ oz / ½ cup butter, unsalted, softened
300 g / 10 ½ oz / 2 ½ cups icing (confectioners') sugar
½ tsp vanilla extract
½ tbsp milk
Maltesers

Chocolate Caramel Teasers

258

- Replace the malteser topping with a chocolate covered soft caramel.

259

MAKES 12

Red Sugar Cupcakes

- Preheat the oven to 200°C (180° fan) / 400F / gas 6 and line a cupcake tin with paper cases.
- Cream butter and sugar until pale and fluffy with an electric whisk.
- Gradually mix in the egg.
- Gently mix in the flour adding the milk.
- Spoon cupcake mix into each paper case.
- Bake, for 15 minutes. Test with a wooden toothpick, if it comes out clean, the cake is done.
- Place on a wire rack to cool.
- To make the buttercream, beat butter with a whisk until soft then gradually beat in icing sugar, vanilla and milk.
- Pipe on the buttercream.
- Colour sugar with a couple of drops of red food colouring.

PREPARATION TIME 25 MINUTES

COOKING TIME 15 MINUTES

INGREDIENTS

125 g / 4 ½ oz / ½ cup butter unsalted, softened
125 g / 4 ½ oz / ½ cup light muscovado sugar
2 medium eggs, room temperature
125 g / 4 ½ oz / 1 cup wholemeal self-raising flour
2 tbsp milk

TO DECORATE

125 g / 4 ½ oz / ½ cup butter, unsalted, softened
300 g / 10 ½ oz / 2 ½ cups icing (confectioners') sugar
½ tsp vanilla extract
½ tbsp milk
60 g / 2 oz / ¼ cup granulated sugar
red food colouring

Green Sugar Cupcakes

260

- Colour the granulated sugar for the topping green instead of red.

261

MAKES 12

Pink Crown Raspberry Cupcakes

PREPARATION TIME 10 MINUTES

COOKING TIME 15 MINUTES

INGREDIENTS

110 g / 4 oz / ⅔ cup self-raising flour, sifted
110 g / 4 oz / ½ cup margarine, softened
110 g / 4 oz / ½ cup caster (superfine) sugar
1 tsp vanilla extract
2 large eggs
a pinch of salt

FOR THE RASPBERRY BUTTERCREAM
100 g / 3 ½ oz / ½ cup butter, softened
200 g / 7 oz / 2 cups icing (confectioners') sugar
2 tbsp Framboise liqueur

TO GARNISH
200 g / 7 oz / 2 cups raspberries

- Preheat the oven to 180°C (160° fan) / 350F / gas 4.
- Line a 12-hole cupcake tin with 12 cupcake cases.
- Beat together all the ingredients for the batter in a mixing bowl for 2 minutes until smooth and creamy.
- Divide evenly between the paper cases before rapping the tin on a work surface to help settle the batter.
- Bake for 15-18 minutes until risen; test with a wooden toothpick, if it comes out clean, the cakes are done.
- Remove to a wire rack to cool as you prepare the buttercream.
- Beat the softened butter in a mixing bowl for 3-4 minutes until pale.
- Add the icing sugar and the Framboise and beat again until smooth.
- Spoon into a piping bag fitted with a star-shaped nozzle and pipe a rosette on top of each cupcake.
- Garnish the perimeter with raspberries before serving.

262

Redcurrant Truffle Cupcakes

- Substitute the raspberries for redcurrants around the perimeters.

263

Framboise Drizzle Cupcakes

- Drizzle the cupcakes with 3 tbsp of Framboise before cooling and topping with the buttercream.

264

MAKES 18

Chocolate Cigarillo Cupcakes

- Preheat the oven to 180°C (160° fan) / 350F / gas 4 and line an 18-hole cupcake tin with paper cases.
- In a large mixing bowl, whisk up the eggs and sugar for 4 minutes until they are light and fluffy.
- Beat in the grated beetroot and vanilla essence. Add the flour, ground almonds, baking powder, cocoa powder, salt and beat until combined.
- Add the buttermilk. Beat again to ensure everything is well combined.
- Spoon the cupcake mix into each paper case.
- Bake for 20 minutes. Test with a wooden toothpick, if it comes out clean, the cake is done. Leave to cool.
- To make the buttercream, beat the butter with a whisk until soft then gradually beat in the icing sugar, vanilla and milk.
- Pipe on the buttercream. Place the cigarillo.

PREPARATION TIME 30 MINUTES

COOKING TIME 20 MINUTES

INGREDIENTS

3 eggs
150 g / 5 ½ oz / ¾ cup granulated sugar
200 g / 7 oz / 1 ¼ cup beetroot, peeled and grated
½ tsp vanilla extract
180 g / 6 ½ oz /1 ½ cup plain (all purpose) flour
180 g / 6 ½ oz / 2 cups ground almonds
2 tsp baking powder
2 tbsp cocoa powder
¼ tsp salt
284 ml / 10 oz / 1 ¼ cup buttermilk

TO DECORATE

125 g / 4 ½ oz / ½ cup butter, unsalted, softened
300 g / 10 ½ oz / 2 ½ cups icing (confectioners') sugar
½ tsp vanilla extract
½ tbsp milk
chocolate cigarillos

265

Chocolate Mint Cigarillo Cupcakes

- Replace the vanilla essence in the buttercream with peppermint essence.

266

MAKES 12

Peppermint Crisp Cupcakes

- Preheat the oven to 160°C (140° fan) / 325F / gas 3 and line a cupcake tin with paper cases.
- Cream butter and sugar until pale and fluffy with an electric whisk.
- Gradually mix in the egg.
- Gently mix in the flour and cocoa.
- Add milk and peppermint.
- Spoon cupcake mix into each paper case.
- Bake, for 20 minutes. Test with a wooden toothpick, if it comes out clean, the cake is done.
- Place on wire rack to cool.
- To make the buttercream, beat the butter with a whisk until soft then gradually beat in the icing sugar, vanilla and milk.
- Pipe buttercream and place chocolate on top

PREPARATION TIME 25 MINUTES

COOKING TIME 30 MINUTES

INGREDIENTS

80 g / 3 oz / ¼ cup butter, at room temperature
175 g / 6 oz / ¾ cup caster (superfine) sugar
1 large egg
170 g / 6 oz / 1 ¼ cups self-raising flour
1 tbsp cocoa powder
100 ml / 3 ½ fl. oz milk
1 tsp peppermint extract

TO DECORATE

125 g / 4 ½ oz / ½ cup butter, unsalted, softened
300 g / 10 ½ oz / 2 ½ cups icing (confectioners') sugar
½ tsp vanilla extract
½ tbsp milk
peppermint crisp chocolate

267

Double Mint Cupcakes

- Add 1 tsp of peppermint extract instead of vanilla to the buttercream

268

MAKES 18

Chocolate Chip Cream Cupcakes

PREPARATION TIME 30 MINUTES

COOKING TIME 20 MINUTES

INGREDIENTS

150 g / 5 ½ oz / ½ cup butter, unsalted, softened
150 g / 5 ½ oz / ¾ cup light muscovado sugar
3 eggs
115 g / 4 oz / 1 cup self-raising flour
35 g / 1 ½ oz / ¼ cup cocoa powder
½ tsp baking powder
100 g / 3 ½ oz / ¾ cup milk chocolate chips

TO DECORATE

125 g / 4 ½ oz / ½ cup butter, unsalted, softened
300 g / 10 ½ oz / 2 ½ cups icing (confectioners') sugar
½ tsp vanilla extract
½ tbsp milk

- Preheat the oven to 170°C (150° fan) / 325F / gas 3 and line a cupcake tin with paper cases.
- Cream butter and sugar until pale and fluffy with an electric whisk.
- Gradually mix in the egg.
- Gently mix in the flour, cocoa, vanilla, baking powder and chocolate chips.
- Spoon cupcake mix into each paper case.
- Bake, for 20 minutes. Test with a wooden toothpick, if it comes out clean, the cake is done.
- Place on wire rack to cool.
- To make the buttercream, beat the butter with a whisk until soft then gradually beat in the icing sugar, vanilla and milk.
- Pipe buttercream with rose nozzle.

269

Chocolate Cinnamon Cream Cupcakes

- Add 3 tbsp of cocoa and 1 tsp of ground cinnamon to the buttercream for a chocolate icing.

270

MAKES 12

Vanilla Cream Raspberry Cupcakes

PREPARATION TIME 30 MINUTES

COOKING TIME 20 MINUTES

INGREDIENTS

125 g / 4 ½ oz / ½ cup butter unsalted, softened
125 g / 4 ½ oz / ½ cup caster (superfine) sugar
2 medium eggs, room temperature
½ tsp vanilla extract
125 g / 4 ½ oz / 1 cup self-raising flour
2 tbsp cocoa powder
45 ml / 1 ½ fl. oz / ¼ cup milk

TO DECORATE

125 g / 4 ½ oz / ½ cup butter, unsalted, softened
300 g / 10 ½ oz / 2 ½ cups icing (confectioners') sugar
½ tsp vanilla extract
½ tbsp milk
raspberries

- Preheat the oven to 180°C (160° fan) / 350F / gas 4 and line a cupcake tin with paper cases.
- Cream butter and sugar until pale and fluffy with an electric whisk.
- Gradually mix in the egg and vanilla extract.
- Gently mix in the flour and cocoa, adding the milk.
- Spoon cupcake mix into each paper case.
- Bake, for 18-20 minutes. Test with a wooden toothpick, if it comes out clean, the cake is done.
- Place on wire rack to cool.
- To make the buttercream, beat the butter with a whisk until soft then gradually beat in the icing sugar, vanilla and milk.
- Pipe buttercream. Top with a raspberry.

271

Chocolate Cream Raspberry Cupcakes

- Add 3 tbsp of cocoa to the buttercream mixture.

272

MAKES 12

Apricot Jam Cupcakes

PREPARATION TIME 10 MINUTES

COOKING TIME 15 - 18 MINUTES

INGREDIENTS

110 g / 4 oz / ⅔ cup self-raising flour, sifted
110 g / 4 oz / ½ cup margarine, softened
110 g / 4 oz / ½ cup caster (superfine) sugar
2 large eggs
a pinch of salt

FOR THE BUTTERCREAM
100 g / 3 ½ oz / ½ cup butter, softened
200 g / 7 oz / 2 cups icing (confectioners') sugar
2 tbsp apricot jam
a few drops of orange food colouring

TO GARNISH
150 g / 5 oz / ⅔ cup apricot jam

- Preheat the oven to 180°C (160° fan) / 350F / gas 4.
- Line a 12-hole cupcake tin with 12 cupcake cases.
- Beat together all the ingredients for the batter in a mixing bowl for 2 minutes until smooth and creamy.
- Divide evenly between the paper cases before rapping the tin on a work surface to help settle the batter.
- Bake for 15-18 minutes until risen; test with a wooden toothpick, if it comes out clean, the cakes are done.
- Remove to a wire rack to cool as you prepare the buttercream.
- Beat the softened butter for 2 minutes until creamy and pale.
- Add the icing sugar and apricot jam and beat again until smooth.
- Add a few drops of the food colouring and beat well until uniformly orange.
- Spoon into a piping bag fitted with a small star-shaped nozzle.
- Pipe small stars around the perimeter of the cupcakes before filling the centres with apricot jam.

Apricot and Coconut Cupcakes

273

- Add ⅔ cup of desiccated coconut and 2 tbsp whole milk to the batter.

Strawberry Jam Cupcakes

274

- Replace the apricot jam for the topping and buttercream with strawberry jam.

275

MAKES 12

Lemon and Poppy Seed Star Cupcakes

PREPARATION TIME 30 MINUTES

COOKING TIME 20 MINUTES

INGREDIENTS

150 g / 5 ½ oz / ½ cup butter, unsalted, softened
150 g / 5 ½ oz / ½ cup golden caster (superfine) sugar
3 eggs
150 g / 5 ½ oz / 1 cup self-raising flour
30 g / 1 oz / ¼ cup poppy seeds
3 tbsp yoghurt
1 lemon, juiced and zested
3 tbsp golden caster (superfine) sugar

TO DECORATE

125 g / 4 ½ oz / ½ cup butter, unsalted, softened
300 g / 10 ½ oz / 2 ½ cups icing (confectioners') sugar
½ tsp lemon extract
½ tbsp milk
fondant stars

- Preheat the oven to 180°C (160° fan) / 350F / gas 4 and line a cupcake tin with paper cases.
- Cream butter and sugar until pale and fluffy with an electric whisk.
- Gradually mix in the egg.
- Gently mix in the flour, baking powder, lemon zest, poppy seeds and yoghurt until smooth.
- Spoon cupcake mix into each paper case.
- Bake, for 20 – 25 minutes. Test with a wooden toothpick, if it comes out clean, the cake is done.
- Warm the lemon juice with the sugar in a small pan until the sugar has dissolved. With a toothpick make a few holes in the cupcake and spoon a little over each cake.
- Place on a wire rack to cool.
- To make the buttercream, beat the butter with a whisk until soft then gradually beat in the icing sugar, vanilla and milk.
- Pipe the buttercream and add a star.

276

MAKES 12

Strawberry Jam Frosted Cupcakes

PREPARATION TIME 30 MINUTES

COOKING TIME 25 MINUTES

INGREDIENTS

15 g / ½ oz / ¼ cup freeze dried strawberries
150 g / 5 ½ oz / ½ cup butter, unsalted, softened
150 g / 5 ½ oz / ½ cup caster (superfine) sugar
3 eggs
150 g / 5 ½ oz / 1 cup self-raising flour
½ tsp baking powder

TO DECORATE

125 g / 4 ½ oz / ½ cup butter
300 g / 10 ½ oz / 2 ½ cups icing (confectioners') sugar
½ tsp vanilla extract
½ tbsp milk
strawberry jam

- Preheat the oven to 180°C (160° fan) / 350F / gas 4 and line a cupcake tin with paper cases.
- Crush the strawberries in a pestle and mortar until finely ground but not completely powdered.
- Cream butter and sugar until pale and fluffy with an electric whisk.
- Gradually mix in the eggs.
- Add strawberries and all flour.
- Spoon cupcake mix into each paper case.
- Bake, for 20 -25 minutes. Test with a wooden toothpick, if it comes out clean, the cake is done.
- Place on wire rack to cool.
- To make the buttercream, beat the butter with a whisk until soft then gradually beat in the icing sugar, vanilla and milk.
- Pipe on buttercream swirls and a tsp of strawberry jam.

277

Summer Fruit Crème Fraiche Cupcakes

MAKES 12

- Preheat the oven to 190°C (170° fan) / 375F / gas 5 and line a 12-hole cupcake tin with foil cases.
- Combine the flour, sugar, butter, eggs and vanilla in a bowl and whisk together for 2 minutes or until smooth.
- Divide the mixture between the cases and bake for 15 – 20 minutes.
- Test with a wooden toothpick, if it comes out clean, the cakes are done. Transfer the cakes to a wire rack and leave to cool completely.
- Spoon the crème fraiche on top of the cakes and decorate each one with a raspberry, a blueberry and a slice of banana.

PREPARATION TIME 25 MINUTES

COOKING TIME 15 - 20 MINUTES

INGREDIENTS

110 g / 4 oz / ⅔ cup self-raising flour, sifted
110 g / 4 oz / ½ cup caster (superfine) sugar
110 g / 4 oz / ½ cup butter, softened
2 large eggs
1 tsp vanilla extract
300 ml / 10 ½ fl. oz / 1 ¼ cups crème fraiche
12 raspberries
12 blueberries
1 banana, sliced

278

Glace Icing for Cupcakes

MAKES ENOUGH TO ICE 12 CUPCAKES

PREPARATION TIME 10 MINUTES

SETTING TIME 1 – 2 HOURS

INGREDIENTS

200 g / 7 oz / 2 cups icing (confectioners') sugar

- Sieve the icing sugar into a bowl to remove any lumps then add just enough water to make a thick, spreadable icing.
- Spoon the icing onto your cupcakes and spread it out with the back of the spoon.
- Decorate the cakes with sugar flowers, sweets or cake sprinkles while the icing is still wet, then leave to set for 1 – 2 hours.

279

Chocolate Cookies Cupcakes

MAKES 12

PREPARATION TIME 1 HOUR

COOKING TIME 15 - 20 MINUTES

INGREDIENTS

110 g / 4 oz / ⅔ cup self-raising flour, sifted
110 g / 4 oz / ½ cup caster (superfine) sugar
110 g / 4 oz / ½ cup butter, softened
2 large eggs
2 tbsp unsweetened cocoa powder

TO DECORATE:

100 g / 3 ½ oz / ½ cup butter, softened
200 g / 7 oz / 2 cups icing (confectioners') sugar
½ tsp vanilla extract
1 tbsp unsweetened cocoa powder
12 Oreo cookies

- Preheat the oven to 190°C (170° fan) / 375F / gas 5 and line a 12-hole cupcake tin with paper cases.
- Combine the flour, sugar, butter, eggs and cocoa powder in a bowl and whisk together for 2 minutes or until smooth. Divide the mixture between the cases, then transfer the tin to the oven and bake for 15 – 20 minutes.
- Test with a wooden toothpick, if it comes out clean, the cakes are done. Transfer the cakes to a wire rack and leave to cool completely.
- Beat the butter until smooth, then gradually whisk in the icing sugar and vanilla extract.
- Spoon half the mixture into a separate bowl and whisk in 1 tbsp of cocoa powder.
- Spoon the plain buttercream into one side of a piping bag fitted with a large star nozzle and spoon the cocoa buttercream into the other side.
- Pipe the buttercream into a big swirl on top of each cake and top each one with an Oreo cookie.

280

MAKES 12

White Chocolate Champagne Cupcakes

PREPARATION TIME 45 MINUTES

COOKING TIME 15 - 20 MINUTES

INGREDIENTS

110 g / 4 oz / ⅔ cup self-raising flour, sifted
110 g / 4 oz / ½ cup caster (superfine) sugar
110 g / 4 oz / ½ cup butter, softened
2 large eggs
4 tbsp champagne
75 g / 2 ½ oz white chocolate, melted

TO DECORATE:
100 g / 3 ½ oz / ½ cup butter, softened
200 g / 7 oz / 2 cups icing (confectioners') sugar
1 tbsp champagne
3 tbsp white chocolate, grated

- Preheat the oven to 190°C (170° fan) / 375F / gas 5 and line a 12-hole cupcake tin with paper cases.
- Combine all of the cake ingredients in a bowl and whisk together for 2 minutes or until smooth.
- Divide the mixture between the cases and bake for 15 – 20 minutes.
- Test with a wooden toothpick, if it comes out clean, the cakes are done. Transfer the cakes to a wire rack and leave to cool completely.
- Beat the butter until smooth, then gradually whisk in the icing sugar and champagne.
- Pipe a swirl of buttercream onto each cake and sprinkle with grated chocolate.

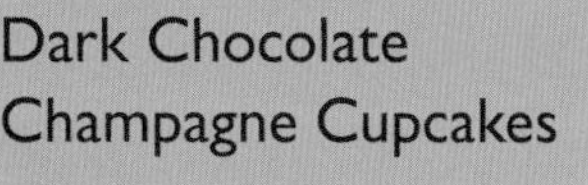

Dark Chocolate Champagne Cupcakes

281

- Replace the white chocolate with dark chocolate and add cocoa to buttercream.

282

MAKES 12

Dark Chocolate Delight Cupcakes

PREPARATION TIME 45 MINUTES

COOKING TIME 20 MINUTES

INGREDIENTS

125 g / 4 ½ oz / ½ cup unsalted butter, softened
125 g / 4 ½ oz / ½ cup caster (superfine) sugar
2 medium eggs, room temperature
½ tsp vanilla extract
125 g / 4 ½ oz / 1 cup self-raising flour
2 tbsp cocoa
45 ml / 1 ½ fl. oz / ¼ cup milk

TO DECORATE
125 g / 4 ½ oz / ½ cup unsalted butter, unsalted, softened
300 g / 10 ½ oz / 2 ½ cups icing (confectioners') sugar
½ tsp vanilla extract
½ tbsp milk
50 g / 2 oz / ¼ cup chocolate grated

- Preheat the oven to 180°C (160° fan) / 350F / gas 4 and line a cupcake tin with paper cases.
- Cream butter and sugar until pale and fluffy with an electric whisk.
- Gradually mix in the egg and vanilla extract.
- Gently mix in the flour and cocoa, adding the milk.
- Spoon cupcake mix into each paper case.
- Bake, for 18-20 minutes. Test with a wooden toothpick, if it comes out clean, the cake is done.
- Place on wire rack to cool.
- To make the buttercream, beat the butter with a whisk until soft then gradually beat in the icing sugar, vanilla and milk.
- Pipe buttercream sprinkle chocolate.

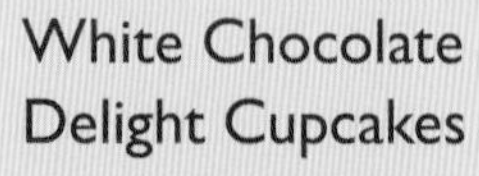

White Chocolate Delight Cupcakes

283

- Instead of dark chocolate sprinkle with grated white chocolate.

284

MAKES 12

Blueberry Dream Cupcakes

- Preheat the oven to 180°C (160° fan) / 350F / gas 4 and line a cupcake tin with paper cases.
- Sift the flour, baking powder and bicarbonate of soda together into a bowl.
- Cream the butter and sugar together until pale and fluffy. Add the vanilla essence, egg and a spoonful of flour and mix.
- Add a third of the flour along with a third of the buttermilk and mix again. Repeat the process again twice until you have used all the flour and buttermilk.
- Spoon cupcake mix into each paper case and divide the blueberries evenly between the cakes scattering them on top.
- Bake, for 15-20 minutes.
- Place on wire rack to cool.
- To make the buttercream, beat the butter with a whisk until soft then gradually beat in the icing sugar, vanilla and milk.
- Pipe buttercream swirls. Place Blueberry on top.

PREPARATION TIME 45 MINUTES

COOKING TIME 45 MINUTES

INGREDIENTS

150 g / 5 ½ oz / 1 ¼ cup plain (all purpose) flour
½ tsp baking powder (baking)
½ tsp bicarbonate of soda
55 g / 2 oz / ¼ cup butter softened
115 g / 4 oz / ½ cup caster (superfine) sugar
½ tsp vanilla extract
1 egg, beaten
125 ml / 4 ½ oz / ½ cup buttermilk
100 g / 4 oz / 1 cup blueberries

TO DECORATE

125 g / 4 ½ oz / ½ cup butter
300 g / 10 ½ oz / 2 ½ cups icing (confectioners') sugar
½ tsp vanilla extract
½ tbsp milk
blueberries

285

Blueberry Almond Cream Cupcakes

- Instead of vanilla extract, use almond essence when mixing the buttercream.

286

MAKES 12

Walnut Whip Cupcakes

- Preheat the oven to 180°C (160° fan) / 350F / gas 4 and line a cupcake tin with paper cases.
- Beat the butter, sugar, flour and eggs with 4 tsp of the coffee and a pinch of salt until creamy. Stir in the chopped walnuts.
- Spoon cupcake mix into each paper case.
- Bake, for 18-20 minutes. Test with a wooden toothpick, if it comes out clean, the cake is done.
- Place on wire rack to cool.
- To make the buttercream, beat the butter with a whisk until soft then gradually beat in the icing sugar, vanilla and milk.
- Pipe buttercream swirls. Place 12 walnut halves on top.

PREPARATION TIME 10 MINUTES

COOKING TIME 20 MINUTES

INGREDIENTS

100 g / 4 oz / ½ cup butter, unsalted, softened
100 g / 4 oz / ½ cup light muscovado sugar
100 g / 4 oz / 1 cup self-raising flour
2 large eggs
2 tsp instant coffee, mixed with 100ml / 3 fl. ox / ½ cup boiling water, then cooled
25 g / 1 oz / ½ cup walnut halves, chopped

TO DECORATE

125 g / 4 ½ oz / ½ cup butter
300 g / 10 ½ oz / 2 ½ cups icing (confectioners') sugar
½ tsp vanilla extract
½ tbsp milk
walnut halves

287

Coffee Walnut Cupcakes

- Replace buttercream with 200 g mascarpone whisked with 2 tbsp light muscovado sugar and 3 tsp coffee.

MAKES 24

Very Blueberry Cupcakes

Very Blackberry Cupcakes

289

- Instead of using blueberries, substitute them with very ripe blackberries.

Very Raspberry Cupcakes

290

- Replace the blueberries with raspberries.

PREPARATION TIME 25 MINUTES

COOKING TIME 22 MINUTES

INGREDIENTS

375 g / 13 ½ oz / 3 cups plain (all-purpose) flour
400 g / 14 oz /2 cups granulated sugar
1 tbsp baking powder
¾ tsp salt
225 g / 8 oz /1 cup unsalted butter
4 large eggs
240 ml / 8 ½ /1 cup whole milk
2 tsp pure vanilla extract
250 g / 9 oz / 1 ½ cups fresh blueberries
2 tbsp plain (all purpose) flour

TO DECORATE

225 g /8 oz / 1 cup cream cheese
225 g / 8 oz /1 cup unsalted butter, softened
900 g /2 lbs / 7 ¼ cups icing (confectioners') sugar, sifted
2 tsp vanilla extract
purple food colouring paste
24 blueberries

- Preheat the oven to 190°C (170° fan) / 375F / gas 5 and line two 12-hole cupcake tins with paper cases.
- Put the flour, sugar, baking powder and salt in a bowl with the butter and mix briefly with an electric whisk.
- Mix together the eggs, milk and vanilla extract, then gradually pour it onto the dry ingredients, whisking all the time.
- Toss the blueberries in the flour then fold them into the cake mixture.
- Divide the cake mixture between the paper cases and bake for 18 – 22 minutes.
- Test with a wooden toothpick, if it comes out clean, the cakes are done. Transfer the cakes to a wire rack to cool completely.
- To make the frosting, beat the cream cheese with the butter then incorporate the icing sugar, vanilla extract and a little purple food colouring.
- Pipe a swirl of frosting on top of each cake and decorate with the blueberries.

291

MAKES 12

White Choc Raspberry Liquorice Cupcake

- Preheat the oven to 170°C (150° fan) / 325F / gas 3 and line a cupcake tin with paper cases.
- Mix flour, sugar, chocolate, baking powder and butter until you have a sandy consistency.
- In a separate bowl mix milk, framboise liqueur, egg and vanilla.
- Drizzle into flour while mixing until smooth.
- Spoon cupcake mix into each paper case.
- Bake, for 18-20 minutes. Test with a wooden toothpick, if it comes out clean, the cake is done.
- Place on wire rack to cool.
- To make the buttercream, beat the butter with a whisk until soft then gradually beat in the icing sugar, vanilla and milk.
- Pipe buttercream swirls and sprinkle grated chocolate.

PREPARATION TIME 45 MINUTES

COOKING TIME 20 MINUTES

INGREDIENTS

130 g plain (all purpose) flour
140 g caster (superfine) sugar
1 ½ tsp baking powder
40 g butter, unsalted, softened
1 egg
100 ml whole milk
20 ml framboise liqueur
10 ml vanilla extract
100 g white chocolate grated

TO DECORATE

125 g / 4 ½ oz / ½ cup butter
300 g / 10 ½ oz / 2 ½ cups icing (confectioners') sugar
½ tsp vanilla extract
½ tbsp milk
pieces of raspberry liquorice

292

White Chocolate and Black Liquorice Cupcakes

- Replace the raspberry liquorice with black liquorice and add 2 tbsp of Pernod to the buttercream mixture.

293

MAKES 12

Date and Rum Cupcakes

- Preheat the oven to 180°C (160° fan) / 350F / gas 4.
- Line a 12-hole cupcake tin with 12 cupcake cases.
- Beat together all the ingredients for the batter apart from the rum in a mixing bowl for 2 minutes until smooth.
- Add the rum and beat again for a further minute.
- Divide evenly between the paper cases before rapping the tin on a work surface to help settle the batter.
- Bake for 15-18 minutes until risen.
- Remove to a wire rack to cool.
- Beat the softened butter for 3-4 minutes in a mixing bowl until pale and creamy.
- Add the icing sugar and white rum and beat again until smooth.
- Spoon into a piping bag fitted with a straight-sided nozzle.
- Pipe pillows of buttercream on top of the cupcakes before garnishing with pieces of chopped dates.

PREPARATION TIME 45 MINUTES

COOKING TIME 15 - 20 MINUTES

INGREDIENTS

110 g / 4 oz / ⅔ cup self-raising flour, sifted
110 g / 4 oz / ½ cup margarine, softened
110 g / 4 oz / ½ cup caster (superfine) sugar
1 tsp vanilla extract
55 ml / 2 fl. oz / ¼ cup dark rum
2 large eggs
a pinch of salt

FOR THE BUTTERCREAM

100 g / 3 ½ oz / ½ cup butter, softened
200 g / 7 oz / 2 cups icing (confectioners') sugar
30 ml / 1 fl. oz / 2 tbsp white rum

TO GARNISH

12 chopped dates, stones removed

294

Coconut Rum Cupcakes

- Substitute the dark rum and the white rum for Malibu.

295

MAKES 12

Chocolate Butterfly Cupcakes

PREPARATION TIME 45 MINUTES

COOKING TIME 15 - 18 MINUTES

INGREDIENTS

110 g / 4 oz / ⅔ cup self-raising flour, sifted
110 g / 4 oz / ½ cup margarine, softened
110 g / 4 oz / ½ cup caster (superfine) sugar
1 tsp vanilla extract
2 large eggs
a pinch of salt

FOR THE BUTTERCREAM

100 g / 3 ½ oz / ½ cup butter, softened
200 g / 7 oz / 2 cups icing (confectioners') sugar
50 g / 2 oz / ⅓ cup cocoa powder
2 tbsp whole milk

TO GARNISH

chocolate or fondant butterflies

- Preheat the oven to 180°C (160° fan) / 350F / gas 4.
- Line a 12-hole cupcake tin with 12 cupcake cases.
- Beat together all the ingredients for the batter in a mixing bowl for 2 minutes until smooth and creamy.
- Divide evenly between the paper cases before rapping the tin on a work surface to help settle the batter.
- Bake for 15-18 minutes until risen; test with a wooden toothpick, if it comes out clean, the cakes are done.
- Remove to a wire rack to cool as you prepare the buttercream.
- Beat the softened butter with the cocoa powder, icing sugar and milk in a mixing bowl until smooth and creamy.
- Spoon into a piping bag fitted with a straight-sided nozzle and pipe in round mounds on top of the cupcakes.
- Garnish the buttercream with a chocolate butterfly before serving.

Two Chocolate Butterfly Cupcakes

296

- Add 50 g / 2 oz / ⅓ cup of cocoa powder and 30 ml / 1 fl. oz / 2 tbsp whole milk to the cupcake batter as you mix.

297

MAKES 12

Coffee Truffle Cupcakes

PREPARATION TIME 45 MINUTES

COOKING TIME 15 - 18 MINUTES

INGREDIENTS

110 g / 4 oz / ⅔ cup self-raising flour, sifted
110 g / 4 oz / ½ cup margarine
110 g / 4 oz / ½ cup caster (superfine) sugar
55 g / 2 oz / ⅓ cup cocoa powder
55 ml / 2 fl. oz / ¼ cup whole milk
2 large eggs, a pinch of salt

FOR THE BUTTERCREAM

100 g / 3 ½ oz / ½ cup butter, softened
200 g / 7 oz / 2 cups icing (confectioners') sugar
50 g / 2 oz / ⅓ cup cocoa powder
30 ml / 1 fl. oz / 2 tbsp whole milk
1 tsp strong instant espresso powder
1 tsp pink sugar pearls
1 tsp white sugar pearls

- Preheat the oven to 180°C (160° fan) / 350F / gas 4.
- Line a 12-hole cupcake tin with 12 cupcake cases.
- Beat together all the ingredients for the batter apart from the milk in a mixing bowl for 2 minutes.
- Add the milk and beat again for a further minute.
- Divide evenly between the paper cases before rapping the tin on a work surface to help settle the batter.
- Bake for 15-18 minutes until risen.
- Remove to a wire rack to cool.
- Beat the softened butter with the cocoa powder, icing sugar and milk in a mixing bowl until smooth.
- Mix together the espresso powder with the boiling water until smooth, then beat into the buttercream.
- Spoon into a piping bag fitted with a star-shaped nozzle and pipe a swirled mound on top of each cupcake.
- Garnish the buttercream with a few sugar pearls.

Crushed Almond and Chocolate Cupcakes

298

- Substitute the sugar pearls garnish for a sprinkle of crushed almonds on top of the buttercream.

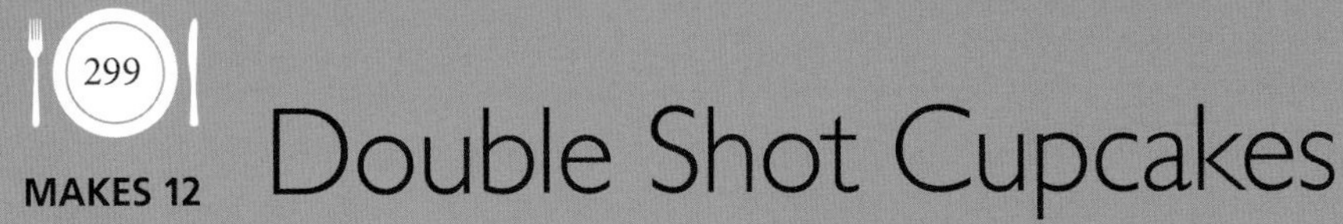

299

MAKES 12

Double Shot Cupcakes

300 Coffee and White Chocolate Cupcakes

- Garnish the cupcakes with white chocolate buttons instead of hundreds and thousands.

301 Hazelnut Latte Cupcakes

- Add 2 tbsp of hazelnut syrup to the buttercream and sprinkle the cakes with chopped roasted hazelnuts.

PREPARATION TIME 45 MINUTES

COOKING TIME 15 - 18 MINUTES

INGREDIENTS

110 g / 4 oz / ⅔ cup self-raising flour, sifted
110 g / 4 oz / ½ cup margarine, softened
110 g / 4 oz / ½ cup caster (superfine) sugar
1 tsp vanilla extract
2 large eggs
a pinch of salt

FOR THE BUTTERCREAM
100 g / 3 ½ oz / ½ cup butter, softened
200 g / 7 oz / 2 cups icing (confectioners') sugar
2 tsp strong instant espresso powder

TO GARNISH
1 tbsp hundreds and thousands

- Preheat the oven to 180°C (160° fan) / 350F / gas 4.
- Line a 12-hole cupcake tin with 12 cupcake cases.
- Beat together all the ingredients in a mixing bowl for 2 minutes until smooth and creamy.
- Divide evenly between the paper cases before rapping the tin on a work surface to help settle the batter.
- Bake for 15-18 minutes until risen; test with a wooden toothpick, if it comes out clean, the cakes are done.
- Remove to a wire rack to cool as you prepare the buttercream.
- Beat the softened butter with the icing sugar in a mixing bowl until smooth.
- Mix together the espresso powder with the boiling water until smooth, then beat into the buttercream.
- Spoon into a piping bag fitted with a star-shaped nozzle.
- Carefully remove any peaks on the cupcakes with a serrated knife and pipe a swirled mound on buttercream on top.
- Garnish with a sprinkle of hundreds and thousands.

302

MAKES 12

Mochaccino Cupcakes

PREPARATION TIME 45 MINUTES

COOKING TIME 15 - 18 MINUTES

INGREDIENTS

110 g / 4 oz / ⅔ cup self-raising flour, sifted
110 g / 4 oz / ½ cup margarine
110 g / 4 oz / ½ cup caster (superfine) sugar
55 g / 2 oz / ⅓ cup cocoa powder
55 ml / 2 fl. oz / ¼ cup whole milk
2 large eggs, a pinch of salt

FOR THE COFFEE BUTTERCREAM
100 g / 3 ½ oz / ½ cup butter, softened
200 g / 7 oz / 2 cups icing (confectioners') sugar
1 tsp strong instant espresso powder
55 g / 2 oz / ⅓ cup dark chocolate, melted

- Preheat the oven to 180°C (160° fan) / 350F / gas 4.
- Line a 12-hole cupcake tin with 12 cupcake cases.
- Beat together all the ingredients for the batter apart from the milk in a mixing bowl for 2 minutes.
- Add the milk and beat again for a further minute.
- Divide evenly between the paper cases before rapping the tin on a work surface to help settle the batter.
- Bake for 15-18 minutes until risen.
- Remove to a wire rack to cool.
- Beat the softened butter with the icing sugar in a mixing bowl until smooth.
- Mix together the espresso powder with the boiling water until smooth, then beat into the buttercream.
- Spoon into a piping bag fitted with a straight-sided nozzle and pipe a mound on top of each cupcake.
- Pipe small blobs of chocolate on top of the buttercream.

Baileys and Chocolate Cupcakes

303

- Add 2 tbsp Baileys (or other Irish cream liqueur) to the buttercream before using.

304

MAKES 12

Raspberry Jelly Tot Cupcakes

PREPARATION TIME 45 MINUTES

COOKING TIME 15 - 18 MINUTES

INGREDIENTS

FOR THE BATTER
110 g / 4 oz / ⅔ cup self-raising flour, sifted
110 g / 4 oz / ½ cup margarine, softened
110 g / 4 oz / ½ cup caster (superfine) sugar
1 tsp vanilla extract
2 large eggs
a pinch of salt

FOR THE PINK BUTTERCREAM
100 g / 3 ½ oz / ½ cup butter, softened
200 g / 7 oz / 2 cups icing (confectioners') sugar
a few drops of red food colouring

TO GARNISH
12 raspberry Jelly Tots

- Preheat the oven to 180°C (160° fan) / 350F / gas 4.
- Line a 12-hole cupcake tin with 12 cupcake cases.
- Beat together all the ingredients for the batter in a mixing bowl for 2 minutes until smooth and creamy.
- Divide evenly between the paper cases.
- Bake for 15-18 minutes until risen.
- Remove to a wire rack to cool.
- Beat the softened butter in a mixing bowl for 3-4 minutes until pale.
- Add the icing sugar and beat well before beating in the food colouring until you reach a light pink colour.
- Spread evenly on top of the cupcakes using a small palette knife, reserving about a third of the icing.
- Spoon the remaining icing into a piping bag and pipe a blob of icing on top of the icing and garnish with a Jelly Tot.

Red Wine Gum Cupcakes

305

- Substitute the Jelly Tot for a red wine gum on top.

306

MAKES 18

Macchiato Cupcakes

- Preheat the oven to 180°C (160° fan) / 350F / gas 4.
- Line a 12-hole cupcake tin with 12 cupcake cases.
- Beat together all the ingredients for the batter apart from the milk in a mixing bowl for 2 minutes.
- Add the milk and beat again for a further minute.
- Divide evenly between the paper cases.
- Bake for 15-18 minutes until risen.
- Remove to a wire rack to cool.
- Beat the softened butter with the icing sugar until smooth.
- Add the cocoa powder and boiling water and beat again
- Spoon about one third of the buttercream into a piping bag fitted with a star-shaped nozzle.
- Spread the tops of the cupcakes evenly with the remaining buttercream.
- Pipe a swirl of buttercream on top of the flat icing before garnishing the top with a Malteser.

Chocolate Minstrel Cupcakes

307

- Substitute the Maltesers with Minstrels on top of the cupcakes.

PREPARATION TIME 45 MINUTES

COOKING TIME 15 - 18 MINUTES

INGREDIENTS

FOR THE BATTER
110 g / 4 oz / ⅔ cup self-raising flour, sifted
110 g / 4 oz / ½ cup margarine
110 g / 4 oz / ½ cup caster (superfine) sugar
55 g / 2 oz / ⅓ cup cocoa powder
55 ml / 2 fl. oz / ¼ cup whole milk
2 large eggs
a pinch of salt

FOR THE COFFEE BUTTERCREAM
100 g / 3 ½ oz / ½ cup butter, softened
200 g / 7 oz / 2 cups icing (confectioners') sugar
1 tbsp cocoa powder
1 tsp strong instant espresso powder
12 Maltesers

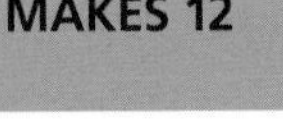

308

MAKES 12

White-Choc Coffee Cupcakes

- Preheat the oven to 180°C (160° fan) / 350F / gas 4.
- Line a 12-hole cupcake tin with 12 cupcake cases.
- Beat together all the ingredients for the batter in a mixing bowl for 2 minutes until smooth and creamy.
- Divide evenly between the paper cases.
- Bake for 15-18 minutes until risen.
- Beat the softened butter with the icing sugar and vanilla extract until smooth and set to one side.
- Beat together the butter with the icing sugar for the coffee buttercream; mix together the espresso powder with the boiling water before beating into the butter, making sure you leave it rippled.
- Spoon into a piping bag fitted.
- Spread the tops of the cupcakes with the vanilla buttercream before piping a round of icing on top.
- Garnish with a white chocolate button.

Coffee and Vanilla Cupcakes

309

- Add a sprinkle of instant espresso powder on top of the cupcakes.

PREPARATION TIME 45 MINUTES

COOKING TIME 15 - 18 MINUTES

INGREDIENTS

110 g / 4 oz / ⅔ cup self-raising flour, sifted
110 g / 4 oz / ½ cup margarine
110 g / 4 oz / ½ cup caster (superfine) sugar
1 tsp vanilla extract
2 large eggs, a pinch of salt

VANILLA BUTTERCREAM
175 g / 6 oz / ¾ cup unsalted butter
125 g / 4 ½ oz / 1 cup icing (confectioners') sugar
1 tsp vanilla extract

TO DECORATE:
100 g / 3 ½ oz / ½ cup butter, softened
200 g / 7 oz / 2 cups icing (confectioners') sugar
1 tsp vanilla extract
1 tsp instant espresso powder
12 white chocolate buttons

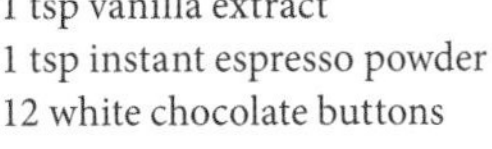

310

MAKES 12

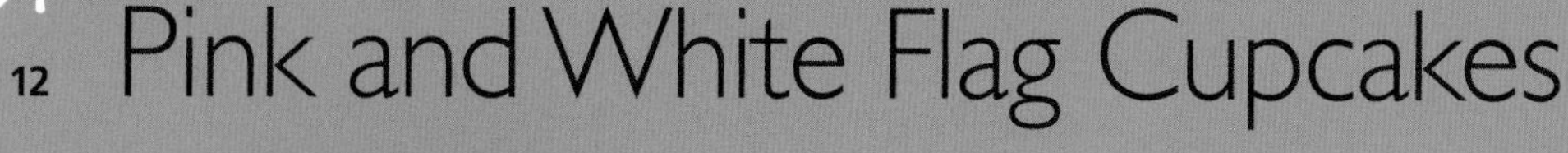

Pink and White Flag Cupcakes

Grated Chocolate and Vanilla Cupcakes

311

- Substitute the pink glitter for grated dark chocolate on top.

Chocolate Flag Cupcakes

312

- Add 2 tbsp of cocoa powder to the cake mixture before baking and 1 tbsp of cocoa to the buttercream.

PREPARATION TIME 45 MINUTES

COOKING TIME 15 - 18 MINUTES

INGREDIENTS

FOR THE BATTER

110 g / 4 oz / ⅔ cup self-raising flour, sifted
110 g / 4 oz / ½ cup margarine
110 g / 4 oz / ½ cup caster (superfine) sugar
1 tsp vanilla extract
2 large eggs, a pinch of salt

FOR THE BUTTERCREAM

55 g / 2 oz / ½ cup butter, softened
55 g / 2 oz / ¼ cup Greek yoghurt
200 g / 7 oz / 2 cups icing (confectioners') sugar
1 tsp vanilla extract
1 tsp pink edible glitter
small flags to garnish

- Preheat the oven to 180°C (160° fan) / 350F / gas 4.
- Line a 12-hole cupcake tin with 12 cupcake cases.
- Beat together all the ingredients for the batter in a mixing bowl for 2 minutes until smooth and creamy.
- Divide evenly between the paper cases before rapping the tin on a work surface to help settle the batter.
- Bake for 15-18 minutes until risen; test with a wooden toothpick, if it comes out clean, the cakes are done.
- Remove to a wire rack to cool as you prepare the vanilla buttercream.
- Beat the softened butter for 3-4 minutes until creamy and pale.
- Add the icing sugar, plain yoghurt and vanilla extract before beating again until smooth.
- Spoon into a piping bag fitted with a petal tip before piping ruffled rosettes on top of the cupcakes.
- Garnish with a light dusting of the glitter and top with the flags.

313

MAKES 12

Sour Cream Cupcakes

- Preheat the oven to 180°C (160° fan) / 350F / gas 4.
- Line a 12-hole cupcake tin with 12 cupcake cases.
- Beat together all the ingredients for the batter in a mixing bowl for 2 minutes until smooth and creamy.
- Divide evenly between the paper cases.
- Bake for 15-18 minutes until risen. Leave to cool.
- Beat the cream cheese and sour cream in a mixing bowl before adding the icing sugar and vanilla extract.
- Spoon most of the icing into a piping bag fitted with a star-shaped nozzle.
- Add drops of the food colouring to the remaining icing, beating well until purple in colour.
- Spoon into a small piping bag fitted with a small straight-sided nozzle.
- Pipe the plain vanilla icing in a swirl on top of the cupcakes before dotting with beads of purple icing.

Sour Cream and Raspberry Cupcakes

314

- Substitute the vanilla extract in the batter and icing for 30 ml / 1 fl. oz / 2 tbsp framboise.

PREPARATION TIME 10 MINUTES

COOKING TIME 20 MINUTES

INGREDIENTS

FOR THE BATTER
110 g / 4 oz / ⅔ cup self-raising flour, sifted
110 g / 4 oz / ½ cup margarine, softened
110 g / 4 oz / ½ cup caster (superfine) sugar
1 tsp vanilla extract
2 large eggs
a pinch of salt

FOR THE ICING
30 g / 1 oz / ¼ cup butter, softened
75 ml / 2 ½ fl. oz / ⅓ cup sour cream
300 g / 10 ½ oz / 3 cups icing (confectioners') sugar
1 tsp vanilla extract
a few drops violet food colouring

315

MAKES 12

Indigo Sugar Cupcakes

- Preheat the oven to 180°C (160° fan) / 350F / gas 4.
- Line a 12-hole cupcake tin with 12 cupcake cases.
- Beat together all the ingredients for the batter in a mixing bowl for 2 minutes until smooth and creamy.
- Divide evenly between the paper cases before rapping the tin on a work surface to help settle the batter.
- Bake for 15-18 minutes until risen.
- Remove to a wire rack to cool.
- Beat the butter with the icing sugar, lemon juice and drops of food colouring until you have an even light purple butter.
- Spread the tops of the cupcake evenly with ½ of the buttercream before spooning the remainder into a piping bag fitted with a small star-shaped nozzle.
- Pipe stars of buttercream around the perimeter of the cupcakes before sprinkling the centres with sugar.

Cream Cheese Purple Cupcakes

316

- Substitute the butter for the same amount of cream cheese in the buttercream

PREPARATION TIME 45 MINUTES

COOKING TIME 15 - 18 MINUTES

INGREDIENTS

FOR THE BATTER
110 g / 4 oz / ⅔ cup self-raising flour, sifted
110 g / 4 oz / ½ cup margarine, softened
110 g / 4 oz / ½ cup caster (superfine) sugar
1 tsp vanilla extract
2 large eggs
a pinch of salt

FOR THE BUTTERCREAM
225 g / 8 oz / 1 cup unsalted butter, softened
180 g / 6 oz / 1 ½ cups icing (confectioners') sugar
1 tbsp lemon juice
a few drops of purple food colouring

TO GARNISH
2 tbsp purple sugar sprinkles

317

MAKES 12

White Choc Raspberry Drizzle Cupcakes

PREPARATION TIME 45 MINUTES

COOKING TIME 15 - 18 MINUTES

INGREDIENTS

FOR THE BATTER
110 g / 4 oz / ⅔ cup self-raising flour, sifted
110 g / 4 oz / ½ cup margarine, softened
110 g / 4 oz / ½ cup caster (superfine) sugar
1 tsp vanilla extract
2 large eggs
a pinch of salt

FOR THE BUTTERCREAM
100 g / 3 ½ oz / ½ cup butter, softened
200 g / 7 oz / 2 cups icing (confectioners') sugar
12 raspberry button boiled sweets
30 g / 1 oz / 2 tbsp raspberry jam, warmed

- Preheat the oven to 180°C (160° fan) / 350F / gas 4.
- Line a 12-hole cupcake tin with 12 cupcake cases.
- Beat together all the ingredients for the batter in a mixing bowl for 2 minutes until smooth and creamy.
- Divide evenly between the paper cases.
- Bake for 15-18 minutes until risen.
- Remove to a wire rack to cool.
- Melt the chocolate in a heatproof bowl set atop a saucepan of simmering water, stirring occasionally.
- Remove from the heat and leave to cool for 5 minutes.
- Beat the butter with the icing sugar until creamy before folding through the cooled, melted chocolate.
- Spoon into a piping bag fitted with a star-shaped nozzle before piping spiral swirls on the cupcakes.
- Garnish with a raspberry button boiled sweets and a drizzle of jam.

Red, White and Blue Cupcakes

318

- Use a mixture of raspberries and blueberries instead of boiled sweets to garnish.

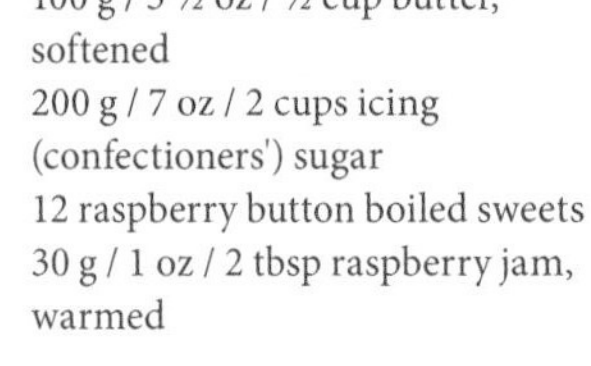

319

MAKES 12

Raspberry Yoghurt Cupcakes

PREPARATION TIME 45 MINUTES

COOKING TIME 15 - 18 MINUTES

INGREDIENTS

FOR THE BATTER
110 g / 4 oz / ⅔ cup self-raising flour, sifted
110 g / 4 oz / ½ cup margarine
110 g / 4 oz / ½ cup caster (superfine) sugar
1 tsp vanilla extract
2 large eggs
a pinch of salt

FOR THE BUTTERCREAM
100 g / 3 ½ oz / ½ cup butter, softened
200 g / 7 oz / 2 cups icing (confectioners') sugar
4 tbsp thick raspberry yogurt
1 tsp vanilla extract
12 raspberries
½ tsp pink edible glitter

- Preheat the oven to 180°C (160° fan) / 350F / gas 4.
- Line a 12-hole cupcake tin with 12 cupcake cases.
- Beat together all the ingredients for the batter in a mixing bowl for 2 minutes until smooth and creamy.
- Divide evenly between the paper cases before rapping the tin on a work surface to help settle the batter.
- Bake for 15-18 minutes until risen.
- Remove to a wire rack to cool.
- Beat the softened butter for 3-4 minutes until creamy.
- Add the icing sugar, vanilla yoghurt and vanilla extract before beating again until smooth.
- Spoon into a piping bag fitted with a petal tip before piping petals on top to form roses.
- Garnish with a light dusting of the glitter and a raspberry in the middle.

Blueberry Vanilla Cupcakes

320

- Substitute the raspberries for a blueberry in the middle.

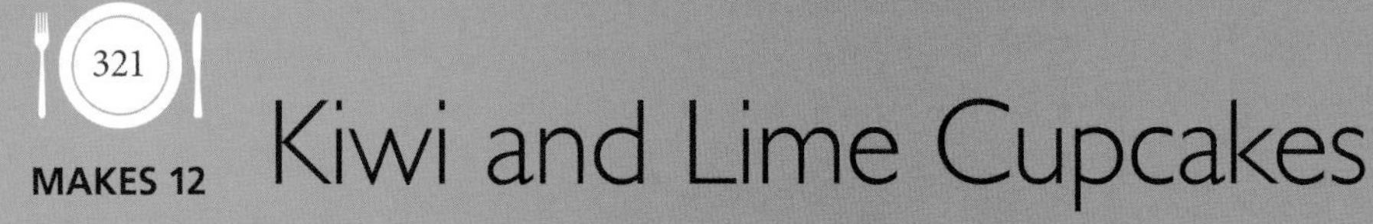

321

MAKES 12

Kiwi and Lime Cupcakes

Lime and Ginger Cupcakes

322

- Substitute the kiwi fruit garnish for a piece of crystallised ginger on top of the cupcakes.

Kiwi and Ginger Cupcakes

323

- Add 2 tsp of ground ginger to the cake mixture and sprinkle the icing with finely chopped crystallised ginger before topping with the kiwi slice.

PREPARATION TIME 10 MINUTES

COOKING TIME 20 MINUTES

INGREDIENTS

FOR THE BATTER

110 g / 4 oz / ⅔ cup self-raising flour, sifted
110 g / 4 oz / ½ cup margarine, softened
110 g / 4 oz / ½ cup caster (superfine) sugar
1 tsp vanilla extract
2 large eggs
a pinch of salt

FOR THE BUTTERCREAM

100 g / 3 ½ oz / ½ cup butter, softened
200 g / 7 oz / 2 cups icing (confectioners') sugar
30 ml / 1 fl. oz / 2 tbsp lime cordial

TO GARNISH

1 kiwi fruit, cut into 12 semi-circles

- Preheat the oven to 180°C (160° fan) / 350F / gas 4.
- Line a 12-hole cupcake tin with 12 cupcake cases.
- Beat together all the ingredients for the batter in a mixing bowl for 2 minutes until smooth and creamy.
- Divide evenly between the paper cases before rapping the tin on a work surface to help settle the batter.
- Bake for 15-18 minutes until risen; test with a wooden toothpick, if it comes out clean, the cakes are done.
- Remove to a wire rack to cool as you prepare the buttercream.
- Beat the softened butter for 2 minutes until creamy and pale.
- Add the icing sugar and lime cordial and beat well until smooth.
- Spoon into a piping bag fitted with a star-shaped nozzle before levelling the cupcakes.
- Pipe a flat swirl on top of the cupcakes before garnishing with a semi-circle of kiwi fruit.

324

MAKES 12

Chocolate Cookies and Cream Cupcakes

PREPARATION TIME 10 MINUTES

COOKING TIME 20 MINUTES

INGREDIENTS

FOR THE BATTER
110 g / 4 oz / ⅔ cup self-raising flour, sifted
110 g / 4 oz / ½ cup margarine, softened
110 g / 4 oz / ½ cup caster (superfine) sugar
55 g / 2 oz / ⅓ cup cocoa powder
30 ml / 1 fl. oz / 2 tbsp whole milk
2 large eggs
a pinch of salt

FOR THE BUTTERCREAM
225 g / 8 oz / 1 cup unsalted butter, softened
180 g / 6 oz / 1 ½ cups icing (confectioners') sugar
1 Bourbon biscuit, crushed

TO GARNISH
6 Bourbon biscuits, lightly crushed

- Preheat the oven to 180°C (160° fan) / 350F / gas 4.
- Line a 12-hole cupcake tin with 12 cupcake cases.
- Beat together all the ingredients for the batter apart from the milk in a mixing bowl for 2 minutes until smooth and creamy.
- Add the milk and beat again for a further minute.
- Divide evenly between the paper cases before rapping the tin on a work surface to help settle the batter.
- Bake for 15-18 minutes until risen; test with a wooden toothpick, if it comes out clean, the cakes are done.
- Remove to a wire rack to cool as you prepare the buttercream.
- Beat the softened butter for 3-4 minutes in a mixing bowl until pale and creamy.
- Add the icing sugar and beat again until smooth before folding through the crushed bourbon biscuit.
- Spread the tops of the cupcakes with the icing before garnishing the top with lightly crushed bourbon biscuits.

325

Digestive Biscuit Cupcakes

- Substitute the bourbon biscuits for digestive biscuits.

326

Peanut Brittle Cupcakes

- Replace the Bourbon biscuits with peanut brittle.

327

MAKES 12

Ginger Cream Cupcakes

- Preheat the oven to 180°C (160° fan) / 350F / gas 4.
- Line a 12-hole cupcake tin with 12 cupcake cases.
- Beat together all the ingredients for the batter in a mixing bowl for 2 minutes until smooth and creamy.
- Divide evenly between the paper cases before rapping the tin on a work surface to help settle the batter.
- Bake for 15-18 minutes until risen; test with a wooden toothpick, if it comes out clean, the cakes are done.
- Remove to a wire rack to cool as you prepare the ginger buttercream.
- Beat the softened butter for 3-4 minutes until creamy.
- Add the icing sugar, vanilla extract and ground ginger before beating again until smooth.
- Spoon into a piping bag fitted with a petal tip before ruffles on top of the cupcakes.
- Garnish with a little crushed ginger nut and a cigarillo.

Ginger and Orange Cupcakes

328

- Add 1 tsp orange flower water to the buttercream and the batter.

PREPARATION TIME 45 MINUTES

COOKING TIME 15 - 18 MINUTES

INGREDIENTS

110 g / 4 oz / ⅔ cup self-raising flour, sifted
110 g / 4 oz / ½ cup margarine
110 g / 4 oz / ½ cup caster (superfine) sugar
1 tsp ground ginger
2 large eggs, a pinch of salt

FOR THE BUTTERCREAM
100 g / 3 ½ oz / ½ cup butter, softened
200 g / 7 oz / 2 cups icing (confectioners') sugar
1 tsp vanilla extract
a pinch of ground ginger
12 white and dark chocolate cigarillos
2-3 ginger nut biscuits, crushed

329

MAKES 12

Chocolate Rum Cupcakes

- Preheat the oven to 180°C (160° fan) / 350F / gas 4.
- Line a 12-hole cupcake tin with 12 cupcake cases.
- Beat together all the ingredients for the batter apart from the rum in a mixing bowl for 2 minutes until smooth and creamy.
- Add the rum and beat again for a further minute.
- Divide evenly between the paper cases.
- Bake for 15-18 minutes until risen.
- Beat the softened butter for 3-4 minutes in a mixing bowl until pale and creamy.
- Add the icing sugar and rum and beat again until smooth.
- Spoon into a piping bag fitted with a straight-sided nozzle.
- Pipe pillows of buttercream on top of the cupcakes before garnishing with a raisin and a pinch of cocoa powder.

Coconut Rum Cupcakes

330

- Substitute the dark rum and the white rum for Malibu.

PREPARATION TIME 10 MINUTES

COOKING TIME 20 MINUTES

INGREDIENTS

FOR THE BATTER
110 g / 4 oz / ⅔ cup self-raising flour, sifted
110 g / 4 oz / ½ cup margarine, softened
110 g / 4 oz / ½ cup caster (superfine) sugar
55 g / 2 oz / ⅓ cup cocoa powder
55 ml / 2 fl. oz / ¼ cup dark rum
2 large eggs
a pinch of salt

FOR THE BUTTERCREAM
100 g / 3 ½ oz / ½ cup butter, softened
200 g / 7 oz / 2 cups icing (confectioners') sugar
30 ml / 1 fl. oz / 2 tbsp white rum

TO GARNISH
12 raisins
1 tsp cocoa powder

331

MAKES 12

Crimson Raspberry Cupcakes

PREPARATION TIME 45 MINUTES

COOKING TIME 15 - 18 MINUTES

INGREDIENTS

FOR THE BATTER
110 g / 4 oz / ⅔ cup self-raising flour, sifted
110 g / 4 oz / ½ cup margarine, softened
110 g / 4 oz / ½ cup caster (superfine) sugar
1 tsp vanilla extract
2 medium eggs
a pinch of salt
a few drops of red food colouring
3 tbsp framboise

FOR THE BUTTERCREAM
100 g / 3 ½ oz / ½ cup butter, softened
200 g / 7 oz / 2 cups icing (confectioners') sugar
1 tsp vanilla extract
12 raspberries

- Preheat the oven to 180°C (160° fan) / 350F / gas 4.
- Line a 12-hole cupcake tin with 12 cupcake cases.
- Beat together all the ingredients for the batter apart from the food colouring in a mixing bowl for 2 minutes.
- Add drops of food colouring, beating well, until you have a pink coloured batter.
- Divide evenly between the paper cases.
- Bake for 15-18 minutes until risen.
- Remove to a wire rack to cool.
- Beat the softened butter for 3-4 minutes until creamy and pale.
- Add the icing sugar and vanilla extract and beat until smooth.
- Spoon into a piping bag fitted with a straight nozzle before piping pillows of buttercream on top.
- Garnish with a raspberry on top.

Pink Rose Cupcakes

332

- Add 1 tsp rosewater the batter and buttercream instead of vanilla extract.

333

MAKES 12

Honey Buttercream Cupcakes

PREPARATION TIME 10 MINUTES

COOKING TIME 20 MINUTES

INGREDIENTS

FOR THE BATTER
110 g / 4 oz / ⅔ cup self-raising flour, sifted
110 g / 4 oz / ½ cup margarine, softened
75 g / 3 oz / ⅓ cup caster (superfine) sugar
30 g / 1 oz / 2 tbsp honey
1 tsp almond extract
2 large eggs
a pinch of salt

FOR THE HONEY BUTTERCREAM
100 g / 3 ½ oz / ½ cup butter, softened
200 g / 7 oz / 2 cups icing (confectioners') sugar
55 g / 2 oz / ¼ cup honey

TO GARNISH
12 physalis

- Preheat the oven to 180°C (160° fan) / 350F / gas 4.
- Line a 12-hole cupcake tin with 12 cupcake cases.
- Beat together all the ingredients for the batter in a mixing bowl for 2 minutes until smooth and creamy.
- Divide evenly between the paper cases before rapping the tin on a work surface to help settle the batter.
- Bake for 15-18 minutes until risen.
- Remove to a wire rack to cool.
- Beat the softened butter for 2-3 minutes until creamy and pale.
- Add the icing sugar and honey and beat again until smooth.
- Spoon half into a piping bag fitted with a straight-sided nozzle before spreading the remainder evenly on the cupcakes.
- Pipe pillows of buttercream on top before garnishing with a physalis.

Orange and Physalis Cupcakes

334

- Add a skinned segment of orange on top of the cupcakes as well as the physalis.

335

MAKES 12

Chocolate Lime Cupcakes

Lime and Chocolate Chip Cupcakes

336

- Stud the top of the buttercream with chocolate chips instead of jelly beans.

Chocolate Lime Drizzle Cupcakes

337

- Omit the jelly beans and drizzle the buttercream with lime flavoured sundae sauce.

PREPARATION TIME 45 MINUTES

COOKING TIME 15 - 18 MINUTES

INGREDIENTS

FOR THE BATTER
110 g / 4 oz / ⅔ cup self-raising flour, sifted
110 g / 4 oz / ½ cup margarine, softened
110 g / 4 oz / ½ cup caster (superfine) sugar
30 g / 1 oz / 2 tbsp cocoa powder
2 tbsp whole milk
2 large eggs
a pinch of salt

FOR THE BUTTERCREAM
100 g / 3 ½ oz / ½ cup butter, softened
200 g / 7 oz / 2 cups icing (confectioners') sugar
30 ml / 1 fl. oz / 2 tbsp lime cordial

TO GARNISH
36 lime jelly beans
½ tsp edible glitter

- Preheat the oven to 180°C (160° fan) / 350F / gas 4.
- Line a 12-hole cupcake tin with 12 cupcake cases.
- Beat together all the ingredients for the batter in a mixing bowl for 2 minutes until smooth and creamy.
- Divide evenly between the paper cases before rapping the tin on a work surface to help settle the batter.
- Bake for 15-18 minutes until risen; test with a wooden toothpick, if it comes out clean, the cakes are done.
- Remove to a wire rack to cool as you prepare the buttercream.
- Beat the softened butter for 2 minutes until creamy and pale.
- Add the icing sugar and lime cordial and beat well until smooth before spooning into a piping bag fitted with a petal tip.
- Garnish the tops of the cupcakes with a little glitter before piping a ruffled mound of lime buttercream on top.
- Garnish with 3 jelly beans on top of the buttercream.

338

MAKES 12

Lime and Ginger Jelly Bean Cupcakes

PREPARATION TIME 45 MINUTES

COOKING TIME 15 - 18 MINUTES

INGREDIENTS

FOR THE BATTER

110 g / 4 oz / ⅔ cup self-raising flour, sifted
110 g / 4 oz / ½ cup margarine, softened
110 g / 4 oz / ½ cup caster (superfine) sugar
1 tsp vanilla extract
1 tsp ground ginger
2 large eggs
a pinch of salt

FOR THE BUTTERCREAM

100 g / 3 ½ oz / ½ cup butter, softened
200 g / 7 oz / 2 cups icing (confectioners') sugar
30 ml / 1 fl. oz / 2 tbsp lime juice
1 tbsp ginger cordial
60 assorted jelly beans

- Preheat the oven to 180°C (160° fan) / 350F / gas 4.
- Line a 12-hole cupcake tin with 12 cupcake cases.
- Beat together all the ingredients for the batter in a mixing bowl for 2 minutes until smooth and creamy.
- Divide evenly between the paper cases before rapping the tin on a work surface to help settle the batter.
- Bake for 15-18 minutes until risen; test with a wooden toothpick, if it comes out clean, the cakes are done.
- Remove to a wire rack to cool as you prepare the buttercream.
- Beat the softened butter for 2 minutes until creamy and pale.
- Add the icing sugar, lime juice and ginger cordials and beat well until smooth.
- Spoon into a piping bag fitted with a star-shaped nozzle before levelling the cupcakes.
- Pipe ice-cream swirls of buttercream on top before garnishing each with 5 jelly beans.

339

MAKES 12

Banoffee Pie Cupcakes

PREPARATION TIME 30 MINUTES

COOKING TIME 15 - 20 MINUTES

INGREDIENTS

3 very ripe bananas
100 g / 3 ½ oz / 1/2 cup soft light brown sugar
2 large eggs
125 ml / 4 ½ fl. oz / ½ cup sunflower oil
225 g / 8 oz / 1 ½ cups plain (all-purpose) flour
1 tsp bicarbonate of (baking) soda
75 ml / 2 ½ fl. oz / 1/3 cup toffee sundae sauce
300 ml / 10 ½ fl. oz / 1 ¼ cups double (heavy) cream
dried banana chips to decorate

- Preheat the oven to 200°C (180° fan) / 400F / gas 6 and line a 12-hole cupcake tin with paper cases.
- Mash the bananas with a fork then whisk in the sugar, eggs and oil.
- Sieve the flour and bicarbonate of soda into the bowl and stir just enough to evenly mix all the ingredients together.
- Divide the mixture between the paper cases, then transfer the tin to the oven and bake for 15 – 20 minutes.
- Test with a wooden toothpick, if it comes out clean, the cakes are done.
- Spoon half of the toffee sauce over the cakes, then transfer them to a wire rack and leave to cool completely.
- Whip the cream until it holds its shape, then spoon it into a piping bag, fitted with a plain nozzle.
- Pipe a swirl of cream onto each cake, then drizzle with the rest of the toffee sauce and arrange the banana chips on top.

340

MAKES 12

Dried Cranberry and Almond Cupcakes

- Preheat the oven to 190°C (170° fan) / 375F / gas 5 and line a 12-hole cupcake tin with foil cases.
- Combine the flour, sugar, butter, eggs and ground almonds in a bowl and whisk together for 2 minutes or until smooth.
- Divide the mixture between the cases and bake for 15 – 20 minutes.
- Test with a wooden toothpick, if it comes out clean, the cakes are done.
- Transfer the cakes to a wire rack and leave to cool completely then top with the dried cranberries and sprinkle with icing sugar.

PREPARATION TIME 15 MINUTES

COOKING TIME 15 - 20 MINUTES

INGREDIENTS

110 g / 4 oz / ⅔ cup self-raising flour, sifted
110 g / 4 oz / ½ cup caster (superfine) sugar
110 g / 4 oz / ½ cup butter, softened
2 large eggs
2 tbsp ground almonds
75 g / 2 ½ oz / ⅓ cup dried cranberries
icing (confectioners') sugar for dusting

Lime Green Sugar Cupcakes

341

MAKES 12

PREPARATION TIME 45 MINUTES

COOKING TIME 15 - 20 MINUTES

INGREDIENTS

110 g / 4 oz / ⅔ cup self-raising flour, sifted
110 g / 4 oz / ½ cup caster (superfine) sugar
110 g / 4 oz / ½ cup butter, softened
2 large eggs
1 lime, juiced and zest finely grated

TO DECORATE:
100 g / 3 ½ oz / ½ cup butter, softened
200 g / 7 oz / 2 cups icing (confectioners') sugar
1 lime, juiced and zest finely grated
green food colouring
green sugar sprinkles

- Preheat the oven to 190°C (170° fan) / 375F / gas 5 and line a 12-hole cupcake tin with paper cases.
- Combine the flour, sugar, butter, eggs and lime juice and zest in a bowl and whisk together for 2 minutes or until smooth. Divide the mixture between the cases, then transfer the tin to the oven and bake for 15 – 20 minutes.
- Test with a wooden toothpick, if it comes out clean, the cakes are done. Transfer the cakes to a wire rack and leave to cool completely.
- Beat the butter until smooth, then gradually whisk in the icing sugar, lime juice and zest and a little green food colouring.
- Spoon the mixture into a piping bag, fitted with a large star nozzle and pipe a swirl of buttercream on top of each cake.
- Sprinkle the cupcakes generously with green sugar sprinkles.

Nectarine Cupcakes

342

MAKES 12

PREPARATION TIME 45 MINUTES

COOKING TIME 15 - 20 MINUTES

INGREDIENTS

110 g / 4 oz / ⅔ cup self-raising flour, sifted
110 g / 4 oz / ½ cup caster (superfine) sugar
110 g / 4 oz / ½ cup butter, softened
2 large eggs
2 nectarines, stoned and finely chopped

TO DECORATE:
100 g / 3 ½ oz / ½ cup butter, softened
200 g / 7 oz / 2 cups icing (confectioners') sugar
½ lemon, juiced and zest finely grated
orange sugar pearls

- Preheat the oven to 190°C (170° fan) / 375F / gas 5 and line a 12-hole cupcake tin with paper cases.
- Combine the flour, sugar, butter and eggs in a bowl and whisk together for 2 minutes or until smooth. Fold in the nectarines then divide the mixture between the cases and bake for 15 – 20 minutes.
- Test with a wooden toothpick, if it comes out clean, the cakes are done. Transfer the cakes to a wire rack and leave to cool completely.
- Beat the butter until smooth, then gradually whisk in the icing sugar, lemon juice and zest.
- Spoon the mixture into a piping bag, fitted with a large star nozzle and pipe a swirl of buttercream on top of each cake.
- Sprinkle the cupcakes generously with orange sugar pearls.

CELEBRATION & PARTY

343

MAKES 12

Strawberry Jam Lattice Cupcakes

PREPARATION TIME 30 MINUTES

COOKING TIME 15 - 20 MINUTES

INGREDIENTS

110 g / 4 oz / ⅔ cup self-raising flour, sifted
110 g / 4 oz / ½ cup caster (superfine) sugar
110 g / 4 oz / ½ cup butter, softened
2 large eggs
1 tsp vanilla extract

TO DECORATE:
200 g / 7 oz / ⅔ cup strawberry jam (jelly)

- Preheat the oven to 190°C (170° fan) / 375F / gas 5 and line a 12-hole cupcake tin with paper cases.
- Combine the flour, sugar, butter, eggs and vanilla extract in a bowl and whisk together for 2 minutes or until smooth.
- Divide the mixture between the cases, then transfer the tin to the oven and bake for 15 – 20 minutes.
- Test with a wooden toothpick, if it comes out clean, the cakes are done.
- Transfer the cakes to a wire rack and leave to cool completely.
- Put the strawberry jam in a food processor and blend to a smooth gel.
- Spoon the gel into a piping bag, fitted with a small plain nozzle, and pipe a lattice design on top of the cakes.

344

Strawberry Jam Spiral Cupcakes

- Pipe the strawberry gel in a spiral on top of the cakes.

345

MAKES 12

Rose Cupcakes

PREPARATION TIME 25 MINUTES

COOKING TIME 15 - 20 MINUTES

INGREDIENTS

110 g / 4 oz / ⅔ cup self-raising flour, sifted
110 g / 4 oz / ½ cup caster (superfine) sugar
110 g / 4 oz / ½ cup butter, softened
2 large eggs
1 tsp rose water

TO DECORATE:
200 g / 7 oz / 2 cups icing (confectioners') sugar
1 – 2 tsp rose water
a few drops of pink food colouring
12 sugar paste roses
sugar pearls to decorate

- Preheat the oven to 190°C (170° fan) / 375F / gas 5 and line a 12-hole cupcake tin with paper cases.
- Combine the flour, sugar, butter, eggs and rose water in a bowl and whisk together for 2 minutes or until smooth.
- Divide the mixture between the cases, then transfer the tin to the oven and bake for 15 – 20 minutes.
- Test with a wooden toothpick, if it comes out clean, the cakes are done.
- Transfer the cakes to a wire rack and leave to cool completely.
- Sieve the icing sugar into a bowl and add just enough rose water to make a thick, pourable icing.
- Colour the icing with a few drops of pink food colouring then spoon it on top of the cupcakes to come level with the top of the paper case.
- Press a rose into the centre of each cake and decorate with sugar pearls before leaving the icing to set.

346

Champagne and Roses Cupcakes

- Add 1 tbsp of marc de champagne to the cake mixture when whisking.

347

MAKES 12

Rose and Pearl Cupcakes

- Preheat the oven to 190°C (170° fan) / 375F / gas 5 and line a 12-hole cupcake tin with paper cases.
- Combine the flour, sugar, butter, eggs and rose water in a bowl and whisk together for 2 minutes.
- Divide the mixture between the cases, then transfer the tin to the oven and bake for 15 – 20 minutes.
- Transfer the cakes to a wire rack and leave to cool.
- Sieve the icing sugar into a bowl and add just enough rose water to make a thick, pourable icing.
- Colour the icing with a few drops of blue food colouring then spoon it on top of the cupcakes to come level with the top of the paper case.
- Press a rose into each cake and leave to set.
- Meanwhile, roll the fondant icing into small balls and spray with edible lustre. Leave to dry for 1 hour, then attach to the cakes with a little icing.

Black Pearl Cupcakes

348

- Omit the sugar paste roses and colour the icing black instead of blue.

PREPARATION TIME 45 MINUTES

COOKING TIME 15 - 20 MINUTES

INGREDIENTS

110 g / 4 oz / ⅔ cup self-raising flour, sifted
110 g / 4 oz / ½ cup caster (superfine) sugar
110 g / 4 oz / ½ cup butter, softened
2 large eggs
1 tsp rose water

TO DECORATE:
200 g / 7 oz / 2 cups icing (confectioners') sugar
1 – 2 tsp rose water
a few drops of blue food colouring
12 sugar paste roses
150 g / 5 ½ oz fondant icing
pearl edible lustre spray

349

MAKES 12

Strawberry Glace-Iced Orange Cupcakes

- Preheat the oven to 180°C (160° fan) / 350F / gas 4 and line a 12-hole cupcake tin with paper cases.
- Beat the egg in a jug with the orange zest, oil and milk until well mixed.
- Mix the flour, baking powder and sugar in a bowl, then pour in the egg mixture and stir just enough to combine.
- Spoon the mixture into the tin, then bake in the oven for 20 – 25 minutes.
- Test with a wooden toothpick, if it comes out clean, the cakes are done.
- Transfer the cakes to a wire rack and leave to cool completely.
- Sieve the icing sugar into a bowl and stir in just enough strawberry syrup to make a runny icing.
- Spoon the icing over the cakes and sprinkle with purple hearts.

Strawberry Glace-Iced Lemon Muffin Cupcakes

350

- Replace the orange zest with lemon zest.

PREPARATION TIME 25 MINUTES

COOKING TIME 20 – 25 MINUTES

INGREDIENTS

1 large egg
1 orange, zest finely grated
125 ml / 4 ½ fl. oz / ½ cup sunflower oil
125 ml / 4 ½ fl. oz / ½ cup milk
375 g / 13 oz / 2 ½ cups self-raising flour, sifted
1 tsp baking powder
200 g / 7 oz / ¾ cup caster (superfine) sugar

TO DECORATE:
200 g / 7 oz / 2 cups icing (confectioners') sugar
2 – 3 tsp strawberry syrup
purple heart-shaped cake sprinkles

351

MAKES 12

Vanilla Cupcakes with Rolled Icing

PREPARATION TIME 1 HOUR

COOKING TIME 15 - 20 MINUTES

INGREDIENTS

110 g / 4 oz / ⅔ cup self-raising flour, sifted
110 g / 4 oz / ½ cup caster (superfine) sugar
110 g / 4 oz / ½ cup butter, softened
2 large eggs
1 tsp vanilla extract

TO DECORATE:
200 g / 7 oz ready to roll fondant icing
yellow and pink food colouring
icing (confectioners') sugar for dusting

- Preheat the oven to 190°C (170° fan) / 375F / gas 5 and line a 12-hole cupcake tin with paper cases.
- Combine the flour, sugar, butter, eggs and vanilla in a bowl and whisk together for 2 minutes or until smooth.
- Divide the mixture between the cases, then transfer the tin to the oven and bake for 15 – 20 minutes.
- Test with a wooden toothpick, if it comes out clean, the cakes are done.
- Transfer the cakes to a wire rack and leave to cool completely.
- Divide the fondant icing into 2 pieces and knead a little food colouring into each.
- Dust the work surface lightly with icing sugar and roll out the icing, then cut out 6 large yellow flours and 6 large pink flowers.
- Wet the backs and stick one to the top of each cake. Use a small flower cutter to add a contrasting coloured smaller flower to each cake.
- Roll any off-cuts into small balls to use as the centres and attach with a dab of water.

352

Strawberry Cupcakes with Rolled Icing

- Add 2 tbsp of strawberry syrup to the cake mixture instead of the vanilla extract and cut the fondant icing into the shapes of your choice.

353

Apple Cupcakes with Rolled Icing

- Add a peeled, grated apple to the cake mixture. Colour the icing green and cut out an apple shape for the top of each cake.

354

MAKES 12

Coconut Star Cupcakes

- Preheat the oven to 190°C (170° fan) / 375F / gas 5 and line a 12-hole cupcake tin with paper cases.
- Combine the flour, sugar, butter, eggs and coconut in a bowl and whisk together for 2 minutes or until smooth.
- Divide the mixture between the cases, then transfer the tin to the oven and bake for 15 – 20 minutes.
- Transfer the cakes to a wire rack and leave to cool.
- Reserve a quarter of the fondant icing and knead a little blue food colouring into the rest.
- Dust the work surface lightly with icing sugar and roll out the icing, then cut out 12 circles the same diameter as the top of the cupcakes with a fluted cookie cutter.
- Wet the backs and stick one to the top of each cake, then sprinkle with coconut.
- Colour the reserved icing yellow and cut out 12 stars, then stick them to the cakes with a dab of water.

PREPARATION TIME 1 HOUR

COOKING TIME 15 - 20 MINUTES

INGREDIENTS

110 g / 4 oz / ⅔ cup self-raising flour, sifted
110 g / 4 oz / ½ cup caster (superfine) sugar
110 g / 4 oz / ½ cup butter, softened
2 large eggs
2 tbsp desiccated coconut

TO DECORATE:
200 g / 7 oz ready to roll fondant icing
a few drops of blue and yellow food colouring
icing (confectioners') sugar for dusting
2 tbsp desiccated coconut

Coconut and Blueberry Star Cupcakes

355

- Add 75 g of blueberries to the cake mixture before baking.

356

MAKES 12

Vanilla Rose Cupcakes

- Preheat the oven to 190°C (170° fan) / 375F / gas 5 and line a 12-hole cupcake tin with paper cases.
- Combine the flour, sugar, butter, eggs and vanilla extract in a bowl and whisk together for 2 minutes or until smooth.
- Divide the mixture between the cases, then transfer the tin to the oven and bake for 15 – 20 minutes.
- Transfer the cakes to a wire rack and leave to cool completely.
- Sieve the icing sugar into a bowl and add just enough recently boiled water to make a thick, pourable icing.
- Stir in a few drops of vanilla extract then spoon it on top of the cupcakes to come level with the top of the paper cases.
- Press a rose into the centre of each cake and leave the icing to set.

PREPARATION TIME 25 MINUTES

COOKING TIME 15 - 20 MINUTES

INGREDIENTS

110 g / 4 oz / ⅔ cup self-raising flour, sifted
110 g / 4 oz / ½ cup caster (superfine) sugar
110 g / 4 oz / ½ cup butter, softened
2 large eggs
1 tsp vanilla extract

TO DECORATE:
200 g / 7 oz / 2 cups icing (confectioners') sugar
1 – 2 tsp recently boiled water
a few drops of vanilla extract
12 sugar paste roses with leaves

Vanilla Pod Cupcakes

357

- Use the seeds from a vanilla pod instead of the vanilla extract in the cake mixture. Cut the pod into thin slivers and use to decorate the cases in place of the roses.

358

MAKES 12

Colourful Rose Cupcakes

PREPARATION TIME 30 MINUTES

COOKING TIME 15 - 20 MINUTES

INGREDIENTS

110 g / 4 oz / ⅔ cup self-raising flour, sifted
110 g / 4 oz / ½ cup caster (superfine) sugar
110 g / 4 oz / ½ cup butter, softened
2 large eggs
1 tsp rose water

TO DECORATE:
200 g / 7 oz fondant icing
a few drops of blue food colouring
12 white sugar paste roses
12 red sugar paste roses
12 pink sugar paste roses
24 sugar paste rose leaves
red ribbons to decorate

- Preheat the oven to 190°C (170° fan) / 375F / gas 5 and line a 12-hole cupcake tin with paper cases.
- Combine the flour, sugar, butter, eggs and rose water in a bowl and whisk together for 2 minutes or until smooth.
- Divide the mixture between the cases, then transfer the tin to the oven and bake for 15 – 20 minutes.
- Test with a wooden toothpick, if it comes out clean, the cakes are done.
- Transfer the cakes to a wire rack and leave to cool completely.
- Colour the fondant icing blue then roll it out between 2 sheets of greaseproof paper.
- Cut out 12 circles, the same diameter as the top of the cupcakes, then wet the backs and attach to the top of the cakes.
- Top the cakes with the roses and rose leaves and tie a red ribbon round each one.

359

Colourful Flower Cupcakes

- Add 1 tsp of orange flower water to the cake mixture and use a mixture of sugar paste flowers to decorate the cakes.

360

MAKES 12

Blackcurrant Buttercream Cupcakes

PREPARATION TIME 30 MINUTES

COOKING TIME 15 - 20 MINUTES

INGREDIENTS

110 g / 4 oz / ⅔ cup self-raising flour, sifted
110 g / 4 oz / ½ cup caster (superfine) sugar
110 g / 4 oz / ½ cup butter, softened
2 large eggs
1 tsp vanilla extract

TO DECORATE:
100 g / 3 ½ oz / ½ cup butter, softened
200 g / 7 oz / 2 cups icing (confectioners') sugar
2 tbsp blackcurrant syrup
pink cake sprinkles and candles to decorate

- Preheat the oven to 190°C (170° fan) / 375F / gas 5 and line a 12-hole cupcake tin with paper cases.
- Combine the flour, sugar, butter, eggs and vanilla extract in a bowl and whisk together for 2 minutes or until smooth.
- Divide the mixture between the cases and bake for 15 – 20 minutes.
- Transfer the cakes to a wire rack and leave to cool completely.
- Beat the butter until smooth, then gradually whisk in the icing sugar and blackcurrant syrup.
- Spoon the mixture into a piping bag, fitted with a large star nozzle, and pipe the icing in a spiral on top of each cake.
- Scatter over the cake sprinkles and top each cake with a candle to finish.

361

Almond Cupcakes with Blackcurrant Buttercream

- Add 3 tbsp of ground almonds and ½ tsp of almond extract to the cake mixture.

362

MAKES 12

Vanilla Cupcakes with Vanilla Buttercream

Strawberry Cupcakes with Vanilla Buttercream

363

- Add 100 g of chopped strawberries to the cake mixture and top each cake with a whole strawberry.

Vanilla Ice Cream Cupcakes

364

- Leave out the buttercream and top each cupcake with a scoop of good quality vanilla ice cream.

PREPARATION TIME 30 MINUTES

COOKING TIME 15 - 20 MINUTES

INGREDIENTS

110 g / 4 oz / ⅔ cup self-raising flour, sifted
110 g / 4 oz / ½ cup caster (superfine) sugar
110 g / 4 oz / ½ cup butter, softened
2 large eggs
1 tsp vanilla extract

TO DECORATE:
100 g / 3 ½ oz / ½ cup butter, softened
200 g / 7 oz / 2 cups icing (confectioners') sugar
1 tsp vanilla extract
purple sugar cake sprinkles

- Preheat the oven to 190°C (170° fan) / 375F / gas 5 and line a 12-hole cupcake tin with paper cases.
- Combine the flour, sugar, butter, eggs and vanilla extract in a bowl and whisk together for 2 minutes or until smooth.
- Divide the mixture between the cases and bake for 15 – 20 minutes.
- Test with a wooden toothpick, if it comes out clean, the cakes are done.
- Transfer the cakes to a wire rack and leave to cool completely.
- Beat the butter until smooth, then gradually whisk in the icing sugar and vanilla extract.
- Spoon the mixture into a piping bag, fitted with a large star nozzle, and pipe a swirl of icing on top of each cake. Sprinkle with the purple sugar cake sprinkles.

365

Black and Orange Flower Cupcakes

MAKES 12

PREPARATION TIME 30 MINUTES

COOKING TIME 15 - 20 MINUTES

INGREDIENTS

110 g / 4 oz / ⅔ cup self-raising flour, sifted
110 g / 4 oz / ½ cup caster (superfine) sugar
110 g / 4 oz / ½ cup butter, softened
2 large eggs
1 tsp orange flower water
a few drops of orange food colouring

TO DECORATE:
100 g / 3 ½ oz / ½ cup butter, softened
200 g / 7 oz / 2 cups icing (confectioners') sugar
200 g / 7 oz fondant icing
a few drops of black and orange food colouring
black and silver food colouring pens
silver balls and red ribbons to decorate

- Preheat the oven to 190°C (170° fan) / 375F / gas 5 and line a 12-hole cupcake tin with paper cases.
- Combine the flour, sugar, butter, eggs, orange flower water and food colouring in a bowl and whisk for 2 minutes.
- Divide the mixture between the cases, then transfer the tin to the oven and bake for 15 – 20 minutes.
- Transfer the cakes to a wire rack and leave to cool.
- Beat the smooth, then gradually whisk in the icing sugar.
- Spoon the mixture into a piping bag, fitted with a large star nozzle, and pipe a swirl of icing on top of each cake.
- Divide the fondant icing in half and colour one piece black and the other orange. Roll out the icing between 2 sheets of greaseproof paper and cut out small flowers with a plunger cutter, adding the centres with the pens.
- Top the cakes with the flowers and silver balls and tie a ribbon round each.

366

Orange Flower Cupcakes

- Add 1 tsp of orange flower water to the icing and decorate with only the orange flowers.

367

Glace-Iced Gluten-Free Cupcakes

MAKES 12

PREPARATION TIME 25 MINUTES

COOKING TIME 15 - 20 MINUTES

INGREDIENTS

110 g / 4 oz / ⅔ cup gluten free plain (all purpose) flour, sifted
1 ½ tsp baking powder
110 g / 4 oz / ½ cup caster (superfine) sugar
110 g / 4 oz / ½ cup butter, softened
2 large eggs
1 tsp vanilla extract

TO DECORATE:
200 g / 7 oz / 2 cups icing (confectioners') sugar
sugar star-shaped cake sprinkles to decorate

- Preheat the oven to 190°C (170° fan) / 375F / gas 5 and line a 12-hole cupcake tin with paper cases.
- Combine the flour, sugar, butter, eggs and vanilla extract in a bowl and whisk together for 2 minutes or until smooth.
- Divide the mixture between the cases and bake for 15 – 20 minutes.
- Test with a wooden toothpick, if it comes out clean, the cakes are done.
- Transfer the cakes to a wire rack and leave to cool completely.
- Sieve the icing sugar into a bowl and add just enough water to make a thick, spreadable icing.
- Spread the icing onto the cakes and decorate with cake sprinkles.

368

Glace-Iced Lemon Gluten-Free Cupcakes

- Add the grated zest of a lemon to the cake mixture and use lemon juice instead of water to make the icing.

369

MAKES 12

Chocolate Syrup Cream Cupcakes

- Preheat the oven to 190°C (170° fan) / 375F / gas 5 and line a 12-hole cupcake tin with silicone cases.
- Sieve the flour, bicarbonate of soda and cocoa together.
- Put the golden syrup, butter and brown sugar in a small saucepan and boil gently for 2 minutes, stirring to dissolve the sugar.
- Pour the butter and sugar mixture onto the flour with the eggs and milk, then fold with the chocolate chunks.
- Divide the mixture between the cases and bake for 20 – 25 minutes.
- Transfer the cakes to a wire rack and leave to cool.
- Heat the cream until it starts to simmer, then pour it over the chopped chocolate and stir until smooth.
- Leave to cool and thicken to a pipable consistency, then spoon it into a piping bag. Pipe a big swirl onto each cake and decorate with chocolate cigarillos and balls.

Triple Chocolate Chunk Cupcakes

370

- Use 50 g of dark chocolate chunks, 50 g of milk chocolate chunks and 50 g of white chocolate chunks. Top the cakes with a jumble of chocolate chunks.

PREPARATION TIME 30 MINUTES

COOKING TIME 20 – 25 MINUTES

INGREDIENTS

250 g / 9 oz / 1 ¾ cups self-raising flour
1 tsp bicarbonate of (baking) soda
3 tbsp unsweetened cocoa powder
200 g / 8 ½ oz / ½ cup golden syrup
125 g / 4 ½ oz / ½ cup butter
125 g / 4 ½ oz / ¾ cup dark brown sugar
2 large eggs, beaten
250 ml / 9 fl. oz / 1 cup milk
150 g / 5 ½ oz dark chocolate chunks

TO DECORATE:
200 ml / 7 fl. oz / 3/4 cup double (heavy) cream
200 g / 7 oz dark chocolate, minimum 60% cocoa solids, chopped
chocolate cigarillos and chocolate balls to decorate

371

MAKES 12

Blue Butterfly Cupcakes

- Preheat the oven to 190°C (170° fan) / 375F / gas 5 and line a 12-hole cupcake tin with foil cases.
- Combine the flour, sugar, butter, eggs and vanilla extract in a bowl and whisk together for 2 minutes or until smooth.
- Divide the mixture between the cases, then transfer the tin to the oven and bake for 15 – 20 minutes.
- Transfer the cakes to a wire rack and leave to cool completely.
- Colour 2 thirds of the icing blue and roll it out between 2 sheets of greaseproof paper.
- Cut out 12 circles the same diameter as the top of the cupcakes with a fluted cutter, then wet the backs and attach them to the top of the cakes.
- Roll out the white icing and cut out 12 butterflies, then attach them to the top of the cakes with a dab of water.

Peppermint Butterfly Cupcakes

372

- Use a few drops of peppermint extract instead of the vanilla extract and colour the icing pale green instead of blue.

PREPARATION TIME 35 MINUTES

COOKING TIME 15 - 20 MINUTES

INGREDIENTS

110 g / 4 oz / ⅔ cup self-raising flour, sifted
110 g / 4 oz / ½ cup caster (superfine) sugar
110 g / 4 oz / ½ cup butter, softened
2 large eggs
1 tsp vanilla extract

TO DECORATE:
150 g / 5 ½ oz fondant icing
a few drops of blue food colouring

373

MAKES 12

Coconut Pearl Cupcakes

PREPARATION TIME 25 MINUTES

COOKING TIME 15 - 20 MINUTES

INGREDIENTS

110 g / 4 oz / ⅔ cup self-raising flour, sifted
110 g / 4 oz / ½ cup caster (superfine) sugar
110 g / 4 oz / ½ cup butter, softened
2 large eggs
2 tbsp desiccated coconut

TO DECORATE:
100 g / 3 ½ oz / ½ cup butter, softened
200 g / 7 oz / 2 cups icing (confectioners') sugar
2 tbsp desiccated coconut
sugar pearls to decorate

- Preheat the oven to 190°C (170° fan) / 375F / gas 5 and line a 12-hole cupcake tin with paper cases.
- Combine the flour, sugar, butter, eggs and coconut in a bowl and whisk together for 2 minutes or until smooth.
- Divide the mixture between the cases, then transfer the tin to the oven and bake for 15 – 20 minutes.
- Test with a wooden toothpick, if it comes out clean, the cakes are done.
- Transfer the cakes to a wire rack and leave to cool completely.
- Beat the butter until smooth, then gradually whisk in the icing sugar and coconut.
- Spoon the mixture into a piping bag, fitted with a large star nozzle, and pipe a swirl of icing on top of each cake. Decorate with sugar pearls.

374

Coconut and Pineapple Pearl Cupcakes

- Add 75 g of finely chopped glace pineapple to the cake mixture.

375

Chocolate Orange Syrup Cupcakes

- Add the grated zest of an orange to the cake mixture. Make a batch of orange buttercream and swirl half and half with the chocolate ganache.

376

Vanilla & Blackberry Buttercream Cupcakes

MAKES 12

- Preheat the oven to 190°C (170° fan) / 375F / gas 5 and line a 12-hole cupcake tin with paper cases.
- Combine the flour, sugar, butter, eggs and vanilla extract in a bowl and whisk together for 2 minutes or until smooth.
- Divide the mixture between the cases and bake for 15 – 20 minutes.
- Test with a wooden toothpick, if it comes out clean, the cakes are done.
- Transfer the cakes to a wire rack and leave to cool completely.
- Beat the butter until smooth, then gradually whisk in the icing sugar and blackberry syrup.
- Spoon the mixture into a piping bag, fitted with a large star nozzle, and pipe a swirl of icing on top of each cake.
- Top each cake with an edible crystal.

PREPARATION TIME 30 MINUTES

COOKING TIME 15 - 20 MINUTES

INGREDIENTS

110 g / 4 oz / ⅔ cup self-raising flour, sifted
110 g / 4 oz / ½ cup caster (superfine) sugar
110 g / 4 oz / ½ cup butter, softened
2 large eggs
1 tsp vanilla extract

TO DECORATE:

100 g / 3 ½ oz / ½ cup butter, softened
200 g / 7 oz / 2 cups icing (confectioners') sugar
2 tbsp blackberry syrup
12 edible crystals

Vanilla Cupcakes with Grenadine Buttercream

377

- Use grenadine in place of the blackberry syrup.

378

White Rose Cupcakes

MAKES 12

- Preheat the oven to 190°C (170° fan) / 375F / gas 5 and line a 12-hole cupcake tin with paper cases.
- Combine the flour, sugar, butter, eggs and rose water in a bowl and whisk together for 2 minutes or until smooth.
- Divide the mixture between the cases, then transfer the tin to the oven and bake for 15 – 20 minutes.
- Test with a wooden toothpick, if it comes out clean, the cakes are done.
- Transfer the cakes to a wire rack and leave to cool completely.
- Roll out the fondant icing between 2 sheets of grease proof paper and cut out 12 circles the same diameter as the top of the cupcakes.
- Wet the back of the icing circles and attach them to the top of the cakes, then top with the sugar paste roses.
- Glue a ribbon bow onto the front of each paper case.

PREPARATION TIME 35 MINUTES

COOKING TIME 15 - 20 MINUTES

INGREDIENTS

110 g / 4 oz / ⅔ cup self-raising flour, sifted
110 g / 4 oz / ½ cup caster (superfine) sugar
110 g / 4 oz / ½ cup butter, softened
2 large eggs
1 tsp rose water

TO DECORATE:

150 g / 5 ½ oz fondant icing
12 sugar paste roses
purple ribbon bows to decorate

Green Rose Cupcakes

379

- Use a few drops of green food colouring to colour the icing pale green and use green sugar paste roses to decorate.

380

MAKES 12

Rhubarb Syrup Cream Cheese Cupcakes

PREPARATION TIME 30 MINUTES

COOKING TIME 15 - 20 MINUTES

INGREDIENTS

110 g / 4 oz / ⅔ cup self-raising flour, sifted
110 g / 4 oz / ½ cup caster (superfine) sugar
110 g / 4 oz / ½ cup butter, softened
2 large eggs
3 tbsp rhubarb syrup

TO DECORATE:
110 g / 4 oz / ½ cup cream cheese
55 g / 2 oz / ¼ cup butter, softened
110 g / 4 oz / 1 cup icing (confectioners') sugar
1 tsp vanilla extract
3 tbsp rhubarb syrup

- Preheat the oven to 190°C (170° fan) / 375F / gas 5 and line a 12-hole cupcake tin with paper cases.
- Combine the flour, sugar, butter, eggs and rhubarb syrup in a bowl and whisk together for 2 minutes or until smooth.
- Divide the mixture between the cases and bake for 15 – 20 minutes.
- Transfer the cakes to a wire rack and leave to cool.
- Beat the cream cheese and butter together until light and fluffy then beat in the icing sugar a quarter at a time.
- Add the vanilla extract then whip the mixture for 2 minutes or until smooth and light.
- Spoon the icing into a piping bag, fitted with a large star nozzle, and pipe a swirl of icing on top of each cake.
- Drizzle over the rhubarb syrup.

381

Peach Syrup Cream Cheese Cupcakes

- Replace the rhubarb syrup with peach syrup.

382

MAKES 12

Vanilla Cupcakes with Coffee Buttercream

PREPARATION TIME 30 MINUTES

COOKING TIME 15 - 20 MINUTES

INGREDIENTS

110 g / 4 oz / ⅔ cup self-raising flour, sifted
110 g / 4 oz / ½ cup caster (superfine) sugar
110 g / 4 oz / ½ cup butter, softened
2 large eggs
1 tsp vanilla extract

TO DECORATE:
100 g / 3 ½ oz / ½ cup butter, softened
200 g / 7 oz / 2 cups icing (confectioners') sugar
1 tbsp instant espresso powder
chocolate cake sprinkles
12 sugar paste roses

- Preheat the oven to 190°C (170° fan) / 375F / gas 5 and line a 12-hole cupcake tin with paper cases.
- Combine the flour, sugar, butter, eggs and vanilla extract in a bowl and whisk together for 2 minutes or until smooth.
- Divide the mixture between the cases, then transfer the tin to the oven and bake for 15 – 20 minutes.
- Test with a wooden toothpick, if it comes out clean, the cakes are done.
- Transfer the cakes to a wire rack and leave to cool completely.
- Beat the butter until smooth, then gradually whisk in the icing sugar and espresso powder.
- Spread the buttercream onto the cakes and sprinkle with chocolate sprinkles before topping each one with a rose.

383

Vanilla Cupcakes with Cinnamon Buttercream

- Replace the espresso powder with 1 tsp ground cinnamon.

384

MAKES 12

Strawberry Heart Cupcakes

Apricot Heart Cupcakes

385

- Replace the strawberry jam and syrup with apricot jam and syrup. Decorate with orange sugar hearts.

Banana Heart Cupcakes

386

- Add a chopped banana to the cake mixture and use banana syrup instead of strawberry syrup in the icing. Top with yellow sugar hearts.

PREPARATION TIME 30 MINUTES

COOKING TIME 15 - 20 MINUTES

INGREDIENTS

110 g / 4 oz / ⅔ cup self-raising flour, sifted
110 g / 4 oz / ½ cup caster (superfine) sugar
110 g / 4 oz / ½ cup butter, softened
2 large eggs
1 tsp vanilla extract
200 g / 7 oz / ⅔ cup strawberry jam (jelly)

TO DECORATE:
100 g / 3 ½ oz / ½ cup butter, softened
200 g / 7 oz / 2 cups icing (confectioners') sugar
2 tbsp strawberry syrup
red and pink sugar hearts and white cake sprinkles
red ribbons

- Preheat the oven to 190°C (170° fan) / 375F / gas 5 and line a 12-hole cupcake tin with paper cases.
- Combine the flour, sugar, butter, eggs and vanilla extract in a bowl and whisk together for 2 minutes or until smooth.
- Divide half the mixture between the cases and add a big spoonful of jam to each one.
- Top with the rest of the cake mixture, then transfer the tin to the oven and bake for 15 – 20 minutes.
- Test with a wooden toothpick, if it comes out clean, the cakes are done.
- Transfer the cakes to a wire rack and leave to cool completely.
- Beat the butter until smooth, then gradually whisk in the icing sugar and strawberry syrup.
- Spoon the icing into a piping bag, fitted with a large star nozzle, and pipe a swirl of icing on top of each cake.
- Decorate the cakes with hearts and sprinkles and tie a ribbon round each case.

387

MAKES 12

Chocolate Cupcakes with Rose Buttercream

PREPARATION TIME 30 MINUTES

COOKING TIME 15 - 20 MINUTES

INGREDIENTS

110 g / 4 oz / ⅔ cup self-raising flour, sifted
110 g / 4 oz / ½ cup caster (superfine) sugar
110 g / 4 oz / ½ cup butter, softened
2 large eggs
2 tbsp unsweetened cocoa powder

TO DECORATE:
100 g / 3 ½ oz / ½ cup butter, softened
200 g / 7 oz / 2 cups icing (confectioners') sugar
1 tbsp rose water
12 sugar paste roses

- Preheat the oven to 190°C (170° fan) / 375F / gas 5 and line a 12-hole cupcake tin with paper cases.
- Combine the flour, sugar, butter, eggs and cocoa in a bowl and whisk together for 2 minutes or until smooth.
- Divide the mixture between the cases, then transfer the tin to the oven and bake for 15 – 20 minutes.
- Test with a wooden toothpick, if it comes out clean, the cakes are done.
- Transfer the cakes to a wire rack and leave to cool completely.
- Beat the butter until smooth, then gradually whisk in the icing sugar and rose water.
- Spoon the mixture into a piping bag, fitted with a large star nozzle, and pipe a swirl on top of each cake. Top each cake with a sugar paste rose.

388

Chocolate Cupcakes with Lavender Buttercream

- Replace the rose water with a few drops of lavender extract and sprinkle the cakes with lavender flowers instead of the sugar roses.

389

MAKES 12

Strawberry and Vanilla Cupcakes

PREPARATION TIME 30 MINUTES

COOKING TIME 15 - 20 MINUTES

INGREDIENTS

110 g / 4 oz / ⅔ cup self-raising flour, sifted
110 g / 4 oz / ½ cup caster (superfine) sugar
110 g / 4 oz / ½ cup butter, softened
2 large eggs
1 tsp vanilla extract
2 tbsp strawberry syrup

TO DECORATE:
100 g / 3 ½ oz / ½ cup butter, softened
200 g / 7 oz / 2 cups icing (confectioners') sugar
2 tbsp strawberry syrup
coloured sugar strands to decorate

- Preheat the oven to 190°C (170° fan) / 375F / gas 5 and line a 12-hole cupcake tin with paper cases.
- Combine the flour, sugar, butter, eggs, vanilla extract and strawberry syrup in a bowl and whisk together for 2 minutes or until smooth.
- Divide the mixture between the cases, then transfer the tin to the oven and bake for 15 – 20 minutes.
- Test with a wooden toothpick, if it comes out clean, the cakes are done.
- Transfer the cakes to a wire rack and leave to cool completely.
- Beat the butter until smooth, then gradually whisk in the icing sugar and strawberry syrup.
- Spoon the icing into a piping bag, fitted with a large star nozzle, and pipe a swirl of icing on top of each cake.
- Decorate the cakes with sugar strands.

390

Strawberry and Orange Cupcakes

- Replace the vanilla extract with the finely grated zest of an orange.

391

MAKES 12

Red Velvet Cupcakes

- Preheat the oven to 190°C (170° fan) / 375F / gas 5 and line a 12-hole cupcake tin with paper cases.
- Combine the flour, sugar, butter, eggs, cinnamon and food colouring in a bowl and whisk together for 2 minutes or until smooth.
- Divide the mixture between the cases, then transfer the tin to the oven and bake for 15 – 20 minutes.
- Transfer the cakes to a wire rack and leave to cool.
- Beat the cream cheese and butter until light and fluffy then beat in the icing sugar a quarter at a time.
- Add the vanilla extract then whip the mixture for 2 minutes or until smooth and light.
- Spoon the icing into a piping bag, fitted with a large plain nozzle, and pipe a swirl of icing on top of each cake.
- Sprinkle with a little bit of ground cinnamon.

PREPARATION TIME 30 MINUTES

COOKING TIME 15 - 20 MINUTES

INGREDIENTS

110 g / 4 oz / ⅔ cup self-raising flour, sifted
110 g / 4 oz / ½ cup caster (superfine) sugar
110 g / 4 oz / ½ cup butter, softened
2 large eggs
1 tsp ground cinnamon
1 tbsp red food colouring

TO DECORATE:
110 g / 4 oz / ½ cup cream cheese
55 g / 2 oz / ¼ cup butter, softened
110 g / 4 oz / 1 cup icing (confectioners') sugar
1 tsp vanilla extract
ground cinnamon for dusting

Blue Suede Cupcakes

392

- Replace the red food colouring with blue food colouring and use the grated zest of an orange in place of the ground cinnamon in the cake mixture.

393

MAKES 12

Chocolate Truffle Cupcakes

- Preheat the oven to 190°C (170° fan) / 375F / gas 5 and line a 12-hole cupcake tin with paper cases.
- Combine the flour, sugar, butter, eggs and cocoa in a bowl and whisk together for 2 minutes or until smooth.
- Divide the mixture between the cases, then transfer the tin to the oven and bake for 15 – 20 minutes.
- Test with a wooden toothpick, if it comes out clean, the cakes are done.
- Transfer the cakes to a wire rack and leave to cool completely.
- Heat the cream with the rum until it starts to simmer, then pour it over the chopped chocolate and stir until smooth. Leave to cool to room temperature, then chill until thick enough to pipe.
- Spoon the ganache into a piping bag fitted with a large plain nozzle and pipe a swirl on top of each cake. Sprinkle with sugar strands.

PREPARATION TIME 30 MINUTES

COOKING TIME 15 - 20 MINUTES

INGREDIENTS

110 g / 4 oz / ⅔ cup self-raising flour, sifted
110 g / 4 oz / ½ cup caster (superfine) sugar
110 g / 4 oz / ½ cup butter, softened
2 large eggs
2 tbsp unsweetened cocoa powder

TO DECORATE:
200 ml / 7 fl. oz / 3/4 cup double (heavy) cream
2 tbsp dark rum
200 g / 7 oz dark chocolate, minimum 60% cocoa solids, chopped
sugar strands for sprinkling

Champagne Truffle Cupcakes

394

- Replace the rum with marc de champagne.

395

Raspberry Rose and Pearl Cupcakes

MAKES 12

Strawberry Rose and Pearl Cupcakes

396

- Use strawberry jam in place of the raspberry jam.

Apricot Rose and Pearl Cupcakes

397

- Use apricot jam instead of the raspberry jam and decorate with orange roses.

PREPARATION TIME 35 MINUTES

COOKING TIME 15 - 20 MINUTES

INGREDIENTS

110 g / 4 oz / ⅔ cup self-raising flour, sifted
110 g / 4 oz / ½ cup caster (superfine) sugar
110 g / 4 oz / ½ cup butter, softened
2 large eggs
1 tsp rose water
200 g / 7 oz / ⅔ cup raspberry jam (jelly)

TO DECORATE:
150 g / 5 ½ oz fondant icing
12 sugar paste roses
sugar pearls and pink ribbons to decorate

- Preheat the oven to 190°C (170° fan) / 375F / gas 5 and line a 12-hole cupcake tin with paper cases.
- Combine the flour, sugar, butter, eggs and rose water in a bowl and whisk together for 2 minutes or until smooth.
- Divide half the mixture between the cases, then add a big spoonful of raspberry jam to each.
- Top with the rest of the cake mixture then transfer the tin to the oven and bake for 15 – 20 minutes.
- Test with a wooden toothpick, if it comes out clean, the cakes are done.
- Transfer the cakes to a wire rack and leave to cool completely.
- Roll out the fondant icing between 2 sheets of grease proof paper and cut out 12 circles, the diameter of the top of the cupcakes, with a round fluted edge cutter.
- Wet the back of the icing circles and attach them to the top of the cakes, then decorate with the roses and sugar pearls.
- Tie a ribbon around each cake and stick a sugar pearl to the centre of each bow with glue.

398

MAKES 12

Chocolate and Coffee Cupcakes

- Preheat the oven to 190°C (170° fan) / 375F / gas 5 and line a 12-hole cupcake tin with paper cases.
- Combine the flour, sugar, butter, eggs and cocoa in a bowl and whisk together for 2 minutes or until smooth.
- Divide the mixture between the cases, then transfer the tin to the oven and bake for 15 – 20 minutes.
- Test with a wooden toothpick, if it comes out clean, the cakes are done.
- Transfer the cakes to a wire rack and leave to cool completely.
- Beat the butter until smooth, then gradually whisk in the icing sugar and espresso powder.
- Spoon the icing into a piping bag fitted with a large star nozzle and pipe a big swirl on top of each cake.

PREPARATION TIME 30 MINUTES

COOKING TIME 15 - 20 MINUTES

INGREDIENTS

110 g / 4 oz / ⅔ cup self-raising flour, sifted
110 g / 4 oz / ½ cup caster (superfine) sugar
110 g / 4 oz / ½ cup butter, softened
2 large eggs
2 tbsp unsweetened cocoa powder

TO DECORATE:
100 g / 3 ½ oz / ½ cup butter, softened
200 g / 7 oz / 2 cups icing (confectioners') sugar
1 tbsp instant espresso powder

399

Chocolate Cupcakes with Cinnamon Buttercream

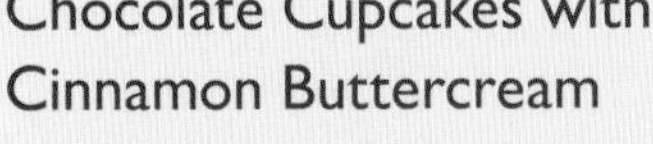

- Replace the espresso powder with 1 tsp ground cinnamon.

400

MAKES 12

Pretty Flower Cupcakes

- Preheat the oven to 190°C (170° fan) / 375F / gas 5 and line a 12-hole cupcake tin with paper cases.
- Combine the flour, sugar, butter, eggs and flower extracts in a bowl and whisk together for 2 minutes or until smooth.
- Divide the mixture between the cases, then transfer the tin to the oven and bake for 15 – 20 minutes.
- Test with a wooden toothpick, if it comes out clean, the cakes are done.
- Transfer the cakes to a wire rack and leave to cool completely.
- Beat the butter until smooth, then gradually whisk in the icing sugar.
- Spoon the mixture into a piping bag, fitted with a large star nozzle, and pipe a swirl of icing on top of each cake.
- Decorate the cakes with the sugar flowers and decorate the cases with pink ribbons and pearls.

PREPARATION TIME 30 MINUTES

COOKING TIME 15 - 20 MINUTES

INGREDIENTS

110 g / 4 oz / ⅔ cup self-raising flour, sifted
110 g / 4 oz / ½ cup caster (superfine) sugar
110 g / 4 oz / ½ cup butter, softened
2 large eggs
a few drops of lavender and violet extracts

TO DECORATE:
100 g / 3 ½ oz / ½ cup butter, softened
200 g / 7 oz / 2 cups icing (confectioners') sugar
blue, pink and purple sugar flowers
pink ribbons and pearls to decorate the cases

401

Layered Flower Cupcakes

- Remove the cakes from their cases and slice each one into 3 layers. Sandwich back together with rose petal jam and decorate as before.

402

Raspberry Rose Cream Cheese Cupcakes

MAKES 12

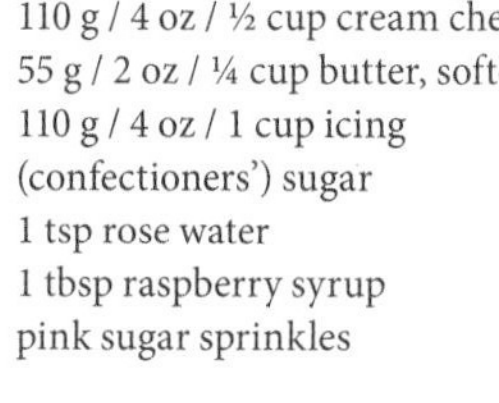

PREPARATION TIME 30 MINUTES

COOKING TIME 15 - 20 MINUTES

INGREDIENTS

110 g / 4 oz / ⅔ cup self-raising flour, sifted
110 g / 4 oz / ½ cup caster (superfine) sugar
110 g / 4 oz / ½ cup butter, softened
2 large eggs
1 tbsp rose water
75 g / 2 ½ oz / ½ cup raspberries

TO DECORATE:
110 g / 4 oz / ½ cup cream cheese
55 g / 2 oz / ¼ cup butter, softened
110 g / 4 oz / 1 cup icing (confectioners') sugar
1 tsp rose water
1 tbsp raspberry syrup
pink sugar sprinkles

- Preheat the oven to 190°C (170° fan) / 375F / gas 5 and line a 12-hole cupcake tin with paper cases.
- Combine the flour, sugar, butter, eggs and rose water in a bowl and whisk together for 2 minutes or until smooth.
- Fold in the raspberries then divide the mixture between the cases and bake for 15 – 20 minutes.
- Transfer the cakes to a wire rack and leave to cool.
- Beat the cream cheese and butter together until light and fluffy then beat in the icing sugar a quarter at a time.
- Add the rose water and raspberry syrup then whip the mixture for 2 minutes or until smooth and light.
- Spoon the icing into a piping bag, fitted with a large star nozzle, and pipe a swirl of icing on top of each cake, then sprinkle with pink sugar sprinkles.

403

Raspberry Violet Cream Cheese Cupcakes

- Add Replace the rose water with violet syrup.

404

Raspberry Sorbet Cupcakes

MAKES 12

PREPARATION TIME 15 MINUTES

COOKING TIME 15 - 20 MINUTES

INGREDIENTS

110 g / 4 oz / ⅔ cup self-raising flour, sifted
110 g / 4 oz / ½ cup caster (superfine) sugar
110 g / 4 oz / ½ cup butter, softened
2 large eggs
1 tsp vanilla extract
500 ml / 17 ½ fl. oz tub raspberry sorbet
sugar cake sprinkles to decorate

- Preheat the oven to 190°C (170° fan) / 375F / gas 5 and line a 12-hole cupcake tin with paper cases.
- Combine the flour, sugar, butter, eggs and vanilla extract in a bowl and whisk together for 2 minutes or until smooth.
- Divide the mixture between the cases, then transfer the tin to the oven and bake for 15 – 20 minutes.
- Test with a wooden toothpick, if it comes out clean, the cakes are done.
- Transfer the cakes to a wire rack and leave to cool completely.
- Take the sorbet out of the freezer and leave to soften for 20 minutes, then spoon it into a food processor and process until smooth and soft.
- Spoon the sorbet into a piping bag and quickly pipe a swirl on top of each cake.
- Sprinkle with cake sprinkles and serve immediately.

405

Lemon Sorbet Cupcakes

- Use lemon sorbet instead of raspberry sorbet.

406

MAKES 18

Pink Party Cupcakes

PREPARATION TIME 30 MINUTES

COOKING TIME 15 - 20 MINUTES

INGREDIENTS

175 g / 6 oz / 1 ¼ cups self-raising flour, sifted
175 g / 6 oz / 3/4 cup caster (superfine) sugar
175 g / 6 oz / 3/4 cup butter, softened
3 large eggs
1 tsp vanilla extract

TO DECORATE:
100 g / 3 ½ oz / ½ cup butter, softened
200 g / 7 oz / 2 cups icing (confectioners') sugar
a few drops of pink food colouring
small sweets and sugar sprinkles to decorate

- Preheat the oven to 190°C (170° fan) / 375F / gas 5 and line an 18-hole cupcake tin with paper cases.
- Combine the flour, sugar, butter, eggs and vanilla extract in a bowl and whisk together for 2 minutes or until smooth.
- Divide the mixture between the cases, then transfer the tin to the oven and bake for 15 – 20 minutes.
- Test with a wooden toothpick, if it comes out clean, the cakes are done.
- Transfer the cakes to a wire rack and leave to cool completely.
- Beat the butter until smooth, then gradually whisk in the icing sugar and food colouring.
- Spoon the mixture into a piping bag, fitted with a large star nozzle, and pipe a swirl of icing on top of each cake.
- Decorate each cake with a combination of sweets and sugar sprinkles.

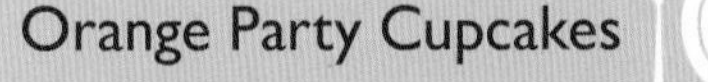

Orange Party Cupcakes

407

- Colour the butter icing orange and replace the vanilla extract with the grated zest of an orange.

Lemon Party Cupcakes

408

- Add the grated zest of a lemon to the cake mixture and icing and colour the icing yellow.

409

MAKES 12

Coconut Cupcakes with Rolled Icing

PREPARATION TIME 1 HOUR

COOKING TIME 15 - 20 MINUTES

INGREDIENTS

110 g / 4 oz / ⅔ cup self-raising flour, sifted
110 g / 4 oz / ½ cup caster (superfine) sugar
110 g / 4 oz / ½ cup butter, softened
2 large eggs
2 tbsp desiccated coconut

TO DECORATE:
a few drops of blue food colouring
200 g / 7 oz ready to roll fondant icing
icing (confectioners') sugar for dusting
2 tbsp desiccated coconut

- Preheat the oven to 190°C (170° fan) / 375F / gas 5 and line a 12-hole cupcake tin with paper cases.
- Combine the flour, sugar, butter, eggs and coconut in a bowl and whisk together for 2 minutes or until smooth.
- Divide the mixture between the cases, then transfer the tin to the oven and bake for 15 – 20 minutes.
- Test with a wooden toothpick, if it comes out clean, the cakes are done.
- Transfer the cakes to a wire rack and leave to cool completely.
- Knead a little blue food colouring into the fondant icing.
- Dust the work surface lightly with icing sugar and roll out the icing, then cut out 12 circles the same diameter as the top of the cupcakes with a fluted cookie cutter.
- Wet the backs and stick one to the top of each cake, then sprinkle with coconut.

Lemon Cupcakes with Rolled Icing

410

- Omit the coconut and add the grated zest of a lemon to the cupcake mixture. Sprinkle the icing with finely pared lemon zest instead of the coconut.

411

MAKES 12

Blueberry and Redcurrant Cupcakes

PREPARATION TIME 30 MINUTES

COOKING TIME 15 - 20 MINUTES

INGREDIENTS

110 g / 4 oz / ⅔ cup self-raising flour, sifted
110 g / 4 oz / ½ cup caster (superfine) sugar
110 g / 4 oz / ½ cup butter, softened
2 large eggs
1 tsp vanilla extract
75 g / 2 ½ oz / ½ cup blueberries
75 g / 2 ½ oz / ½ cup redcurrants

TO DECORATE:
100 g / 3 ½ oz / ½ cup butter, softened
200 g / 7 oz / 2 cups icing (confectioners') sugar
2 tbsp blueberry syrup

- Preheat the oven to 190°C (170° fan) / 375F / gas 5 and line a 12-hole cupcake tin with paper cases.
- Combine the flour, sugar, butter, eggs and vanilla extract in a bowl and whisk together for 2 minutes or until smooth. Reserve a few of the berries for decoration and fold in the rest.
- Divide the mixture between the cases, then transfer the tin to the oven and bake for 15 – 20 minutes.
- Test with a wooden toothpick, if it comes out clean, the cakes are done.
- Transfer the cakes to a wire rack and leave to cool completely.
- Beat the butter until smooth, then gradually whisk in the icing sugar and blueberry syrup.
- Spoon the icing into a piping bag, fitted with a large star nozzle, and pipe a swirl of icing on top of each cake.
- Decorate with the reserved blueberries and redcurrants.

Raspberry and Redcurrant Cupcakes

412

- Replace the blueberries with raspberries and use raspberry syrup in the icing.

413

MAKES 12

White Chocolate Sprinkle Cupcakes

- Preheat the oven to 190°C (170° fan) / 375F / gas 5 and line a 12-hole cupcake tin with paper cases.
- Combine the flour, sugar, butter, eggs and cocoa in a bowl and whisk together for 2 minutes or until smooth.
- Divide the mixture between the cases, then transfer the tin to the oven and bake for 15 – 20 minutes.
- Test with a wooden toothpick, if it comes out clean, the cakes are done.
- Transfer the cakes to a wire rack and leave to cool completely.
- Beat the butter until smooth, then gradually whisk in the icing sugar.
- Spoon the mixture into a piping bag, fitted with a large star nozzle, and pipe a swirl of icing on top of each cake, then decorate with the white chocolate sprinkles, sugar strands and mini chocolate buttons.

PREPARATION TIME 30 MINUTES

COOKING TIME 15 - 20 MINUTES

INGREDIENTS

110 g / 4 oz / ⅔ cup self-raising flour, sifted
110 g / 4 oz / ½ cup caster (superfine) sugar
110 g / 4 oz / ½ cup butter, softened
2 large eggs
2 tbsp unsweetened cocoa powder

TO DECORATE:
100 g / 3 ½ oz / ½ cup butter, softened
200 g / 7 oz / 2 cups icing (confectioners') sugar
white chocolate sprinkles
chocolate sugar strands
mini chocolate buttons

414

White Chocolate Chip Sprinkle Cupcakes

- Add 75 g of white chocolate chips to the cake mixture before baking.

415

MAKES 12

Coconut and Mint Buttercream Cupcakes

- Preheat the oven to 190°C (170° fan) / 375F / gas 5 and line a 12-hole cupcake tin with paper cases.
- Combine the flour, sugar, butter, eggs, mint syrup and coconut in a bowl and whisk together for 2 minutes or until smooth.
- Divide the mixture between the cases, then transfer the tin to the oven and bake for 15 – 20 minutes.
- Test with a wooden toothpick, if it comes out clean, the cakes are done.
- Transfer the cakes to a wire rack and leave to cool completely.
- Beat the butter until smooth, then gradually whisk in the icing sugar, mint syrup and coconut.
- Spoon the mixture into a piping bag, fitted with a large star nozzle, and pipe a swirl of icing on top of each cake. Sprinkle with the blue sugar sprinkles.

PREPARATION TIME 30 MINUTES

COOKING TIME 15 - 20 MINUTES

INGREDIENTS

110 g / 4 oz / ⅔ cup self-raising flour, sifted
110 g / 4 oz / ½ cup dark brown sugar
110 g / 4 oz / ½ cup butter, softened
2 large eggs
1 tbsp mint syrup
2 tbsp desiccated coconut

TO DECORATE:
100 g / 3 ½ oz / ½ cup butter, softened
200 g / 7 oz / 2 cups icing (confectioners') sugar
1 tbsp mint syrup
2 tbsp desiccated coconut
blue sugar cake sprinkles

416

Coconut and Ginger Buttercream Cupcakes

- Omit the mint syrup and chop 3 pieces of stem ginger and stir it into the cake mixture.

417

MAKES 18

Lemon and Lime Buttercream Cupcakes

PREPARATION TIME 30 MINUTES

COOKING TIME 15 - 20 MINUTES

INGREDIENTS

110 g / 4 oz / ⅔ cup self-raising flour, sifted
110 g / 4 oz / ½ cup caster (superfine) sugar
110 g / 4 oz / ½ cup butter, softened
2 large eggs
1 lime, juiced and zest finely grated
1 lemon, zest finely grated

TO DECORATE:
100 g / 3 ½ oz / ½ cup butter, softened
200 g / 7 oz / 2 cups icing (confectioners') sugar
2 tsp lime juice
2 tsp lemon juice
a few drops of green food colouring
sugar cake sprinkles to decorate

- Preheat the oven to 190°C (170° fan) / 375F / gas 5 and line a 12-hole cupcake tin with paper cases.
- Combine the flour, sugar, butter, eggs, lime juice and zest and lemon zest in a bowl and whisk together for 2 minutes or until smooth.
- Divide the mixture between the cases, then transfer the tin to the oven and bake for 15 – 20 minutes.
- Test with a wooden toothpick, if it comes out clean, the cakes are done.
- Transfer the cakes to a wire rack and leave to cool completely.
- Beat the butter until smooth, then gradually whisk in the icing sugar and citrus juices.
- Colour the icing a very pale green then spoon the mixture into a piping bag, fitted with a large star nozzle, and pipe a swirl of icing on top of each cake.
- Decorate with sugar cake sprinkles.

418

Lime and Orange Buttercream Cupcakes

- Replace the lemon zest and juice with orange zest and juice.

419

Grapefruit and Lime Buttercream Cupcakes

- Replace the lemon zest and juice with grapefruit zest and juice.

420

Vanilla and Strawberry Cupcakes

MAKES 12

- Preheat the oven to 190°C (170° fan) / 375F / gas 5 and line a 12-hole cupcake tin with paper cases.
- Combine the flour, sugar, butter, eggs and vanilla extract in a bowl and whisk together for 2 minutes or until smooth.
- Divide the mixture between the cases and bake for 15 – 20 minutes.
- Test with a wooden toothpick, if it comes out clean, the cakes are done.
- Transfer the cakes to a wire rack and leave to cool completely.
- Beat the butter until smooth, then gradually whisk in the icing sugar and strawberry syrup.
- Spoon the mixture into a piping bag, fitted with a large star nozzle, and pipe a swirl of icing on top of each cake.
- Top each cake with a chocolate heart and a red ribbon bow.

PREPARATION TIME 30 MINUTES

COOKING TIME 15 - 20 MINUTES

INGREDIENTS

110 g / 4 oz / ⅔ cup self-raising flour, sifted
110 g / 4 oz / ½ cup caster (superfine) sugar
110 g / 4 oz / ½ cup butter, softened
2 large eggs
1 tsp vanilla extract

TO DECORATE:
100 g / 3 ½ oz / ½ cup butter, softened
200 g / 7 oz / 2 cups icing (confectioners') sugar
2 tbsp strawberry syrup
12 chocolate hearts
12 red ribbon bows

421

Strawberry and Orange Buttercream

- Add the finely grated zest of an orange to the buttercream. Top the cakes with a strawberry and orange zest.

422

Chocolate Pearl Cupcakes

MAKES 12

- Preheat the oven to 190°C (170° fan) / 375F / gas 5 and line a 12-hole cupcake tin with paper cases.
- Combine the flour, sugar, butter, eggs and cocoa in a bowl and whisk together for 2 minutes or until smooth.
- Divide the mixture between the cases, then transfer the tin to the oven and bake for 15 – 20 minutes.
- Test with a wooden toothpick, if it comes out clean, the cakes are done.
- Transfer the cakes to a wire rack and leave to cool completely.
- Beat the butter until smooth, then gradually whisk in the icing sugar and cocoa powder.
- Spoon the mixture into a piping bag, fitted with a large star nozzle, and pipe a swirl of icing on top of each cake, then decorate with the sugar pearls and chocolate strands.

PREPARATION TIME 30 MINUTES

COOKING TIME 15 - 20 MINUTES

INGREDIENTS

110 g / 4 oz / ⅔ cup self-raising flour, sifted
110 g / 4 oz / ½ cup caster (superfine) sugar
110 g / 4 oz / ½ cup butter, softened
2 large eggs
2 tbsp unsweetened cocoa powder

TO DECORATE:
100 g / 3 ½ oz / ½ cup butter, softened
200 g / 7 oz / 2 cups icing (confectioners') sugar
1 tbsp cocoa powder
sugar pearls and chocolate sugar strands

423

Double Chocolate Pearl Cupcakes

- Add 75 g of white chocolate chunks to the cake mixture before baking.

424

MAKES 12

Strawberry Syrup Cream Cheese Cupcakes

PREPARATION TIME 30 MINUTES

COOKING TIME 15 - 20 MINUTES

INGREDIENTS

110 g / 4 oz / 2/3 cup self-raising flour, sifted
110 g / 4 oz / ½ cup caster (superfine) sugar
110 g / 4 oz / ½ cup butter, softened
2 large eggs
3 tbsp strawberry syrup

TO DECORATE:
110 g / 4 oz / ½ cup cream cheese
55 g / 2 oz / 1/4 cup butter, softened
110 g / 4 oz / 1 cup icing (confectioners') sugar
1 tsp vanilla extract
3 tbsp strawberry syrup

- Preheat the oven to 190°C (170° fan) / 375F / gas 5 and line a 12-hole cupcake tin with paper cases.
- Combine the flour, sugar, butter, eggs and strawberry syrup in a bowl and whisk together for 2 minutes or until smooth.
- Divide the mixture between the cases and bake for 15 – 20 minutes.
- Transfer the cakes to a wire rack and leave to cool.
- Beat the cream cheese and butter together until light and fluffy then beat in the icing sugar a quarter at a time.
- Add the vanilla extract then whip the mixture for 2 minutes or until smooth and light.
- Spoon the icing into a piping bag, fitted with a large star nozzle, and pipe a swirl of icing on top of each cake.
- Drizzle over the strawberry syrup.

Raspberry Syrup Cream Cheese Cupcakes

425

- Replace the strawberry syrup with raspberry syrup.

426

MAKES 12

Milk and White Chocolate Cupcakes

PREPARATION TIME 30 MINUTES

COOKING TIME 15 - 20 MINUTES

INGREDIENTS

110 g / 4 oz / ⅔ cup self-raising flour, sifted
110 g / 4 oz / ½ cup caster (superfine) sugar
110 g / 4 oz / ½ cup butter, softened
2 large eggs
2 tbsp unsweetened cocoa powder

TO DECORATE:
100 g / 3 ½ oz / ½ cup butter, softened
200 g / 7 oz / 2 cups icing (confectioners') sugar
1 tbsp unsweetened cocoa powder
white chocolate sprinkles

- Preheat the oven to 190°C (170° fan) / 375F / gas 5 and line a 12-hole cupcake tin with paper cases.
- Combine the flour, sugar, butter, eggs and cocoa in a bowl and whisk together for 2 minutes or until smooth.
- Divide the mixture between the cases, then transfer the tin to the oven and bake for 15 – 20 minutes.
- Test with a wooden toothpick, if it comes out clean, the cakes are done.
- Transfer the cakes to a wire rack and leave to cool completely.
- Beat the butter until smooth, then gradually whisk in the icing sugar and cocoa powder.
- Spoon the mixture into a piping bag, fitted with a large star nozzle, and pipe a swirl of icing on top of each cake, then decorate with the white chocolate sprinkles.

Dark and White Chocolate Cupcakes

427

- Drizzle the finished cupcakes with dark chocolate before topping with the white chocolate sprinkles.

MAKES 12

Violet and Lemon Cupcakes

Violet and Cinnamon Cupcakes

429

- Replace the lemon zest with 1 tsp ground cinnamon.

Violet and Ginger Cupcakes

430

- Replace the lemon zest with 1 tsp ground ginger.

PREPARATION TIME 30 MINUTES

COOKING TIME 15 - 20 MINUTES

INGREDIENTS

110 g / 4 oz / ⅔ cup self-raising flour, sifted
110 g / 4 oz / ½ cup caster (superfine) sugar
110 g / 4 oz / ½ cup butter, softened
2 large eggs
1 lemon, zest finely grated

TO DECORATE:
200 g / 7 oz / 2 cups icing (confectioners') sugar
1 – 2 tsp violet syrup
a few drops of purple food colouring
sugar flowers to decorate

- Preheat the oven to 190°C (170° fan) / 375F / gas 5 and line a 12-hole cupcake tin with paper cases.
- Combine the flour, sugar, butter, eggs and lemon zest in a bowl and whisk together for 2 minutes or until smooth.
- Divide the mixture between the cases, then transfer the tin to the oven and bake for 15 – 20 minutes.
- Test with a wooden toothpick, if it comes out clean, the cakes are done.
- Transfer the cakes to a wire rack and leave to cool completely.
- Sieve the icing sugar into a bowl and add just enough violet syrup to make a thick, pourable icing.
- Spoon the icing onto the cakes and decorate with the sugar flowers.

431

Mocha Cupcakes

MAKES 12

PREPARATION TIME 30 MINUTES

COOKING TIME 15 - 20 MINUTES

INGREDIENTS

110 g / 4 oz / ⅔ cup self-raising flour, sifted
110 g / 4 oz / ½ cup caster (superfine) sugar
110 g / 4 oz / ½ cup butter, softened
2 large eggs
2 tbsp unsweetened cocoa powder
1 tbsp instant espresso powder

TO DECORATE:
100 g / 3 ½ oz / ½ cup butter, softened
200 g / 7 oz / 2 cups icing (confectioners') sugar
2 tsp instant espresso powder
milk and white chocolate balls to decorate

- Preheat the oven to 190°C (170° fan) / 375F / gas 5 and line a 12-hole cupcake tin with paper cases.
- Combine the flour, sugar, butter, eggs, cocoa and espresso powder in a bowl and whisk together for 2 minutes or until smooth.
- Divide the mixture between the cases, then transfer the tin to the oven and bake for 15 – 20 minutes.
- Test with a wooden toothpick, if it comes out clean, the cakes are done.
- Transfer the cakes to a wire rack and leave to cool completely.
- Beat the butter until smooth, then gradually whisk in the icing sugar and espresso powder.
- Spoon the mixture into a piping bag, fitted with a large star nozzle, and pipe a swirl of icing on top of each cake, then decorate with the chocolate balls.

432

Cream Cheese Frosting for Cupcakes

MAKES ENOUGH TO ICE 12 CUPCAKES

PREPARATION TIME 10 MINUTES

INGREDIENTS

110 g / 4 oz / ½ cup cream cheese
55 g / 2 oz / ¼ cup butter, softened
110 g / 4 oz / 1 cup icing (confectioners') sugar, sifted
1 tsp vanilla extract

- Beat the cream cheese and butter together until smooth and well whipped.
- Beat in the icing sugar a quarter at a time until it is fully incorporated with no lumps remaining.
- Add the vanilla extract then whip the mixture for 2 minutes or until smooth and light.
- Spread or pipe the icing onto your cupcakes and add the decorations of your choice.

433

MAKES 24

Gel-Iced Mini Cupcakes

- Preheat the oven to 180°C (160° fan) / 350F / gas 4 and line a 24-hole mini cupcake tin with paper cases.
- Combine the flour, sugar, butter and eggs in a bowl and whisk together for 2 minutes or until smooth.
- Divide the mixture between the cases and bake for 12 - 15 minutes.
- Test with a wooden toothpick, if it comes out clean, the cakes are done.
- Transfer the cakes to a wire rack and leave to cool completely.
- Draw a spiral on top of each cake with the gel icing and sprinkle with hundreds and thousands.

PREPARATION TIME 15 MINUTES

COOKING TIME 12 - 15 MINUTES

INGREDIENTS

110 g / 4 oz / ⅔ cup self-raising flour, sifted
110 g / 4 oz / ½ cup caster (superfine) sugar
110 g / 4 oz / ½ cup butter, softened
2 large eggs

TO DECORATE:
1 tube of red gel icing
hundreds and thousands for sprinkling

Fondant Roses for Cupcakes

434

MAKES 12

PREPARATION TIME 2 HOURS

INGREDIENTS

200 g / 7 oz ready to roll fondant icing
1 tsp gum tragacanth
icing (confectioners') sugar for dusting
a few drops of green food colouring

- Knead the icing with the gum tragacanth until smoothly combined.
- Break off a marble-sized piece of paste and flatten it into an oval. Curl the oval up into a spiral and turn out the top edges.
- This will form the centre of the rose – repeat to make 12 more.
- Break off a marble-sized piece of paste and flatten it into a circle. Wet the centre and attach it to one of the rose centres, then turn out the top edge.
- Repeat twice more to complete the first rose, then add 3 petals to the rest of the rose centres. Pinch off and remove any excess icing from the base of the roses.
- Dust the work surface with icing sugar. Colour the remaining icing green and roll it out on the work surface.
- Use a star-shaped cutter to cut out 12 calyxes, then attach them to the bottom of the roses with a dab of water.
- Leave the roses to dry and harden for 1 day before using to decorate your cakes.

Elderflower Cupcakes

435

MAKES 12

PREPARATION TIME 30 MINUTES

COOKING TIME 15 - 20 MINUTES

INGREDIENTS

110 g / 4 oz / ⅔ cup self-raising flour, sifted
110 g / 4 oz / ½ cup caster (superfine) sugar
110 g / 4 oz / ½ cup butter, softened
2 large eggs
1 tbsp elderflower cordial

TO DECORATE:
200 g / 7 oz / 2 cups icing (confectioners') sugar
1 – 2 tsp elderflower cordial
48 yellow sugar flowers

- Preheat the oven to 190°C (170° fan) / 375F / gas 5 and line a 12-hole cupcake tin with paper cases.
- Combine the flour, sugar, butter, eggs and elderflower cordial in a bowl and whisk together for 2 minutes or until smooth.
- Divide the mixture between the cases, then transfer the tin to the oven and bake for 15 – 20 minutes.
- Test with a wooden toothpick, if it comes out clean, the cakes are done.
- Transfer the cakes to a wire rack and leave to cool completely.
- Sieve the icing sugar into a bowl and add just enough elderflower cordial to make a thick icing.
- Spoon the icing onto the cakes and top each one with 4 yellow flowers.

436

Lemon Baby Shower Cupcakes

MAKES 12

PREPARATION TIME 35 MINUTES

COOKING TIME 15 - 20 MINUTES

INGREDIENTS

110 g / 4 oz / ⅔ cup self-raising flour, sifted
110 g / 4 oz / ½ cup caster (superfine) sugar
110 g / 4 oz / ½ cup butter, softened
2 large eggs
1 lemon, juiced and zest finely grated

TO DECORATE:
100 g / 3 ½ oz / ½ cup butter, softened
200 g / 7 oz / 2 cups icing (confectioners') sugar
1 tsp vanilla extract
24 blue baby feet edible cake toppers

- Preheat the oven to 190°C (170° fan) / 375F / gas 5 and line a 12-hole cupcake tin with paper cases.
- Combine the flour, sugar, butter, eggs and lemon juice and zest in a bowl and whisk together for 2 minutes or until smooth.
- Divide the mixture between the cases, then transfer the tin to the oven and bake for 15 – 20 minutes.
- Test with a wooden toothpick, if it comes out clean, the cakes are done.
- Transfer the cakes to a wire rack and leave to cool completely.
- Beat the butter until smooth, then gradually whisk in the icing sugar and vanilla extract.
- Spoon the mixture into a piping bag fitted with a large star nozzle and pipe a big swirl on top of the cakes, then position 2 feet on top of each cake.

Chocolate Baby Shower Cupcakes

437

- Omit the lemon juice and zest and add 2 tbsp of cocoa powder to the cake mixture.

438

Giant Chocolate Cupcake

MAKES 1

PREPARATION TIME 35 MINUTES

COOKING TIME 30 - 40 MINUTES

INGREDIENTS

225 g / 8 oz / 1 ½ cups self-raising flour, sifted
50 g / 1 ¾ oz / ½ cup unsweetened cocoa powder
225 g / 8 oz / 1 cup caster (superfine) sugar
225 g / 8 oz / 1 cup butter, softened
4 large eggs
1 tsp vanilla extract

TO DECORATE:
200 ml / 7 fl. oz / 3/4 cup double (heavy) cream
200 g / 7 oz dark chocolate, minimum 60% cocoa solids, chopped
sugar pearls to decorate

- Preheat the oven to 190°C (170° fan) / 375F / gas 5 and oil a 2-part giant cupcake mould.
- Combine the flour, cocoa, sugar, butter, eggs and vanilla extract in a bowl and whisk together for 2 minutes or until smooth.
- Spoon the mixture into the moulds and level the top, then bake for 30 - 40 minutes.
- Test with a wooden toothpick, if it comes out clean, the cakes are done.
- Transfer the cakes to a wire rack and leave to cool completely.
- Heat the cream until it starts to simmer, then pour it over the chopped chocolate and stir until smooth.
- Leave the ganache to cool a little then use half of it to sandwich the 2 parts of the cake together.
- Spread the rest of the ganache over the top and decorate with the sugar pearls.

Giant Spotted Cupcake

439

- Add 200 g of white chocolate chips to the cake mixture and decorate the cake with white chocolate buttons.

440

MAKES 12

Wholemeal Baby Shower Cupcakes

- Preheat the oven to 190°C (170° fan) / 375F / gas 5 and line a 12-hole cupcake tin with paper cases.
- Combine the flour, baking powder, sugar, butter, eggs and vanilla extract in a bowl and whisk together for 2 minutes or until smooth.
- Divide the mixture between the cases, then transfer the tin to the oven and bake for 15 – 20 minutes.
- Test with a wooden toothpick, if it comes out clean, the cakes are done.
- Transfer the cakes to a wire rack and leave to cool completely.
- Beat the butter until smooth, then gradually whisk in the icing sugar and vanilla extract.
- Spoon the mixture into a piping bag fitted with a large star nozzle and pipe a big swirl on top of the cakes, then position a sugar pram on top of each cake.

PREPARATION TIME 35 MINUTES

COOKING TIME 15 - 20 MINUTES

INGREDIENTS

110 g / 4 oz / ⅔ cup stoneground wholemeal flour
2 tsp baking powder
110 g / 4 oz / ½ cup caster (superfine) sugar
110 g / 4 oz / ½ cup butter, softened
2 large eggs
1 tsp vanilla extract

TO DECORATE:
100 g / 3 ½ oz / ½ cup butter, softened
200 g / 7 oz / 2 cups icing (confectioners') sugar
1 tsp vanilla extract
12 pram-shaped cake toppers

Spiced Wholemeal Baby Shower Cupcakes

441

- Add 1 tsp of mixed spice to the cake mixture.

442

MAKES 12

Vanilla Cupcakes with Peach Buttercream

- Preheat the oven to 190°C (170° fan) / 375F / gas 5 and line a 12-hole cupcake tin with paper cases.
- Combine the flour, sugar, butter, eggs and vanilla extract in a bowl and whisk together for 2 minutes or until smooth.
- Divide the mixture between the cases and bake for 15 – 20 minutes.
- Test with a wooden toothpick, if it comes out clean, the cakes are done.
- Transfer the cakes to a wire rack and leave to cool completely.
- Beat the butter until smooth, then gradually whisk in the icing sugar and peach syrup.
- Spoon the mixture into a piping bag, fitted with a large star nozzle, and pipe a swirl of icing on top of each cake. Top with the halved wafer cigars.

PREPARATION TIME 30 MINUTES

COOKING TIME 15 - 20 MINUTES

INGREDIENTS

110 g / 4 oz / ⅔ cup self-raising flour, sifted
110 g / 4 oz / ½ cup caster (superfine) sugar
110 g / 4 oz / ½ cup butter, softened
2 large eggs
1 tsp vanilla extract

TO DECORATE:
100 g / 3 ½ oz / ½ cup butter, softened
200 g / 7 oz / 2 cups icing (confectioners') sugar
2 tbsp peach syrup
12 wafer cigars, halved

Vanilla Cupcakes with Butterscotch Buttercream

443

- Replace the peach syrup with butterscotch syrup. Top each cake with a butterscotch sweet.

444

MAKES 12

Chocolate Cream Cupcakes

PREPARATION TIME 30 MINUTES

COOKING TIME 15 - 20 MINUTES

INGREDIENTS

110 g / 4 oz / ⅔ cup self-raising flour, sifted
110 g / 4 oz / ½ cup caster (superfine) sugar
110 g / 4 oz / ½ cup butter, softened
2 large eggs
2 tbsp unsweetened cocoa powder

TO DECORATE:
300 ml / 10 ½ fl. oz / 1 ¼ cups double (heavy) cream
200 g / 7 oz dark chocolate, minimum 60% cocoa solids, chopped
sugar flowers to decorate

- Preheat the oven to 190°C (170° fan) / 375F / gas 5 and line a 12-hole cupcake tin with paper cases.
- Combine the flour, sugar, butter, eggs and cocoa in a bowl and whisk together for 2 minutes or until smooth.
- Divide the mixture between the cases, then transfer the tin to the oven and bake for 15 – 20 minutes.
- Test with a wooden toothpick, if it comes out clean, the cakes are done.
- Transfer the cakes to a wire rack and leave to cool completely.
- Heat half of the cream until it starts to simmer, then pour it over the chopped chocolate and stir until smooth. Leave to cool to room temperature, then combine with the rest of the cream and whisk until it holds its shape.
- Spoon the chocolate cream into a piping bag fitted with a large star nozzle and pipe a swirl on top of each cake. Decorate with the sugar flowers.

445

Chocolate and Orange Cream Cupcakes

- Add the finely grated zest of an orange to the cake mixture and cream topping.

446

Chocolate and Honey Cream Cupcakes

- Add 2 tbsp of runny honey to the chocolate ganache before whisking.

447

MAKES 12

Glace-Iced Honey Cupcakes

- Preheat the oven to 190°C (170° fan) / 375F / gas 5 and line a 12-hole cupcake tin with paper cases.
- Sieve the flour and bicarbonate of soda together into a bowl.
- Put the honey, butter and brown sugar in a small saucepan and boil gently for 2 minutes, stirring to dissolve the sugar.
- Pour the honey mixture onto the flour with the eggs and milk, then fold it all together until smooth.
- Divide the mixture between the cases, then transfer the tin to the oven and bake for 20 – 25 minutes.
- Transfer the cakes to a wire rack and leave to cool.
- Sieve the icing sugar into a bowl and add just enough water to make a thick, pourable icing.
- Spoon the icing onto the cakes and decorate with the cake sprinkles.

PREPARATION TIME 30 MINUTES

COOKING TIME 20 – 25 MINUTES

INGREDIENTS

250 g / 9 oz / 1 ¾ cups self-raising flour
1 tsp bicarbonate of (baking) soda
200 g / 8 ½ oz / ½ cup runny honey
125 g / 4 ½ oz / ½ cup butter
125 g / 4 ½ oz / ¾ cup light brown sugar
2 large eggs, beaten
250 ml / 9 fl. oz / 1 cup milk

TO DECORATE:
200 g / 7 oz / 2 cups icing (confectioners') sugar
pastel coloured cake sprinkles to decorate

Honey Cream Cheese Cupcakes

448

- Beat 200 g of cream cheese with 100 g of runny honey and use the mixture to ice the cupcakes.

449

MAKES 12

Rich Chocolate Cream Cupcakes

- Preheat the oven to 190°C (170° fan) / 375F / gas 5 and line a 12-hole cupcake tin with paper cases.
- Combine the flour, sugar, butter, eggs, melted chocolate and cocoa in a bowl and whisk together for 2 minutes or until smooth.
- Divide the mixture between the cases, then transfer the tin to the oven and bake for 15 – 20 minutes.
- Transfer the cakes to a wire rack and leave to cool completely.
- Heat half of the cream until it starts to simmer, then pour it over the chopped chocolate and stir until smooth. Leave to cool to room temperature, then combine with the rest of the cream and whisk until it holds its shape.
- Spoon the chocolate cream into a piping bag fitted with a large star nozzle and pipe a swirl on top of each cake. Decorate with the chocolate chips.

PREPARATION TIME 30 MINUTES

COOKING TIME 15 - 20 MINUTES

INGREDIENTS

110 g / 4 oz / ⅔ cup self-raising flour, sifted
110 g / 4 oz / ½ cup caster (superfine) sugar
110 g / 4 oz / ½ cup butter, softened
2 large eggs
100 g / 3 ½ oz dark chocolate (minimum 60% cocoa solids), melted
2 tbsp unsweetened cocoa powder

TO DECORATE:
300 ml / 10 ½ fl. oz / 1 ¼ cups double (heavy) cream
200 g / 7 oz dark chocolate, minimum 60% cocoa solids, chopped
3 tbsp milk chocolate chips

Triple Chocolate Cream Cupcakes

450

- Add 75 g of white chocolate chips to the cake mixture and top the cakes with dark, milk and white chocolate chips.

451

MAKES 12

Marzipan Butterfly Cupcakes

PREPARATION TIME 30 MINUTES

COOKING TIME 20 – 25 MINUTES

INGREDIENTS

250 g / 9 oz / 1 ¾ cups self-raising flour
1 tsp bicarbonate of (baking) soda
200 g / 7 oz / ⅔ cup golden syrup
125 g / 4 ½ oz / ½ cup butter
125 g / 4 ½ oz / ¾ cup dark brown sugar
2 large eggs, beaten
250 ml / 9 fl. oz / 1 cup milk
1 tsp almond extract

TO DECORATE:
icing (confectioners') sugar for dusting
200 g / 7 oz marzipan
a few drops of food colouring

- Preheat the oven to 190°C (170° fan) / 375F / gas 5 and line a 12-hole cupcake tin with paper cases.
- Sieve the flour and bicarbonate of soda together.
- Put the golden syrup, butter and brown sugar in a small saucepan and boil for 2 minutes, to dissolve the sugar.
- Pour the butter mixture onto the flour with the eggs, milk and almond extract, then fold it all together.
- Divide the mixture between the cases, then transfer the tin to the oven and bake for 20 – 25 minutes.
- Transfer the cakes to a wire rack and leave to cool.
- Dust the work surface with icing sugar and roll out the marzipan. Cut out 12 circles the same diameter as the top of the cakes, then attach one to each cake.
- Colour the marzipan off-cuts with the food colouring of your choice, then roll it out again and cut out small butterfly shapes. Attach the butterflies to the cakes.

Marzipan Duck Cupcakes

452

- Colour the offcuts yellow and cut out small rubber duck shapes to top the cakes.

453

MAKES 12

Dairy-Free Chocolate Cupcakes

PREPARATION TIME 15 MINUTES

COOKING TIME 15 - 20 MINUTES

INGREDIENTS

110 g / 4 oz / ⅔ cup self-raising flour, sifted
1 tbsp unsweetened cocoa powder
110 g / 4 oz / ½ cup caster (superfine) sugar
110 g / 4 oz / ½ cup dairy-free baking spread
2 large eggs
icing (confectioners') sugar for dusting
12 sugar paste roses with leaves

- Preheat the oven to 190°C (170° fan) / 375F / gas 5 and line a 12-hole cupcake tin with paper cases.
- Combine the flour, cocoa, sugar, baking spread and eggs in a bowl and whisk together for 2 minutes or until smooth.
- Divide the mixture between the cases, then transfer the tin to the oven and bake for 15 – 20 minutes.
- Test with a wooden toothpick, if it comes out clean, the cakes are done.
- Transfer the cakes to a wire rack and leave to cool completely before dusting with icing sugar and positioning the roses on top.

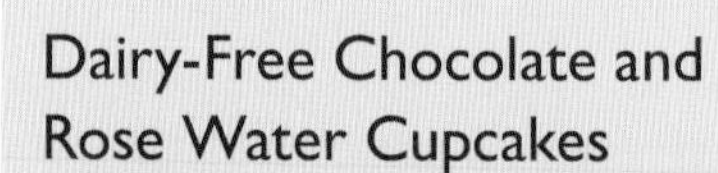

Dairy-Free Chocolate and Rose Water Cupcakes

454

- Add 1 tbsp of rose water to the cake mixture. Ice the cakes with 200 g of icing sugar mixed with 1 – 2 tsp rose water before topping with the sugar paste roses.

455

MAKES 12

Gluten-Free Cupcakes

PREPARATION TIME 15 MINUTES

COOKING TIME 15 - 20 MINUTES

INGREDIENTS

110 g / 4 oz / ⅔ cup gluten-free self-raising flour, sifted
110 g / 4 oz / ½ cup caster (superfine) sugar
110 g / 4 oz / ½ cup butter, softened
2 large eggs

- Preheat the oven to 190°C (170° fan) / 375F / gas 5 and line a 12-hole cupcake tin with paper cases.
- Combine the flour, sugar and eggs in a bowl and whisk together for 2 minutes or until smooth.
- Divide the mixture between the cases, then transfer the tin to the oven and bake for 15 – 20 minutes.
- Test with a wooden toothpick, if it comes out clean, the cakes are done.
- Decorate with the toppings of your choice.

Dairy-Free Cupcakes

456

- Replace the butter with dairy-free baking spread.

Spiced Gluten-Free Cupcakes

457

- Add 1 tsp of mixed spice to the cake mixture.

458

MAKES 12

Chocolate and Watermelon Cupcakes

PREPARATION TIME 30 MINUTES

COOKING TIME 20 – 25 MINUTES

INGREDIENTS

250 g / 9 oz / 1 ¾ cups self-raising flour
1 tsp bicarbonate of (baking) soda
2 tbsp unsweetened cocoa powder
200 g / 8 ½ oz / ½ cup golden syrup
125 g / 4 ½ oz / ½ cup butter
125 g / 4 ½ oz / ¾ cup dark brown sugar
2 large eggs, beaten
250 ml / 9 fl. oz / 1 cup milk
2 tbsp watermelon syrup

TO DECORATE:
250 ml / 9 fl. oz / 1 cup double (heavy) cream
icing (confectioners') sugar for dusting
12 chunks of fresh watermelon, seeded
chocolate vermicelli for sprinkling

- Preheat the oven to 190°C (170° fan) / 375F / gas 5 and line a 12-hole cupcake tin with silicone cases.
- Sieve the flour, bicarbonate of soda and cocoa powder together into a bowl.
- Put the golden syrup, butter and brown sugar in a saucepan and boil for 2 minutes, to dissolve the sugar.
- Pour the butter and sugar mixture onto the flour with the eggs, milk and watermelon syrup, then fold it all together until smooth.
- Divide the mixture between the cases, then transfer the tin to the oven and bake for 20 – 25 minutes.
- Transfer the cakes to a wire rack and leave to cool.
- Whip the cream until it holds its shape, then spoon it into a piping bag, fitted with a large star nozzle.
- Pipe a swirl of cream onto the cakes then top each one with a chunk of watermelon and a sprinkle of chocolate.

Chocolate and Blueberry Cream Cupcakes

459

- Add 100 g of blueberries to the cake mixture and omit the watermelon syrup. Top the cakes with more fresh blueberries.

460

MAKES 12

Frosted Chocolate Muffin Cupcakes

PREPARATION TIME 30 MINUTES

COOKING TIME 20 – 25 MINUTES

INGREDIENTS

1 large egg
125 ml / 4 ½ fl. oz / ½ cup sunflower oil
125 ml / 4 ½ fl. oz / ½ cup milk
375 g / 13 oz / 2 ½ cups self-raising flour, sifted
50 g / 1 ¾ oz / ½ cup unsweetened cocoa powder, sifted
1 tsp baking powder
200 g / 7 oz / ¾ cup caster (superfine) sugar

TO DECORATE:
150 g / 5 ½ oz / 1 ½ cups royal icing powder
blue, pink and yellow sugar flowers

- Preheat the oven to 180°C (160° fan) / 350F / gas 4 and line a 12-hole cupcake tin with paper cases.
- Beat the egg in a jug with the oil and milk until well mixed.
- Mix the flour, cocoa, baking powder and sugar in a bowl, then pour in the egg mixture and stir just enough to combine.
- Divide the mixture between the cases, then bake in the oven for 20 – 25 minutes.
- Test with a wooden toothpick, if it comes out clean, the cakes are done.
- Transfer the cakes to a wire rack and leave to cool completely.
- Whisk the royal icing powder with 25 ml of cold water for 5 minutes with an electric whisk until smooth and thick.
- Spread the icing onto the cakes with a spoon and top with the sugar flowers.

Frosted Double Chocolate Muffin Cupcakes

461

- Add 100 g of dark chocolate chunks to the cake mixture when you combine the liquid and dry ingredients.

462

MAKES 12

Strawberry Frosted Muffin Cupcakes

- Preheat the oven to 180°C (160° fan) / 350F / gas 4 and line a 12-hole cupcake tin with paper cases.
- Beat the egg in a jug with the vanilla extract, oil and milk until well mixed.
- Mix the flour, baking powder and sugar in a bowl, then pour in the egg mixture and stir just enough to combine.
- Divide the mixture between the cases, then bake in the oven for 20 – 25 minutes.
- Transfer the cakes to a wire rack and leave to cool completely.
- Beat the butter until smooth, then gradually whisk in the icing sugar and strawberry syrup.
- Spoon the mixture into a piping bag, fitted with a large star nozzle, and pipe a swirl of icing on top of each cake, then finish with a sugar flower.

PREPARATION TIME 30 MINUTES

COOKING TIME 20 – 25 MINUTES

INGREDIENTS

1 large egg
1 tsp vanilla extract
125 ml / 4 ½ fl. oz / ½ cup sunflower oil
125 ml / 4 ½ fl. oz / ½ cup milk
375 g / 13 oz / 2 ½ cups self-raising flour, sifted
1 tsp baking powder
200 g / 7 oz / ¾ cup caster (superfine) sugar

TO DECORATE:
100 g / 3 ½ oz / ½ cup butter, softened
200 g / 7 oz / 2 cups icing (confectioners') sugar
2 tbsp strawberry syrup
12 sugar flowers to decorate

Double Strawberry Muffin Cupcakes

463

- Add 75 g of chopped dried strawberries to the muffin mixture when you combine the liquid and dry ingredients.

464

MAKES 12

Chocolate, Almond and Rose Buttercream Cupcakes

- Preheat the oven to 190°C (170° fan) / 375F / gas 5 and line a 12-hole cupcake tin with paper cases.
- Combine all of the cake ingredients in a bowl and whisk together for 2 minutes or until smooth.
- Divide the mixture between the cases, then transfer the tin to the oven and bake for 15 – 20 minutes.
- Test with a wooden toothpick, if it comes out clean, the cakes are done.
- Transfer the cakes to a wire rack and leave to cool completely.
- Beat the butter until smooth, then gradually whisk in the icing sugar, almond extract and rose water.
- Spoon the mixture into a piping bag fitted with a large star nozzle and pipe a big swirl on top of each cake.
- Arrange the sugar paste roses and leaves on top.

PREPARATION TIME 30 MINUTES

COOKING TIME 15 - 20 MINUTES

INGREDIENTS

110 g / 4 oz / ⅔ cup self-raising flour, sifted
110 g / 4 oz / ½ cup caster (superfine) sugar
110 g / 4 oz / ½ cup butter, softened
2 large eggs
2 tbsp unsweetened cocoa powder
2 tbsp ground almonds

TO DECORATE:
100 g / 3 ½ oz / ½ cup butter, softened
200 g / 7 oz / 2 cups icing (confectioners') sugar
½ tsp almond extract
1 tsp rose water
12 sugar paste roses and leaves

Chocolate, Almond and Mint Buttercream Cupcakes

- Omit the rose water and add a few drops of peppermint extract to the cake mixture and icing.

466

MAKES 12

Walnut Cream Cupcakes

PREPARATION TIME 30 MINUTES

COOKING TIME 15 - 20 MINUTES

INGREDIENTS

110 g / 4 oz / ⅔ cup self-raising flour, sifted
110 g / 4 oz / ½ cup caster (superfine) sugar
110 g / 4 oz / ½ cup butter, softened
2 large eggs
50 g / 1 ¾ oz / ½ cup walnuts, chopped

TO DECORATE:
300 ml / 10 ½ fl. oz / 1 ¼ cups double (heavy) cream
3 tbsp walnut syrup
chocolate vermicelli for sprinkling

- Preheat the oven to 190°C (170° fan) / 375F / gas 5 and line a 12-hole cupcake tin with paper cases.
- Combine the flour, sugar, butter, eggs and chopped walnuts in a bowl and whisk together for 2 minutes or until smooth.
- Divide the mixture between the cases and bake for 15 – 20 minutes.
- Test with a wooden toothpick, if it comes out clean, the cakes are done.
- Transfer the cakes to a wire rack and leave to cool completely.
- Whip the cream with the walnut syrup until it holds its shape.
- Spoon the mixture into a piping bag, fitted with a large star nozzle, and pipe a swirl of cream on top of each cake. Sprinkle with chocolate vermicelli.

467

Hazelnut Cream Cupcakes

- Replace the walnuts and walnut syrup with hazelnuts (cob nuts) and hazelnut syrup.

468

Pistachio Cream Cupcakes

- Replace the walnuts and walnut syrup with pistachio nuts and pistachio syrup.

469

MAKES 12

Chocolate Syrup Cream Cupcakes

- Preheat the oven to 190°C (170° fan) / 375F / gas 5 and line a 12-hole cupcake tin with silicone cases.
- Sieve the flour, bicarbonate of soda and cocoa powder together into a bowl.
- Put the golden syrup, butter and brown sugar in a saucepan and boil for 2 minutes, to dissolve the sugar.
- Pour the butter and sugar mixture onto the flour with the eggs and milk, then fold it all together until smooth.
- Divide the mixture between the cases, then transfer the tin to the oven and bake for 20 – 25 minutes.
- Transfer the cakes to a wire rack and leave to cool.
- Whip the cream until it holds its shape, then spoon it into a piping bag, fitted with a large star nozzle.
- Pipe a swirl of cream on top of each cake and decorate with the silver balls and cake sprinkles before dusting with icing sugar.

PREPARATION TIME 30 MINUTES

COOKING TIME 20 – 25 MINUTES

INGREDIENTS

250 g / 9 oz / 1 ¾ cups self-raising flour
1 tsp bicarbonate of (baking) soda
2 tbsp unsweetened cocoa powder
200 g / 8 ½ oz / ½ cup golden syrup
125 g / 4 ½ oz / ½ cup butter
125 g / 4 ½ oz / ¾ cup dark brown sugar
2 large eggs, beaten
250 ml / 9 fl. oz / 1 cup milk

TO DECORATE:
250 ml / 9 fl. oz / 1 cup double (heavy) cream
icing (confectioners') sugar for dusting
silver balls and cake sprinkles to decorate

470

Double Chocolate Syrup Cupcakes

- Add 100 g of dark chocolate chunks to the cake mixture.

471

MAKES 12

Jelly Tot Temptation Cupcakes

- Preheat the oven to 180°C (160° fan) / 350F / gas 4 and line a cupcake tin with paper cases.
- Cream butter and sugar until pale and fluffy with an electric whisk.
- Gradually mix in the egg and vanilla extract.
- Gently mix in the flour adding the milk.
- Spoon cupcake mix into each paper case.
- Bake, for 18-20 minutes. Test with a wooden toothpick, if it comes out clean, the cake is done.
- Place on wire rack to cool.
- With an apple corer bore out 1½ cm deep hole in top of cupcake.
- Fill hole with 1 tsp of jam.
- To make the buttercream, beat butter with a whisk until soft then gradually beat in icing sugar, vanilla and milk.
- Pipe buttercream swirls. Place jelly tot on top.

PREPARATION TIME 30 MINUTES

COOKING TIME 20 MINUTES

INGREDIENTS

125 g / 4 ½ oz / ½ cup butter unsalted, softened
1 tsp vanilla extract
125 g / 4 ½ oz/ ½ cup caster (superfine) sugar
2 eggs
125 g/ 4 ½ oz / 1 cup self-raising flour
200 g/ 7 oz / 1 ½ cup strawberry jam

TO DECORATE
125 g / 4 ½ oz / ½ cup butter, unsalted, softened
300 g / 10 ½ oz / 2 ½ cups icing (confectioners') sugar
½ tsp vanilla extract
½ tbsp milk
Jelly tots

472

Raspberry Tot Temptation

- Replace the strawberry jam with raspberry jam

473

MAKES 12

Popcorn Cupcakes

PREPARATION TIME 30 MINUTES

COOKING TIME 15 - 20 MINUTES

INGREDIENTS

110 g / 4 oz / 2/3 cup self-raising flour, sifted
110 g / 4 oz / ½ cup caster (superfine) sugar
110 g / 4 oz / ½ cup butter, softened
2 large eggs
1 tsp vanilla extract

TO DECORATE
100 g / 3 ½ oz / ½ cup butter, softened
200 g / 7 oz / 2 cups icing (confectioners') sugar
1 tsp vanilla extract
75 g / 2 ½ oz / 2 cups popcorn

- Preheat the oven to 190°C (170° fan) / 375F / gas 5 and line a 12-hole cupcake tin with paper cases.
- Combine the cake ingredients in a bowl and whisk together for 2 minutes or until smooth.
- Divide the mixture between the cases and bake for 15 – 20 minutes.
- Test with a wooden toothpick, if it comes out clean, the cakes are done. Transfer the cakes to a wire rack and leave to cool.
- Beat the butter until smooth, then gradually whisk in the icing sugar and vanilla extract.
- Spoon the mixture into a piping bag, fitted with a large star nozzle, and pipe rosettes of icing onto the cakes.
- Top the buttercream with popcorn.

Peanut Popcorn Cupcakes

474

- Add 4 tbsp of peanut butter to the cake mixture.

475

MAKES 48

Simple Iced Wedding Muffin Cupcakes

PREPARATION TIME 1 HOUR 30 MINUTES

COOKING TIME 20 – 25 MINUTES

INGREDIENTS

4 large eggs
4 tsp vanilla extract
500 ml / 17 ½ fl. oz / 2 cups sunflower oil
500 ml / 17 ½ fl. oz / 2 cups milk
1.5 kg / 3 lb 5 oz / 10 ½ cups self-raising flour, sifted
4 tsp baking powder
800 g / 1 lb 12 oz / 3 ½ cups caster (superfine) sugar

TO DECORATE:
icing (confectioners') sugar for dusting
1.5 kg / 3 lb 5 oz ready to roll fondant icing
pink and orange food colouring

- Preheat the oven to 180°C (160° fan) / 350F / gas 4 and line 4 x 12-hole cupcake tins with foil cases.
- Beat the eggs in a large jug with the vanilla extract, oil and milk until well mixed.
- Mix the flour, baking powder and sugar in a bowl, pour in the egg mixture and stir just enough to combine.
- Divide the mixture between the cases, then bake in the oven for 20 – 25 minutes.
- Transfer the cakes to a wire rack and leave to cool.
- Dust the work surface lightly with icing sugar and roll out half of the icing. Cut out 24 circles a little larger than the top of the cakes, then wet the backs with water and mould them onto the cupcakes.
- Repeat with the rest of the icing to cover the remaining cakes, then knead the offcuts well.
- Colour one half pink and the other orange, then roll out as before and cut out small circles for decoration.

Orange and Strawberry Muffin Cupcakes

476

- Add 200 g of chopped dried strawberries and the grated zest of 4 oranges to the muffin mixture when you combine the liquid and dry ingredients.

477

MAKES 12

Crystallised Rose Petal Cupcakes

Crystallised Violet Cupcakes

478

- Replace the crystallised rose petals with crystallised violets and use violet syrup in place of the rose water.

Chocolate and Crystallised Rose Petal Cupcakes

479

- Add 2 tbsp of cocoa powder to the cake mixture.

PREPARATION TIME 30 MINUTES

COOKING TIME 15 - 20 MINUTES

INGREDIENTS

110 g / 4 oz / ⅔ cup self-raising flour, sifted
110 g / 4 oz / ½ cup caster (superfine) sugar
110 g / 4 oz / ½ cup butter, softened
2 large eggs
1 tbsp rose water

TO DECORATE:
100 g / 3 ½ oz / ½ cup butter, softened
200 g / 7 oz / 2 cups icing (confectioners') sugar
1 tbsp rose water
24 crystallised rose petals

- Preheat the oven to 190°C (170° fan) / 375F / gas 5 and line a 12-hole cupcake tin with paper cases.
- Combine the flour, sugar, butter, eggs and rose water in a bowl and whisk together for 2 minutes or until smooth.
- Divide the mixture between the cases, then transfer the tin to the oven and bake for 15 – 20 minutes.
- Test with a wooden toothpick, if it comes out clean, the cakes are done.
- Transfer the cakes to a wire rack and leave to cool completely.
- Beat the butter until smooth, then gradually whisk in the icing sugar and rose water.
- Crush 12 of the crystallised roses with a pestle and mortar and stir them into the icing.
- Spoon the buttercream into a piping bag, fitted with a large star nozzle, and pipe a swirl of icing on top of each cake.
- Decorate the cakes with the remaining crystallised rose petals.

480

MAKES 12

Honey Nut Chocolate Cupcakes

PREPARATION TIME 30 MINUTES

COOKING TIME 15 - 20 MINUTES

INGREDIENTS

110 g / 4 oz / ⅔ cup self-raising flour, sifted
110 g / 4 oz / ½ cup caster (superfine) sugar
110 g / 4 oz / ½ cup butter, softened
2 large eggs
2 tbsp unsweetened cocoa powder
75 g / 2 ½ oz / ⅔ cup honey-roasted peanuts, chopped

TO DECORATE:
200 ml / 7 fl. oz / 3/4 cup double (heavy) cream
200 g / 7 oz dark chocolate, minimum 60% cocoa solids, chopped
12 honey-roasted peanuts

- Preheat the oven to 190°C (170° fan) / 375F / gas 5 and line a 12-hole cupcake tin with paper cases.
- Combine the flour, sugar, butter, eggs and cocoa in a bowl and whisk together for 2 minutes or until smooth.
- Fold in the chopped nuts and divide the mixture between the cases, then bake for 15 – 20 minutes.
- Transfer the cakes to a wire rack and leave to cool completely.
- Heat the cream until it starts to simmer, then pour it over the chopped chocolate and stir until smooth. Leave to cool to room temperature, then whisk until thick enough to pipe.
- Spoon the ganache into a piping bag fitted with a large plain nozzle and pipe a swirl on top of each cake. Top each one with a peanut.

Honey Nut Cupcakes

481

- Omit the cocoa powder and spread the cakes with honey instead of the ganache, before sprinkling with extra honey-roasted peanuts.

482

MAKES 12

Grenadine, Orange Chocolate Cupcakes

PREPARATION TIME 30 MINUTES

COOKING TIME 15 - 20 MINUTES

INGREDIENTS

110 g / 4 oz / ⅔ cup self-raising flour, sifted
110 g / 4 oz / ½ cup caster (superfine) sugar
110 g / 4 oz / ½ cup butter, softened
2 large eggs
2 tbsp unsweetened cocoa powder
1 orange, zest finely grated

TO DECORATE:
110 g / 4 oz / ½ cup cream cheese
55 g / 2 oz / ¼ cup butter, softened
110 g / 4 oz / 1 cup icing (confectioners') sugar
2 tbsp grenadine
pink sugar sprinkles

- Preheat the oven to 190°C (170° fan) / 375F / gas 5 and line a 12-hole cupcake tin with paper cases.
- Combine the flour, sugar, butter, eggs, cocoa and orange zest in a bowl and whisk together for 2 minutes or until smooth.
- Divide the mixture between the cases and bake for 15 – 20 minutes.
- Transfer the cakes to a wire rack and leave to cool.
- Beat the cream cheese and butter together until light and fluffy then beat in the icing sugar a quarter at a time.
- Add the grenadine then whip the mixture for 2 minutes or until smooth and light.
- Spoon the icing into a piping bag, fitted with a large star nozzle, and pipe a swirl of icing on top of each cake, then sprinkle with pink sugar sprinkles.

Grenadine, Orange and Raspberry Cupcakes

483

- Omit the cocoa and fold 100 g of raspberries into the cake mixture. Top the cakes with fresh raspberries and finely pared orange zest.

484

MAKES 12

Forest Fruits Buttercream Cupcakes

- Preheat the oven to 190°C (170° fan) / 375F / gas 5 and line a 12-hole cupcake tin with paper cases.
- Combine the flour, sugar, butter, eggs and fruit syrups in a bowl and whisk together for 2 minutes or until smooth.
- Divide the mixture between the cases and bake for 15 – 20 minutes.
- Test with a wooden toothpick, if it comes out clean, the cakes are done.
- Transfer the cakes to a wire rack and leave to cool completely.
- Beat the butter until smooth, then gradually whisk in the icing sugar and fruit syrups.
- Spoon the mixture into a piping bag, fitted with a large star nozzle, and pipe a swirl of icing on top of each cake.
- Sprinkle with the pink cake sprinkles to finish.

PREPARATION TIME 30 MINUTES

COOKING TIME 15 - 20 MINUTES

INGREDIENTS

110 g / 4 oz / ⅔ cup self-raising flour, sifted
110 g / 4 oz / ½ cup caster (superfine) sugar
110 g / 4 oz / ½ cup butter, softened
2 large eggs
1 tbsp blueberry syrup
1 tbsp raspberry syrup
1 tbsp blackberry syrup

TO DECORATE:
100 g / 3 ½ oz / ½ cup butter, softened
200 g / 7 oz / 2 cups icing (confectioners') sugar
2 tsp blueberry syrup
2 tsp raspberry syrup
2 tsp blackberry syrup
pink cake sprinkles to decorate

485

Fresh Forest Fruits Buttercream Cupcakes

- Add 100 g of mixed forest fruits to the cake mixture and top the buttercream with extra berries.

486

MAKES 12

Rocky Road Topped Muffin Cupcakes

- Preheat the oven to 180°C (160° fan) / 350F / gas 4 and line a 12-hole cupcake tin with thick paper cases.
- Beat the egg in a jug with the oil and milk until well mixed.
- Mix the flour, cocoa, baking powder and sugar in a bowl, then pour in the egg mixture and stir just enough to combine.
- Divide the mixture between the cases, then bake in the oven for 20 – 25 minutes.
- Transfer the cakes to a wire rack and leave to cool completely.
- Stir the chocolate, butter and honey together over a low heat until it forms a smooth sauce, then drizzle it over the cakes.
- Scatter over the pistachios, walnuts, toffee pieces and mini marshmallows.

PREPARATION TIME 30 MINUTES

COOKING TIME 20 – 25 MINUTES

INGREDIENTS

1 large egg
125 ml / 4 ½ fl. oz / ½ cup sunflower oil
125 ml / 4 ½ fl. oz / ½ cup milk
375 g / 13 oz / 2 ½ cups self-raising flour, sifted
50 g / 1 ¾ oz / ½ cup unsweetened cocoa powder, sifted
1 tsp baking powder
200 g / 7 oz / ¾ cup caster (superfine) sugar
100 g / 3 ½ oz dark chocolate (minimum 60% cocoa solids), chopped
2 tbsp butter, 2 tbsp honey
25 g / 1 oz / ¼ cup pistachio nuts, roughly chopped
25 g / 1 oz / ¼ cup walnuts, chopped
25 g / 1 oz / ¼ cup toffee pieces
24 mini marshmallows

487

Rocky Road Muffin Cupcakes

- Stir the nuts, toffee and marshmallows into the cake mixture before baking, along with 50 g of halved glace cherries and 4 roughly chopped digestive biscuits.

488

MAKES 12

Chocolate and Toffee Cupcakes

PREPARATION TIME 30 MINUTES

COOKING TIME 15 - 20 MINUTES

INGREDIENTS

110 g / 4 oz / ⅔ cup self-raising flour, sifted
110 g / 4 oz / ½ cup caster (superfine) sugar
110 g / 4 oz / ½ cup butter, softened
2 large eggs
2 tbsp unsweetened cocoa powder
75 g / 2 ½ oz / ½ cup toffee, chopped

TO DECORATE:
100 g / 3 ½ oz dark chocolate (minimum 60 % cocoa solids), chopped
100 g / 3 ½ oz / ½ cup dulce de leche
30 g / 1 oz milk chocolate

- Preheat the oven to 190°C (170° fan) / 375F / gas 5 and line a 12-hole cupcake tin with paper cases.
- Combine the flour, sugar, butter, eggs, cocoa powder and chopped toffee in a bowl and whisk together for 2 minutes or until smooth.
- Divide the mixture between the cases, then transfer the tin to the oven and bake for 15 – 20 minutes.
- Test with a wooden toothpick, if it comes out clean, the cakes are done.
- Transfer the cakes to a wire rack and leave to cool completely.
- Melt the chocolate in a microwave or bain marie then stir in the dulce de leche and spread the mixture on top of the cakes.
- Use a vegetable peeler to shave over the milk chocolate.

489

Coffee and Toffee Cupcakes

- Use 1 tbsp of instant espresso powder instead of the cocoa powder and sprinkle with chocolate-coated coffee beans instead of the milk chocolate shavings.

490

Chocolate, Toffee and Banana Cupcakes

- Add a chopped banana to the cake mixture before baking and top each cake with a banana slice.

491

MAKES 12

Blueberry Syrup Cream Cheese Cupcakes

- Preheat the oven to 190°C (170° fan) / 375F / gas 5 and line a 12-hole cupcake tin with paper cases.
- Combine the flour, sugar, butter, eggs and vanilla extract in a bowl and whisk together for 2 minutes or until smooth.
- Divide the mixture between the cases and bake for 15 – 20 minutes.
- Transfer the cakes to a wire rack and leave to cool.
- Beat the cream cheese and butter together until light and fluffy then beat in the icing sugar a quarter at a time.
- Add the blueberry syrup then whip the mixture for 2 minutes or until smooth and light.
- Spoon the icing into a piping bag, fitted with a large star nozzle, and pipe a swirl of icing on top of each cake. Decorate with the purple sweets.

PREPARATION TIME 30 MINUTES

COOKING TIME 15 - 20 MINUTES

INGREDIENTS

110 g / 4 oz / ⅔ cup self-raising flour, sifted
110 g / 4 oz / ½ cup light brown sugar
110 g / 4 oz / ½ cup butter, softened
2 large eggs
½ tsp vanilla extract

TO DECORATE:
110 g / 4 oz / ½ cup cream cheese
55 g / 2 oz / ¼ cup butter, softened
110 g / 4 oz / 1 cup icing (confectioners') sugar
3 tbsp blueberry syrup
small purple sweets to decorate

Bubble Gum Cream Cheese Cupcakes

492

- Replace the blueberry syrup with bubble gum syrup and colour the icing blue. Top each cake with a bubble gum ball.

493

MAKES 12

Coffee Syrup Cream Cupcakes

- Preheat the oven to 190°C (170° fan) / 375F / gas 5 and line a 12-hole cupcake tin with thick paper cases.
- Sieve the flour, bicarbonate of soda and espresso powder together into a bowl.
- Put the golden syrup, butter and brown sugar in a small saucepan and boil gently for 2 minutes, stirring to dissolve the sugar.
- Pour the butter and sugar mixture onto the flour with the eggs and milk, then fold it all together until smooth.
- Divide the mixture between the cases, then transfer the tin to the oven and bake for 20 – 25 minutes.
- Transfer the cakes to a wire rack and leave to cool.
- Whip the cream until it holds its shape, then spoon it into a piping bag, then pipe a swirl on top of each cake.
- Put the sugar in a small pan with 3 tbsp of water and bring to the boil.
- Stir in the espresso powder then spoon over the cream.

PREPARATION TIME 30 MINUTES

COOKING TIME 20 – 25 MINUTES

INGREDIENTS

250 g / 9 oz / 1 ¾ cups self-raising flour
1 tsp bicarbonate of (baking) soda
2 tbsp instant espresso powder
200 g / 8 ½ oz / ½ cup golden syrup
125 g / 4 ½ oz / ½ cup butter
125 g / 4 ½ oz / ¾ cup dark brown sugar
2 large eggs, beaten
250 ml / 9 fl. oz / 1 cup milk

TO DECORATE:
250 ml / 9 fl. oz / 1 cup double (heavy) cream
3 tbsp caster (superfine) sugar
1 tsp instant espresso powder

Fennel and Coffee Syrup Cupcakes

494

- Add 1 tsp of ground fennel seeds to the cake mixture with the flour.

495

Chocolate Crispy Cupcakes

MAKES 12

PREPARATION TIME 25 MINUTES
COOKING TIME 15 - 20 MINUTES
SETTING TIME 30 MINUTES

INGREDIENTS

110 g / 4 oz / ⅔ cup self-raising flour, sifted
110 g / 4 oz / ½ cup caster (superfine) sugar
110 g / 4 oz / ½ cup butter, softened
2 large eggs
2 tbsp unsweetened cocoa powder

TO DECORATE:
200 g / 7 oz dark chocolate, minimum 60% cocoa solids, chopped
50 g / 1 ¾ oz / 1 cup cornflakes
50 g / 1 ¾ oz / 1 cup sugar puffs
50 g / 1 ¾ oz / ½ cup walnuts, roughly chopped

- Preheat the oven to 190°C (170° fan) / 375F / gas 5 and line a 12-hole cupcake tin with paper cases.
- Combine the flour, sugar, butter, eggs and cocoa in a bowl and whisk together for 2 minutes or until smooth.
- Divide the mixture between the cases, then transfer the tin to the oven and bake for 15 – 20 minutes.
- Test with a wooden toothpick, if it comes out clean, the cakes are done.
- Transfer the cakes to a wire rack and leave to cool completely.
- Melt the butter in a microwave or bain marie, then stir in the corn flakes, sugar puffs and walnuts.
- Spoon the mixture on top of the cupcakes and leave to set for 30 minutes.

496

White Chocolate Crispy Cupcakes

- Replace the dark chocolate with white chocolate.

497

Glace-Iced Apple Muffin Cupcakes

MAKES 12

PREPARATION TIME 25 MINUTES
COOKING TIME 20 – 25 MINUTES

INGREDIENTS

1 large egg
1 lemon, zest finely grated
125 ml / 4 ½ fl. oz / ½ cup sunflower oil
125 ml / 4 ½ fl. oz / ½ cup milk
375 g / 13 oz / 2 ½ cups self-raising flour, sifted
1 tsp baking powder
200 g / 7 oz / ¾ cup caster (superfine) sugar
1 eating apple, peeled and grated

TO DECORATE:
200 g / 7 oz / 2 cups icing (confectioners') sugar
pearlescent cake sprinkles to decorate

- Preheat the oven to 180°C (160° fan) / 350F / gas 4 and line a 12-hole cupcake tin with paper cases.
- Beat the egg in a jug with the lemon zest, oil and milk until well mixed.
- Mix the flour, baking powder and sugar in a bowl, then pour in the egg mixture and grated apple, and stir just enough to combine.
- Spoon the mixture into the cases, then bake in the oven for 20 – 25 minutes.
- Test with a wooden toothpick, if it comes out clean, the cakes are done.
- Transfer the cakes to a wire rack and leave to cool completely.
- Sieve the icing sugar into a bowl and add just enough water to make a thick, spreadable icing.
- Spoon the icing onto the cakes and scatter over the cake sprinkles.

498

Glace-Iced Pear Muffin Cupcakes

- Swap the grated apple for a peeled, grated pear.

499

MAKES 12

Coffee and Rose Water Cupcakes

Cardamom and Rose Water Cupcakes

500

- Replace the espresso powder in the cake mixture with ½ tsp of ground cardamom and add a pinch of ground cardamom to the icing instead of the espresso powder.

Pistachio and Rose Water Cupcakes

501

- Replace the espresso powder in the cake mixture and icing with 2 tbsp of ground pistachio nuts.

PREPARATION TIME 30 MINUTES

COOKING TIME 15 - 20 MINUTES

INGREDIENTS

110 g / 4 oz / ⅔ cup self-raising flour, sifted
110 g / 4 oz / ½ cup caster (superfine) sugar
110 g / 4 oz / ½ cup butter, softened
2 large eggs
1 tbsp instant espresso powder
1 tsp rose water

TO DECORATE:
100 g / 3 ½ oz / ½ cup butter, softened
200 g / 7 oz / 2 cups icing (confectioners') sugar
2 tsp instant espresso powder
½ tsp rose water
12 sugar flowers

- Preheat the oven to 190°C (170° fan) / 375F / gas 5 and line a 12-hole cupcake tin with paper cases.
- Combine the flour, sugar, butter, eggs, espresso powder and rose water in a bowl and whisk together for 2 minutes or until smooth.
- Divide the mixture between the cases, then transfer the tin to the oven and bake for 15 – 20 minutes.
- Test with a wooden toothpick, if it comes out clean, the cakes are done.
- Transfer the cakes to a wire rack and leave to cool completely.
- Beat the butter until smooth, then gradually whisk in the icing sugar, espresso powder and rose water.
- Spread the buttercream onto the cakes and top each one with a sugar flower.

502

MAKES 12

Glace-Iced Oat Muffin Cupcakes

PREPARATION TIME 25 MINUTES

COOKING TIME 20 – 25 MINUTES

INGREDIENTS

1 large egg
125 ml / 4 ½ fl. oz / ½ cup sunflower oil
125 ml / 4 ½ fl. oz / ½ cup milk
375 g / 13 oz / 2 ½ cups self-raising flour, sifted
1 tsp baking powder
200 g / 7 oz / ¾ cup caster (superfine) sugar
4 tbsp rolled porridge oats

TO DECORATE:
200 g / 7 oz / 2 cups icing (confectioners') sugar
75 g / 2 ½ oz dark chocolate, melted

- Preheat the oven to 180°C (160° fan) / 350F / gas 4 and line a 12-hole cupcake tin with paper cases.
- Beat the egg in a jug with the oil and milk until well mixed.
- Mix the flour, baking powder, sugar and oats in a bowl, then pour in the egg mixture and stir just enough to combine.
- Spoon the mixture into the cases, then bake in the oven for 20 – 25 minutes.
- Test with a wooden toothpick, if it comes out clean, the cakes are done.
- Transfer the cakes to a wire rack and leave to cool completely.
- Sieve the icing sugar into a bowl and add just enough water to make a thick, spreadable icing.
- Spoon the icing onto the cakes, followed by the melted chocolate.

503

Glace-Iced Muesli Muffin Cupcakes

- Use 50 g of muesli instead of the porridge oats.

504

MAKES 12

Lemon, Lime and Chocolate Cupcakes

PREPARATION TIME 30 MINUTES

COOKING TIME 20 – 25 MINUTES

INGREDIENTS

250 g / 9 oz / 1 ¾ cups self-raising flour
1 tsp bicarbonate of (baking) soda
2 tbsp unsweetened cocoa powder
200 g / 8 ½ oz / ½ cup golden syrup
125 g / 4 ½ oz / ½ cup butter
125 g / 4 ½ oz / ¾ cup dark brown sugar
2 large eggs, beaten
200 ml / 7 fl. oz / 3/4 cup milk
75 g / 2 ½ oz / ½ cup mixed candied peel
1 lime, juiced and zest finely pared
1 lemon, juiced and zest finely pared

- Preheat the oven to 190°C (170° fan) / 375F / gas 5 and line a deep 12-hole cupcake tin with paper cases.
- Sieve the flour, bicarbonate of soda and cocoa powder together into a bowl.
- Put the golden syrup, butter and brown sugar in a small saucepan and boil gently for 2 minutes, stirring to dissolve the sugar.
- Pour the butter and sugar mixture onto the flour with the eggs and milk. Reserve a little candied peel for the topping and add the rest to the bowl with the lime and lemon juices, then fold it all together until smooth.
- Divide the mixture between the cases, then transfer the tin to the oven and bake for 20 – 25 minutes.
- Allow to cool completely, then sprinkle with the pared lime and lemon zest and the reserved candied peel.

505

Lemon, Lime and Ginger Cupcakes

- Omit the cocoa and add 2 tsp of ground ginger to the cake mixture.

506

MAKES 12

Flower-Iced Vanilla Cupcakes

- Preheat the oven to 190°C (170° fan) / 375F / gas 5 and line a 12-hole cupcake tin with paper cases.
- Combine the flour, sugar, butter, eggs and vanilla extract in a bowl and whisk together for 2 minutes or until smooth.
- Divide the mixture between the cases, then transfer the tin to the oven and bake for 15 – 20 minutes.
- Transfer the cakes to a wire rack and leave to cool.
- Beat the butter until smooth, then gradually whisk in the icing sugar and vanilla extract.
- Colour the icing with a little pink food colouring, then spoon the mixture into a piping bag, fitted with a large star nozzle.
- Hold the piping bag vertically above the first cake and pipe the icing in a spiral, without twisting the bag, so that it looks like a rose. Repeat with the other cakes.

PREPARATION TIME 30 MINUTES

COOKING TIME 15 - 20 MINUTES

INGREDIENTS

110 g / 4 oz / ⅔ cup self-raising flour, sifted
110 g / 4 oz / ½ cup caster (superfine) sugar
110 g / 4 oz / ½ cup butter, softened
2 large eggs
1 tsp vanilla extract

TO DECORATE:
100 g / 3 ½ oz / ½ cup butter, softened
200 g / 7 oz / 2 cups icing (confectioners') sugar
1 tsp vanilla extract
a few drops of pink food colouring

Plain-Iced Vanilla Cupcakes

507

- Omit the food colouring and spread the icing onto the cakes with a palette knife. Top with purple sweets.

508

MAKES 12

White Rose Cupcakes

- Preheat the oven to 190°C (170° fan) / 375F / gas 5 and line a 12-hole cupcake tin with paper cases.
- Combine the flour, sugar, butter, eggs and rose water in a bowl and whisk together for 2 minutes or until smooth.
- Divide the mixture between the cases, then transfer the tin to the oven and bake for 15 – 20 minutes.
- Test with a wooden toothpick, if it comes out clean, the cakes are done.
- Transfer the cakes to a wire rack and leave to cool completely.
- Sieve the icing sugar into a bowl and add just enough rose water to make a thick, pourable icing.
- Spoon the icing onto the cakes and top each one with a sugar paste rose.

PREPARATION TIME 30 MINUTES

COOKING TIME 15 - 20 MINUTES

INGREDIENTS

110 g / 4 oz / ⅔ cup self-raising flour, sifted
110 g / 4 oz / ½ cup caster (superfine) sugar
110 g / 4 oz / ½ cup butter, softened
2 large eggs
1 tbsp rose water

TO DECORATE:
200 g / 7 oz / 2 cups icing (confectioners') sugar
1 – 2 tsp rose water
12 sugar paste roses with leaves

Hibiscus Cupcakes

509

- Replace the rose water with hibiscus syrup and top the cakes with fresh hibiscus flowers.

510

MAKES 12

Lemon Fondant Flower Cupcakes

PREPARATION TIME 1 HOUR

COOKING TIME 15 - 20 MINUTES

INGREDIENTS

110 g / 4 oz / ⅔ cup self-raising flour, sifted
110 g / 4 oz / ½ cup caster (superfine) sugar
110 g / 4 oz / ½ cup butter, softened
2 large eggs
1 lemon, juiced and zest finely grated

TO DECORATE:
200 g / 7 oz / 2 cups icing (confectioners') sugar
200 g / 7 oz ready to roll fondant icing
a few drops of yellow and pink food colouring
icing (confectioners') sugar for dusting

- Preheat the oven to 190°C (170° fan) / 375F / gas 5 and line a 12-hole cupcake tin with paper cases.
- Combine the flour, sugar, butter, eggs and lemon juice and zest in a bowl and whisk together for 2 minutes or until smooth.
- Divide the mixture between the cases, then transfer the tin to the oven and bake for 15 – 20 minutes.
- Test with a wooden toothpick, if it comes out clean, the cakes are done.
- Transfer the cakes to a wire rack and leave to cool completely.
- Sieve the icing sugar into a bowl and add just enough water to make a thick, pourable icing, then spoon the icing onto the cakes.
- Divide the fondant icing into 2 pieces and knead a little food colouring into each.
- Dust the work surface lightly with icing sugar and roll out the icing, then use flower-shaped cutters to cut out the flowers and arrange them on top of the cakes.

511

Lime Fondant Flower Cupcakes

- Replace the lemon juice and zest with lime juice and zest.

512

Spiced Fondant Flower Cupcakes

- Replace the lemon juice and zest with 1 tsp of mixed spice.

513

MAKES 12

Raspberry Curd Cupcakes

- Preheat the oven to 190°C (170° fan) / 375F / gas 5 and line a 12-hole cupcake tin with paper cases.
- Combine the flour, sugar, butter and eggs in a bowl and whisk together for 2 minutes or until smooth.
- Fold in the raspberries and divide the mixture between the cases then bake for 15 – 20 minutes.
- Transfer the cakes to a wire rack and leave to cool.
- While the cakes are cooling, reserve 12 raspberries for decoration and press the rest through a sieve.
- Dissolve cornflour in 100 ml of the sieved raspberry pulp and put it in a pan with the rest of the ingredients.
- Stir constantly over a medium heat.
- After 6 or 7 minutes the mixture should thicken. Stir until it bubbles then cool to room temperature.
- Spoon the curd onto the cupcakes and decorate each one with a raspberry and heart-shaped sprinkles.

Gooseberry Curd Cupcakes

514

- Poach 150 g of gooseberries in 2 tbsp of water for 5 minutes, then press through a sieve and use in place of the raspberries.

PREPARATION TIME 30 MINUTES

COOKING TIME 15 - 20 MINUTES

INGREDIENTS

110 g / 4 oz / ⅔ cup self-raising flour, sifted
110 g / 4 oz / ½ cup caster (superfine) sugar
110 g / 4 oz / ½ cup butter, softened
2 large eggs
100 g / 3 ½ oz / ⅔ cup raspberries

TO DECORATE:
150 g / 5 ½ oz / 1 cup raspberries
1 tsp cornflour (cornstarch)
2 large eggs, beaten
110 g / 4 oz / 1 cup butter
85 g / 3 oz / ⅓ cup caster (superfine) sugar
heart-shaped sugar sprinkles

515

MAKES 12

Pomegranate Cream Cheese Cupcakes

- Preheat the oven to 190°C (170° fan) / 375F / gas 5 and line a 12-hole cupcake tin with paper cases.
- Combine the flour, sugar, butter and eggs in a bowl and whisk together for 2 minutes or until smooth.
- Divide the mixture between the cases, then transfer the tin to the oven and bake for 15 – 20 minutes.
- Test with a wooden toothpick, if it comes out clean, the cakes are done.
- Transfer the cakes to a wire rack and leave to cool completely.
- Beat the cream cheese and butter together until light and fluffy then beat in the icing sugar a quarter at a time.
- Add the vanilla extract then whip the mixture for 2 minutes or until smooth and light.
- Pipe a big swirl onto the cakes then sprinkle over the pomegranate seeds and purple sprinkles.

Pomegranate and Date Cupcakes

516

- Add 100 g of stoned, chopped medjool dates to the cake mixture and top each cake with a stoned medjool date instead of the sugar sprinkles.

PREPARATION TIME 30 MINUTES

COOKING TIME 15 - 20 MINUTES

INGREDIENTS

110 g / 4 oz / ⅔ cup self-raising flour, sifted
110 g / 4 oz / ½ cup caster (superfine) sugar
110 g / 4 oz / ½ cup butter, softened
2 large eggs
2 tbsp grenadine

TO DECORATE:
110 g / 4 oz / ½ cup cream cheese
55 g / 2 oz / ¼ cup butter, softened
110 g / 4 oz / 1 cup icing (confectioners') sugar
1 tsp vanilla extract
100 g / 3 ½ oz / ⅔ cup pomegranate seeds
purple sugar sprinkles

517

MAKES 12

Raspberry Buttercream Cupcakes

PREPARATION TIME 30 MINUTES

COOKING TIME 15 - 20 MINUTES

INGREDIENTS

110 g / 4 oz / ⅔ cup self-raising flour, sifted
110 g / 4 oz / ½ cup caster (superfine) sugar
110 g / 4 oz / ½ cup butter, softened
2 large eggs
100 g / 3 ½ oz / ⅔ cup raspberries

TO DECORATE:
100 g / 3 ½ oz / ½ cup butter, softened
200 g / 7 oz / 2 cups icing (confectioners') sugar
2 tbsp raspberry syrup
3 tbsp freeze-dried raspberry pieces
12 fresh raspberries
sugar pearls to decorate

- Preheat the oven to 190°C (170° fan) / 375F / gas 5 and line a 12-hole cupcake tin with paper cases.
- Combine the flour, sugar, butter and eggs in a bowl and whisk together for 2 minutes or until smooth.
- Fold in the raspberries and divide the mixture between the cases, then bake for 15 – 20 minutes.
- Transfer the cakes to a wire rack and leave to cool.
- Beat the butter until smooth, then gradually whisk in the icing sugar and raspberry syrup.
- Spoon the mixture into a piping bag, fitted with a large plain nozzle, and pipe a swirl of icing on top of each cake.
- Pound the freeze-dried raspberries in a pestle and mortar then sprinkle over the cakes.
- Top each cake with a raspberry and decorate with the sugar pearls.

518

Raspberry and Violet Buttercream Cupcakes

- Replace the freeze-dried raspberries with crystallised violets, pounding as before with a pestle and mortar.

519

MAKES 12

Chocolate, Orange and Strawberry Cupcakes

PREPARATION TIME 15 MINUTES

COOKING TIME 20 – 25 MINUTES

INGREDIENTS

1 large egg
1 orange, zest finely grated
125 ml / 4 ½ fl. oz / ½ cup sunflower oil
125 ml / 4 ½ fl. oz / ½ cup milk
350 g / 12 ½ oz / 2 ⅓ cups self-raising flour, sifted
50 g / 1 ¾ oz / ½ cup unsweetened cocoa powder, sifted
1 tsp baking powder
200 g / 7 oz / ¾ cup caster (superfine) sugar
150 g / 5 ½ oz strawberries, chopped

TO DECORATE:
300 ml / 10 ½ fl. oz / 1 ¼ cups double (heavy) cream
2 tbsp icing (confectioners') sugar
1 tsp vanilla extract
6 strawberries, halved
chocolate flakes for sprinkling

- Preheat the oven to 180°C (160° fan) / 350F / gas 4 and line a 12-hole cupcake tin with paper cases.
- Beat the egg in a jug with the orange zest, oil and milk until well mixed.
- Mix the flour, cocoa, baking powder and sugar in a bowl, then pour in the egg mixture and strawberry pieces and stir just enough to combine.
- Divide the mixture between the cases, then bake in the oven for 20 – 25 minutes.
- Test with a wooden toothpick, if it comes out clean, the cakes are done.
- Transfer the cakes to a wire rack and leave to cool completely.
- Whip the cream with the icing sugar and vanilla until it holds its shape, then spoon it into a piping bag, fitted with a large star nozzle.
- Pipe a big swirl on top of the cakes and top each one with half a strawberry and a sprinkle of chocolate flakes.

520

Chocolate, Orange and Raspberry Muffin Cupcakes

- Replace the chopped strawberries with raspberries and top each cake with a raspberry.

521

MAKES 12

Chocolate Cupcakes with Buttercream

Chocolate Cupcakes with Orange Buttercream

522

- Replace the vanilla extract in the buttercream with the zest and juice of half an orange.

Chocolate Muffin Cupcakes with Strawberry Buttercream

523

- Add 2 tbsp of strawberry syrup to the buttercream and top the cakes with fresh strawberries.

PREPARATION TIME 35 MINUTES

COOKING TIME 20 – 25 MINUTES

INGREDIENTS

1 large egg
125 ml / 4 ½ fl. oz / ½ cup sunflower oil
125 ml / 4 ½ fl. oz / ½ cup milk
350 g / 12 ½ oz / 2 ⅓ cups self-raising flour, sifted
50 g / 1 ¾ oz / ½ cup unsweetened cocoa powder, sifted
1 tsp baking powder
200 g / 7 oz / ¾ cup caster (superfine) sugar
150 g / 5 ½ oz dark chocolate chunks (minimum 60% cocoa solids)

TO DECORATE:
100 g / 3 ½ oz / ½ cup butter, softened
200 g / 7 oz / 2 cups icing (confectioners') sugar
1 tsp vanilla extract
purple star-shaped cake sprinkles

- Preheat the oven to 180°C (160° fan) / 350F / gas 4 and line a 12-hole cupcake tin with paper cases.
- Beat the egg in a jug with the oil and milk until well mixed.
- Mix the flour, cocoa, baking powder and sugar in a bowl, then pour in the egg mixture and chocolate chunks and stir just enough to combine.
- Divide the mixture between the cases, then bake in the oven for 20 – 25 minutes.
- Test with a wooden toothpick, if it comes out clean, the cakes are done.
- Transfer the cakes to a wire rack and leave to cool completely.
- Beat the butter until smooth, then gradually whisk in the icing sugar. Add the vanilla extract and whisk for 2 minutes or until smooth and well whipped.
- Spoon the buttercream into a piping bag and pipe a big swirl on top of each cake before scattering over the cake sprinkles.

524

MAKES 12

Candied Fruit Cupcakes

PREPARATION TIME 30 MINUTES

COOKING TIME 15 - 20 MINUTES

INGREDIENTS

110 g / 4 oz / ⅔ cup self-raising flour, sifted
110 g / 4 oz / ½ cup caster (superfine) sugar
110 g / 4 oz / ½ cup butter, softened
2 large eggs
1 tsp vanilla extract
50 g / 1 ¾ oz / ⅓ cup mixed candied peel, chopped
50 g / 1 ¾ oz / ⅓ cup candied angelica, chopped
50 g / 1 ¾ oz / ⅓ cup candied melon, chopped
50 g / 1 ¾ oz / ⅓ cup glacé cherries, chopped

TO DECORATE:
200 g / 7 oz / 2 cups icing (confectioners') sugar

- Preheat the oven to 190°C (170° fan) / 375F / gas 5 and line a 12-hole cupcake tin with paper cases.
- Combine the flour, sugar, butter, eggs and vanilla in a bowl and whisk together for 2 minutes or until smooth.
- Mix the candied and glacé fruits together and reserve half for decoration, then fold the rest into the cake mixture.
- Divide the mixture between the cases, then transfer the tin to the oven and bake for 15 – 20 minutes.
- Test with a wooden toothpick, if it comes out clean, the cakes are done.
- Transfer the cakes to a wire rack and leave to cool completely before peeling off the papers.
- Sieve the icing sugar into a bowl and add just enough water to make a thick, pourable icing.
- Spoon the icing onto the cakes and decorate with the reserved candied fruit.

525

MAKES 12

Grenadine Cream Cheese Cupcakes

PREPARATION TIME 30 MINUTES

COOKING TIME 15 - 20 MINUTES

INGREDIENTS

110 g / 4 oz / ⅔ cup self-raising flour, sifted
110 g / 4 oz / ½ cup caster (superfine) sugar
110 g / 4 oz / ½ cup butter, softened
2 large eggs

TO DECORATE:
110 g / 4 oz / ½ cup cream cheese
55 g / 2 oz / ¼ cup butter, softened
110 g / 4 oz / 1 cup icing (confectioners') sugar
1 tbsp grenadine
pink and purple cake sprinkles to decorate

- Preheat the oven to 190°C (170° fan) / 375F / gas 5 and line a 12-hole cupcake tin with thick paper cases.
- Combine the flour, sugar, butter and eggs in a bowl and whisk together for 2 minutes or until smooth.
- Divide the mixture between the cases, then transfer the tin to the oven and bake for 15 – 20 minutes.
- Test with a wooden toothpick, if it comes out clean, the cakes are done.
- Transfer the cakes to a wire rack and leave to cool completely.
- Beat the cream cheese and butter together until light and fluffy then beat in the icing sugar a quarter at a time.
- Add the grenadine then whip the mixture for 2 minutes or until smooth and light.
- Spoon or pipe the icing onto the cakes and decorate with the cake sprinkles.

526

MAKES 12

Strawberry Ripple Cupcakes

- Preheat the oven to 190°C (170° fan) / 375F / gas 5 and line a 12-hole cupcake tin with foil cases.
- Combine the cake ingredients in a bowl and whisk together for 2 minutes.
- Divide the mixture between the cases and bake for 15 – 20 minutes.
- Test with a wooden toothpick, if it comes out clean, the cakes are done. Transfer the cakes to a wire rack and leave to cool.
- Beat the butter with the icing sugar until smooth then ripple through the strawberry syrup.
- Spoon the mixture into a piping bag, fitted with a large star nozzle, and pipe a swirl of icing on top of each cake before topping with the flowers.

PREPARATION TIME 30 MINUTES

COOKING TIME 15-20 MINUTES

INGREDIENTS

110 g / 4 oz / 2/3 cup self-raising flour
110 g / 4 oz / ½ cup caster (superfine) sugar
110 g / 4 oz / ½ cup butter, softened
2 large eggs
100 g / 3 ½ oz strawberries, chopped
To decorate:
100 g / 3 ½ oz / ½ cup butter, softened
200 g / 7 oz / 2 cups icing (confectioners') sugar
2 tbsp strawberry syrup
12 sugar flowers

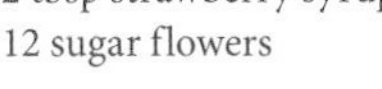

Ginger and Lime Cupcakes

527

MAKES 12

PREPARATION TIME 30 MINUTES

COOKING TIME 15 - 20 MINUTES

INGREDIENTS

110 g / 4 oz / ⅔ cup self-raising flour, sifted
110 g / 4 oz / ½ cup caster (superfine) sugar
110 g / 4 oz / ½ cup butter, softened
2 large eggs
3 pieces of stem ginger, chopped
1 lime, juiced and zest finely grated
100 g / 3 ½ oz / ½ cup butter
200 g / 7 oz / 2 cups icing (confectioners') sugar
1 tbsp stem ginger syrup
1 tbsp lime juice
green food dye
gold sugar pearls

- Preheat the oven to 190°C (170° fan) / 375F / gas 5 and line a 12-hole cupcake tin with paper cases.
- Combine the flour, sugar, butter, eggs, stem ginger and lime juice and zest in a bowl and whisk together for 2 minutes or until smooth.
- Divide the mixture between the cases, then transfer the tin to the oven and bake for 15 – 20 minutes.
- Transfer the cakes to a wire rack and leave to cool completely.
- Beat the butter until smooth, then gradually whisk in the icing sugar, ginger syrup and lime juice.
- Colour the icing a very pale green then spoon the mixture into a piping bag, fitted with a large star nozzle, and pipe a swirl of icing on top of each cake.
- Decorate with gold sugar pearls.

Lemon Pink Cupcakes

528

MAKES 12

PREPARATION TIME 1 HOUR 10 MINUTES

COOKING TIME 15 - 20 MINUTES

INGREDIENTS

110 g / 4 oz / ⅔ cup self-raising flour, sifted
110 g / 4 oz / ½ cup caster (superfine) sugar
110 g / 4 oz / ½ cup butter, softened
2 large eggs
1 lemon, juiced and zest finely grated
100 g / 3 ½ oz / ½ cup butter
200 g / 7 oz / 2 cups icing (confectioners') sugar
½ lemon, juiced and zested
110 g / 4 oz fondant icing
pink food colouring
sugar sprinkles

- Preheat the oven to 190°C (170° fan) / 375F / gas 5 and line a 12-hole cupcake tin with paper cases.
- Combine the flour, sugar, butter, eggs and lemon juice and zest in a bowl and whisk together for 2 minutes or until smooth. Divide the mixture between the cases, then bake for 15 – 20 minutes.
- Transfer the cakes to a wire rack and leave to cool completely.
- Beat the butter with the icing sugar, lemon juice and zest.
- Spoon the mixture into a piping bag, fitted with a large star nozzle and pipe a swirl of buttercream on top of each cake.
- Colour the fondant icing pink and roll it out on a work surface that has been lightly dusted with icing sugar.
- Use a small daisy cutter to cut out 12 flowers and attach one to the top of each cake.
- Sprinkle with sugar sprinkles.

529

MAKES 12

Dolly Mixture Daydream Cupcakes

PREPARATION TIME 30 MINUTES

COOKING TIME 15-20 MINUTES

INGREDIENTS

10 g / 4 oz / 2/3 cup self-raising flour, sifted
110 g / 4 oz / ½ cup caster (superfine) sugar
110 g / 4 oz / ½ cup butter, softened
2 large eggs
1 tsp vanilla extract

To decorate:
100 g / 3 ½ oz / ½ cup butter, softened
200 g / 7 oz / 2 cups icing (confectioners') sugar
1 tsp vanilla extract
Dolly Mixtures

- Preheat the oven to 190°C (170° fan) / 375F / gas 5 and line a 12-hole cupcake tin with paper cases.
- Combine the cake ingredients in a bowl and whisk together for 2 minutes or until smooth.
- Divide the mixture between the cases and bake for 15 – 20 minutes.
- Test with a wooden toothpick, if it comes out clean, the cakes are done.
- Transfer the cakes to a wire rack and leave to cool.
- Beat the butter until smooth, then gradually whisk in the icing sugar and vanilla extract.
- Spoon the mixture into a piping bag, fitted with a large star nozzle, and pipe a swirl of icing on top of each cake. Top with the Dolly Mixtures.

530

Sweet Tooth Cupcakes

- Instead of Dolly Mixtures,use a mixture of different sweets.

531

MAKES 12

Chocolate Vermicelli Cupcakes

PREPARATION TIME 30 MINUTES

COOKING TIME 15 - 20 MINUTES

INGREDIENTS

110 g / 4 oz / ⅔ cup self-raising flour, sifted
110 g / 4 oz / ½ cup caster (superfine) sugar
110 g / 4 oz / ½ cup butter, softened
2 large eggs
2 tbsp unsweetened cocoa powder

TO DECORATE:
100 g / 3 ½ oz / ½ cup butter, softened
200 g / 7 oz / 2 cups icing (confectioners') sugar
1 tbsp unsweetened cocoa powder
2 tbsp chocolate vermicelli

- Preheat the oven to 190°C (170° fan) / 375F / gas 5 and line a 12-hole cupcake tin with paper cases.
- Combine the flour, sugar, butter, eggs and cocoa in a bowl and whisk together for 2 minutes or until smooth.
- Divide the mixture between the cases, then transfer the tin to the oven and bake for 15 – 20 minutes.
- Test with a wooden toothpick, if it comes out clean, the cakes are done.
- Transfer the cakes to a wire rack and leave to cool completely.
- Beat the butter until smooth, then gradually whisk in the icing sugar and cocoa powder.
- Spread the mixture into the cakes, swirling with the back of the spoon, then sprinkle with vermicelli.

532

Chocolate Almond Buttercream Cupcakes

- Add 1 tsp of almond extract to the cake mixture and decorate the cakes with toasted flaked (slivered) almonds instead of the chocolate vermicelli.

533

MAKES 12

Strawberry Cream Cheese Cupcakes

- Preheat the oven to 190°C (170° fan) / 375F / gas 5 and line a 12-hole cupcake tin with paper cases.
- Combine the flour, sugar, butter and eggs in a bowl and whisk together for 2 minutes or until smooth.
- Fold in the strawberries then divide the mixture between the cases and bake for 15 – 20 minutes.
- Transfer the cakes to a wire rack and leave to cool.
- Beat the cream cheese and butter together until light and fluffy then beat in the icing sugar a quarter at a time.
- Add the strawberry syrup then whip the mixture for 2 minutes or until smooth and light.
- Spoon the icing into a piping bag, fitted with a large star nozzle, and pipe a swirl of icing on top of each cake, then top each one with a sugar flower.

PREPARATION TIME 30 MINUTES

COOKING TIME 15 - 20 MINUTES

INGREDIENTS

110 g / 4 oz / ⅔ cup self-raising flour, sifted
110 g / 4 oz / ½ cup caster (superfine) sugar
110 g / 4 oz / ½ cup butter, softened
2 large eggs
75 g / 2 ½ oz / ½ cup strawberries, chopped

TO DECORATE:
110 g / 4 oz / ½ cup cream cheese
55 g / 2 oz / ¼ cup butter, softened
110 g / 4 oz / 1 cup icing (confectioners') sugar
2 tbsp strawberry syrup
12 pink sugar flowers

Strawberry and Rose Cupcakes

534

- Add 1 tbsp rose water to the cake mixture and 2 tsp of rose water to the buttercream.

535

MAKES 12

Classic Strawberry Sprinkles Cupcakes

- Preheat the oven to 180°C (160° fan) / 350F / gas 4 and line a cupcake tin with paper cases
- In a bowl, whisk flour, baking powder, and salt.
- In a small bowl, mix together milk, vanilla, and strawberry puree.
- Cream butter and sugar until light and fluffy.
- Gradually mix in egg and egg whites.
- Add half the flour mixture. Add the milk mixture; mix until just blended. Add remaining mixture.
- Spoon cupcake mix into each paper case.
- Bake, for 20-25 minutes then place on wire rack to cool.
- To make buttercream beat butter with a whisk until soft gradually beat in icing sugar, vanilla and milk.
- Pipe buttercream swirls. Sprinkle sprinkles on top.

PREPARATION TIME 30 MINUTES

COOKING TIME 25 MINUTES

INGREDIENTS

75 ml / 2 ½ fl. oz strawberry puree
200 g / 7 oz / 1 ½ cups plain (all-purpose) flour
1 tsp baking powder
60 ml / 2 fl. oz /¼ cup whole milk,
1 tsp pure vanilla extract
125 g / 4 ½ oz / ½ cup unsalted butter, softened
225 g / 8 oz / 1 cup caster (superfine) sugar
1 large egg, room temperature
2 large egg whites, room temperature
125 g / 4 ½ oz / ½ cup butter, unsalted, softened
300 g / 10 ½ oz / 2 ½ cups icing (confectioners') sugar
½ tsp vanilla extract
½ tbsp milk
sprinkles

Raspberry Sprinkles

536

- Use raspberry puree instead of strawberry.

537

MAKES 12

Birthday Blues Cupcakes

PREPARATION TIME 30 MINUTES

COOKING TIME 20 MINUTES

INGREDIENTS

115 g / 4 oz / ½ cup butter, unsalted, softened
115 g / 4 oz / ½ cup caster (superfine) sugar
2 large eggs
1 tsp vanilla extract
115 g / 4 oz / 1 cup plain (all purpose) flour
1 tsp baking powder
2-3 tbsp milk
2-3 tsp cinnamon
75 g / 3 oz / ½ Demerara sugar

TO DECORATE

125 g / 4 ½ oz / ½ cup butter, unsalted, softened
300 g / 10 ½ oz / 2 ½ cups icing (confectioners') sugar
½ tsp vanilla extract
½ tbsp milk
edible glitter

- Preheat the oven to 180°C (160° fan) / 350F / gas 4 and line a cupcake tin with paper cases.
- Cream butter and sugar until pale and fluffy with an electric whisk.
- Gradually mix in the egg and vanilla extract.
- Gently mix in the flour and baking powder, adding the milk.
- In a separate bowl mix together demerara sugar and cinnamon.
- Pour a small amount of cupcake mix into case to cover bottom of the case. Add tsp of cinnamon sugar. Repeat and top with a layer of cupcake mixture.
- Take a toothpick and poke into the centre of each cupcake case. Swirl around to stir up mix and cinnamon sugar.
- Bake, for 20 minutes. Test with a wooden toothpick, if it comes out clean, the cake is done.
- Place on wire rack to cool.
- To make buttercream beat butter with a whisk until soft gradually beat in icing sugar, vanilla and milk.
- Pipe buttercream swirls. Sprinkle with edible glitter.

538

Ginger Birthday Cupcakes

- Replace the cinnamon with 2 -3 tsp ground ginger.

539

Birthday Sparkler Cupcakes

- Top the cakes with indoor-use sparklers and light according to the packet instructions.

540

MAKES 12

Vanilla Sprinkles Cupcakes

- Preheat the oven to 180°C (160° fan) / 350F / gas 4 and line a cupcake tin with paper cases.
- Cream butter and sugar until pale and fluffy with an electric whisk.
- Gradually mix in the egg and vanilla extract.
- Gently mix in the flour adding the milk.
- Spoon cupcake mix into each paper case.
- Bake, for 18-20 minutes. Test with a wooden toothpick, if it comes out clean, the cake is done.
- Place on wire rack to cool.
- To make buttercream beat butter with a whisk until soft gradually beat in icing sugar, vanilla and milk.
- Pipe buttercream. Sprinkle sugar strands on top.

PREPARATION TIME 20 MINUTES

COOKING TIME 20 MINUTES

INGREDIENTS

125 g / 4 ½ oz / ½ cup butter unsalted, softened
125 g / 4 ½ oz / ½ cup caster (superfine) sugar
2 medium eggs, room temperature
½ tsp vanilla extract
125 g / 4 ½ oz / 1 cup self-raising flour
45 ml / 1 ½ fl. oz / ¼ cup milk

TO DECORATE
125 g / 4 ½ oz / ½ cup butter, unsalted, softened
300 g / 10 ½ oz / 2 ½ cups icing (confectioners') sugar
½ tsp vanilla extract
½ tbsp. milk
sugar strands

Chocolate Vanilla Dreams

541

- Instead of coloured sugar strands, top with some grated chocolate.

542

MAKES 12

Carrot and Milk Chocolate Cupcakes

- Preheat the oven to 190°C (170° fan) / 375F / gas 5 and line a 12-hole cupcake tin with thick paper cases.
- Whisk the sugar, eggs and oil together for 3 minutes.
- Fold in the flour, baking powder and cocoa, followed by the grated carrots and chocolate.
- Divide the mixture between the paper cases, then transfer the tin to the oven and bake for 20 - 25 minutes.
- Transfer the cakes to a wire rack and leave to cool.
- Heat half of the cream until it starts to simmer, then pour it over the chopped chocolate and stir until smooth. Leave to cool to room temperature, then combine with the rest of the cream and whisk until it holds its shape.
- Spoon the chocolate cream into a piping bag fitted with a large star nozzle and pipe a swirl on top of each cake, then dust with cocoa.

PREPARATION TIME 35 MINUTES

COOKING TIME 20 – 25 MINUTES

COOLING TIME 1 HOUR

INGREDIENTS

175 g / 6 oz / 1 cup soft brown sugar
2 large eggs
150 ml / 5 fl. oz / ⅔ cup sunflower oil
175 g / 6 oz / 1 ¼ cups wholemeal flour
3 tsp baking powder
1 tsp unsweetened cocoa powder
200 g / 7 oz / 1 ⅔ cups carrots, peeled and coarsely grated
75 g / 2 ½ oz milk chocolate, grated

TO DECORATE:
300 ml / 10 ½ fl. oz / 1 ¼ cups double (heavy) cream
200 g / 7 oz dark chocolate, minimum 60% cocoa solids, chopped
cocoa powder to dust

Parsnip and Chocolate Cream Cupcakes

543

- Replace the carrots with grated parsnip and add 1 tsp of ground ginger to the cake mixture when you add the cocoa.

544

Rhubarb Rose Cupcakes

MAKES 18

PREPARATION TIME 10 MINUTES

COOKING TIME 45 MINUTES

INGREDIENTS

250 g / 8 oz butter, unsalted, softened
175 g / 6 oz light muscovado sugar
3 eggs
225 g / 7 ½ oz self-raising flour
2 tsp ground ginger
175 ml / 6 fl.oz milk
rhubarb compote
125 g / 4 ½ oz rhubarb, trimmed and cut into small dice
40 g / 1 ½ oz golden caster (superfine) sugar
1 tsp ground ginger
1 tbsp water

TO DECORATE

125 g / 4 ½ oz / ½ cup butter, unsalted, softened
300 g / 10 ½ oz / 2 ½ cups icing (confectioners') sugar
½ tsp vanilla extract
½ tbsp. milk

- Preheat the oven to 200°C (180° fan) / 400F / gas 6 and line a cupcake tin with paper cases.
- Cream butter and sugar. Gradually mix in the egg.
- Gently mix in the flour and ginger, adding the milk.
- Spoon cupcake mix into each paper case.
- Bake, for 18-20 minutes. Place on wire rack to cool.
- To make the compote: place all the ingredients in a pan and heat to boiling point. Leave to bubble and reduce for 2–3 minutes.
- Once the rhubarb has softened and the liquid has gone syrupy, remove from the heat and leave to cool.
- With an apple corer bore out 1½ cm deep hole in top of cupcake.
- To make buttercream beat butter with a whisk until soft gradually beat in icing sugar, vanilla and milk.
- Pipe buttercream with rose nozzle.

545

Apple Vanilla Rose

- Replace the rhubarb compote with apple

546

Glacé-Iced Dairy-Free Cupcakes

MAKES 12

PREPARATION TIME 30 MINUTES

COOKING TIME 20 – 25 MINUTES

INGREDIENTS

1 large egg
1 tsp vanilla extract
125 ml / 4 ½ fl. oz / ½ cup sunflower oil
125 ml / 4 ½ fl. oz / ½ cup coconut milk
375 g / 13 oz / 2 ½ cups self-raising flour, sifted
1 tsp baking powder
200 g / 7 oz / ¾ cup caster (superfine) sugar

TO DECORATE:

200 g / 7 oz / 2 cups icing (confectioners') sugar
food colouring of your choice
colourful cake sprinkles to decorate

- Preheat the oven to 180°C (160° fan) / 350F / gas 4 and line a 12-hole cupcake tin with paper cases.
- Beat the egg in a jug with the vanilla extract, oil and coconut milk until well mixed.
- Mix the flour, baking powder and sugar in a bowl, then pour in the egg mixture and stir just enough to combine.
- Divide the mixture between the cases, then bake in the oven for 20 – 25 minutes.
- Test with a wooden toothpick, if it comes out clean, the cakes are done.
- Transfer the cakes to a wire rack and leave to cool completely.
- Sieve the icing sugar into a bowl and add just enough water to make a thick, spreadable icing.
- Colour the icing with a few drops of food colouring and spread it onto the cakes, then decorate with cake sprinkles.

547

Glacé-Iced Lemon Dairy-Free Cupcakes

- Add the grated zest of a lemon to the cake mixture and use lemon juice instead of water to make the icing.

548

MAKES 12

Chocolate-Glazed Lavender Cupcakes

Chocolate-Glazed Raspberry and Lavender Cupcakes

549

- Add 75 g of raspberries to the cake mixture and top the cakes with raspberry pieces.

Chocolate-glazed Apricot and Lavender Cupcakes

550

- Add 75 g of chopped dried apricots to the cake mixture.

PREPARATION TIME 30 MINUTES

COOKING TIME 20 – 25 MINUTES

INGREDIENTS

1 large egg
125 ml / 4 ½ fl. oz / ½ cup sunflower oil
125 ml / 4 ½ fl. oz / ½ cup milk
a few drops of lavender extract
375 g / 13 oz / 2 ½ cups self-raising flour, sifted
1 tsp baking powder
200 g / 7 oz / ¾ cup caster (superfine) sugar

TO DECORATE:
200 g / 7 oz dark chocolate (minimum 60% cocoa solids), chopped
50 g / 1 ¾ oz / ¼ cup butter
4 tbsp runny honey
purple and white sugar sprinkles to decorate

- Preheat the oven to 180°C (160° fan) / 350F / gas 4 and line a 12-hole cupcake tin with paper cases.
- Beat the egg in a jug with the oil, milk and lavender extract until well mixed.
- Mix the flour, baking powder and sugar in a bowl, then pour in the egg mixture and stir just enough to combine.
- Divide the mixture between the cases, then bake in the oven for 20 – 25 minutes.
- Test with a wooden toothpick, if it comes out clean, the cakes are done.
- Transfer the cakes to a wire rack and leave to cool completely.
- Stir the chocolate, butter and honey together over a low heat until it forms a smooth glaze.
- Leave the mixture to cool to body temperature, then spoon it over the cakes to fully coat the tops. Scatter over the sugar sprinkles.

551

MAKES 12

Wholemeal Chocolate Muffin Cupcakes

PREPARATION TIME 30 MINUTES

COOKING TIME 20 – 25 MINUTES

INGREDIENTS

1 large egg
125 ml / 4 ½ fl. oz / ½ cup sunflower oil
125 ml / 4 ½ fl. oz / ½ cup milk
200 g / 7 oz / 1 ⅓ cups stone-ground wholemeal flour
175 g / 6 oz / 1 ¼ cups self-raising flour, sifted
50 g / 1 ¾ oz / ½ cup unsweetened cocoa powder, sifted
2 tsp baking powder
200 g / 7 oz / ¾ cup caster (superfine) sugar
icing (confectioners') sugar for dusting

- Preheat the oven to 180°C (160° fan) / 350F / gas 4 and line a 12-hole cupcake tin with paper cases.
- Beat the egg in a jug with the oil and milk until well mixed.
- Mix the flours, cocoa, baking powder and sugar in a bowl, then pour in the egg mixture and stir just enough to combine.
- Divide the mixture between the cases, then bake in the oven for 20 – 25 minutes.
- Test with a wooden toothpick, if it comes out clean, the cakes are done.
- Transfer the cakes to a wire rack and leave to cool completely before dusting with icing sugar.

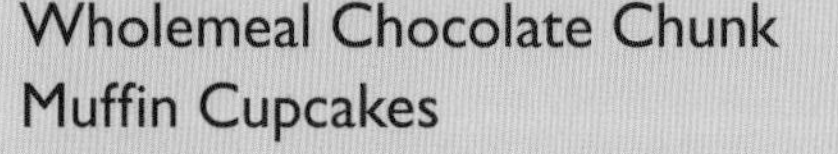

Wholemeal Chocolate Chunk Muffin Cupcakes

552

- Add 50 g of white chocolate chunks and 50 g of milk chocolate chunks to the cake mixture.

553

MAKES 12

Strawberry Surprise Cupcakes

PREPARATION TIME 40 MINUTES

COOKING TIME 25 MINUTES

INGREDIENTS

8 large strawberries
2 eggs
200 g /7 oz / ¾ cup caster (superfine) sugar
75 ml / 2 ½ oz / ¼ cup vegetable oil
½ tsp vanilla extract
½ tsp grated lemon zest
200 g / 7 oz / 1 ½ cup plain (all purpose) flour
2 tsp baking powder
¼ tsp salt
3 tbsp custard powder

TO DECORATE

175 g / 6 oz / ¾ cup cream cheese, softened
30 g / 1 oz / ¼ cup butter, unsalted, softened
60 g / 2 oz / ½ cup icing (confectioners') sugar
½ tsp vanilla extract

- Preheat the oven to 170°C (150° fan) / 325F / gas 3 and line a cupcake tin with paper cases.
- Blend strawberries until smooth. Poor the puree through a sieve to remove seeds.
- Beat together the eggs, sugar, oil, vanilla extract, lemon zest and strawberry puree until well combined.
- Stir in the flour, baking powder, salt, custard powder.
- Spoon cupcake mix into each paper case.
- Bake, for 20 minutes. Test with a wooden toothpick, if it comes out clean, the cake is done.
- Place on wire rack to cool.
- To make cream cheese icing beat butter and cream cheese together until smooth gradually mix in icing sugar and vanilla.
- Pipe icing onto cupcakes.

Raspberry Surprise Cupcakes

554

- Replace the strawberries with the same weight of raspberries.

555

MAKES 14

Vanilla Chocolate Cupcakes

- Preheat oven to 160°C (140° fan) / 325F / gas 3 and line cupcake tins with paper cases.
- Cream butter and sugar together until light and fluffy.
- Gradually mix in eggs and flour.
- Divide batter into two bowls.
- Melt white chocolate in microwave. Combine with the batter in one of the bowls. Repeat with dark chocolate and combine with batter in the other bowl.
- Spoon a small amount of dark chocolate batter into each cupcake case. Add a small amount of white chocolate batter to each case. Repeat like this until all the batter has been used. Using a skewer, swirl the batter in each cupcake case to create the marbled effect. Bake for 30 minutes.
- To make buttercream beat butter with a whisk until soft gradually beat in icing sugar, vanilla and milk.
- Pipe buttercream and top with sugar rose.

PREPARATION TIME 30 MINUTES

COOKING TIME 30 MINUTES

INGREDIENTS

150 g / 5 ½ oz / ½ cup unsalted butter, softened
150 g / 5 ½ oz / ½ cup caster (superfine) sugar
3 medium eggs
150 g / 5 ½ oz / 1 ¼ cups self-raising flour
60 g / 2 oz good quality white chocolate
60 g / 2 oz good quality dark chocolate
1 tbsp cocoa powder

TO DECORATE
100 g / 3 ½ oz / ½ cup butter
200 g / 7 oz / 1 2 cups icing (confectioners') sugar
½ tsp vanilla extract
½ tbsp. milk
2 sugar roses

Triple Chocolate Cupcakes

556

- Add 5 tbsp of chocolate chips to the cupcake batter.

557

MAKES 12

Pumpkin and Cinnamon Cupcakes

- Preheat the oven to 190°C (170° fan) / 375F / gas 5 and line a 12-hole cupcake tin with paper cases.
- Whisk the sugar, eggs and oil together for 3 minutes.
- Fold in the flour, baking powder, orange zest and cinnamon, followed by the grated pumpkin.
- Divide the mixture between the paper cases, then transfer the tin to the oven and bake for 20 - 25 minutes.
- Test with a wooden toothpick, if it comes out clean, the cakes are done.
- Transfer the cakes to a wire rack and leave to cool completely.
- Beat the cream cheese and butter together until light and fluffy then beat in the icing sugar a quarter at a time. Add the vanilla extract and whip for 2 minutes.
- Spoon the icing onto the cakes, top with the pumpkin seeds and sprinkle with ground cinnamon.

PREPARATION TIME 35 MINUTES

COOKING TIME 20 – 25 MINUTES

INGREDIENTS

175 g / 6 oz / 1 cup soft brown sugar
2 large eggs
150 ml / 5 ½ fl. oz / ⅔ cup sunflower oil
175 g / 6 oz / 1 ¼ cups wholemeal flour
3 tsp baking powder
1 orange, zest finely grated
1 tsp ground cinnamon
200 g / 7 oz / 1 ⅔ cups pumpkin or squash, peeled and coarsely grated

TO DECORATE:
110 g / 4 oz / ½ cup cream cheese
55 g / 2 oz / ¼ cup butter, softened
110 g / 4 oz / 1 cup icing (confectioners') sugar
1 tsp vanilla extract
2 tbsp pumpkin seeds
ground cinnamon for sprinkling

Pumpkin and Clove Cream Cheese Cupcakes

558

- Replace the cinnamon with half the amount of ground cloves.

559

Double Chocolate Pillow Cupcakes

MAKES 12

PREPARATION TIME 45 MINUTES

COOKING TIME 15-18 MINUTES

INGREDIENTS

110 g / 4 oz / ⅔ cup self-raising flour, sifted
110 g / 4 oz / ½ cup margarine, softened
110 g / 4 oz / ½ cup caster (superfine) sugar
55 g / 2 oz / ⅓ cup cocoa powder
55 ml / 2 fl. oz / ¼ cup whole milk
2 large eggs
a pinch of salt

FOR THE BUTTERCREAM

100 g / 3 ½ oz / ½ cup butter, softened
200 g / 7 oz / 2 cups icing (confectioners') sugar
50 g / 2 oz / ⅓ cup cocoa powder
30 ml / 1 fl. oz / 2 tbsp whole milk
assorted milk chocolate decorations

- Preheat the oven to 180°C (160° fan) / 350F / gas 4.
- Line a 12-hole cupcake tin with 12 cupcake cases.
- Beat together all the ingredients for the batter apart from the milk in a mixing bowl for 2 minutes until smooth and creamy.
- Add the milk and beat again for a further minute.
- Divide evenly between the paper cases before rapping the tin on a work surface to help settle the batter.
- Bake for 15-18 minutes until risen; test with a wooden toothpick, if it comes out clean, the cakes are done.
- Remove to a wire rack to cool as you prepare the buttercream.
- Beat the softened butter with the cocoa powder, icing sugar and milk in a mixing bowl until smooth and creamy.
- Spoon into a piping bag fitted with a large plain nozzle and pipe in mounds on top of the cupcakes.
- Garnish the buttercream with a chocolate decoration before serving.

560

Two Chocolate Cupcakes

- Grate white chocolate on top of the cupcakes instead of using the decorations.

561

Chocolate Orange Pillow Cupcakes

- Add the grated zest of an orange to the cake mixture and buttercream.

562

MAKES 12

Chocolate Heart Cupcakes

- Preheat the oven to 200°C (180° fan) / 400 F / gas 6 and line a cupcake tin with paper cases.
- In a large saucepan, melt the chocolate and butter over medium heat, stirring to prevent burning. Allow this to cool for a few minutes
- Stir in the sugar until well mixed. Add the eggs, one at a time, until you have a smooth batter. Sift the baking powder, flour and cocoa into the batter and mix until smooth. Fold in the chocolate chips
- Spoon cupcake mix into each paper case.
- Bake, for 20 – 25 minutes. Place on wire rack to cool.
- To make cream cheese icing beat butter and cream cheese together until smooth gradually mix in icing sugar and vanilla.
- Pipe icing, add chocolate heart on top.

PREPARATION TIME 20 MINUTES

COOKING TIME 25 MINUTES

INGREDIENTS

75 g / 3 oz / ½ cup dark chocolate
200 g / 7 oz / 1 cup butter, unsalted, softened
225 g / 8 oz / 1 cup caster (superfine) sugar
3 eggs
½ tsp baking powder
175 g / 6 oz / 1 ½ cups plain (all purpose) flour
25 g / 1 oz / ¼ cup cocoa powder
50 g /2 oz / ½ cup dark chocolate chips

TO DECORATE

175 g / 6 oz / ¾ cup cream cheese
30 g / 1 oz / ¼ cup butter, unsalted, softened
60 g / 2 oz / ½ cup icing (confectioners') sugar
½ tsp vanilla extract
12 chocolate hearts

Chocolate Star Cupcakes

563

- Instead of topping with chocolate hearts, top with dark chocolate stars.

564

MAKES 12

Lemon Drop Cupcakes

- Preheat the oven to 180°C (160° fan) / 350F / gas 4 and line a cupcake tin with paper cases.
- Cream butter and sugar until pale and fluffy with an electric whisk.
- Gradually mix in the egg and vanilla.
- Gently mix in the flour and lemon zest until smooth.
- Spoon cupcake mix into each paper case. Add tsp of lemon curd to top of each cupcake.
- Bake, for 15 minutes.
- Warm the lemon juice with the sugar in a pan until the sugar has dissolved. With a toothpick make a few holes in the cupcake and spoon a little over each cake.
- To make buttercream beat butter with a whisk until soft gradually beat in icing sugar, vanilla and milk.
- Pipe buttercream. Add a few drops of food colouring to sugar and sprinkle sugar.

PREPARATION TIME 15 MINUTES

COOKING TIME 20 MINUTES

INGREDIENTS

100g / 4 oz / ½ cup butter, unsalted, softened
100 g / 4 oz / ½ cup caster (superfine) sugar
1 tsp vanilla extract
2 eggs
100 g / 4 oz / 1 cup self-raising flour
1 lemon, unwaxed, zest only
50 g / 2 oz / ¼ cup lemon curd

TO DECORATE

125 g / 4 ½ oz / ½ cup butter, unsalted, softened
300 g / 10 ½ oz / 2 ½ cups icing (confectioners') sugar
½ tsp lemon extract
½ tbsp. milk
100 g / 4 oz / ½ cup granulated sugar
yellow sugar cake sprinkles

Orange Drop Cupcakes

565

- Replace the lemon zest with orange zest and replace the yellow sugar sprinkles with orange ones.

566

MAKES 12

Treacle Cream Cheese Cupcakes

PREPARATION TIME 30 MINUTES

COOKING TIME 20 – 25 MINUTES

INGREDIENTS

250 g / 9 oz / 1 ¾ cups self-raising flour
1 tsp bicarbonate of (baking) soda
200 g / 8 ½ oz / ½ cup treacle
125 g / 4 ½ oz / ½ cup butter
125 g / 4 ½ oz / ¾ cup dark brown sugar
2 large eggs, beaten
250 ml / 9 fl. oz / 1 cup milk

TO DECORATE:

110 g / 4 oz / ½ cup cream cheese
55 g / 2 oz / ¼ cup butter, softened
110 g / 4 oz / 1 cup icing (confectioners') sugar
1 tsp vanilla extract

- Preheat the oven to 190°C (170° fan) / 375F / gas 5 and line a 12-hole cupcake tin with paper cases.
- Sieve the flour and bicarbonate of soda together.
- Put the treacle, butter and brown sugar in a small saucepan and boil gently for 2 minutes, stirring to dissolve the sugar.
- Pour the butter and sugar mixture onto the flour with the eggs and milk, then fold it all together until smooth.
- Divide the mixture between the cases, then transfer the tin to the oven and bake for 20 – 25 minutes.
- Transfer the cakes to a wire rack and leave to cool.
- Beat the cream cheese and butter together until light and fluffy then beat in the icing sugar a quarter at a time. Add the vanilla extract and whip for 2 minutes.
- Pile the frosting on top of the cakes and make a peak with the back of the spoon.

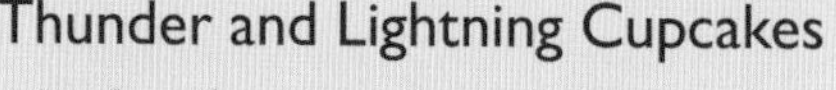

Thunder and Lightning Cupcakes

567

- Replace the cream cheese frosting with a thick layer of clotted cream and an extra drizzle of treacle.

568

MAKES 12

Strawberry Jam-filled Cupcakes

PREPARATION TIME 20 MINUTES

COOKING TIME 20 MINUTES

INGREDIENTS

125 g / 4 ½ oz / ½ cup butter unsalted, softened
125 g / 4 ½ oz / ½ cup caster (superfine) sugar
2 medium eggs
½ tsp vanilla extract
125 g / 4 ½ oz / 1 cup self-raising flour
45 ml / 1 ½ fl. oz / ¼ cup milk

TO DECORATE

125 g / 4 ½ oz / ½ cup butter
300 g / 10 ½ oz / 2 ½ cups icing (confectioners') sugar
½ tsp vanilla extract
½ tbsp. milk
150 g / 5 ½ oz / 1 cup strawberry jam

- Preheat the oven to 180°C (160° fan) / 350F / gas 4 and line a cupcake tin with paper cases.
- Cream butter and sugar until pale and fluffy with an electric whisk.
- Gradually mix in the egg and vanilla extract.
- Gently mix in the flour adding the milk.
- Spoon cupcake mix into each paper case.
- Bake, for 18-20 minutes. Test with a wooden toothpick, if it comes out clean, the cake is done.
- Place on wire rack to cool.
- Scoop a small hole out of the cupcake and fill with 1 tsp jam
- To make buttercream beat butter with a whisk until soft gradually beat in icing sugar, vanilla and milk.
- Pipe buttercream and spoon a little more jam into the centre.

Apricot Jam-filled Cupcakes

569

- Instead of using strawberry jam, use apricot jam.

570

MAKES 12

Irresistible Dark Chocolate Cupcakes

Chocolate Pistachios Cupcakes

571

- Substitute the hundreds and thousands for crushed pistachios on top.

Dark Chocolate Chip Cupcakes

572

- Add a tablespoon of chocolate chips to the mixture before baking.

PREPARATION TIME 30 MINUTES

COOKING TIME 15-18 MINUTES

INGREDIENTS

110 g / 4 oz / ⅔ cup self-raising flour, sifted
110 ml / 4 fl. oz / ½ cup sunflower oil
110 g / 4 oz / ½ cup caster (superfine) sugar
75 g / 3 oz / ½ cup cocoa powder
30 g / 1 oz / 2 tbsp cornflour (cornstarch)
1 tbsp distilled vinegar
2 large eggs
a pinch of salt

TO DECORATE

175 g / 6 oz / ¾ cup unsalted butter
125 g / 4 ½ oz / 1 cup icing (confectioner's) sugar
50 g / 2 oz / ⅓ cup cocoa powder
30 ml / 1 fl. oz / 2 tbsp whole milk
sugar strands

- Preheat the oven to 180°C (160° fan) / 350F / gas 4.
- Line a 12-hole cupcake tin with 12 cupcake cases.
- Beat together all the ingredients for the batter in a mixing bowl for 2 minutes until smooth.
- Divide evenly between the paper cases before rapping the tin on a work surface to help settle the batter.
- Bake for 15-18 minutes until risen; test with a wooden toothpick, if it comes out clean, the cakes are done.
- Remove to a wire rack to cool as you prepare the buttercream.
- Beat the softened butter with the cocoa powder, icing sugar and milk in a mixing bowl until smooth and creamy.
- Spoon into a piping bag fitted with a large plain nozzle and pipe in mounds on top of the cupcakes.
- Garnish the buttercream with a sprinkle of sugar strands.

573

MAKES 12

Raspberry Dream Cupcakes

PREPARATION TIME 30 MINUTES

COOKING TIME 15 - 20 MINUTES

INGREDIENTS

110 g / 4 oz / 2/3 cup self-raising flour, sifted
110 g / 4 oz / ½ cup caster (superfine) sugar
110 g / 4 oz / ½ cup butter, softened
2 large eggs
2 tbsp unsweetened cocoa powder
100 g / 3 ½ oz / 2/3 cup raspberries

TO DECORATE:
300 ml / 10 ½ fl. oz / 1 1/4 cups double (heavy) cream
200 g / 7 oz / 1 1/3 cups raspberries

- Preheat the oven to 190°C (170° fan) / 375F / gas 5 and line a 12-hole cupcake tin with paper cases.
- Combine the flour, sugar, butter, eggs and cocoa in a bowl and whisk together for 2 minutes or until smooth.
- Fold in the raspberries and divide between the cases, then bake for 15 – 20 minutes.
- Test with a wooden toothpick, if it comes out clean, the cakes are done.
- Transfer the cakes to a wire rack and leave to cool.
- Whip the cream until it holds its shape. Arrange the raspberries in a ring around the edge of each cake and pipe the cream into the centre.

Loganberry Dream Cupcakes

574

- Instead of raspberries use fresh loganberries.

575

MAKES 12

Pink Grapefruit Cream Cupcakes

PREPARATION TIME 30 MINUTES

COOKING TIME 15 - 20 MINUTES

INGREDIENTS

110 g / 4 oz / ⅔ cup self-raising flour, sifted
110 g / 4 oz / ½ cup caster (superfine) sugar
110 g / 4 oz / ½ cup butter, softened
2 large eggs
1 pink grapefruit, zest finely grated

TO DECORATE:
300 ml / 10 ½ fl. oz / 1 ¼ cups double (heavy) cream
2 tbsp icing (confectioners') sugar
1 pink grapefruit, juiced
a few drops pink food colouring
hundreds and thousands for sprinkling

- Preheat the oven to 190°C (170° fan) / 375F / gas 5 and line a 12-hole cupcake tin with paper cases.
- Combine the flour, sugar, butter, eggs and grapefruit zest in a bowl and whisk together for 2 minutes or until smooth.
- Divide the mixture between the cases, then transfer the tin to the oven and bake for 15 – 20 minutes.
- Test with a wooden toothpick, if it comes out clean, the cakes are done.
- Transfer the cakes to a wire rack and leave to cool completely.
- Whisk the cream with the icing sugar and grapefruit juice until it holds its shape.
- Spoon the cream into a piping bag fitted with a large plain nozzle and pipe a swirl on top of each cake, then sprinkle with hundreds and thousands.

Grapefruit and Gin Cream Cupcakes

576

- Add 2 tbsp of gin to the cake mixture. Reduce the grapefruit juice by half in the icing and add 1 tbsp of gin.

577

MAKES 12

Chocolate and Sunflower Cream Cupcakes

- Preheat the oven to 190°C (170° fan) / 375F / gas 5 and line a 12-hole cupcake tin with paper cases.
- Combine the flour, sugar, butter, eggs and cocoa in a bowl and whisk together for 2 minutes or until smooth.
- Fold in the sunflower seeds then divide the mixture between the cases and bake for 15 – 20 minutes.
- Transfer the cakes to a wire rack and leave to cool completely.
- Heat half of the cream until it starts to simmer, then pour it over the chopped chocolate and stir until smooth. Leave to cool to room temperature, then combine with the rest of the cream and whisk until it holds its shape.
- Spoon the chocolate cream into a piping bag fitted with a large star nozzle and pipe a swirl on top of each cake. Top each one with a sugar sunflower.

PREPARATION TIME 30 MINUTES

COOKING TIME 15 - 20 MINUTES

COOLING TIME 1 HOUR

INGREDIENTS

110 g / 4 oz / ⅔ cup self-raising flour, sifted
110 g / 4 oz / ½ cup caster (superfine) sugar
110 g / 4 oz / ½ cup butter, softened
2 large eggs
2 tbsp unsweetened cocoa powder
3 tbsp sunflower seeds

TO DECORATE:
300 ml / 10 ½ fl. oz / 1 ¼ cups double (heavy) cream
200 g / 7 oz dark chocolate, minimum 60% cocoa solids, chopped
12 sugar sunflowers

578

Chocolate and Pumpkin Seed Cupcakes

- Replace the sunflower seeds with pumpkin seeds and top the cakes with a fresh pumpkin flower petal.

579

MAKES 10

Pink Butterfly Cupcakes

- Preheat the oven to 180°C (160° fan) / 350F / gas 4 and line a cupcake tin with paper cases.
- Cream butter and sugar until pale and fluffy with an electric whisk.
- Gradually mix in the egg and vanilla extract.
- Gently mix in the flour adding the milk.
- Spoon cupcake mix into each paper case.
- Bake, for 18-20 minutes.
- Place on wire rack to cool.
- Cut and remove a strawberry (coned) shaped portion of cupcake from the top of each cupcake, leaving about 2cm of cake in the bottom. Stuff each cake with a strawberry and cover with a little bit of cake.
- To make buttercream beat butter with a whisk until soft gradually beat in icing sugar, vanilla and milk.
- Pipe buttercream and place butterfly.

PREPARATION TIME 35 MINUTES

COOKING TIME 18 - 20 MINUTES

INGREDIENTS

125 g / 4 ½ oz / ½ cup butter unsalted, softened
125 g / 4 ½ oz / ½ cup caster (superfine) sugar
2 medium eggs, room temperature
½ tsp vanilla extract
125 g / 4 ½ oz / 1 cup self-raising flour
45 ml / 1 ½ fl. oz / ¼ cup milk
10 strawberries

TO DECORATE
125 g / 4 ½ oz / ½ cup butter
300 g / 10 ½ oz / 2 ½ cups icing (confectioners') sugar
1 tsp strawberry flavouring
½ tbsp. milk
10 sugar paste butterflies

580

Raspberry Butterfly Cupcakes

- Replace the strawberries with raspberries in the cake mixture and swap the strawberry essence with raspberry essence for the icing.

581

MAKES 12

Chocolate Raspberry Cupcakes

PREPARATION TIME 45 MINUTES

COOKING TIME 15-18 MINUTES

INGREDIENTS

110 g / 4 oz / ⅔ cup self-raising flour, sifted
110 g / 4 oz / ½ cup margarine, softened
110 g / 4 oz / ½ cup caster (superfine) sugar
55 g / 2 oz / ⅓ cup cocoa powder
55 ml / 2 fl. oz / ¼ cup whole milk
2 large eggs
a pinch of salt

FOR THE BUTTERCREAM

100 g / 3 ½ oz / ½ cup butter, softened
200 g / 7 oz / 2 cups icing (confectioners') sugar
50 g / 2 oz / ⅓ cup cocoa powder
2 tbsp whole milk

TO GARNISH

12 raspberries

- Preheat the oven to 180°C (160° fan) / 350F / gas 4.
- Line a 12-hole cupcake tin with 12 cupcake cases.
- Beat together all the ingredients for the batter apart from the milk in a mixing bowl for 2 minutes until smooth and creamy.
- Add the milk and beat again for a further minute.
- Divide evenly between the paper cases before rapping the tin on a work surface to help settle the batter.
- Bake for 15-18 minutes until risen; test with a wooden toothpick, if it comes out clean, the cakes are done.
- Remove to a wire rack to cool as you prepare the buttercream.
- Beat the softened butter with the cocoa powder, icing sugar and milk in a mixing bowl until smooth and creamy.
- Spoon into a piping bag fitted with a large plain nozzle and pipe in swirled mounds on top of the cupcakes
- Garnish the top of the buttercream with a raspberry before serving.

582

Chocolate Strawberry Cupcakes

- Substitute the raspberries for a halved strawberry on top.

583

Chocolate and Blueberry Buttercream Cupcakes

- Replace the raspberries with blueberries for a tangy taste.

584

MAKES 12

Coming Up Roses Cupcakes

- Preheat the oven to 190°C (170° fan) / 375F / gas 5 and line a 12-hole cupcake tin with foil cases.
- Combine the flour, sugar, butter, eggs and earl grey syrup in a bowl and whisk together for 2 minutes or until smooth.
- Divide the mixture between the cases, then transfer the tin to the oven and bake for 15 – 20 minutes.
- Test with a wooden toothpick, if it comes out clean, the cakes are done.
- Transfer the cakes to a wire rack and leave to cool.
- Beat the butter with the icing sugar and tea syrup until smooth.
- Pipe a swirl of icing onto each cake and top with the roses.

PREPARATION TIME 30 MINUTES

COOKING TIME 15-20 MINUTES

INGREDIENTS

110 g / 4 oz / 2/3 cup self-raising flour, sifted
110 g / 4 oz / ½ cup caster (superfine) sugar
110 g / 4 oz / ½ cup butter, softened
2 large eggs
2 tbsp earl grey tea syrup

TO DECORATE:
100 g / 3 ½ oz / ½ cup butter, softened
200 g / 7 oz / 2 cups icing (confectioners') sugar
1 tbsp earl grey tea syrup
12 sugar paste roses

Cinnamon Rose Cupcakes

585

- Replace the Earl Grey Teabags with 2 sticks of cinnamon and ½ tsp of ground cinnamon and gently heat until simmering.

586

Dairy-Free Buttercream for Cupcakes

MAKES ENOUGH TO ICE 12 CUPCAKES

- Beat the baking spread until smooth, then gradually whisk in the icing sugar and vanilla extract.
- Colour the buttercream with the food colouring of your choice, then pipe or spread the icing onto your cooled cakes.

PREPARATION TIME 5 MINUTES

INGREDIENTS

100 g / 3 ½ oz / ½ cup dairy-free baking spread
200 g / 7 oz / 2 cups icing (confectioners') sugar
1 tsp vanilla extract
food colouring of your choice

Dairy-Free Chocolate Buttercream for Cupcakes

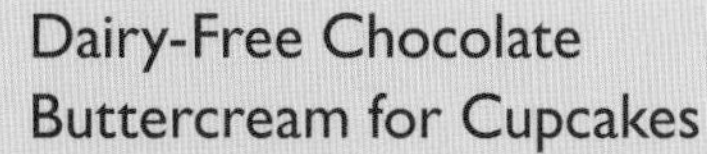

587

- Add 1 tbsp of cocoa powder when you add the icing sugar.

588

MAKES 12

Raspberry Mess Cupcakes

PREPARATION TIME 30 MINUTES

COOKING TIME 15 – 20 MINUTES

INGREDIENTS

175 g /6 ½ oz / ¾ cup butter, unsalted, softened
175 g / 6 ½ oz / ¾ cup caster (superfine) sugar
3 eggs
75 g /2 ½ oz / ½ cup self –raising flour
75 g / 2 ½ oz 1 cup raspberries
3 tbsp milk
75 g / 2 ½ oz / ¼ cup dessicated coconut
25 g / 1 oz almonds, ground

TO DECORATE
300 ml / 10 ½ fl. oz / 1 ¼ cups double cream
2 meringue nests, crushed
100 g / 3 ½ oz / 2/3 cup raspberries, partly crushed

- Preheat the oven to 180°C (160° fan) / 350F / gas 4 and line a 12-hole cupcake tin with foil cases.
- Cream the butter and sugar together until pale and smooth, then gradually beat in the eggs.
- Fold in the flour, raspberries, coconut and almonds then divide the mixture between the cake cases.
- Bake the cakes for 18 – 20 minutes. Test with a wooden toothpick, if it comes out clean, the cakes are done.
- Transfer to cakes to a wire rack and leave to cool.
- Whip the cream until thick then fold in the meringue and raspberries and spoon the mixture on top of the cakes.

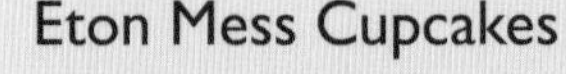

Eton Mess Cupcakes

589

- Replace the raspberries with finely chopped strawberries.

590

MAKES 12

Sugared Blueberry Cupcakes

PREPARATION TIME 30 MINUTES

COOKING TIME 20 MINUTES

INGREDIENTS

110 g / 4 oz / ⅔ cup self-raising flour, sifted
110 g / 4 oz / ½ cup margarine, softened
110 g / 4 oz / ½ cup caster (superfine) sugar
1 tsp vanilla extract
2 large eggs
a pinch of salt

FOR THE BUTTERCREAM
175 g / 6 oz / ¾ cup unsalted butter, softened
125 g / 4 ½ oz / 1 cup icing (confectioner's) sugar
a few drops of purple food colouring

TO GARNISH
150 g / 5 oz / 1 ½ cups blueberries
1 tbsp caster (superfine) sugar

- Preheat the oven to 180°C (160° fan) / 350F / gas 4.
- Line a 12-hole cupcake tin with 12 cupcake cases.
- Beat together all the ingredients for the batter in a mixing bowl for 2 minutes until smooth and creamy.
- Divide evenly between the paper cases before rapping the tin on a work surface to help settle the batter.
- Bake for 15-18 minutes until risen.
- Transfer the cakes to a wire rack and leave to cool.
- Beat the butter with the icing sugar and food colouring until smooth.
- Spread the buttercream on top of the cakes, then sprinkle with blueberries and sugar.

Sugared Redcurrant Cupcakes

591

- Substitute the blueberries for redcurrants.

592

MAKES 12

Coffee Ruffle Cupcakes

PREPARATION TIME 35 MINUTES

COOKING TIME 15-20 MINUTES

INGREDIENTS

110 g / 4 oz / ⅔ cup self-raising flour, sifted
110 g / 4 oz / ½ cup margarine
110 g / 4 oz / ½ cup caster (superfine) sugar
55 g / 2 oz / ⅓ cup cocoa powder
55 ml / 2 fl. oz / ¼ cup whole milk
2 large eggs
a pinch of salt

TO DECORATE
100 g / 3 ½ oz / ½ cup butter, softened
200 g / 7 oz / 2 cups icing (confectioners') sugar
2 tbsp cocoa powder
1 tsp instant espresso powder
2 tbsp milk

- Preheat the oven to 180°C (160° fan) / 350F / gas 4.
- Line a 12-hole cupcake tin with 12 cupcake cases.
- Beat together all the ingredients for the batter apart from the milk in a mixing bowl for 2 minutes until smooth and creamy.
- Add the milk and beat again for a further minute.
- Divide evenly between the paper cases before rapping the tin on a work surface to help settle the batter.
- Bake for 15-18 minutes until risen; test with a wooden toothpick, if it comes out clean, the cakes are done.
- Transfer the cakes to a wire rack and leave to cool.
- Beat the butter with the icing sugar, cocoa, espresso powder and milk until smooth.
- Pipe a ruffle of buttercream onto each cake and top with the chocolate cigarillos.

593

Vanilla and Chocolate Cigarillo Cupcakes

- Use 1 tsp of vanilla extract instead of cocoa in the cake mixture. Omit the espresso powder from the icing.

594

Mocha Cupcakes

- Add 2 tablespoons of chocolate powder to the mixture to make a mocha version.

595

MAKES 12

Violet Tip Cupcakes

PREPARATION TIME 35 MINUTES

COOKING TIME 20 MINUTES

INGREDIENTS

110 g / 4 oz / ⅔ cup self-raising flour, sifted
110 g / 4 oz / ½ cup margarine, softened
110 g / 4 oz / ½ cup caster (superfine) sugar
1 tsp vanilla extract
2 large eggs
a pinch of salt

FOR THE BUTTERCREAM
225 g / 8 oz / 1 cup unsalted butter, softened
180 g / 6 oz / 1 ½ cups icing (confectioner's) sugar
1 tsp vanilla extract
a few drops of purple food colouring
5 drops of violet essence

- Preheat the oven to 190°C (170° fan) / 375F / gas 5 and line a 12-hole cupcake tin with paper cases.
- Combine the cake ingredients and whisk together for 2 minutes.
- Divide the mixture between the cases and bake for 15 – 20 minutes.
- Test with a wooden toothpick, if it comes out clean, the cakes are done.
- Transfer the cakes to a wire rack and leave to cool.
- Beat the butter with the icing sugar and vanilla extract until smooth.
- Pipe two thirds of the icing onto the cakes in small rosettes.
- Add a few drops of food colouring and violet essence to the remaining icing, then pipe purple rosettes on top.

596

Purple Coconut Cupcakes

- Garnish the tops with a sprinkle of desiccated coconut.

597

MAKES 12

Baby Shower Cupcakes

PREPARATION TIME 35 MINUTES

COOKING TIME 15 - 20 MINUTES

INGREDIENTS

110 g / 4 oz / ⅔ cup self-raising flour, sifted
110 g / 4 oz / ½ cup caster (superfine) sugar
110 g / 4 oz / ½ cup butter, softened
2 large eggs
½ tsp vanilla extract

TO DECORATE:
100 g / 3 ½ oz / ½ cup butter, softened
200 g / 7 oz / 2 cups icing (confectioners') sugar
1 tsp vanilla extract
24 pink baby feet edible cake toppers

- Preheat the oven to 190°C (170° fan) / 375F / gas 5 and line a 12-hole cupcake tin with paper cases.
- Combine the flour, sugar, butter, eggs and vanilla extract in a bowl and whisk together for 2 minutes or until smooth.
- Divide the mixture between the cases, then transfer the tin to the oven and bake for 15 – 20 minutes.
- Test with a wooden toothpick, if it comes out clean, the cakes are done.
- Transfer the cakes to a wire rack and leave to cool completely.
- Beat the butter until smooth, then gradually whisk in the icing sugar and vanilla extract.
- Spoon the mixture into a piping bag fitted with a small star nozzle and pipe 3 rings of rosettes on top, then position 2 feet on top of each cake.

598

Cinnamon Baby Shower Cupcakes

- Add 1 tsp of ground cinnamon to the cake mixture and sprinkle a little cinnamon on top before adding the baby feet.

599

MAKES 12

Coffee and Orange Flower Cupcakes

- Preheat the oven to 190°C (170° fan) / 375F / gas 5 and line a 12-hole cupcake tin with cupcake wraps.
- Combine the flour, sugar, butter, eggs, espresso powder and orange flower water in a bowl and whisk together for 2 minutes or until smooth.
- Divide the mixture between the cases, then transfer the tin to the oven and bake for 15 – 20 minutes.
- Test with a wooden toothpick, if it comes out clean, the cakes are done.
- Transfer the cakes to a wire rack and leave to cool completely.
- Beat the butter until smooth, then gradually whisk in the icing sugar, espresso powder and orange flower water.
- Spoon the mixture into a piping bag, fitted with a large star nozzle, and pipe a swirl of icing on top of each cake, then sprinkle with chocolate flakes. Finish each one with a sugar flower.

PREPARATION TIME 30 MINUTES

COOKING TIME 15 - 20 MINUTES

INGREDIENTS

110 g / 4 oz / ⅔ cup self-raising flour, sifted
110 g / 4 oz / ½ cup caster (superfine) sugar
110 g / 4 oz / ½ cup butter, softened
2 large eggs
1 tbsp instant espresso powder
1 tsp orange flower water

TO DECORATE:
100 g / 3 ½ oz / ½ cup butter, softened
200 g / 7 oz / 2 cups icing (confectioners') sugar
2 tsp instant espresso powder
½ tsp orange flower water
chocolate flakes to sprinkle
12 sugar flowers

Cardamom and Orange Flower Cupcakes

600

- Add ½ tsp ground cardamom to the cake mixture and icing instead of the espresso powder.

601

MAKES 12

Lavender Buttercream Cupcakes

- Preheat the oven to 180°C (160° fan) / 350F / gas 4.
- Line a 12-hole cupcake tin with 12 cupcake cases.
- Beat together all the ingredients for the batter in a mixing bowl for 2 minutes until smooth and creamy.
- Divide evenly between the paper cases before rapping the tin on a work surface to help settle the batter.
- Bake for 15-18 minutes until risen.
- Remove to a wire rack to cool.
- Beat the softened butter in a mixing bowl for 3-4 minutes until pale.
- Add the icing sugar, lavender essence and drops of food colouring until you have an even, purple buttercream.
- Spoon into a piping bag.
- Pipe a rosette swirl in the centre of the cupcakes and surround with piped stars before garnishing with a Jelly Tot on top.

PREPARATION TIME 30 MINUTES

COOKING TIME 15-18 MINUTES

INGREDIENTS

110 g / 4 oz / ⅔ cup self-raising flour, sifted
110 g / 4 oz / ½ cup margarine, softened
110 g / 4 oz / ½ cup caster (superfine) sugar
1 tsp vanilla extract
2 large eggs
a pinch of salt

FOR THE BUTTERCREAM
100 g / 3 ½ oz / ½ cup butter, softened
200 g / 7 oz / 2 cups icing (confectioner's) sugar
a few drops of purple food colouring
5 drops of lavender essence

TO GARNISH
12 raspberry Jelly Tots

Framboise Cupcakes

602

- Substitute the purple food colouring and lavender essence for red colouring and 2 tbsp of framboise.

603

MAKES 12

Raspberry Truffle Cupcakes

PREPARATION TIME 30 MINUTES

COOKING TIME 15-18 MINUTES

INGREDIENTS

110 g / 4 oz / ⅔ cup self-raising flour, sifted
110 g / 4 oz / ½ cup margarine, softened
110 g / 4 oz / ½ cup caster (superfine) sugar
1 tsp vanilla extract
2 large eggs
a pinch of salt

FOR THE PINK BUTTERCREAM

100 g / 3 ½ oz / ½ cup butter, softened
200 g / 7 oz / 2 cups icing (confectioners') sugar
a few drops of pink food colouring
1 tbsp whole milk

TO GARNISH

12 raspberries

- Preheat the oven to 180°C (160° fan) / 350F / gas 4.
- Line a 12-hole cupcake tin with 12 cupcake cases.
- Beat together all the ingredients for the batter in a mixing bowl for 2 minutes until smooth and creamy.
- Divide evenly between the paper cases before rapping the tin on a work surface to help settle the batter.
- Bake for 15-18 minutes until risen; test with a wooden toothpick, if it comes out clean, the cakes are done.
- Remove to a wire rack to cool as you prepare the buttercream.
- Beat the softened butter with the icing sugar, food colouring and milk in a mixing bowl until smooth and creamy.
- Spoon into a piping bag fitted with a star-shaped nozzle and pipe in swirls on top of the cupcakes.
- Garnish the tops with a raspberry before serving.

604

Blackberry Truffle Cupcakes

- Substitute the raspberries for blackberries.

605

Tayberry Truffle Cupcakes

- Replace the raspberries with tayberries.

606

MAKES 12

Blueberry Cinnamon Cupcakes

- Preheat the oven to 180°C (160° fan) / 350F / gas 4.
- Line a 12-hole cupcake tin with 12 cupcake cases.
- Beat together all the ingredients for the batter in a mixing bowl for 2 minutes until smooth and creamy.
- Divide evenly between the paper cases before rapping the tin on a work surface to help settle the batter.
- Bake for 15-18 minutes until risen; test with a wooden toothpick, if it comes out clean, the cakes are done.
- Remove to a wire rack to cool as you prepare the icing.
- Beat the cream cheese with the icing sugar, lemon juice and drops of food colouring until you have an even purple icing.
- Spoon into a piping bag fitted with a large plain nozzle before piping spiral swirls on the cupcakes.
- Garnish the perimeter with blueberries before serving.

Red and Blue Cupcakes

607

- Use a mixture of raspberries and strawberries instead of blueberries for the fruit.

PREPARATION TIME 30 MINUTES

COOKING TIME 15-18 MINUTES

INGREDIENTS

110 g / 4 oz / ⅔ cup self-raising flour, sifted
110 g / 4 oz / ½ cup margarine, softened
110 g / 4 oz / ½ cup caster (superfine) sugar
1 tsp vanilla extract
1 tsp ground cinnamon
2 large eggs
a pinch of salt

FOR THE ICING
225 g / 8 oz / 1 cup cream cheese
180 g / 6 oz / 1 ½ cups icing (confectioner's) sugar
1 tbsp lemon juice
a few drops of blue food colouring

TO GARNISH
200 g / 7 oz / 2 cups blueberries

608

MAKES 12

Flower-Iced Blueberry Cupcakes

- Preheat the oven to 190°C (170° fan) / 375F / gas 5 and line a 12-hole cupcake tin with paper cases.
- Combine the flour, sugar, butter, eggs and vanilla extract in a bowl and whisk together for 2 minutes or until smooth.
- Fold in the blueberries and divide the mixture between the cases, then bake for 15 – 20 minutes.
- Transfer the cakes to a wire rack and leave to cool.
- Beat the butter until smooth, then gradually whisk in the icing sugar and vanilla extract.
- Spoon the mixture into a piping bag, fitted with a large.
- Hold the piping bag vertically above the first cake and pipe the icing in a spiral, without twisting the bag, so that it looks like a rose.
- Repeat with the other cakes and top each one with a blue sugar flower.

Flower-Iced Raspberry Cupcakes

609

- Replace the blueberries with raspberries and top each cake with a pink sugar flower.

PREPARATION TIME 30 MINUTES

COOKING TIME 15 - 20 MINUTES

INGREDIENTS

110 g / 4 oz / ⅔ cup self-raising flour, sifted
110 g / 4 oz / ½ cup caster (superfine) sugar
110 g / 4 oz / ½ cup butter, softened
2 large eggs
1 tsp vanilla extract
75 g / 2 ½ oz / ½ cup blueberries

TO DECORATE:
100 g / 3 ½ oz / ½ cup butter, softened
200 g / 7 oz / 2 cups icing (confectioners') sugar
1 tsp vanilla extract
12 blue sugar flowers with leaves

610

Greek Yoghurt Cupcakes

MAKES 12

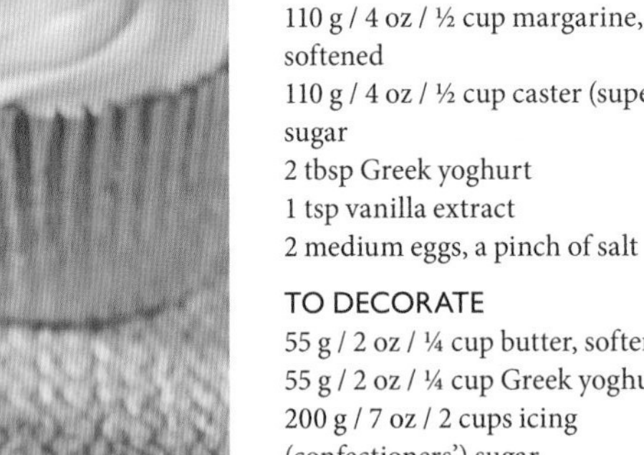

PREPARATION TIME 30 MINUTES

COOKING TIME 15-18 MINUTES

INGREDIENTS

110 g / 4 oz / ⅔ cup self-raising flour, sifted
110 g / 4 oz / ½ cup margarine, softened
110 g / 4 oz / ½ cup caster (superfine) sugar
2 tbsp Greek yoghurt
1 tsp vanilla extract
2 medium eggs, a pinch of salt

TO DECORATE
55 g / 2 oz / ¼ cup butter, softened
55 g / 2 oz / ¼ cup Greek yoghurt
200 g / 7 oz / 2 cups icing (confectioners') sugar
1 tbsp lemon juice
1 tsp pink edible glitter
12 sugar flowers

- Preheat the oven to 190°C (170° fan) / 375F / gas 5 and line a 12-hole cupcake tin with paper cases.
- Combine the cake ingredients and whisk together for 2 minutes.
- Divide the mixture between the cases and bake for 15 – 18 minutes.
- Test with a wooden toothpick, if it comes out clean, the cakes are done.
- Transfer the cakes to a wire rack and leave to cool.
- Beat the butter and yoghurt together then gradually incorporate the icing sugar and lemon juice.
- Pipe a swirl of icing onto each cake and top with the glitter and flowers.

Raspberry Greek Yoghurt Cupcakes

611

- Fold 100 g raspberries into the batter before baking.

612

Latte Butterfly Cupcakes

MAKES 12

PREPARATION TIME 30 MINUTES

COOKING TIME 15 - 20 MINUTES

INGREDIENTS

110 g / 4 oz / ⅔ cup self-raising flour, sifted
110 g / 4 oz / ½ cup caster (superfine) sugar
110 g / 4 oz / ½ cup butter, softened
2 large eggs
1 tbsp dried milk powder
1 tsp instant espresso powder

TO DECORATE:
100 g / 3 ½ oz / ½ cup butter, softened
200 g / 7 oz / 2 cups icing (confectioners') sugar
1 tsp instant espresso powder
12 sugar paste butterflies

- Preheat the oven to 190°C (170° fan) / 375F / gas 5 and line a 12-hole cupcake tin with paper cases.
- Combine the flour, sugar, butter, eggs, dried milk powder and espresso powder in a bowl and whisk together for 2 minutes or until smooth.
- Divide the mixture between the cases, then transfer the tin to the oven and bake for 15 – 20 minutes.
- Test with a wooden toothpick, if it comes out clean, the cakes are done.
- Transfer the cakes to a wire rack and leave to cool completely.
- Beat the butter until smooth, then gradually whisk in the icing sugar and espresso powder.
- Spoon the mixture into a piping bag, fitted with a large star nozzle, and pipe a swirl of icing on top of each cake. Finish each one with a sugar paste butterfly.

Lemon Butterfly Cupcakes

613

- Replace the espresso powder in the cake mixture with the grated zest of a lemon and add 1 tbsp of lemon juice to the icing instead of the espresso powder.

614

MAKES 12

Violet Sprinkle Cupcakes

Magenta Sprinkle Cupcakes

615

- Colour the icing magenta instead of violet.

Neon Sprinkle Cupcakes

616

- Colour the icing lime green and use bright pink sprinkles on top.

PREPARATION TIME 30 MINUTES

COOKING TIME 15-18 MINUTES

INGREDIENTS

110 g / 4 oz / ⅔ cup self-raising flour, sifted
110 g / 4 oz / ½ cup margarine, softened
110 g / 4 oz / ½ cup caster (superfine) sugar
1 tsp vanilla extract
2 large eggs
a pinch of salt

TO DECORATE

100 g / 3 ½ oz / ½ cup butter, softened
200 g / 7 oz / 2 cups icing (confectioners') sugar
1 tsp vanilla extract
a few drops of purple food colouring
1 tbsp purple sugar sprinkles

- Preheat the oven to 180°C (160° fan) / 350F / gas 4.
- Line a 12-hole cupcake tin with 12 cupcake cases.
- Beat together all the ingredients for the batter in a mixing bowl for 2 minutes until smooth and creamy.
- Divide evenly between the paper cases before rapping the tin on a work surface to help settle the batter.
- Bake for 15-18 minutes until risen; test with a wooden toothpick, if it comes out clean, the cakes are done.
- Remove to a wire rack to cool as you prepare the buttercream.
- Beat the softened butter in a mixing bowl for 3-4 minutes until pale.
- Add the icing sugar and vanilla extract, beating well before spooning a quarter of it into a piping bag fitted with a straight-sided nozzle.
- Add drops of the food colouring to the remaining buttercream, beating well until violet.
- Spread evenly on top of the cupcakes using a small palette knife.
- Pipe a blob of icing from the piping bag on top and garnish with a sprinkle of sugar sprinkles.

617

MAKES 12

Fruit and Cream Cupcakes

PREPARATION TIME 30 MINUTES

COOKING TIME 15-18 MINUTES

INGREDIENTS

110 g / 4 oz / ⅔ cup self-raising flour, sifted
110 g / 4 oz / ½ cup margarine
110 g / 4 oz / ½ cup caster (superfine) sugar
1 tsp vanilla extract
2 large eggs, a pinch of salt

TO DECORATE
300 ml / 10 ½ fl. oz / 1 1/4 cups double cream
1 tsp vanilla extract
12 physallis
12 raspberries
12 blackcurrants
1 kiwi fruit, cut into 12 pieces

- Preheat the oven to 180°C (160° fan) / 350F / gas 4.
- Line a 12-hole cupcake tin with 12 cupcake cases.
- Beat together all the ingredients for the batter in a mixing bowl for 2 minutes until smooth and creamy.
- Divide evenly between the paper cases before rapping the tin on a work surface to help settle the batter.
- Bake for 15-18 minutes until risen; test with a wooden toothpick, if it comes out clean, the cakes are done.
- Transfer the cakes to a wire rack and leave to cool.
- Whip the cream until it holds its shape then spread it liberally over the cakes.
- Top the cakes with the fruit and serve straight away.

618

MAKES 12

Strawberry Heart Chocolate Cupcakes

PREPARATION TIME 30 MINUTES

COOKING TIME 15 - 20 MINUTES

COOLING TIME 1 HOUR

INGREDIENTS

110 g / 4 oz / ⅔ cup self-raising flour, sifted
110 g / 4 oz / ½ cup caster (superfine) sugar
110 g / 4 oz / ½ cup butter, softened
2 large eggs
1 tsp vanilla extract
200 g / 7 oz / ⅔ cup strawberry jam (jelly)

TO DECORATE:
300 ml / 10 ½ fl. oz / 1 ¼ cups double (heavy) cream
200 g / 7 oz dark chocolate, minimum 60% cocoa solids, chopped
12 red edible glitter sugar hearts

- Preheat the oven to 190°C (170° fan) / 375F / gas 5 and line a 12-hole cupcake tin with paper cases.
- Combine the flour, sugar, butter, eggs and vanilla extract in a bowl and whisk together for 2 minutes or until smooth.
- Divide half the mixture between the cases and add a big spoonful of jam to each one.
- Top with the rest of the cake mixture, then transfer the tin to the oven and bake for 15 – 20 minutes.
- Test with a wooden toothpick, if it comes out clean, the cakes are done.
- Transfer the cakes to a wire rack and leave to cool completely.
- Heat half of the cream until it starts to simmer, then pour it over the chopped chocolate and stir until smooth. Leave to cool to room temperature, then combine with the rest of the cream and whisk until it holds its shape.
- Spoon the chocolate cream into a piping bag fitted with a large star nozzle and pipe a swirl on top of each cake. Decorate with the sugar hearts.

619

MAKES 12

Fondant Rose Cupcakes

- Preheat the oven to 190°C (170° fan) / 375F / gas 5.
- Line a 12-hole cupcake tin with foil cases.
- Combine the cake ingredients and whisk together for 2 minutes.
- Divide the mixture between the cases and bake for 15 – 20 minutes.
- Transfer the cakes to a wire rack and leave to cool.
- Roll out the icing and cut out 12 circles.
- Wet the backs and stick them to the cakes, then top with the rose buds.

PREPARATION TIME 30 MINUTES

COOKING TIME 15-20 MINUTES

INGREDIENTS

110 g / 4 oz / 2/3 cup self-raising flour, sifted
110 g / 4 oz / ½ cup caster (superfine) sugar
110 g / 4 oz / ½ cup butter, softened
2 large eggs
1 tbsp rose water
To decorate:
200 g / 7 oz ready to roll pink fondant icing
12 dried rose buds

620

White Almond Cupcakes

MAKES 12

PREPARATION TIME 30 MINUTES

COOKING TIME 15-20 MINUTES

INGREDIENTS

110 g / 4 oz / 2/3 cup self-raising flour, sifted
110 g / 4 oz / ½ cup caster (superfine) sugar
110 g / 4 oz / ½ cup butter, softened
2 large eggs
½ tsp almond essence
To decorate:
200 g / 7 oz ready to roll fondant icing
12 white carnations

- Preheat the oven to 190°C (170° fan) / 375F / gas 5.
- Line a 12-hole cupcake tin with foil cases.
- Combine the cake ingredients and whisk together for 2 minutes.
- Divide the mixture between the cases and bake for 15 – 20 minutes.
- Transfer the cakes to a wire rack and leave to cool.
- Roll out the icing and cut out 12 circles.
- Wet the backs and stick them to the cakes, then top with the carnations.

621

Blueberry and Chocolate Cakes

MAKES 12

PREPARATION TIME 30 MINUTES

COOKING TIME 15 - 20 MINUTES

INGREDIENTS

110 g / 4 oz / ⅔ cup self-raising flour, sifted
110 g / 4 oz / ½ cup dark brown sugar
110 g / 4 oz / ½ cup butter, softened
2 large eggs
2 tbsp unsweetened cocoa powder
75 g / 2 ½ oz / ½ cup blueberries
110 g / 4 oz / ½ cup cream cheese
55 g / 2 oz / ¼ cup butter, softened
110 g / 4 oz / 1 cup icing (confectioners') sugar
3 tbsp blueberry syrup
gold sugar pearls to decorate

- Preheat the oven to 190°C (170° fan) / 375F / gas 5 and line a 12-hole cupcake tin with paper cases.
- Combine the flour, sugar, butter, eggs and cocoa in a bowl and whisk together for 2 minutes or until smooth.
- Fold in the blueberries then divide the mixture between the cases and bake for 15 – 20 minutes.
- Test with a wooden toothpick, if it comes out clean, the cakes are done.
- Transfer the cakes to a wire rack and leave to cool completely.
- Beat the cream cheese and butter together until light and fluffy then beat in the icing sugar a quarter at a time.
- Add the blueberry syrup then whip the mixture for 2 minutes or until smooth and light.
- Spoon the icing into a piping bag, fitted with a large star nozzle, and pipe a swirl of icing on top of each cake. Decorate with gold pearls.

622

MAKES 12

Smarties Buttercream Cupcakes

PREPARATION TIME 30 MINUTES

COOKING TIME 15 - 20 MINUTES

INGREDIENTS

110 g / 4 oz / ⅔ cup self-raising flour, sifted
110 g / 4 oz / ½ cup caster (superfine) sugar
110 g / 4 oz / ½ cup butter, softened
2 large eggs
½ tsp vanilla extract

TO DECORATE:
100 g / 3 ½ oz / ½ cup butter, softened
200 g / 7 oz / 2 cups icing (confectioners') sugar
food colouring of your choice
Smarties to decorate

- Preheat the oven to 190°C (170° fan) / 375F / gas 5.
- Line a 12-hole cupcake tin with paper cases.
- Combine the cake ingredients and whisk for 2 minutes.
- Divide the mixture between the cases and bake for 15 – 20 minutes.
- Transfer the cakes to a wire rack and leave to cool.
- Beat the butter until smooth, then gradually whisk in the icing sugar and any food colouring of your choice.
- Pipe or spread the icing on top of the cakes and decorate with Smarties.

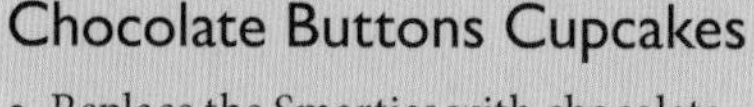

Chocolate Buttons Cupcakes

623

- Replace the Smarties with chocolate buttons

624

MAKES 12

Violet Lemon Jelly Bean Cupcakes

PREPARATION TIME 30 MINUTES

COOKING TIME 15-18 MINUTES

INGREDIENTS

110 g / 4 oz / ⅔ cup self-raising flour, sifted
110 g / 4 oz / ½ cup margarine, softened
110 g / 4 oz / ½ cup caster (superfine) sugar
1 tsp lemon extract
2 large eggs
a pinch of salt

TO DECORATE
225 g / 8 oz / 1 cup unsalted butter, softened
180 g / 6 oz / 1 ½ cups icing (confectioner's) sugar
1 tsp violet extract
a few drops of purple food colouring

TO GARNISH
36 pink jelly beans

- Preheat the oven to 190°C (170° fan) / 375F / gas 5 and line a 12-hole cupcake tin with paper cases.
- Combine the cake ingredients and whisk together for 2 minutes.
- Divide the mixture between the cases and bake for 15 – 18 minutes.
- Test with a wooden toothpick, if it comes out clean, the cakes are done.
- Transfer the cakes to a wire rack and leave to cool.
- Beat the butter with the icing sugar and violet extract until smooth then pipe two thirds of the icing onto the cupcakes.
- Colour the remaining icing violet and pipe a ring of stars around the edge of each cake before topping with the jelly beans.

Violet Meringue Cupcakes

625

- Substitute the jelly beans for crushed ready-made meringue.

626

MAKES 12

Lavender Pillow Cupcakes

- Preheat the oven to 190°C (170° fan) / 375F / gas 5 and line a 12-hole cupcake tin with paper cases.
- Combine the cake ingredients and whisk together for 2 minutes.
- Divide the mixture between the cases and bake for 15 – 18 minutes.
- Test with a wooden toothpick, if it comes out clean, the cakes are done.
- Transfer the cakes to a wire rack and leave to cool.
- Beat the butter with the icing sugar, vanilla extract and lavender extract until smooth then set aside two thirds of the icing.
- Colour the remaining icing pale purple and spread it over the cakes.
- Pipe the reserved white icing onto the cakes and dip the tops in lavender sugar.

PREPARATION TIME 30 MINUTES

COOKING TIME 15-18 MINUTES

INGREDIENTS

110 g / 4 oz / ⅔ cup self-raising flour, sifted
110 g / 4 oz / ½ cup margarine, softened
110 g / 4 oz / ½ cup caster (superfine) sugar
1 tsp lemon extract
2 large eggs
a pinch of salt

FOR THE BUTTERCREAM
100 g / 3 ½ oz / ½ cup butter, softened
200 g / 7 oz / 2 cups icing (confectioners') sugar
½ tsp vanilla extract
½ tsp edible lavender extract
a few drops of purple food colouring
1 tbsp lavender sugar

Lavender and Lemon Cupcakes

627

- Drizzle the cupcakes with lemon curd before serving.

628

MAKES 12

Apricot Buttercream Cupcakes

- Preheat the oven to 190°C (170° fan) / 375F / gas 5 and line a 12-hole cupcake tin with paper cases.
- Combine the flour, sugar, butter, eggs and apricot syrup in a bowl and whisk together for 2 minutes or until smooth.
- Divide the mixture between the cases, then transfer the tin to the oven and bake for 15 – 20 minutes.
- Test with a wooden toothpick, if it comes out clean, the cakes are done.
- Transfer the cakes to a wire rack and leave to cool completely.
- Beat the butter until smooth, then gradually whisk in the icing sugar and apricot syrup.
- Spoon the mixture into a piping bag, fitted with a large star nozzle, and pipe a swirl of icing on top of each cake, then top with the silver balls.

PREPARATION TIME 30 MINUTES

COOKING TIME 15 - 20 MINUTES

INGREDIENTS

110 g / 4 oz / ⅔ cup self-raising flour, sifted
110 g / 4 oz / ½ cup caster (superfine) sugar
110 g / 4 oz / ½ cup butter, softened
2 large eggs
2 tbsp apricot syrup

TO DECORATE:
100 g / 3 ½ oz / ½ cup butter, softened
200 g / 7 oz / 2 cups icing (confectioners') sugar
2 tbsp apricot syrup
edible silver balls to decorate

Dried Apricot Buttercream Cupcakes

629

- Add 75 g of chopped dried apricots to the cake mixture.

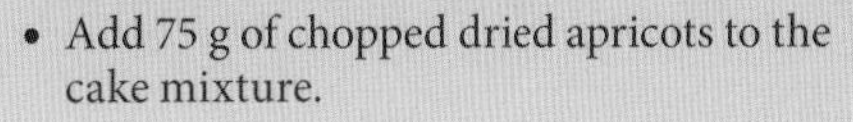

630

MAKES 12

Fondant Flower Cupcakes

PREPARATION TIME 1 HOUR

COOKING TIME 15 - 20 MINUTES

INGREDIENTS

110 g / 4 oz / ⅔ cup self-raising flour, sifted
110 g / 4 oz / ½ cup caster (superfine) sugar
110 g / 4 oz / ½ cup butter, softened
2 large eggs
1 tsp vanilla extract

TO DECORATE:
200 g / 7 oz / 2 cups icing (confectioners') sugar
200 g / 7 oz ready to roll fondant icing
a few drops of yellow and pink icing
icing (confectioners') sugar for dusting

- Preheat the oven to 190°C (170° fan) / 375F / gas 5 and line a 12-hole cupcake tin with paper cases.
- Combine the flour, sugar, butter, eggs and vanilla in a bowl and whisk together for 2 minutes or until smooth.
- Divide the mixture between the cases, then transfer the tin to the oven and bake for 15 – 20 minutes.
- Test with a wooden toothpick, if it comes out clean, the cakes are done.
- Transfer the cakes to a wire rack and leave to cool completely.
- Sieve the icing sugar into a bowl and add just enough water to make a thick, pourable icing, then spoon the icing onto the cakes.
- Divide the fondant icing into 2 pieces and knead a little food colouring into each.
- Dust the work surface lightly with icing sugar and roll out the icing, then use a small blossom plunger cutter to cut out the flowers, pressing them out directly onto the cakes.

Elderflower Cupcakes

631

- Add 2 tbsp of elderflower cordial to the cake mixture and colour the fondant icing pale cream.

Forget-me-not Cupcakes

632

- Colour the fondant icing blue and pipe a yellow icing dot into the centre of each one.

633

MAKES 12

Dairy-Free Party Cupcakes

- Preheat the oven to 180°C (160° fan) / 350F / gas 4 and double line a 12-hole cupcake tin with silicone and paper cases.
- Beat the egg in a jug with the vanilla extract, oil and coconut milk until well mixed.
- Mix the flour, baking powder and sugar in a bowl, then pour in the egg mixture and stir just enough to combine.
- Divide the mixture between the cases, then bake in the oven for 20 – 25 minutes.
- Transfer the cakes to a wire rack and leave to cool.
- Sieve the icing sugar into a bowl and add just enough water to make a thick, spreadable icing.
- Spoon it onto the cakes, then decorate with rainbow drops and edible silver balls. Top each cake with a candle.

PREPARATION TIME 30 MINUTES

COOKING TIME 20 – 25 MINUTES

INGREDIENTS

1 large egg
1 tsp vanilla extract
125 ml / 4 ½ fl. oz / ½ cup sunflower oil
125 ml / 4 ½ fl. oz / ½ cup coconut milk
375 g / 13 oz / 2 ½ cups self-raising flour, sifted
1 tsp baking powder
200 g / 7 oz / ¾ cup caster (superfine) sugar

TO DECORATE:
200 g / 7 oz / 2 cups icing (confectioners') sugar
rainbow drops and edible silver balls
12 candles

Dairy and Gluten-Free Party Cupcakes

634

- Replace the self-raising flour with gluten-free plain flour and double the amount of baking powder.

635

MAKES 12

Jelly Mint Cupcakes

- Preheat the oven to 190°C (170° fan) / 375F / gas 5 and line a 12-hole cupcake tin with paper cases.
- Combine the cake ingredients and whisk together for 2 minutes.
- Divide the mixture between the cases and bake for 15 – 18 minutes.
- Test with a wooden toothpick, if it comes out clean, the cakes are done.
- Transfer the cakes to a wire rack and leave to cool.
- Beat the butter with the icing sugar, vanilla extract and peppermint extract until smooth then set aside two thirds of the icing.
- Colour the remaining icing pale pink and spread it over the cakes.
- Colour the reserved icing pale green and pipe it in a ruffle on top of the cakes.
- Top each cake with a jelly tot.

PREPARATION TIME 30 MINUTES

COOKING TIME 15-18 MINUTES

INGREDIENTS

110 g / 4 oz / ⅔ cup self-raising flour, sifted
110 g / 4 oz / ½ cup margarine, softened
110 g / 4 oz / ½ cup caster (superfine) sugar
1 tsp vanilla extract
2 large eggs
a pinch of salt

TO DECORATE
100 g / 3 ½ oz / ½ cup butter, softened
200 g / 7 oz / 2 cups icing (confectioners') sugar
½ tsp peppermint extract
a few drops of red food colouring
a few drops of green food colouring
12 raspberry Jelly Tots

Humbug Cupcakes

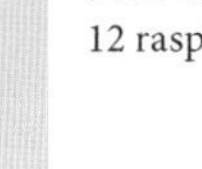

636

- Top each cupcake with a humbug instead of the jelly tot.

637

Coconut and Orange Cream Cupcakes

MAKES 12

PREPARATION TIME 30 MINUTES

COOKING TIME 15 – 20 MINUTES

INGREDIENTS

1 orange, juiced
28 g / 1 oz / 1/8 cup desiccated coconut
110 g / 4 oz / 1 cup self-raising flour, sifted
110 g / 4 oz / ½ cup caster (superfine) sugar
110 g / 4 oz / ½ cup butter, softened
2 large eggs

TO DECORATE:
225 ml / 8 fl. oz / ¾ cup double (heavy) cream
2 tbsp icing (confectioners') sugar
2 tbsp sweetened shredded coconut
1 orange, zest finely pared

- Preheat the oven to 190°C (170° fan) / 375F / gas 5 and line a 12-hole cupcake tin with paper cases.
- Pour the orange juice over the coconut and leave to soak for 10 minutes.
- Combine the flour, sugar, butter, eggs and coconut mixture in a bowl and whisk together for 2 minutes.
- Divide the mixture between the paper cases, then transfer the tin to the oven and bake for 15 – 20 minutes.
- Transfer the cakes to a wire rack and leave to cool.
- To make the topping, whisk the cream with the icing sugar until it forms soft peaks.
- Spoon the whipped cream into a piping bag fitted with a large star nozzle and pipe a swirl on top of each cake.
- Sprinkle each cake with shredded coconut and orange zest.

Coconut and Lemon Cream Cupcakes

638

- Replace the orange juice and zest with lemon juice and zest.

639

Malteser Mint Cupcakes

MAKES 12

PREPARATION TIME 30 MINUTES

COOKING TIME 15-18 MINUTES

INGREDIENTS

110 g / 4 oz / ⅔ cup self-raising flour, sifted
110 g / 4 oz / ½ cup margarine
110 g / 4 oz / ½ cup caster (superfine) sugar
55 g / 2 oz / ⅓ cup cocoa powder
55 ml / 2 fl. oz / ¼ cup whole milk
2 large eggs, a pinch of salt

TO DECORATE
100 g / 3 ½ oz / ½ cup butter, softened
200 g / 7 oz / 2 cups icing (confectioners') sugar
a few drops of peppermint essence
2 tbsp cocoa powder
2 tbsp milk
12 Maltesers
12 sprigs of mint

- Preheat the oven to 180°C (160° fan) / 350F / gas 4.
- Line a 12-hole cupcake tin with 12 cupcake cases.
- Beat together all the ingredients for the batter apart from the milk in a mixing bowl for 2 minutes.
- Add the milk and beat again for a further minute.
- Divide evenly between the paper cases.
- Bake for 15-18 minutes. Transfer the cakes to a wire rack and leave to cool.
- Beat the butter with the icing sugar and peppermint essence until smooth.
- Set aside a third of the buttercream and whisk the cocoa and milk into the rest.
- Pipe a ring of cocoa buttercream round the edge of each cake, then spoon the plain buttercream into the centres.
- Top with the Maltesers and mint.

Softmint and Cocoa Cupcakes

640

- Substitute the Malteser on top for a softmint and a dusting of cocoa powder.

641

MAKES 12

Glacé-Iced Rose Petal Cupcakes

Glacé-Iced Violet Cupcakes

642

- Replace the crystallised rose petals with crystallised violets and use violet syrup in place of the rose water.

Crystallised Ginger Cupcakes

643

- Flavour the cakes and icing with ginger syrup and top the cakes with crystallised ginger.

PREPARATION TIME 30 MINUTES

COOKING TIME 15 - 20 MINUTES

INGREDIENTS

110 g / 4 oz / 2/3 cup self-raising flour, sifted
110 g / 4 oz / ½ cup caster (superfine) sugar
110 g / 4 oz / ½ cup butter, softened
2 large eggs
1 tbsp rose water
3 tbsp crystallised rose petals

To decorate:
200 g / 7 oz / 2 cups icing (confectioners') sugar
1 – 2 tsp rose water
a few drops pink food colouring
12 crystallised rose petals

- Preheat the oven to 190°C (170° fan) / 375F / gas 5 and line a 12-hole cupcake tin with paper cases.
- Combine the cake ingredients and whisk together for 2 minutes or until smooth.
- Divide the mixture between the cases, then transfer the tin to the oven and bake for 15 – 20 minutes.
- Test with a wooden toothpick, if it comes out clean, the cakes are done.
- Transfer the cakes to a wire rack and leave to cool.
- Sieve the icing sugar into a bowl and add just enough rose water to make a thick, pourable icing.
- Colour the icing with a few drops of food colouring, then spoon it onto the cakes and top each one with a crystallised rose petal.

644

MAKES 12

Mint Truffle Cupcakes

PREPARATION TIME 30 MINUTES

COOKING TIME 15-18 MINUTES

INGREDIENTS

110 g / 4 oz / ⅔ cup self-raising flour, sifted
110 g / 4 oz / ½ cup margarine
110 g / 4 oz / ½ cup caster (superfine) sugar
1 tsp vanilla extract
2 large eggs, a pinch of salt

TO DECORATE
200 g / 7 oz / 1 cup butter, softened
400 g / 14 oz / 4 cups icing (confectioners') sugar
a few drops of peppermint essence
2 tbsp cocoa powder
2 tbsp milk
a few drops of green food colouring
12 Minstrels
multi-coloured sugar strands

- Preheat the oven to 180°C (160° fan) / 350F / gas 4.
- Line a 12-hole cupcake tin with 12 cupcake cases.
- Beat together all the ingredients for the batter.
- Divide evenly between the paper cases.
- Bake for 15-18 minutes. Transfer the cakes to a wire rack and leave to cool.
- Beat the butter with the icing sugar and peppermint essence until smooth.
- Set aside a third of the buttercream and whisk the cocoa and milk into the rest.
- Pipe a swirl of cocoa buttercream onto each cake.
- Colour the reserved icing green and pipe it on top then garnish with Minstrels and sugar strands.

645

Double Chocolate and Mint Cupcakes

- Substitute the sugar strands with grated white chocolate.

646

MAKES 12

Choc-chip Cream Cheese Muffin Cupcakes

PREPARATION TIME 35 MINUTES

COOKING TIME 20 – 25 MINUTES

INGREDIENTS

1 large egg
125 ml / 4 ½ fl. oz / ½ cup sunflower oil
125 ml / 4 ½ fl. oz / ½ cup milk
375 g / 13 oz / 2 ½ cups self-raising flour, sifted
1 tsp baking powder
200 g / 7 oz / ¾ cup caster (superfine) sugar
150 g / 5 ½ oz dark chocolate chips (minimum 60% cocoa solids)

TO DECORATE:
110 g / 4 oz / ½ cup cream cheese
55 g / 2 oz / ¼ cup butter, softened
110 g / 4 oz / 1 cup icing (confectioners') sugar
1 tsp vanilla extract
50 g / 1 ¾ oz dark chocolate (minimum 60 % cocoa solids), chopped
12 chocolate cigarillos

- Preheat the oven to 180°C (160° fan) / 350F / gas 4 and line a 12-hole cupcake tin with paper cases.
- Beat the egg in a jug with the oil and milk.
- Mix the flour, baking powder and sugar in a bowl, then pour in the egg mixture and chocolate chips and stir just enough to combine.
- Divide the mixture between the cases and bake for 20 – 25 minutes.
- Transfer the cakes to a wire rack and leave to cool.
- Beat the cream cheese and butter together until smooth then beat in the icing sugar a quarter at a time.
- Beat the cream cheese with the butter until smooth, then incorporate the icing sugar and vanilla extract and whip until light.
- Melt the chocolate and drizzle it over the cakes then top each one with a chocolate cigarillo.

647

Orange Cream Cheese Muffin Cupcakes

- Replace the chocolate chips with chopped candied orange peel and add the finely grated zest of a fresh orange.

648

MAKES 12

Peppermint Sugar Cupcakes

- Preheat the oven to 180°C (160° fan) / 350F / gas 4.
- Line a 12-hole cupcake tin with 12 cupcake cases.
- Beat together all the ingredients for the batter.
- Divide evenly between the paper cases.
- Bake for 15-18 minutes. Transfer the cakes to a wire rack and leave to cool.
- Beat the butter with the icing sugar, peppermint essence and food colouring until smooth.
- Set aside half of the buttercream and spread the rest over the cakes. Sprinkle with green sugar.
- Pipe the reserved buttercream around the edge of the cakes.

PREPARATION TIME 30 MINUTES

COOKING TIME 15-18 MINUTES

INGREDIENTS

110 g / 4 oz / ⅔ cup self-raising flour, sifted
110 g / 4 oz / ½ cup margarine, softened
110 g / 4 oz / ½ cup caster (superfine) sugar
1 tsp vanilla extract
2 large eggs
a pinch of salt

TO DECORATE
200 g / 7 oz / 1 cup butter, softened
400 g / 14 oz / 4 cups icing (confectioners') sugar
a few drops of peppermint essence
a few drops of green food colouring
1 tbsp green sugar sprinkles

Mint and Grated Chocolate Cupcakes

649

- Garnish the middle of the cupcakes with grated chocolate instead of green sugar crystals.

650

MAKES 12

Peanut Buttercream Cupcakes

- Preheat the oven to 190°C (170° fan) / 375F / gas 5 and line a 12-hole cupcake tin with paper cases.
- Combine the flour, sugar, butter, eggs and peanut butter in a bowl and whisk together for 2 minutes or until smooth.
- Divide the mixture between the cases, then transfer the tin to the oven and bake for 15 – 20 minutes.
- Test with a wooden toothpick, if it comes out clean, the cakes are done.
- Transfer the cakes to a wire rack and leave to cool completely.
- Beat the butter and peanut butter until smooth, then gradually whisk in the icing sugar.
- Spoon the mixture into a piping bag, fitted with a medium star nozzle, and pipe a spiral of icing on top of each cake, then top each one with a candle.

PREPARATION TIME 30 MINUTES

COOKING TIME 15 - 20 MINUTES

INGREDIENTS

110 g / 4 oz / ⅔ cup self-raising flour, sifted
110 g / 4 oz / ½ cup caster (superfine) sugar
110 g / 4 oz / ½ cup butter, softened
2 large eggs
4 tbsp crunchy peanut butter

TO DECORATE:
50 g / 1 ¾ oz / ¼ cup butter, softened
50 g / 1 ¾ oz / ¼ cup crunchy peanut butter
200 g / 7 oz / 2 cups icing (confectioners') sugar
12 candles

Peanut and Lime Buttercream Cupcakes

651

- Add the grated zest of a lime to the cake mixture and add the grated zest and juice of half a lime to the buttercream.

652

MAKES 12

Chocolate Vermicelli Cupcakes

Chocolate Chip Vermicelli Cupcakes

653

- Add 50 g of white chocolate chips and 50 g of milk chocolate chips to the cake mixture.

Chocolate Orange Vermicelli Cupcakes

654

- Add the grated zest of an orange to the cake mixture.

PREPARATION TIME 30 MINUTES

COOKING TIME 15 - 20 MINUTES

INGREDIENTS

110 g / 4 oz / ⅔ cup self-raising flour, sifted
110 g / 4 oz / ½ cup caster (superfine) sugar
110 g / 4 oz / ½ cup butter, softened
2 large eggs
2 tbsp unsweetened cocoa powder

TO DECORATE:
200 g / 7 oz / 2 cups icing (confectioners') sugar
2 tbsp unsweetened cocoa powder
dark and white chocolate vermicelli for sprinkling

- Preheat the oven to 190°C (170° fan) / 375F / gas 5 and line a 12-hole cupcake tin with paper cases.
- Combine the flour, sugar, butter, eggs and cocoa in a bowl and whisk together for 2 minutes or until smooth.
- Divide the mixture between the cases, then transfer the tin to the oven and bake for 15 – 20 minutes.
- Test with a wooden toothpick, if it comes out clean, the cakes are done.
- Transfer the cakes to a wire rack and leave to cool completely.
- Sieve the icing sugar and cocoa together then add just enough water to make a thick pourable icing.
- Spoon the icing onto the cakes and sprinkle with chocolate vermicelli.

655

Flower Water Glacé Icing for Cupcakes

MAKES ENOUGH TO ICE 12 CUPCAKES

- Sieve the icing sugar into a bowl to remove any lumps then and add just enough flower water to make a thick but pourable icing.
- At this stage you can add a few drops of a coordinating food colouring. Stir until any streaks of colour disappear.
- Spoon the icing onto your cupcakes until the whole of the top is covered by a 3 – 5 mm layer.
- Decorate the cakes with sugar flowers, sweets or cake sprinkles while the icing is still wet, then leave to set for 1 – 2 hours.

PREPARATION TIME 10 MINUTES

SETTING TIME 1 – 2 HOURS

INGREDIENTS

200 g / 7 oz / 2 cups icing (confectioners') sugar
1 – 2 tsp rose water, orange flower water or violet syrup
a few drops of food colouring (optional)

Citrus Glacé Icing for Cupcakes

656

- Follow the same method, using orange, lemon, lime or grapefruit juice in place of the flower water.

657

Mint Julep Cupcakes

MAKES 12

- Preheat the oven to 180°C (160° fan) / 350F / gas 4.
- Line a 12-hole cupcake tin with 12 cupcake cases.
- Beat together all the ingredients for the batter.
- Divide evenly between the paper cases. Bake for 15-18 minutes.
- Transfer the cakes to a wire rack and leave to cool.
- Beat the butter with the icing sugar and peppermint essence until smooth.
- Set aside two thirds of the buttercream and spread the rest over the cakes.
- Colour the reserved buttercream green and pipe a swirl in the centre of each cake.
- Top the cakes with a jelly bean, a sprig of mint and a straw.

PREPARATION TIME 30 MINUTES

COOKING TIME 15-18 MINUTES

INGREDIENTS

110 g / 4 oz / ⅔ cup self-raising flour, sifted
110 g / 4 oz / ½ cup margarine
110 g / 4 oz / ½ cup caster (superfine) sugar
1 tsp vanilla extract
2 large eggs, a pinch of salt

TO DECORATE

200 g / 7 oz / 1 cup butter, softened
400 g / 14 oz / 4 cups icing (confectioners') sugar
a few drops of peppermint essence
a few drops of green food colouring
12 red jelly beans
mint sprigs and straws to garnish

Mint and Bailey's Cupcakes

658

- "Add 2 tbsp of Bailey's to the buttercream.

659

MAKES 12

Chocolate Mint Dream Cupcakes

PREPARATION TIME 10 MINUTES

COOKING TIME 20 MINUTES

INGREDIENTS

FOR THE BATTER
110 g / 4 oz / ⅔ cup self-raising flour
110 g / 4 oz / ½ cup margarine
110 g / 4 oz / ½ cup caster (superfine) sugar
55 g / 2 oz / ⅓ cup cocoa powder
55 ml / 2 fl. oz / ¼ cup whole milk
2 large eggs, a pinch of salt

TO DECORATE
200 g / 7 oz / 1 cup butter, softened
400 g / 14 oz / 4 cups icing (confectioners') sugar
a few drops of peppermint essence
a few drops of green food colouring
12 chocolate cigarillos
24 pieces of chocolate
cocoa powder for dusting

- Preheat the oven to 180°C (160° fan) / 350F / gas 4.
- Line a 12-hole cupcake tin with 12 cupcake cases.
- Beat together all the ingredients for the batter apart from the milk in a mixing bowl for 2 minutes.
- Add the milk and beat again for a further minute.
- Divide evenly between the paper cases before rapping the tin on a work surface to help settle the batter.
- Bake for 15-18 minutes. Transfer the cakes to a wire rack and leave to cool.
- Beat the butter with the icing sugar, peppermint essence and food colouring until smooth then pipe it onto the cakes.
- Top each cake with a cigarillo, 2 pieces of chocolate and a dusting of cocoa.

660

Cocoa, Mint and Raspberry Cupcakes

- Substitute the mini chocolate bars, cigarillos and cocoa powder with 3-4 raspberries on top.

661

MAKES 12

Smartie Truffle Cupcakes

PREPARATION TIME 30 MINUTES

COOKING TIME 15-18 MINUTES

INGREDIENTS

110 g / 4 oz / ⅔ cup self-raising flour, sifted
110 g / 4 oz / ½ cup margarine, softened
110 g / 4 oz / ½ cup caster (superfine) sugar
55 g / 2 oz / ⅓ cup cocoa powder
55 ml / 2 fl. oz / ¼ cup whole milk
2 large eggs
a pinch of salt

TO DECORATE
200 g / 7 oz / 1 cup butter, softened
400 g / 14 oz / 4 cups icing (confectioners') sugar
2 tbsp cocoa powder
1 tbsp milk
green Smarties to decorate

- Preheat the oven to 180°C (160° fan) / 350F / gas 4.
- Line a 12-hole cupcake tin with 12 cupcake cases.
- Beat together all the ingredients for the batter apart from the milk in a mixing bowl for 2 minutes.
- Add the milk and beat again for a further minute.
- Divide evenly between the paper cases.
- Bake for 15-18 minutes. Transfer the cakes to a wire rack and leave to cool.
- Beat the butter with the icing sugar, cocoa and milk until smooth.
- Pipe a ruffle of buttercream onto each cake and decorate with green Smarties.

662

Cigarillo and Smartie Cupcakes

- Add a white and dark chocolate cigarillo to each cupcake.

663

MAKES 12

White Chocolate Muffin Cupcakes

White Chocolate Orange Muffin Cupcakes

664

- Add the grated zest of an orange to the cake mixture and decorate the tops with chopped candied orange peel instead of the sweets.

White Chocolate Lemon Muffin Cupcakes

665

- Add the grated zest of a lemon to the cake mixture and decorate the tops with chopped candied lemon peel instead of the sweets.

PREPARATION TIME 15 MINUTES

COOKING TIME 20 – 25 MINUTES

INGREDIENTS

1 large egg
125 ml / 4 ½ fl. oz / ½ cup sunflower oil
125 ml / 4 ½ fl. oz / ½ cup milk
375 g / 13 oz / 2 ½ cups self-raising flour, sifted
1 tsp baking powder
200 g / 7 oz / ¾ cup caster (superfine) sugar
150 g / 5 ½ oz white chocolate, roughly chopped

TO DECORATE:
100 g / 3 ½ oz white chocolate, chopped
hundreds and thousands, Rainbow Drops and Smarties

- Preheat the oven to 180°C (160° fan) / 350F / gas 4 and line a 12-hole cupcake tin with silicone cases.
- Beat the egg in a jug with the oil and milk until well mixed.
- Mix the flour, baking powder and sugar in a bowl, then pour in the egg mixture.
- Melt half of the white chocolate in a microwave or bain marie and add to the bowl with the remaining chocolate.
- Stir everything together just enough to combine then divide between the cases and bake for 20 – 25 minutes.
- Test with a wooden toothpick, if it comes out clean, the cakes are done.
- Transfer the cakes to a wire rack and leave to cool completely.
- Melt the chocolate in a microwave or bain marie and dip the top of each cupcake in to coat.
- Decorate the tops with hundreds and thousands, Rainbow Drops or Smarties.

666

Ginger Cream Cheese Cupcakes

MAKES 12

PREPARATION TIME 30 MINUTES

COOKING TIME 15 - 20 MINUTES

INGREDIENTS

110 g / 4 oz / ⅔ cup self-raising flour, sifted
110 g / 4 oz / ½ cup caster (superfine) sugar
110 g / 4 oz / ½ cup butter, softened
2 large eggs
1 tsp ground ginger
50 g / 1 ¾ oz / ⅓ cup stem ginger, finely chopped

TO DECORATE:
110 g / 4 oz / ½ cup cream cheese
55 g / 2 oz / ¼ cup butter, softened
110 g / 4 oz / 1 cup icing (confectioners') sugar
1 tbsp syrup from the stem ginger jar
small sweets and cake sprinkles to decorate

- Preheat the oven to 190°C (170° fan) / 375F / gas 5 and line a 12-hole cupcake tin with paper cases.
- Combine the flour, sugar, butter, eggs, ground ginger and stem ginger in a bowl and whisk together for 2 minutes or until smooth.
- Divide the mixture between the cases, then transfer the tin to the oven and bake for 15 – 20 minutes.
- Test with a wooden toothpick, if it comes out clean, the cakes are done.
- Transfer the cakes to a wire rack and leave to cool completely.
- Beat the cream cheese and butter together until light and fluffy then beat in the icing sugar a quarter at a time.
- Add the ginger syrup then whip the mixture for 2 minutes or until smooth and light.
- Spoon the icing into a piping bag fitted with a star nozzle and pipe a swirl onto each cake then decorate with the sweets and cake sprinkles.

667

Ginger and Lemon Cream Cheese Cupcakes

- Add the grated zest of a lemon to the cake mixture and 1 tbsp lemon juice to the icing. Top with roughly chopped crystallised ginger.

668

Ginger Cheesecake Cupcakes

- Top the cupcakes with crumbled ginger nut biscuits instead of the sweets.

669

MAKES 12

Chocolate, Raspberry and Kiwi Cupcakes

- Preheat the oven to 180°C (160° fan) / 350F / gas 4.
- Line a 12-hole cupcake tin with 12 cupcake cases.
- Beat together all the ingredients for the batter in a mixing bowl for 2 minutes until smooth and creamy.
- Divide evenly between the paper cases before rapping the tin on a work surface to help settle the batter.
- Bake for 15-18 minutes until risen; test with a wooden toothpick, if it comes out clean, the cakes are done.
- Remove to a wire rack to cool as you prepare the cream.
- Whip the cream with the icing sugar and vanilla extract until almost clotted.
- Spoon on top of the cupcakes and garnish with the fruit and cigarillos.

PREPARATION TIME 30 MINUTES

COOKING TIME 15-18 MINUTES

INGREDIENTS

110 g / 4 oz / ⅔ cup self-raising flour, sifted
110 g / 4 oz / ½ cup margarine
110 g / 4 oz / ½ cup caster (superfine) sugar
1 tsp vanilla extract
2 large eggs

TO DECORATE
250 ml / 9 fl. oz / 1 cup double (heavy) cream
65 g / 2 ½ oz / ½ cup icing (confectioner's) sugar
1 tsp vanilla extract
12 raspberries
12 chocolate cigarillos
12 sprigs of mint leaves
1 kiwi fruit, cut into 12 semi-circles

Cream and Berry Cupcakes

670

- Substitute the cigarillos, mint leaves and kiwi fruit with strawberries, blackberries and blueberries.

671

MAKES 12

White Chocolate-Topped Cupcakes

- Preheat the oven to 190°C (170° fan) / 375F / gas 5 and line a 12-hole cupcake tin with paper cases.
- Combine the flour, sugar, butter, eggs and cocoa in a bowl and whisk together for 2 minutes or until smooth.
- Divide the mixture between the cases, then transfer the tin to the oven and bake for 15 – 20 minutes.
- Test with a wooden toothpick, if it comes out clean, the cakes are done.
- Transfer the cakes to a wire rack and leave to cool completely.
- Melt the white chocolate in a microwave or bain marie and tip the top of each cake to coat.
- Decorate each cake with your choice of small sweets and cake sprinkles.

PREPARATION TIME 20 MINUTES

COOKING TIME 15 - 20 MINUTES

INGREDIENTS

110 g / 4 oz / ⅔ cup self-raising flour, sifted
110 g / 4 oz / ½ cup caster (superfine) sugar
110 g / 4 oz / ½ cup butter, softened
2 large eggs
2 tbsp unsweetened cocoa powder

TO DECORATE:
100 g / 3 ½ oz white chocolate, chopped
small sweets and cake sprinkles to decorate

White Chocolate Cupcakes

672

- Omit the cocoa and add 75 g white chocolate chunks. Dip in milk chocolate instead of white.

673

Peanut Truffle Cupcakes

MAKES 12

PREPARATION TIME 30 MINUTES

COOKING TIME 15-18 MINUTES

INGREDIENTS

110 g / 4 oz / ⅔ cup self-raising flour, sifted
110 g / 4 oz / ½ cup margarine, softened
110 g / 4 oz / ½ cup caster (superfine) sugar
1 tsp vanilla extract
2 large eggs
a pinch of salt

TO DECORATE

225 g / 8 oz / 1 cup smooth peanut butter
125 g / 4 ½ oz / 1 cup icing (confectioner's) sugar
55 g / 2 oz / ½ cup salted peanuts
2 tbsp Golden Syrup

- Preheat the oven to 180°C (160° fan) / 350F / gas 4.
- Line a 12-hole cupcake tin with 12 cupcake cases.
- Beat together all the ingredients for the batter in a mixing bowl for 2 minutes until smooth and creamy.
- Divide evenly between the paper cases before rapping the tin on a work surface to help settle the batter.
- Bake for 15-18 minutes until risen; test with a wooden toothpick, if it comes out clean, the cakes are done.
- Remove to a wire rack to cool as you prepare the buttercream.
- Beat together the softened peanut butter and icing sugar until smooth.
- Spoon into a piping bag fitted with a star-shaped nozzle before piping a spiral swirl on top of the cupcakes.
- Garnish with peanuts and a drizzle of Golden Syrup.

Maple Pecan Cupcakes

674

- Substitute the peanuts for pecan halves and the Golden Syrup for maple syrup.

675

Mandarin Dream Cupcakes

MAKES 12

PREPARATION TIME 30 MINUTES

COOKING TIME 15-18 MINUTES

INGREDIENTS

110 g / 4 oz / ⅔ cup self-raising flour, sifted
110 g / 4 oz / ½ cup margarine, softened
110 g / 4 oz / ½ cup caster (superfine) sugar
1 tsp orange flower water
2 large eggs
a pinch of salt

TO DECORATE

225 g / 8 oz / 1 cup unsalted butter, softened
180 g / 6 oz / 1 ½ cups icing (confectioner's) sugar
1 tsp orange flower water
12 mandarin segments
12 fondant flowers
1 mandarin, zest julienned

- Preheat the oven to 180°C (160° fan) / 350F / gas 4.
- Line a 12-hole cupcake tin with 12 cupcake cases.
- Beat together all the ingredients for the batter in a mixing bowl for 2 minutes until smooth and creamy.
- Divide evenly between the paper cases before rapping the tin on a work surface to help settle the batter.
- Bake for 15-18 minutes until risen.
- Remove to a wire rack to cool as you prepare the buttercream.
- Beat the softened butter for 2 minutes until creamy.
- Add the icing sugar and orange flower water and beat again until smooth.
- Pipe the icing onto the cakes and top with the mandarin segments, flowers and mandarin zest.

Lime and Mandarin Cupcakes

676

- Substitute the orange flower water in the buttercream lime cordial.

677

MAKES 12

Fondant-Iced Cupcakes

Fondant Fancy Cupcakes

678

- Pipe a small dome of buttercream on top of each cake then chill in the fridge for 30 minutes before dipping in the coloured fondant.

Chocolate Fondant Cupcakes

679

- Add 1 tbsp of cocoa powder to the fondant icing after adding the water.

PREPARATION TIME 30 MINUTES
COOKING TIME 15 - 20 MINUTES
SETTING TIME 1 HOUR

INGREDIENTS

110 g / 4 oz / ⅔ cup self-raising flour, sifted
110 g / 4 oz / ½ cup caster (superfine) sugar
110 g / 4 oz / ½ cup butter, softened
2 large eggs
1 tsp vanilla extract

TO DECORATE:
250 g / 9 oz ready to roll fondant icing, diced
30 – 40 ml water
a few drops of pink or yellow food colouring

- Preheat the oven to 190°C (170° fan) / 375F / gas 5 and line a 12-hole cupcake tin with paper cases.
- Combine the flour, sugar, butter, eggs and vanilla extract in a bowl and whisk together for 2 minutes or until smooth.
- Divide the mixture between the cases, then transfer the tin to the oven and bake for 15 – 20 minutes.
- Test with a wooden toothpick, if it comes out clean, the cakes are done.
- Transfer the cakes to a wire rack and leave to cool completely.
- Beat the fondant icing with an electric mixer then gradually add enough water to make a thick, pourable icing.
- Spoon a third of the icing into a piping bag then colour the remaining 2 thirds with a few drops of food colouring.
- Dip the top of each cake in the coloured fondant, then pipe a design on top with the plain fondant. Leave to set before serving.

680

MAKES 12

Chocolate Cupcakes with Coffee Cream

PREPARATION TIME: 30 MINUTES

COOKING TIME: 15 - 20 MINUTES

CHILLING TIME: 1 HOUR

INGREDIENTS

110 g / 4 oz / ⅔ cup self-raising flour, sifted
110 g / 4 oz / ½ cup caster (superfine) sugar
110 g / 4 oz / ½ cup butter, softened
2 large eggs
100 g / 3 ½ oz dark chocolate (minimum 60% cocoa solids), melted
2 tbsp unsweetened cocoa powder

TO DECORATE:
300 ml / 10 ½ fl. oz / 1 ¼ cups double (heavy) cream
1 tbsp instant espresso powder
2 tbsp icing (confectioners') sugar
12 sugar paste flowers

- Preheat the oven to 190°C (170° fan) / 375F / gas 5 and line a 12-hole cupcake tin with paper cases.
- Combine the flour, sugar, butter, eggs, melted chocolate and cocoa in a bowl and whisk together for 2 minutes or until smooth.
- Divide the mixture between the cases, then transfer the tin to the oven and bake for 15 – 20 minutes.
- Test with a wooden toothpick, if it comes out clean, the cakes are done.
- Transfer the cakes to a wire rack and leave to cool completely.
- Heat half of the cream until it starts to simmer, then stir in the espresso powder and icing sugar to dissolve. Add the rest of the cream then chill for 1 hour.
- Whip the coffee cream until it holds its shape, then spoon it into a piping bag, fitted with a large plain nozzle.
- Pipe a big swirl of coffee cream on top of each cake and decorate with the sugar flowers.

681

MAKES 12

Bonfire Cupcakes

PREPARATION TIME 30 MINUTES

COOKING TIME 15-18 MINUTES

INGREDIENTS

FOR THE BATTER
110 g / 4 oz / ⅔ cup self-raising flour, sifted
110 g / 4 oz / ½ cup margarine, softened
110 g / 4 oz / ½ cup caster (superfine) sugar
1 tsp orange flower water
2 large eggs
a pinch of salt

TO DECORATE
200 g / 7 oz / 1 cup butter, softened
400 g / 14 oz / 4 cups icing (confectioners') sugar
1 tsp orange flower water
a few drops of orange food colouring
75 g / 2 ½ oz milk chocolate, chopped

- Preheat the oven to 180°C (160° fan) / 350F / gas 4.
- Line a 12-hole cupcake tin with 12 cupcake cases.
- Beat together all the ingredients for the batter in a mixing bowl for 2 minutes until smooth and creamy.
- Divide evenly between the paper cases before rapping the tin on a work surface to help settle the batter.
- Bake for 15-18 minutes until risen; test with a wooden toothpick, if it comes out clean, the cakes are done.
- Transfer the cakes to a wire rack and leave to cool.
- Beat the butter with the icing sugar and orange flower water until smooth.
- Set aside half of the buttercream and spread the rest over the cakes.
- Colour the reserved buttercream orange and pipe a ring of teardrops round the outside of each cake.
- Sprinkle the centres with chopped chocolate.

682

MAKES 12

St Clements Cupcakes

PREPARATION TIME 30 MINUTES

COOKING TIME 15-18 MINUTES

INGREDIENTS

110 g / 4 oz / ⅔ cup self-raising flour, sifted
110 g / 4 oz / ½ cup margarine
110 g / 4 oz / ½ cup caster (superfine) sugar
1 tsp lemon extract
2 large eggs, a pinch of salt
200 g / 7 oz / 1 cup butter, softened
400 g / 14 oz / 4 cups icing (confectioners') sugar
1 tbsp Cointreau liqueur
a few drops of orange food colouring
4 mandarins, segmented

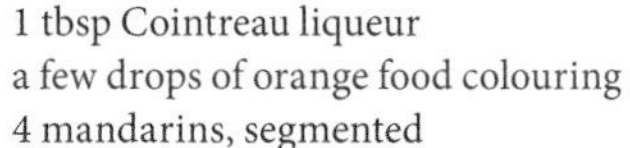

- Preheat the oven to 190°C (170° fan) / 375F / gas 5 and line a 12-hole cupcake tin with paper cases.
- Combine the cake ingredients and whisk together until smooth.
- Divide the mixture between the cases and bake for 15 – 20 minutes.
- Transfer the cakes to a wire rack and leave to cool.
- Beat the butter with the icing sugar, Cointreau and food colouring until smooth.
- Pipe a double ring of icing round each cake, using a petal nozzle, then fill the centres with mandarin segments.

683

Orange Blossom Cupcakes

MAKES 12

PREPARATION TIME 30 MINUTES

COOKING TIME 15-18 MINUTES

INGREDIENTS

110 g / 4 oz / ⅔ cup self-raising flour, sifted
110 g / 4 oz / ½ cup margarine
110 g / 4 oz / ½ cup caster (superfine) sugar
1 tsp orange flower water
2 large eggs, a pinch of salt
200 g / 7 oz / 1 cup butter, softened
400 g / 14 oz / 4 cups icing (confectioners') sugar
1 tsp orange flower water
a few drops of orange food colouring
12 sugar paste flowers

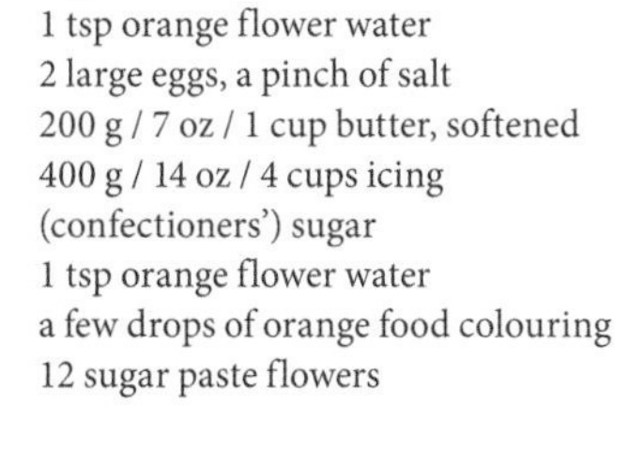

- Preheat the oven to 190°C (170° fan) / 375F / gas 5 and line a 12-hole cupcake tin with paper cases.
- Combine the cake ingredients and whisk together until smooth.
- Divide the mixture between the cases and bake for 15 – 20 minutes.
- Transfer the cakes to a wire rack and leave to cool.
- Beat the butter with the icing sugar, orange flower water and food colouring until smooth.
- Pipe the icing onto the cakes and garnish each one with a flower.

684

Sugar Rose Cupcakes

MAKES 12

PREPARATION TIME 30 MINUTES

COOKING TIME 15-18 MINUTES

INGREDIENTS

110 g / 4 oz / ⅔ cup self-raising flour, sifted
110 g / 4 oz / ½ cup margarine
110 g / 4 oz / ½ cup caster (superfine) sugar
1 tsp vanilla extract
2 large eggs, a pinch of salt
200 g / 7 oz / 1 cup yellow buttercream
200 g / 7 oz / 1 cup red buttercream
12 sugar paste roses

- Preheat the oven to 190°C (170° fan) / 375F / gas 5 and line a 12-hole cupcake tin with paper cases.
- Combine the cake ingredients and whisk together until smooth.
- Divide the mixture between the cases and bake for 15 – 20 minutes.
- Transfer the cakes to a wire rack and leave to cool.
- Spoon the yellow buttercream into one side of a piping bag, fitted with a star nozzle, and the red into the other.
- Pipe a swirl onto each cake and garnish with the roses.

UNIQUE AND NOVELTY

685

MAKES 12

Bastille Day Cupcakes

PREPARATION TIME 30 MINUTES

COOKING TIME 15 - 20 MINUTES

INGREDIENTS

110 g / 4 oz / ⅔ cup self-raising flour, sifted
110 g / 4 oz / ½ cup caster (superfine) sugar
110 g / 4 oz / ½ cup butter, softened
2 large eggs
1 tsp vanilla extract

TO DECORATE:
200 g / 7 oz fondant icing
a few drops of red food colouring
red, blue and white sugar balls
paper Tricolour flags to decorate

- Preheat the oven to 190°C (170° fan) / 375F / gas 5 and line a 12-hole cupcake tin with paper cases.
- Combine the flour, sugar, butter, eggs and vanilla extract in a bowl and whisk together for 2 minutes or until smooth.
- Divide the mixture between the cases, then transfer the tin to the oven and bake for 15 – 20 minutes.
- Transfer the cakes to a wire rack and leave to cool.
- Divide the icing in half and colour one piece red. Roll out the icing between 2 sheets of greaseproof paper and cut 6 circles out of each, the same diameter as the top of the cupcakes.
- Wet the back of the icing disks and attach to the top of the cakes.
- Decorate the cakes with contrasting colour sugar balls and top with the Tricolour flags.

Independence Day Cupcakes

686

- Use American flags and blue and white sugar stars to top the cakes.

687

MAKES 18

Forest Fruits Buttercream Cupcakes

PREPARATION TIME 30 MINUTES

COOKING TIME 15 - 20 MINUTES

INGREDIENTS

110 g / 4 oz / ⅔ cup self-raising flour, sifted
110 g / 4 oz / ½ cup caster (superfine) sugar
110 g / 4 oz / ½ cup butter, softened
2 large eggs
1 tsp vanilla extract

TO DECORATE:
100 g / 3 ½ oz / ½ cup butter, softened
200 g / 7 oz / 2 cups icing (confectioners') sugar
2 tsp blueberry syrup
2 tsp raspberry syrup
2 tsp blackberry syrup
hundreds and thousands for sprinkling
12 chocolate mini eggs
12 sugar paste leaves
12 green ribbon bows

- Preheat the oven to 190°C (170° fan) / 375F / gas 5 and line a 12-hole cupcake tin with paper cases.
- Combine the flour, sugar, butter, eggs and vanilla extract in a bowl and whisk together for 2 minutes or until smooth.
- Divide the mixture between the cases and bake for 15 – 20 minutes.
- Test with a wooden toothpick, if it comes out clean, the cakes are done.
- Transfer the cakes to a wire rack and leave to cool completely.
- Beat the butter until smooth, then gradually whisk in the icing sugar and fruit syrups.
- Spoon the mixture into a piping bag, fitted with a large star nozzle, and pipe a swirl of icing on top of each cake.
- Scatter over the cake sprinkles then decorate each cake with an egg, a leaf and a bow.

Vanilla Cupcakes with Raspberry Buttercream

688

- Omit the blueberry and blackberry syrups and use 2 tbsp of raspberry syrup. Top the cakes with fresh raspberries.

689

MAKES 12

Fruity Easter Buttercream Cupcakes

- Preheat the oven to 190°C (170° fan) / 375F / gas 5 and line a 12-hole cupcake tin with paper cases.
- Combine the flour, sugar, butter, eggs and vanilla extract in a bowl and whisk together for 2 minutes or until smooth.
- Divide the mixture between the cases and bake for 15 – 20 minutes.
- Test with a wooden toothpick, if it comes out clean, the cakes are done.
- Transfer the cakes to a wire rack and leave to cool completely.
- Beat the butter until smooth, then gradually whisk in the icing sugar and fruit syrups.
- Spoon the mixture into a piping bag, fitted with a large star nozzle, and pipe a swirl of icing on top of the cakes, then top each one with a chocolate mini egg.

PREPARATION TIME 30 MINUTES

COOKING TIME 15 - 20 MINUTES

INGREDIENTS

110 g / 4 oz / ⅔ cup self-raising flour, sifted
110 g / 4 oz / ½ cup caster (superfine) sugar
110 g / 4 oz / ½ cup butter, softened
2 large eggs
1 tsp vanilla extract

TO DECORATE:
100 g / 3 ½ oz / ½ cup butter, softened
200 g / 7 oz / 2 cups icing (confectioners') sugar
2 tsp raspberry syrup
2 tsp blackberry syrup
12 chocolate mini eggs

Baileys Buttercream Cupcakes

690

- Replace the fruit Syrups with 2 tbsp of Baileys cream liqueur.

691

MAKES 12

Jubilee Cupcakes

- Preheat the oven to 190°C (170° fan) / 375F / gas 5 and line a 12-hole cupcake tin with paper cases.
- Combine the flour, sugar, butter, eggs and vanilla extract in a bowl and whisk together for 2 minutes or until smooth.
- Divide the mixture between the cases, then transfer the tin to the oven and bake for 15 – 20 minutes.
- Test with a wooden toothpick, if it comes out clean, the cakes are done.
- Transfer the cakes to a wire rack and leave to cool.
- Beat the butter until smooth, then gradually whisk in the icing sugar.
- Spoon the mixture into a piping bag, fitted with a large star nozzle, and pipe a swirl of icing on top of each cake.
- Decorate the cakes with sugar balls and top with the union flags.

PREPARATION TIME 30 MINUTES

COOKING TIME 15 - 20 MINUTES

INGREDIENTS

110 g / 4 oz / ⅔ cup self-raising flour, sifted
110 g / 4 oz / ½ cup caster (superfine) sugar
110 g / 4 oz / ½ cup butter, softened
2 large eggs
1 tsp vanilla extract

TO DECORATE:
100 g / 3 ½ oz / ½ cup butter, softened
200 g / 7 oz / 2 cups icing (confectioners') sugar
red and blue sugar balls
paper Union flags to decorate

St George's Day Cupcakes

692

- Use only red sugar balls and top the cakes with the flag of St George.

693

Smiley Cupcakes

MAKES 18

PREPARATION TIME 15 MINUTES

COOKING TIME 15 - 20 MINUTES

SETTING TIME 2 HOURS

INGREDIENTS

175 g / 6 oz / 1 ¼ cups self-raising flour, sifted
175 g / 6 oz / ¾ cup caster (superfine) sugar
175 g / 6 oz / ¾ cup butter, softened
3 large eggs
1 tsp vanilla extract

TO DECORATE:

200 g / 7 oz / 2 cups icing (confectioners') sugar
a few drops of yellow food colouring
4 tbsp dark chocolate, melted
36 chocolate balls

- Preheat the oven to 190°C (170° fan) / 375F / gas 5 and line an 18-hole cupcake tin with paper cases.
- Combine the flour, sugar, butter, eggs and vanilla extract in a bowl and whisk together for 2 minutes or until smooth.
- Divide the mixture between the cases, then transfer the tin to the oven and bake for 15 – 20 minutes.
- Test with a wooden toothpick, if it comes out clean, the cakes are done.
- Transfer the cakes to a wire rack and leave to cool completely.
- Sieve the icing sugar into a bowl and add just enough water to make a thick, spreadable icing.
- Colour the icing with a few drops of yellow food colouring then spoon it on top of the cupcakes.
- Spoon the melted chocolate into a small piping bag and pipe a smile onto each cake. Use the chocolate balls for the eyes then leave the icing to set.

694

E-Motions Cupcakes

- Use the melted chocolate to pipe a different facial expression onto each cupcake.

695

Sunshine Cupcakes

- Make up a batch of yellow buttercream and pipe the sun's rays round the outside with a petal nozzle.

696

MAKES 12

Orange Buttercream Cupcakes

- Preheat the oven to 190°C (170° fan) / 375F / gas 5 and line a 12-hole cupcake tin with paper cases.
- Combine the flour, sugar, butter, eggs and orange zest in a bowl and whisk together for 2 minutes or until smooth.
- Divide the mixture between the cases, then transfer the tin to the oven and bake for 15 – 20 minutes.
- Test with a wooden toothpick, if it comes out clean, the cakes are done.
- Transfer the cakes to a wire rack and leave to cool completely.
- Beat the butter until smooth, then gradually whisk in the icing sugar and orange juice.
- Spoon the mixture into a piping bag, fitted with a large star nozzle, and pipe a swirl of icing on top of each cake, then top with the orange sweets.

PREPARATION TIME 30 MINUTES

COOKING TIME 15 - 20 MINUTES

INGREDIENTS

110 g / 4 oz / ⅔ cup self-raising flour, sifted
110 g / 4 oz / ½ cup caster (superfine) sugar
110 g / 4 oz / ½ cup butter, softened
2 large eggs
1 orange, zest finely grated

TO DECORATE:
100 g / 3 ½ oz / ½ cup butter, softened
200 g / 7 oz / 2 cups icing (confectioners') sugar
1 tbsp orange juice
orange jelly sweets to decorate

Lemon Buttercream Cupcakes

697

- Replace the orange zest and juice with lemon zest and juice and decorate with lemon jelly sweets.

698

MAKES 12

Chocolate, Honey and Pecan Cupcakes

- Preheat the oven to 180°C (160° fan) / 350F / gas 4 and line a 12-hole cupcake tin with paper cases.
- Beat the egg in a jug with the oil and milk until well mixed.
- Mix the flour, cocoa, baking powder and sugar in a bowl, then pour in the egg mixture, chocolate chunks and chopped pecans and stir just enough to combine.
- Divide the mixture between the cases, then bake in the oven for 20 – 25 minutes.
- Transfer the cakes to a wire rack and leave to cool.
- Beat the butter until smooth, then gradually whisk in the icing sugar. Add the vanilla extract and whisk for 2 minutes or until smooth and well whipped.
- Spoon the buttercream into a piping bag and pipe a big swirl on top of the cakes, then drizzle each cake with 1 tsp of honey and top with a pecan nut.

PREPARATION TIME 35 MINUTES

COOKING TIME 20 – 25 MINUTES

INGREDIENTS

1 large egg
125 ml / 4 ½ fl. oz / ½ cup sunflower oil
125 ml / 4 ½ fl. oz / ½ cup milk
350 g / 12 ½ oz / 2 ⅓ cups self-raising flour, sifted
50 g / 1 ¾ oz / ½ cup unsweetened cocoa powder, sifted
1 tsp baking powder
200 g / 7 oz / ¾ cup caster (superfine) sugar
150 g / 5 ½ oz dark chocolate chunks (minimum 60% cocoa solids)
50 g / 1 ¾ oz / ½ cup pecan nuts, chopped

TO DECORATE:
100 g / 3 ½ oz / ½ cup butter, softened
200 g / 7 oz / 2 cups icing (confectioners') sugar
1 tsp vanilla extract
4 tbsp honey, 12 pecan nuts

Chocolate, Maple and Pecan Buttercream Cupcakes

- Replace the honey with maple syrup.

700

Chocolate Cross Cupcakes

MAKES 12

PREPARATION TIME 30 MINUTES

COOKING TIME 15 - 20 MINUTES

INGREDIENTS

110 g / 4 oz / ⅔ cup self-raising flour, sifted
110 g / 4 oz / ½ cup caster (superfine) sugar
110 g / 4 oz / ½ cup butter, softened
2 large eggs
2 tbsp unsweetened cocoa powder

TO DECORATE:
100 g / 3 ½ oz ready to roll fondant icing
icing (confectioners') sugar for dusting

- Preheat the oven to 190°C (170° fan) / 375F / gas 5 and line a 12-hole cupcake tin with paper cases.
- Combine the flour, sugar, butter, eggs and cocoa in a bowl and whisk together for 2 minutes or until smooth.
- Divide the mixture between the cases, then transfer the tin to the oven and bake for 15 – 20 minutes.
- Test with a wooden toothpick, if it comes out clean, the cakes are done.
- Transfer the cakes to a wire rack and leave to cool completely.
- Roll the icing into 24 thin sausages and lay 2 across each cake, attaching with a dab of water.
- Dust the cakes with icing sugar.

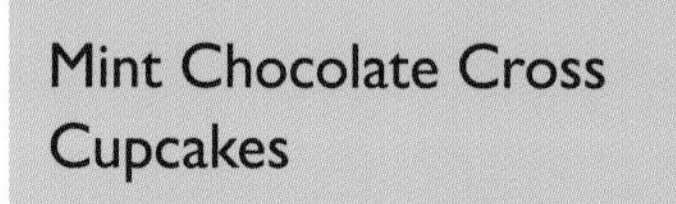

Mint Chocolate Cross Cupcakes

701

- Add a few drops of peppermint extract to the cake mixture.

702

Orange Flower Water Cupcakes

MAKES 12

PREPARATION TIME 30 MINUTES

COOKING TIME 15 - 20 MINUTES

INGREDIENTS

110 g / 4 oz / ⅔ cup self-raising flour, sifted
110 g / 4 oz / ½ cup caster (superfine) sugar
110 g / 4 oz / ½ cup butter, softened
2 large eggs
1 tbsp orange flower water

TO DECORATE:
100 g / 3 ½ oz / ½ cup butter, softened
200 g / 7 oz / 2 cups icing (confectioners') sugar
½ tsp orange flower water
chocolate flakes to sprinkle
12 sugar flowers

- Preheat the oven to 190°C (170° fan) / 375F / gas 5 and line a 12-hole cupcake tin with paper cases.
- Combine the flour, sugar, butter, eggs and orange flower water in a bowl and whisk together for 2 minutes or until smooth.
- Divide the mixture between the cases, then transfer the tin to the oven and bake for 15 – 20 minutes.
- Test with a wooden toothpick, if it comes out clean, the cakes are done.
- Transfer the cakes to a wire rack and leave to cool completely.
- Beat the butter until smooth, then gradually whisk in the icing sugar and orange flower water.
- Spoon the mixture into a piping bag, fitted with a large star nozzle, and pipe a swirl of icing on top of each cake, then sprinkle with chocolate flakes. Finish each one with a sugar flower.

Limoncello Cupcakes

703

- Drizzle the cakes with limoncello liqueur when they come out of the oven and add 1 tbsp of limoncello to the buttercream instead of the orange flower water.

704

MAKES 12

Puppy Love Cupcakes

- Preheat the oven to 190°C (170° fan) / 375F / gas 5 and line a 12-hole cupcake tin with paper cases.
- Combine the flour, sugar, butter, eggs and vanilla extract in a bowl and whisk together for 2 minutes.
- Divide the mixture between the cases, then transfer the tin to the oven and bake for 15 – 20 minutes.
- Transfer the cakes to a wire rack and leave to cool.
- Divide the icing into 3 and colour one ivory.
- Roll out the ivory icing between 2 sheets of greaseproof paper and cut out 12 circles the same diameter as the top of the cupcakes with a fluted cutter.
- Wet the back of the icing circles and attach to the top.
- Divide one of the remaining pieces of icing into 2 and colour one half red and one black.
- Model 12 puppies out of the black and remaining white icing and complete with a red heart and tongue.

PREPARATION TIME 1 HOUR 35 MINUTES

COOKING TIME 15 - 20 MINUTES

INGREDIENTS

110 g / 4 oz / ⅔ cup self-raising flour, sifted
110 g / 4 oz / ½ cup caster (superfine) sugar
110 g / 4 oz / ½ cup butter, softened
2 large eggs
1 tsp vanilla extract

TO DECORATE:
250 g / 9 oz fondant icing
ivory, black and red food colouring

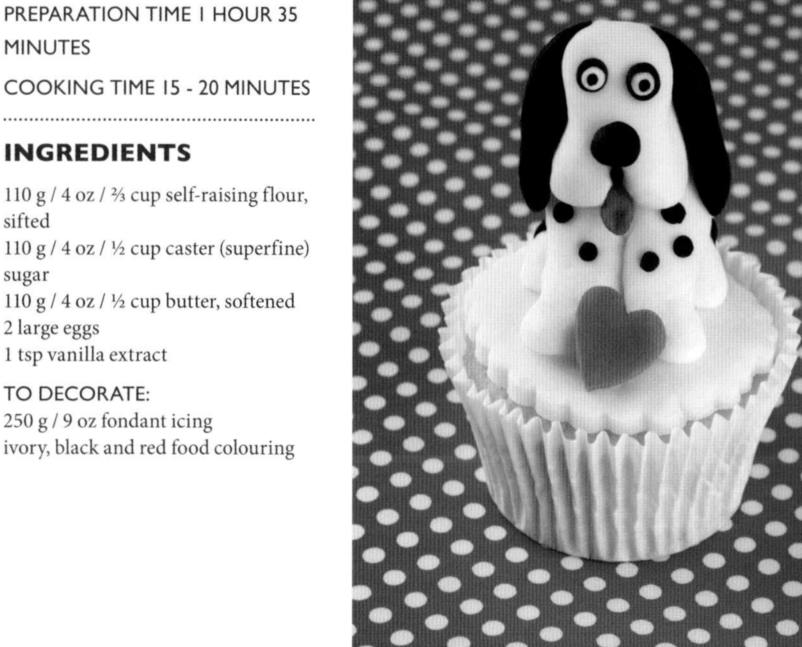

Cute Kitten Cupcakes

705

- Use the black and white icing to model 12 black and white kittens.

706

MAKES 12

Almond and White Chocolate Cupcakes

- Preheat the oven to 190°C (170° fan) / 375F / gas 5 and line a 12-hole cupcake tin with paper cases.
- Combine the flour, sugar, butter, ground almonds and eggs in a bowl and whisk together for 2 minutes or until smooth.
- Fold in the white chocolate then divide the mixture between the cases and bake for 15 – 20 minutes.
- Test with a wooden toothpick, if it comes out clean, the cakes are done.
- Transfer the cakes to a wire rack and leave to cool completely.
- Melt the chocolate in a microwave or bain marie and spread it on top of the cakes.
- Scatter over the almonds and leave the chocolate to set before dusting with icing sugar.

PREPARATION TIME 30 MINUTES

COOKING TIME 15 - 20 MINUTES

SETTING TIME 30 MINUTES

INGREDIENTS

110 g / 4 oz / ⅔ cup self-raising flour, sifted
110 g / 4 oz / ½ cup light muscovado sugar
110 g / 4 oz / ½ cup butter, softened
2 tbsp ground almonds
2 large eggs
75 g / 2 ½ oz / ⅔ cup white chocolate, melted

TO DECORATE:
75 g / 2 ½ oz / ⅔ cup white chocolate, chopped
50 g / 1 ¾ oz / ⅔ cup flaked (slivered) almonds
icing (confectioners') sugar for dusting

Pistachio and White Chocolate Cupcakes

707

- Replace the ground almonds with ground pistachios and top the cakes with slivered pistachios.

708

MAKES 12

Prune Cupcakes

PREPARATION TIME 15 MINUTES

COOKING TIME 15 - 20 MINUTES

INGREDIENTS

110 g / 4 oz / ⅔ cup self-raising flour, sifted
110 g / 4 oz / ½ cup caster (superfine) sugar
110 g / 4 oz / ½ cup butter, softened
2 large eggs
12 stoned prunes

- Preheat the oven to 190°C (170° fan) / 375F / gas 5 and line a 12-hole oval cupcake tin with oval paper cases.
- Combine the flour, sugar, butter and eggs in a bowl and whisk together for 2 minutes or until smooth.
- Divide the mixture between the cases and press a prune into the top of each one, then transfer the tin to the oven and bake for 15 – 20 minutes.
- Test with a wooden toothpick, if it comes out clean, the cakes are done.
- Transfer the cakes to a wire rack and leave to cool completely.

709

Prune and Orange Cupcakes

- Add the finely grated zest of an orange to the cake mixture.

710

MAKES 12

White Chocolate Cream Cheese Cupcakes

PREPARATION TIME 30 MINUTES

COOKING TIME 15 - 20 MINUTES

INGREDIENTS

110 g / 4 oz / ⅔ cup self-raising flour, sifted
110 g / 4 oz / ½ cup light muscovado sugar
110 g / 4 oz / ½ cup butter, softened
2 large eggs
75 g / 2 ½ oz / ⅔ cup white chocolate, melted

TO DECORATE:
110 g / 4 oz / ½ cup cream cheese
55 g / 2 oz / ¼ cup butter, softened
110 g / 4 oz / 1 cup icing (confectioners') sugar
75 g / 2 ½ oz / ⅔ cup white chocolate, melted
dark chocolate curls to decorate

- Preheat the oven to 190°C (170° fan) / 375F / gas 5 and line a 12-hole cupcake tin with paper cases.
- Combine the flour, sugar, butter and eggs in a bowl and whisk together for 2 minutes or until smooth.
- Fold in the white chocolate then divide the mixture between the cases and bake for 15 – 20 minutes.
- Test with a wooden toothpick, if it comes out clean, the cakes are done.
- Transfer the cakes to a wire rack and leave to cool completely.
- Beat the cream cheese and butter together until light and fluffy then beat in the icing sugar a quarter at a time.
- Add the melted chocolate then whip the mixture for 2 minutes or until smooth and light.
- Spoon the mixture into a piping bag fitted with a large star nozzle and pipe a big swirl on top of each cake. Decorate with chocolate curls.

711

White Chocolate and Orange Cream Cheese Cupcakes

- Add the grated zest of an orange to the cake mixture and icing. Top with white chocolate curls instead of dark chocolate curls.

712

MAKES 12

Apple Cupcakes

Spiced Apple Cupcakes

713

- Add 1 tsp of ground cinnamon to the cake mixture before whisking.

Apple Snow Cupcakes

714

- Top the cupcakes with whipped cream and a dusting of icing sugar.

PREPARATION TIME 15 MINUTES

COOKING TIME 15 - 20 MINUTES

INGREDIENTS

110 g / 4 oz / ⅔ cup self-raising flour, sifted
110 g / 4 oz / ½ cup caster (superfine) sugar
110 g / 4 oz / ½ cup butter, softened
2 large eggs
1 tsp vanilla extract
1 eating apple, peeled, cored and chopped

- Preheat the oven to 190°C (170° fan) / 375F / gas 5 and line a 12-hole cupcake tin with silicone cases.
- Combine the flour, sugar, butter, eggs and vanilla extract in a bowl and whisk together for 2 minutes or until smooth.
- Fold in the chopped apple then divide the mixture between the cases and bake for 15 – 20 minutes.
- Test with a wooden toothpick, if it comes out clean, the cakes are done.
- Transfer the cakes to a wire rack and leave to cool completely.

715

MAKES 12

Violet Cream Cupcakes

PREPARATION TIME 30 MINUTES

COOKING TIME 15 - 20 MINUTES

INGREDIENTS

110 g / 4 oz / ⅔ cup self-raising flour, sifted
110 g / 4 oz / ½ cup caster (superfine) sugar
110 g / 4 oz / ½ cup butter, softened
2 large eggs
1 tsp vanilla extract

TO DECORATE:
300 ml / 10 ½ fl. oz / 1 ¼ cups double (heavy) cream
3 tbsp violet syrup
sugar paste roses and leaves to decorate

- Preheat the oven to 190°C (170° fan) / 375F / gas 5 and line a 12-hole cupcake tin with paper cases.
- Combine the flour, sugar, butter, eggs and vanilla in a bowl and whisk together for 2 minutes or until smooth.
- Divide the mixture between the cases, then transfer the tin to the oven and bake for 15 – 20 minutes.
- Test with a wooden toothpick, if it comes out clean, the cakes are done.
- Transfer the cakes to a wire rack and leave to cool completely.
- Whip the cream with the violet syrup until it holds its shape, then spoon the mixture into a piping bag, fitted with a large star nozzle.
- Pipe a big swirl onto each cake and top each one with a sugar paste rose and leaf.

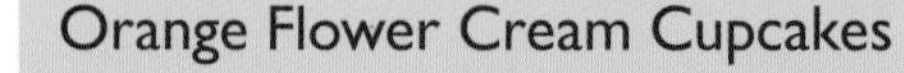

Orange Flower Cream Cupcakes

716

- Replace the violet syrup with 1 tbsp of orange flower water and 2 tbsp of icing sugar.

717

MAKES 12

Chocolate and Blueberry Cupcakes

PREPARATION TIME 30 MINUTES

COOKING TIME 15 - 20 MINUTES

INGREDIENTS

110 g / 4 oz / ⅔ cup self-raising flour, sifted
110 g / 4 oz / ½ cup caster (superfine) sugar
110 g / 4 oz / ½ cup butter, softened
2 large eggs
2 tbsp unsweetened cocoa powder

TO DECORATE:
100 g / 3 ½ oz / ½ cup butter, softened
200 g / 7 oz / 2 cups icing (confectioners') sugar
2 tbsp blueberry syrup
100 g / 3 ½ oz / ⅔ cup fresh blueberries

- Preheat the oven to 190°C (170° fan) / 375F / gas 5 and line a 12-hole cupcake tin with paper cases.
- Combine the flour, sugar, butter, eggs and cocoa in a bowl and whisk together for 2 minutes or until smooth.
- Divide the mixture between the cases and bake for 15 – 20 minutes.
- Test with a wooden toothpick, if it comes out clean, the cakes are done.
- Transfer the cakes to a wire rack and leave to cool completely.
- Beat the butter until smooth, then gradually whisk in the icing sugar and blueberry syrup.
- Spoon the mixture into a piping bag, fitted with a large star nozzle, and pipe a swirl of icing on top of each cake, then decorate with fresh blueberries.

Blueberry Buttercream Chocolate Curl Cupcakes

718

- Omit the cocoa powder and add 1 tsp of vanilla extract to the cake mixture. Top the cakes with chocolate curls instead of the fresh blueberries.

719

Lavender Cream Cheese Cupcakes

MAKES 12

- Preheat the oven to 190°C (170° fan) / 375F / gas 5 and double line a 12-hole cupcake tin with paper cases.
- Combine the flour, sugar, butter, eggs and lavender syrup in a bowl and whisk together for 2 minutes.
- Divide the mixture between the cases, then transfer the tin to the oven and bake for 15 – 20 minutes.
- Transfer the cakes to a wire rack and leave to cool.
- Beat the cream cheese and butter together until light and fluffy then beat in the icing sugar a quarter at a time.
- Add the lavender syrup then whip the mixture for 2 minutes or until smooth and light.
- Spoon the icing into a piping bag, fitted with a large star nozzle, and pipe a dome onto each cake.
- Sprinkle the cakes with lavender flowers and top each one with a lavender sweet.

PREPARATION TIME 30 MINUTES

COOKING TIME 15 - 20 MINUTES

INGREDIENTS

110 g / 4 oz / ⅔ cup self-raising flour, sifted
110 g / 4 oz / ½ cup caster (superfine) sugar
110 g / 4 oz / ½ cup butter, softened
2 large eggs
1 tbsp lavender syrup

TO DECORATE:
110 g / 4 oz / ½ cup cream cheese
55 g / 2 oz / ¼ cup butter, softened
110 g / 4 oz / 1 cup icing (confectioners') sugar
1 tbsp lavender syrup
lavender flowers for sprinkling
12 lavender flavoured sweets

Rose Cream Cheese Cupcakes

720

- Replace the lavender syrup in the cake mixture and icing with rose water and garnish the cakes with crystallised rose petals.

721

Blueberry, Hazelnut and Lemon Cupcakes

MAKES 12

- Preheat the oven to 190°C (170° fan) / 375F / gas 5 and line a 12-hole cupcake tin with paper cases.
- Combine the flour, sugar, butter, eggs and half the lemon zest in a bowl and whisk together for 2 minutes or until smooth.
- Fold in the blueberries and half the chopped hazelnuts then divide the mixture between the cases and bake for 15 – 20 minutes.
- Test with a wooden toothpick, if it comes out clean, the cakes are done.
- Transfer the cakes to a wire rack, sprinkle with the rest of the chopped hazelnuts and lemon zest and leave to cool completely.

PREPARATION TIME 15 MINUTES

COOKING TIME 15 - 20 MINUTES

INGREDIENTS

110 g / 4 oz / ⅔ cup self-raising flour, sifted
110 g / 4 oz / ½ cup caster (superfine) sugar
110 g / 4 oz / ½ cup butter, softened
2 large eggs
1 lemon, zest finely grated
75 g / 2 ½ oz / ½ cup blueberries
75 g / 2 ½ oz / ⅔ cup hazelnuts (cob nuts), chopped

Blueberry, Hazelnut and Orange Cupcakes

722

- Replace the lemon zest with orange zest.

723

MAKES 12

Christmas Buttercream Cupcakes

PREPARATION TIME 30 MINUTES

COOKING TIME 15 - 20 MINUTES

INGREDIENTS

110 g / 4 oz / ⅔ cup self-raising flour, sifted
110 g / 4 oz / ½ cup caster (superfine) sugar
110 g / 4 oz / ½ cup butter, softened
2 large eggs
1 tsp vanilla extract

TO DECORATE:
100 g / 3 ½ oz / ½ cup butter, softened
200 g / 7 oz / 2 cups icing (confectioners') sugar
2 tbsp cherry syrup
1 tsp ground cinnamon
multi-coloured sugar strands for sprinkling
12 Christmas cake toppers

- Preheat the oven to 190°C (170° fan) / 375F / gas 5 and line a 12-hole cupcake tin with paper cases.
- Combine the flour, sugar, butter, eggs and vanilla extract in a bowl and whisk together for 2 minutes or until smooth.
- Divide the mixture between the cases, then transfer the tin to the oven and bake for 15 – 20 minutes.
- Test with a wooden toothpick, if it comes out clean, the cakes are done.
- Transfer the cakes to a wire rack and leave to cool completely.
- Beat the butter until smooth, then gradually whisk in the icing sugar, cherry syrup and cinnamon.
- Spoon the mixture into a piping bag, fitted with a large star nozzle, and pipe a swirl of icing on top of each cake.
- Decorate with sugar strands and top each cake with a Christmas cake topper.

724

Spiced Blueberry Buttercream Cupcakes

- Replace the cinnamon with mixed spice and use blueberry syrup instead of the cherry syrup.

725

Cinnamon Cherry Buttercream Cupcakes

- Top the cakes with a fresh cherry and a sprinkle of cinnamon.

726

MAKES 12

Oreo Cookie Cupcakes

- Preheat the oven to 190°C (170° fan) / 375F / gas 5 and line a 12-hole cupcake tin with paper cases.
- Combine the flour, sugar, butter, eggs and chocolate chips in a bowl and whisk together for 2 minutes.
- Divide the mixture between the cases, then transfer the tin to the oven and bake for 15 – 20 minutes.
- Transfer the cakes to a wire rack and leave to cool.
- Beat the cream cheese and butter until light and fluffy then beat in the icing sugar a quarter at a time.
- Add the vanilla extract then whip for 2 minutes.
- Finely chop 6 of the cookies and fold them into the icing. Cut the rest in half and reserve for decoration.
- Spoon the icing into a piping bag, fitted with a large star nozzle, and pipe a swirl of icing on top of each cake.
- Finish each cake with half an Oreo cookie.

PREPARATION TIME 30 MINUTES

COOKING TIME 15 - 20 MINUTES

INGREDIENTS

110 g / 4 oz / ⅔ cup self-raising flour, sifted
110 g / 4 oz / ½ cup light muscovado sugar
110 g / 4 oz / ½ cup butter, softened
2 large eggs
75 g / 2 ½ oz / ⅔ cup chocolate chips

TO DECORATE:
110 g / 4 oz / ½ cup cream cheese
55 g / 2 oz / ¼ cup butter, softened
110 g / 4 oz / 1 cup icing (confectioners') sugar
1 tsp vanilla extract
12 Oreo cookies

Jaffa Cake Cupcakes

727

- Use Jaffa Cakes instead of the Oreo cookies and add the grated zest of an orange to the cake mixture.

728

MAKES 12

Lime Buttercream Cupcakes

- Preheat the oven to 190°C (170° fan) / 375F / gas 5 and line a 12-hole cupcake tin with paper cases.
- Combine the flour, sugar, butter, eggs and lime juice and zest in a bowl and whisk together for 2 minutes or until smooth.
- Divide the mixture between the cases, then transfer the tin to the oven and bake for 15 – 20 minutes.
- Transfer the cakes to a wire rack and leave to cool completely.
- Beat the butter until smooth, then gradually whisk in the icing sugar and lime juice.
- Colour the icing a very pale green then spoon the mixture into a piping bag, fitted with a large star nozzle, and pipe a swirl of icing on top of each cake.
- Decorate with sugar pearls and top each cake with a Christmas cake topper.

PREPARATION TIME 30 MINUTES

COOKING TIME 15 - 20 MINUTES

INGREDIENTS

110 g / 4 oz / ⅔ cup self-raising flour, sifted
110 g / 4 oz / ½ cup caster (superfine) sugar
110 g / 4 oz / ½ cup butter, softened
2 large eggs
1 lime, juiced and zest finely grated

TO DECORATE:
100 g / 3 ½ oz / ½ cup butter, softened
200 g / 7 oz / 2 cups icing (confectioners') sugar
1 tbsp lime juice
a few drops of green food colouring
sugar pearls and Christmas cake toppers to decorate

Lime and Mint Buttercream Cupcakes

729

- Add 1 tbsp of finely shredded mint leaves to the cake mixture and icing.

730

MAKES 12

Pomegranate and Pistachio Cupcakes

PREPARATION TIME 30 MINUTES

COOKING TIME 15 - 20 MINUTES

INGREDIENTS

110 g / 4 oz / ⅔ cup self-raising flour, sifted
110 g / 4 oz / ½ cup caster (superfine) sugar
110 g / 4 oz / ½ cup butter, softened
2 large eggs
75 g / 2 ½ oz / ½ cup pomegranate seeds

TO DECORATE:
100 g / 3 ½ oz / ½ cup butter, softened
200 g / 7 oz / 2 cups icing (confectioners') sugar
2 tbsp pomegranate molasses
4 tbsp pistachio nuts, chopped

- Preheat the oven to 190°C (170° fan) / 375F / gas 5 and line a 12-hole cupcake tin with paper cases.
- Combine the flour, sugar, butter and eggs in a bowl and whisk together for 2 minutes or until smooth.
- Fold in the pomegranate seeds and divide the mixture between the cases, then transfer the tin to the oven and bake for 15 – 20 minutes.
- Test with a wooden toothpick, if it comes out clean, the cakes are done.
- Transfer the cakes to a wire rack and leave to cool completely.
- Beat the butter until smooth, then gradually whisk in the icing sugar and pomegranate molasses.
- Spoon the mixture into a piping bag, fitted with a large star nozzle, and pipe a swirl of icing on top of each cake, then top with the chopped pistachios.

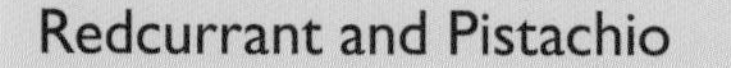

Redcurrant and Pistachio Cupcakes

731

- Replace the pomegranate seeds with redcurrants and use redcurrant jelly instead of the pomegranate molasses.

732

MAKES 12

Chestnut Cream Cupcakes

PREPARATION TIME 30 MINUTES

COOKING TIME 15 – 20 MINUTES

INGREDIENTS

110 g / 4 oz / 1 cup self-raising flour, sifted
110 g / 4 oz / ½ cup caster (superfine) sugar
110 g / 4 oz / ½ cup butter, softened
2 large eggs
1 tsp vanilla extract

TO DECORATE:
225 ml / 8 fl. oz / ¾ cup double (heavy) cream
200 g / 7 oz / ¾ cup sweetened chestnut puree
12 Christmas cake toppers

- Preheat the oven to 190°C (170° fan) / 375F / gas 5 and line a 12-hole cupcake tin with paper cases.
- Combine the flour, sugar, butter, eggs and vanilla extract in a bowl and whisk together for 2 minutes or until smooth.
- Divide the mixture between the paper cases, then transfer the tin to the oven and bake for 15 – 20 minutes.
- Test with a wooden toothpick, if it comes out clean, the cakes are done.
- Transfer the cakes to a wire rack and leave to cool completely.
- To make the topping, whisk the cream until it holds its shape, then fold in the chestnut puree.
- Spoon the chestnut cream into a piping bag fitted with a large star nozzle and pipe a swirl on top of each cake, then top with the Christmas cake toppers.

Chocolate Chip and Chestnut Cream Cupcakes

733

- Add 100 g of mixed chocolate chips to the cake mixture.

734

Chocolate Christmas Buttercream Cupcakes

MAKES 12

- Preheat the oven to 190°C (170° fan) / 375F / gas 5 and line a 12-hole cupcake tin with paper cases.
- Combine the flour, sugar, butter, eggs and cocoa in a bowl and whisk together for 2 minutes or until smooth.
- Divide the mixture between the cases, then transfer the tin to the oven and bake for 15 – 20 minutes.
- Test with a wooden toothpick, if it comes out clean, the cakes are done.
- Transfer the cakes to a wire rack and leave to cool completely.
- Beat the butter until smooth, then gradually whisk in the icing sugar, cherry syrup and cinnamon.
- Spoon the mixture into a piping bag, fitted with a large star nozzle, and pipe a swirl of icing on top of each cake.
- Decorate with sugar pearls and top each cake with a Christmas cake topper.

PREPARATION TIME 30 MINUTES

COOKING TIME 15 - 20 MINUTES

INGREDIENTS

110 g / 4 oz / ⅔ cup self-raising flour, sifted
110 g / 4 oz / ½ cup caster (superfine) sugar
110 g / 4 oz / ½ cup butter, softened
2 large eggs
2 tbsp unsweetened cocoa powder

TO DECORATE:
100 g / 3 ½ oz / ½ cup butter, softened
200 g / 7 oz / 2 cups icing (confectioners') sugar
2 tbsp cherry syrup
1 tsp ground cinnamon
gold sugar pearls and Christmas cake toppers to decorate

735

Spiced Cherry Buttercream Cupcakes

- Replace the cinnamon with mixed spice and add a tsp of mixed spice and 100 g of chopped stoned cherries to the cake mixture.

736

Coconut and Lime Buttercream Cupcakes

MAKES 12

- Preheat the oven to 190°C (170° fan) / 375F / gas 5 and line a 12-hole cupcake tin with paper cases.
- Combine the flour, sugar, butter, eggs, lime juice and zest and coconut in a bowl and whisk together for 2 minutes or until smooth.
- Divide the mixture between the cases, then transfer the tin to the oven and bake for 15 – 20 minutes.
- Transfer the cakes to a wire rack and leave to cool completely.
- Beat the butter until smooth, then gradually whisk in the icing sugar, lime juice and coconut.
- Colour the icing a very pale green then spoon the mixture into a piping bag, fitted with a large star nozzle, and pipe a swirl of icing on top of each cake.
- Sprinkle with more desiccated coconut and top each cake with a rum truffle.

PREPARATION TIME 30 MINUTES

COOKING TIME 15 - 20 MINUTES

INGREDIENTS

110 g / 4 oz / ⅔ cup self-raising flour, sifted
110 g / 4 oz / ½ cup dark brown sugar
110 g / 4 oz / ½ cup butter, softened
2 large eggs
1 lime, juiced and zest finely grated
2 tbsp desiccated coconut

TO DECORATE:
100 g / 3 ½ oz / ½ cup butter, softened
200 g / 7 oz / 2 cups icing (confectioners') sugar
1 tbsp lime juice
2 tbsp desiccated coconut, plus extra for sprinkling
a few drops of green food colouring
12 rum truffles

737

Coconut and Pineapple Buttercream Cupcakes

- Add 100 g of chopped fresh pineapple to the cake mixture and top each cake with dried pineapple instead of the rum truffle.

738

Strawberry Buttercream Heart Cupcakes

MAKES 12

PREPARATION TIME 45 MINUTES

COOKING TIME 15 - 20 MINUTES

INGREDIENTS

110 g / 4 oz / ⅔ cup self-raising flour, sifted
110 g / 4 oz / ½ cup caster (superfine) sugar
110 g / 4 oz / ½ cup butter, softened
2 large eggs
1 tsp vanilla extract

TO DECORATE:
150 g / 5 ½ oz ready to roll fondant icing
a few drops of red food colouring
100 g / 3 ½ oz / ½ cup butter, softened
200 g / 7 oz / 2 cups icing (confectioners') sugar
2 tbsp strawberry syrup

- Preheat the oven to 190°C (170° fan) / 375F / gas 5 and line a 12-hole cupcake tin with paper cases.
- Combine the flour, sugar, butter, eggs and vanilla in a bowl and whisk together for 2 minutes or until smooth.
- Divide the mixture between the cases, then transfer the tin to the oven and bake for 15 – 20 minutes.
- Transfer the cakes to a wire rack and leave to cool completely.
- Knead the icing with the food colouring until all the streaks disappear, then roll it out and cut out heart shapes with different sized cutters.
- Beat the butter until smooth, then gradually whisk in the icing sugar and strawberry syrup.
- Spoon the mixture into a piping bag, fitted with a large star nozzle, and pipe a swirl of icing on top of each cake, then top with the fondant hearts.

Lemon Buttercream Star Cupcakes

739

- Replace the strawberry syrup with lemon juice and cut star shapes out of fondant icing that you've coloured bright yellow.

740

Ginger Beer Cupcakes

MAKES 12

PREPARATION TIME 30 MINUTES

COOKING TIME 15 - 20 MINUTES

INGREDIENTS

110 g / 4 oz / ⅔ cup self-raising flour, sifted
110 g / 4 oz / ½ cup caster (superfine) sugar
110 g / 4 oz / ½ cup butter, softened
2 large eggs
1 tsp ground ginger
2 tbsp ginger beer

TO DECORATE:
110 g / 4 oz / ½ cup cream cheese
55 g / 2 oz / ¼ cup butter, softened
110 g / 4 oz / 1 cup icing (confectioners') sugar
1 tsp ginger syrup
12 pieces crystallised ginger

- Preheat the oven to 190°C (170° fan) / 375F / gas 5 and line a 12-hole cupcake tin with paper cases.
- Combine the flour, sugar, butter, eggs, ground ginger and ginger beer in a bowl and whisk together for 2 minutes or until smooth.
- Divide the mixture between the cases, then transfer the tin to the oven and bake for 15 – 20 minutes.
- Transfer the cakes to a wire rack and leave to cool.
- Beat the cream cheese and butter together until light and fluffy then beat in the icing sugar a quarter at a time.
- Add the ginger syrup then whip the mixture for 2 minutes or until smooth and light.
- Spoon the icing into a piping bag, fitted with a large plain nozzle, and pipe a swirl of icing on top of each cake.
- Top each one with a piece of crystallised ginger and 2 short pieces of drinking straw.

Root Beer Cupcakes

741

- Replace the ginger beer with root beer and omit the ground ginger and crystallised ginger. Use root beer to flavour the icing instead of the ginger syrup.

742

MAKES 12

'Egg and Ketchup' Cupcakes

'French Fries and Ketchup' Cupcakes

743

- Colour some of the icing yellow, roll it out thickly and cut it into French fries with a sharp knife. Leave the fondant to stiffen and dry for a few hours before arranging on the cakes.

'Egg and Soldiers' Cupcakes

744

- Roll out some pale brown icing and cut it into 'toast soldiers' before arranging on the cakes.

PREPARATION TIME 30 MINUTES

COOKING TIME 15 - 20 MINUTES

INGREDIENTS

110 g / 4 oz / ⅔ cup self-raising flour, sifted
110 g / 4 oz / ½ cup caster (superfine) sugar
110 g / 4 oz / ½ cup butter, softened
2 large eggs
1 tsp vanilla extract

TO DECORATE:
200 g / 7 oz ready to roll fondant icing
black, yellow and red food colouring

- Preheat the oven to 190°C (170° fan) / 375F / gas 5 and line a 12-hole cupcake tin with paper cases.
- Combine the flour, sugar, butter, eggs and vanilla extract in a bowl and whisk together for 2 minutes or until smooth.
- Divide the mixture between the cases, then transfer the tin to the oven and bake for 15 – 20 minutes.
- Test with a wooden toothpick, if it comes out clean, the cakes are done.
- Transfer the cakes to a wire rack and leave to cool completely.
- Colour half of the icing black and roll it out between 2 sheets of greaseproof paper. Cut out 12 circles then wet the backs and attach to the top of the cakes.
- Roll out half of the remaining icing and cut out the egg whites, attaching with a dab of water.
- Colour some of the remaining icing yellow to make the yolks and the rest red to make the ketchup, attaching as before with a dab of water.

745

MAKES 12

Cherry Syrup Cream Cheese Cupcakes

PREPARATION TIME 30 MINUTES

COOKING TIME 15 - 20 MINUTES

INGREDIENTS

110 g / 4 oz / ⅔ cup self-raising flour, sifted
110 g / 4 oz / ½ cup caster (superfine) sugar
110 g / 4 oz / ½ cup butter, softened
2 large eggs
½ tsp almond extract

TO DECORATE:
110 g / 4 oz / ½ cup cream cheese
55 g / 2 oz / ¼ cup butter, softened
110 g / 4 oz / 1 cup icing (confectioners') sugar
3 tbsp cherry syrup
12 chocolate mini eggs

- Preheat the oven to 190°C (170° fan) / 375F / gas 5 and line a 12-hole cupcake tin with paper cases.
- Combine the flour, sugar, butter, eggs and almond extract in a bowl and whisk together for 2 minutes or until smooth.
- Divide the mixture between the cases and bake for 15 – 20 minutes.
- Transfer the cakes to a wire rack and leave to cool.
- Beat the cream cheese and butter together until light and fluffy then beat in the icing sugar a quarter at a time.
- Add the cherry syrup then whip the mixture for 2 minutes or until smooth and light.
- Spoon the icing into a piping bag, fitted with a large star nozzle, and pipe a swirl of icing on top of each cake. Decorate with the mini eggs.

Blackcurrant Syrup Cream Cheese Cupcakes

746

- Replace the cherry syrup with blackcurrant syrup.

747

MAKES 12

Oaty Cream Cupcakes

PREPARATION TIME 30 MINUTES

COOKING TIME 15 - 20 MINUTES

INGREDIENTS

110 g / 4 oz / ⅔ cup self-raising flour, sifted
110 g / 4 oz / ½ cup caster (superfine) sugar
110 g / 4 oz / ½ cup butter, softened
2 large eggs
50 g / 1 ¾ oz / ½ cup rolled porridge oats

TO DECORATE:
300 ml / 10 ½ fl. oz / 1 ¼ cups double (heavy) cream
2 tbsp icing (confectioners') sugar
1 tsp vanilla extract
holly cake toppers and chocolate vermicelli

- Preheat the oven to 190°C (170° fan) / 375F / gas 5 and line a 12-hole cupcake tin with paper cases.
- Combine the flour, sugar, butter, eggs and oats in a bowl and whisk together for 2 minutes or until smooth.
- Divide the mixture between the cases, then transfer the tin to the oven and bake for 15 – 20 minutes.
- Test with a wooden toothpick, if it comes out clean, the cakes are done.
- Transfer the cakes to a wire rack and leave to cool completely.
- Whip the cream with the icing sugar and vanilla extract, then spoon it into a piping bag fitted with a large star nozzle.
- Pipe the cream onto the cakes and top each one with a cake topper and some chocolate vermicelli.

Oat and Honey Cream Cupcakes

748

- Omit the icing sugar and vanilla and whip the cream with 4 tbsp of runny honey.

749

MAKES 12

Speculoos Cupcakes

- Preheat the oven to 190°C (170° fan) / 375F / gas 5 and line a 12-hole cupcake tin with paper cases.
- Combine the flour, sugar, butter, eggs and Speculoos crumbs in a bowl and whisk together for 2 minutes or until smooth.
- Divide the mixture between the cases, then transfer the tin to the oven and bake for 15 – 20 minutes.
- Transfer the cakes to a wire rack and leave to cool completely.
- Beat the butter until smooth, then gradually whisk in the icing sugar.
- Spoon the mixture into a piping bag, fitted with a large star nozzle, and pipe a swirl of icing on top of each cake.
- Crumble 4 of the biscuits and sprinkle them over the cakes, then top each one with a whole Speculoos biscuit.

PREPARATION TIME 30 MINUTES

COOKING TIME 15 - 20 MINUTES

INGREDIENTS

110 g / 4 oz / ⅔ cup self-raising flour, sifted
110 g / 4 oz / ½ cup caster (superfine) sugar
110 g / 4 oz / ½ cup butter, softened
2 large eggs
50 g / 1 ¾ oz Speculoos biscuits, crushed

TO DECORATE:
100 g / 3 ½ oz / ½ cup butter, softened
200 g / 7 oz / 2 cups icing (confectioners') sugar
16 Speculoos biscuits

Ginger Nut Cupcakes

750

- Replace the Speculoos with ginger nut biscuits and add 1 tsp ground ginger to the cake mixture.

751

MAKES 12

Glacé-Iced Christmas Spice Cupcakes

- Preheat the oven to 190°C (170° fan) / 375F / gas 5 and line a 12-hole cupcake tin with paper cases.
- Combine the flour, sugar, butter, eggs, mixed spice, almond extract and clementine zest in a bowl and whisk together for 2 minutes or until smooth.
- Divide the mixture between the cases, then transfer the tin to the oven and bake for 15 – 20 minutes.
- Test with a wooden toothpick, if it comes out clean, the cakes are done.
- Transfer the cakes to a wire rack and leave to cool completely.
- Sieve the icing sugar into a bowl and add just enough water to make a thick, spreadable icing.
- Spoon the icing onto the cakes and top each one with a bauble.

PREPARATION TIME 30 MINUTES

COOKING TIME 15 - 20 MINUTES

INGREDIENTS

110 g / 4 oz / ⅔ cup self-raising flour, sifted
110 g / 4 oz / ½ cup caster (superfine) sugar
110 g / 4 oz / ½ cup butter, softened
2 large eggs
1 tsp mixed spice
½ tsp almond extract
2 clementines, zest finely grated

TO DECORATE:
200 g / 7 oz / 2 cups icing (confectioners') sugar
12 Christmas baubles

Marzipan and Christmas Spice Cupcakes

752

- Top the cakes with a thick layer of marzipan instead of the glacé icing.

753

MAKES 12

Violet Buttercream Cupcakes

PREPARATION TIME 30 MINUTES

COOKING TIME 15 - 20 MINUTES

INGREDIENTS

110 g / 4 oz / ⅔ cup self-raising flour, sifted
110 g / 4 oz / ½ cup caster (superfine) sugar
110 g / 4 oz / ½ cup butter, softened
2 large eggs
½ tsp violet essence

TO DECORATE:
100 g / 3 ½ oz / ½ cup butter, softened
200 g / 7 oz / 2 cups icing (confectioners') sugar
2 tbsp violet syrup
chocolate sprinkles to decorate

- Preheat the oven to 190°C (170° fan) / 375F / gas 5 and line a 12-hole cupcake tin with paper cases.
- Combine the flour, sugar, butter, eggs and violet essence in a bowl and whisk together for 2 minutes or until smooth.
- Divide the mixture between the cases, then transfer the tin to the oven and bake for 15 – 20 minutes.
- Test with a wooden toothpick, if it comes out clean, the cakes are done.
- Transfer the cakes to a wire rack and leave to cool completely.
- Beat the butter until smooth, then gradually whisk in the icing sugar and violet syrup.
- Spoon the mixture into a piping bag, fitted with a large star nozzle, and pipe a swirl of icing on top of each cake, then top with the chocolate sprinkles.

754

Lavender Buttercream Cupcakes

- Replace the violet essence with a few drops of lavender extract and use lavender syrup instead of the violet syrup.

755

Violet and Clementine Buttercream Cupcakes

- Add the grated zest of 2 clementines to the cake mixture and buttercream.

756

MAKES 12

Fondant Heart Cupcakes

- Preheat the oven to 190°C (170° fan) / 375F / gas 5 and line a 12-hole cupcake tin with paper cases.
- Combine the flour, sugar, butter, eggs and vanilla in a bowl and whisk together for 2 minutes or until smooth.
- Divide the mixture between the cases, then transfer the tin to the oven and bake for 15 – 20 minutes.
- Test with a wooden toothpick, if it comes out clean, the cakes are done.
- Transfer the cakes to a wire rack and leave to cool completely.
- Sieve the icing sugar into a bowl and add just enough water to make a thick, spreadable icing.
- Knead the icing with the food colouring until all the streaks disappear, then roll it out and cut out 24 hearts.
- Top the cakes with the white glacé icing and arrange the hearts and sugar pearls on top.

PREPARATION TIME 30 MINUTES

COOKING TIME 15 - 20 MINUTES

INGREDIENTS

110 g / 4 oz / ⅔ cup self-raising flour, sifted
110 g / 4 oz / ½ cup caster (superfine) sugar
110 g / 4 oz / ½ cup butter, softened
2 large eggs
1 tsp vanilla extract

TO DECORATE:
200 g / 7 oz / 2 cups icing (confectioners') sugar
150 g / 5 ½ oz ready to roll fondant icing
a few drops of red food colouring
sugar pearls to decorate

Playing Card Cupcakes

757

- Colour half the icing black and cut out clubs and spades. Use the red icing to cut out diamonds and hearts.

758

MAKES 12

Fruit Jelly Cupcakes

- Preheat the oven to 190°C (170° fan) / 375F / gas 5 and line a 12-hole cupcake tin with paper cases.
- Combine the flour, sugar, butter, eggs and lemon juice and zest in a bowl and whisk together for 2 minutes or until smooth.
- Divide the mixture between the cases, then transfer the tin to the oven and bake for 15 – 20 minutes.
- Transfer the cakes to a wire rack and leave to cool completely.
- Knead the food colouring into the fondant icing until any streaks disappear.
- Dust the work surface lightly with icing sugar and roll out the icing, then use a flower-shaped cutter to cut out 12 flowers.
- Wet the backs and attach them to the top of the cakes, then top each one with a fruit jelly sweet.

PREPARATION TIME 1 HOUR

COOKING TIME 15 - 20 MINUTES

INGREDIENTS

110 g / 4 oz / ⅔ cup self-raising flour, sifted
110 g / 4 oz / ½ cup caster (superfine) sugar
110 g / 4 oz / ½ cup butter, softened
2 large eggs
1 lemon, juiced and zest finely grated

TO DECORATE:
a few drops of yellow food colouring
200 g / 7 oz ready to roll fondant icing
icing (confectioners') sugar for dusting
12 fruit jelly sweets

Jelly Baby Cupcakes

759

- Replace the fruit jelly sweets with jelly babies.

760

MAKES 12

Blackberry and Lemon Cupcakes

PREPARATION TIME 30 MINUTES

COOKING TIME 15 - 20 MINUTES

INGREDIENTS

110 g / 4 oz / ⅔ cup self-raising flour, sifted
110 g / 4 oz / ½ cup caster (superfine) sugar
110 g / 4 oz / ½ cup butter, softened
2 large eggs
1 lemon, zest finely grated

TO DECORATE:
200 g / 7 oz / 2 cups icing (confectioners') sugar, plus extra for dusting
1 – 2 tsp lemon juice
36 blackberries

- Preheat the oven to 190°C (170° fan) / 375F / gas 5 and line a 12-hole cupcake tin with paper cases.
- Combine the flour, sugar, butter, eggs and lemon zest in a bowl and whisk together for 2 minutes or until smooth.
- Divide the mixture between the cases, then transfer the tin to the oven and bake for 15 – 20 minutes.
- Test with a wooden toothpick, if it comes out clean, the cakes are done.
- Transfer the cakes to a wire rack and leave to cool completely.
- Sieve the icing sugar into a bowl and add just enough lemon juice to make a thick, spreadable icing.
- Spoon the icing onto the cakes then top each one with 3 blackberries and sprinkle with icing sugar.

Blackberry and Orange Cupcakes

761

- Replace the lemon juice and zest with orange juice and zest.

762

MAKES 12

Oat Muffin Cupcakes

PREPARATION TIME 20 MINUTES

COOKING TIME 20 – 25 MINUTES

INGREDIENTS

1 large egg
125 ml / 4 ½ fl. oz / ½ cup sunflower oil
125 ml / 4 ½ fl. oz / ½ cup milk
375 g / 13 oz / 2 ½ cups self-raising flour, sifted
1 tsp baking powder
200 g / 7 oz / ¾ cup caster (superfine) sugar
50 g / 1 ¾ oz / ½ cup rolled porridge oats, plus extra for sprinkling

- Preheat the oven to 180°C (160° fan) / 350F / gas 4 and line a deep 12-hole cupcake tin with paper cases.
- Beat the egg in a jug with the oil and milk until well mixed.
- Mix the flour, baking powder, sugar and oats in a bowl, then pour in the egg mixture and stir just enough to combine.
- Spoon the mixture into the cases, then sprinkle with more oats and bake in the oven for 20 – 25 minutes.
- Test with a wooden toothpick, if it comes out clean, the cakes are done.
- Transfer the cakes to a wire rack and leave to cool completely.

Oat and Honey Muffin Cupcakes

763

- Replace 50 g of the sugar with 75 ml of runny honey. Drizzle the cakes with honey after baking.

764

MAKES 12

Chilli Cream Cupcakes

- Preheat the oven to 190°C (170° fan) / 375F / gas 5 and line a 12-hole cupcake tin with paper cases.
- Combine the flour, sugar, butter, eggs and chilli powder in a bowl and whisk together for 2 minutes or until smooth.
- Divide the mixture between the cases, then transfer the tin to the oven and bake for 15 – 20 minutes.
- Test with a wooden toothpick, if it comes out clean, the cakes are done.
- Transfer the cakes to a wire rack and leave to cool completely.
- Whip the cream with the icing sugar and vanilla extract, then spoon it onto the cakes.
- Arrange 2 dried chillies on top of each cake.

PREPARATION TIME 30 MINUTES

COOKING TIME 15 - 20 MINUTES

INGREDIENTS

110 g / 4 oz / ⅔ cup self-raising flour, sifted
110 g / 4 oz / ½ cup caster (superfine) sugar
110 g / 4 oz / ½ cup butter, softened
2 large eggs
a pinch of chilli (chili) powder

TO DECORATE:
300 ml / 10 ½ fl. oz / 1 ¼ cups double (heavy) cream
2 tbsp icing (confectioners') sugar
1 tsp vanilla extract
24 dried red chillies (chilies)

Orange and Chilli Cream Cupcakes

765

- Add the grated zest of an orange to the cake mixture and 2 tsp of orange juice to the cream instead of the vanilla extract.

766

MAKES 36

Mini Marrons Glacé Cupcakes

- Make the caramel topping in advance. Put the unopened can of condensed milk in a saucepan of water and simmer for 3 hours, adding more water as necessary to ensure it doesn't boil dry. Leave the can to cool completely.
- Preheat the oven to 190°C (170° fan) / 375F / gas 5 and line 2 x 18-hole mini cupcake tins with a double layer of paper cases.
- Combine the flour, sugar, butter, eggs and vanilla extract in a bowl and whisk together for 2 minutes.
- Divide the mixture between the cases, then transfer the tin to the oven and bake for 10 - 12 minutes.
- Transfer the cakes to a wire rack and leave to cool.
- Open the can of condensed milk and beat the caramel.
- Spoon some of the caramel on top of each cupcake and top each one with half a marron glacé.

PREPARATION TIME 15 MINUTES

COOKING TIME 3 HOURS 12 MINUTES

COOLING TIME 1 - 2 HOURS

INGREDIENTS

400 g / 14 oz can of condensed milk
175 g / 6 oz / 1 ¼ cups self-raising flour, sifted
175 g / 6 oz / ¾ cup light muscovado sugar
175 g / 6 oz / ¾ cup butter, softened
3 large eggs
1 tsp vanilla extract
16 marrons glacé, halved

Mini Chestnut Cream Cupcakes

767

- Omit the caramel topping and replace it with softly whipped cream.

768

MAKES 12

Chocolate Frosted Almond Cupcakes

PREPARATION TIME 30 MINUTES

COOKING TIME 15 - 20 MINUTES

INGREDIENTS

110 g / 4 oz / ⅔ cup self-raising flour, sifted
110 g / 4 oz / ½ cup caster (superfine) sugar
110 g / 4 oz / ½ cup butter, softened
2 large eggs
2 tbsp ground almonds
½ tsp almond extract

TO DECORATE:
300 ml / 10 ½ fl. oz / 1 ¼ cups double (heavy) cream
200 g / 7 oz dark chocolate, minimum 60% cocoa solids, chopped
3 tbsp flaked (slivered) almonds

- Preheat the oven to 190°C (170° fan) / 375F / gas 5 and oil a 12-hole silicone cupcake mould.
- Combine the flour, sugar, butter, eggs, ground almonds and almond extract in a bowl and whisk for 2 minutes.
- Spoon the mixture into the mould, then transfer the tin to the oven and bake for 15 – 20 minutes.
- Turn out the cakes onto a wire rack and leave to cool.
- Heat half of the cream until it starts to simmer, then pour it over the chopped chocolate and stir until smooth. Leave to cool to room temperature, then combine with the rest of the cream and whisk until it holds its shape.
- Add a thick layer of chocolate cream to the top of the cakes and spread it flush with the sides.
- Toast the almonds under a hot grill for a few minutes, stirring regularly, then scatter them over the cakes.

769

White Chocolate Frosted Almond Cupcakes

- Replace the dark chocolate in the icing with good quality white chocolate.

770

MAKES 12

St Patrick's Day Cupcakes

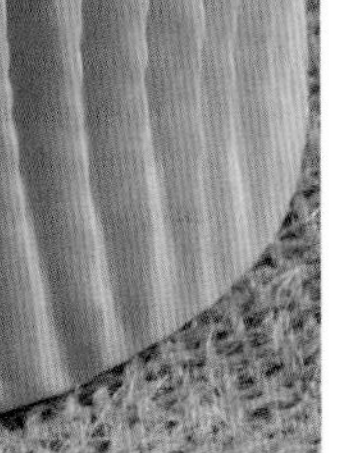

PREPARATION TIME 30 MINUTES

COOKING TIME 15 - 20 MINUTES

INGREDIENTS

110 g / 4 oz / ⅔ cup self-raising flour, sifted
110 g / 4 oz / ½ cup caster (superfine) sugar
110 g / 4 oz / ½ cup butter, softened
2 large eggs
1 tsp vanilla extract

TO DECORATE:
110 g / 4 oz / ½ cup cream cheese
55 g / 2 oz / ¼ cup butter, softened
110 g / 4 oz / 1 cup icing (confectioners') sugar
2 tbsp Guinness
36 sugar paste shamrocks

- Preheat the oven to 190°C (170° fan) / 375F / gas 5 and line a 12-hole cupcake tin with paper cases.
- Combine the flour, sugar, butter, eggs and vanilla extract in a bowl and whisk together for 2 minutes or until smooth.
- Divide the mixture between the cases and bake for 15 – 20 minutes.
- Transfer the cakes to a wire rack and leave to cool.
- Beat the cream cheese and butter together until light and fluffy then beat in the icing sugar a quarter at a time.
- Add the Guinness then whip the mixture for 2 minutes or until smooth and light.
- Spoon the icing into a piping bag, fitted with a large star nozzle, and pipe a swirl of icing on top of each cake. Decorate with the sugar shamrocks.

771

Chocolate and Guinness Cupcakes

- Add 2 tbsp of cocoa powder and 4 tbsp of Guinness to the cake mixture and top the cakes with dark chocolate curls.

772

MAKES 12

Coconut Moon and Star Cupcakes

Peppermint Moon and Star Cupcakes

773

- Omit the coconut from the cake mixture and add 75 g of dark chocolate chips and a few drops of peppermint extract.

Lemon Moon and Star Cupcakes

774

- Replace the coconut in the cake mixture with the zest of a lemon and sprinkle finely grated lemon zest onto the icing instead of coconut.

PREPARATION TIME 1 HOUR

COOKING TIME 15 - 20 MINUTES

INGREDIENTS

110 g / 4 oz / ⅔ cup self-raising flour, sifted
110 g / 4 oz / ½ cup caster (superfine) sugar
110 g / 4 oz / ½ cup butter, softened
2 large eggs
2 tbsp desiccated coconut

TO DECORATE:
a few drops of blue food colouring
200 g / 7 oz ready to roll fondant icing
icing (confectioners') sugar for dusting
2 tbsp desiccated coconut
yellow sugar stars to decorate

- Preheat the oven to 190°C (170° fan) / 375F / gas 5 and line a 12-hole cupcake tin with paper cases.
- Combine the flour, sugar, butter, eggs and coconut in a bowl and whisk together for 2 minutes or until smooth.
- Divide the mixture between the cases, then transfer the tin to the oven and bake for 15 – 20 minutes.
- Test with a wooden toothpick, if it comes out clean, the cakes are done.
- Transfer the cakes to a wire rack and leave to cool completely.
- Reserve a quarter of the fondant icing and knead a little blue food colouring into the rest.
- Dust the work surface lightly with icing sugar and roll out the icing, then cut out 12 circles the same diameter as the top of the cupcakes with a fluted cookie cutter.
- Wet the backs and stick one to the top of each cake. Roll out the reserved white icing and cut out 12 crescent moons, then stick them to the cakes with a dab of water.
- Sprinkle with desiccated coconut and add a few sugar stars to each one.

775

MAKES 12

Heart Cream Cupcakes

PREPARATION TIME 45 MINUTES

COOKING TIME 15 - 20 MINUTES

INGREDIENTS

110 g / 4 oz / ⅔ cup self-raising flour, sifted
110 g / 4 oz / ½ cup caster (superfine) sugar
110 g / 4 oz / ½ cup butter, softened
2 large eggs
1 tsp vanilla extract

TO DECORATE:
150 g / 5 ½ oz ready to roll fondant icing
a few drops of red food colouring
300 ml / 10 ½ fl. oz / 1 ¼ cups double (heavy) cream
2 tbsp icing (confectioners') sugar
1 tsp vanilla extract

- Preheat the oven to 190°C (170° fan) / 375F / gas 5 and line a 12-hole cupcake tin with paper cases.
- Combine the flour, sugar, butter, eggs and vanilla in a bowl and whisk together for 2 minutes or until smooth.
- Divide the mixture between the cases, then transfer the tin to the oven and bake for 15 – 20 minutes.
- Test with a wooden toothpick, if it comes out clean, the cakes are done.
- Transfer the cakes to a wire rack and leave to cool completely.
- Knead the icing with the food colouring until all the streaks disappear, then roll it out and cut out 12 heart shapes.
- Whip the cream with the icing sugar and vanilla until it holds its shape, then spoon it onto the cakes and top each one with a fondant heart.

Star Cream Cupcakes

776

- Colour the icing bright yellow and cut out 12 star shapes.

777

MAKES 12

'Pasta and Peas' Chocolate Cupcakes

PREPARATION TIME 30 MINUTES

COOKING TIME 15 - 20 MINUTES

INGREDIENTS

110 g / 4 oz / ⅔ cup self-raising flour, sifted
110 g / 4 oz / ½ cup caster (superfine) sugar
110 g / 4 oz / ½ cup butter, softened
2 large eggs
2 tbsp unsweetened cocoa powder

TO DECORATE:
100 g / 3 ½ oz marzipan
a little green food colouring

- Preheat the oven to 190°C (170° fan) / 375F / gas 5 and line a 12-hole cupcake tin with paper cases.
- Combine the flour, sugar, butter, eggs and cocoa in a bowl and whisk together for 2 minutes or until smooth.
- Divide the mixture between the cases, then transfer the tin to the oven and bake for 15 – 20 minutes.
- Test with a wooden toothpick, if it comes out clean, the cakes are done.
- Transfer the cakes to a wire rack and leave to cool completely.
- Roll 2/3 of the marzipan into 36 thin sausages and arrange them on top of the cakes, attaching with a dab of water.
- Colour the rest of the marzipan green and roll it into pea shapes, then attach them to the cake with a dab of water.

'Bacon and Egg' Chocolate Cupcakes

778

- Colour some of the marzipan pink and shape into bacon rashers. Colour the rest of the marzipan yellow to make the egg yolks and make the whites from fondant icing.

779

MAKES 12

Liquorice Frosted Parsnip Cupcakes

- Preheat the oven to 190°C (170° fan) / 375F / gas 5 and line a 12-hole cupcake tin with paper cases.
- Whisk the sugar, eggs and oil together for 3 minutes.
- Fold in the flour, baking powder and star anise, followed by the grated parsnips.
- Divide the mixture between the paper cases, then transfer the tin to the oven and bake for 20 - 25 minutes.
- Transfer the cakes to a wire rack and leave to cool.
- Beat the cream cheese and butter until fluffy then beat in the icing sugar gradually for 2 minutes.
- Put the liquorice in a pan with 2 tbsp water and stir over a medium heat until liquorice has dissolved.
- Leave to cool a little then beat half of it into the cream cheese mixture. Swirl through the other half of the liquorice, then spoon the mixture on top of the cakes and garnish with mint leaves.

PREPARATION TIME 35 MINUTES

COOKING TIME 20 – 25 MINUTES

INGREDIENTS

175 g / 6 oz / 1 cup soft brown sugar
2 large eggs
150 ml / 5 fl. oz / ⅔ cup sunflower oil
175 g / 6 oz / 1 ¼ cups wholemeal flour
3 tsp baking powder
1 tsp ground star anise
200 g / 7 oz / 1 ⅔ cups parsnips, peeled and coarsely grated

TO DECORATE:
110 g / 4 oz / ½ cup cream cheese
55 g / 2 oz / ¼ cup butter, softened
110 g / 4 oz / 1 cup icing (confectioners') sugar
110 g / 4 oz black liquorice, chopped
mint leaves to garnish

780

Liquorice Frosted Carrot Cupcakes

- Replace the parsnips with carrots and add the finely grated zest of an orange.

781

MAKES 12

Ice Cream Sundae Chocolate Cupcakes

- Preheat the oven to 190°C (170° fan) / 375F / gas 5 and line a 12-hole cupcake tin with paper cases.
- Combine the flour, sugar, butter, eggs and cocoa in a bowl and whisk together for 2 minutes or until smooth.
- Divide the mixture between the cases, then transfer the tin to the oven and bake for 15 – 20 minutes.
- Transfer the cakes to a wire rack and leave to cool.
- Divide the marzipan in half and colour one piece green and the other red. Model 12 calyxes out of the green marzipan and 12 lotus flowers out of the red marzipan.
- Leave the ice cream to soften for 20 minutes, then spoon it into a food processor and process until smooth.
- Spoon the ice cream into a piping bag and quickly pipe a swirl on top of each cake.
- Top with the lotus calyxes and flowers, then decorate with strawberry sauce and mini marshmallows.

PREPARATION TIME 15 MINUTES

COOKING TIME 15 - 20 MINUTES

INGREDIENTS

110 g / 4 oz / ⅔ cup self-raising flour, sifted
110 g / 4 oz / ½ cup caster (superfine) sugar
110 g / 4 oz / ½ cup butter, softened
2 large eggs
2 tbsp unsweetened cocoa powder

TO DECORATE:
200 g / 7 oz marzipan
a few drops of food colouring
500 ml / 17 ½ fl. oz tub vanilla ice cream
strawberry sauce for drizzling
mini marshmallows for sprinkling

782

Knickerbocker Glory Cupcakes

- Omit the marzipan flowers and top the ice cream with chunks of fresh fruit and a final swirl of whipped cream.

783

MAKES 12

Half and Half Cupcakes

Half and Half Buttercream Cupcakes

784

- Spoon vanilla buttercream into one side of a piping bag and chocolate buttercream into the other side. Pipe a swirl onto each cake for a 2-tone effect.

Half and Half Cream Cupcakes

785

- Decorate one side of each cake with whipped cream and the other side with chocolate spread.

PREPARATION TIME 30 MINUTES
COOKING TIME 15 - 20 MINUTES
SETTING TIME 1 HOUR

INGREDIENTS

110 g / 4 oz / ⅔ cup self-raising flour, sifted
110 g / 4 oz / ½ cup caster (superfine) sugar
110 g / 4 oz / ½ cup butter, softened
2 large eggs
1 tsp vanilla extract
1 tbsp cocoa powder

TO DECORATE:
200 g / 7 oz / 2 cups icing (confectioners') sugar
edible metallic balls to decorate
50 g / 1 ¾ oz milk chocolate, finely grated

- Preheat the oven to 190°C (170° fan) / 375F / gas 5 and line a 12-hole cupcake tin with paper cases.
- Combine the flour, sugar, butter, eggs and vanilla in a bowl and whisk together for 2 minutes or until smooth.
- Divide half the mixture between the cases, then whisk the cocoa powder into the other half.
- Spoon the cocoa cake mixture into the cases and bake for 15 – 20 minutes.
- Test with a wooden toothpick, if it comes out clean, the cakes are done.
- Transfer the cakes to a wire rack and leave to cool completely.
- Sieve the icing sugar into a bowl and add just enough water to make a thick, pourable icing.
- Spoon the icing onto the cakes and decorate one half with edible metallic balls.
- Leave the icing to set for 1 hour, then sprinkle the other half of each cake with the grated chocolate.

786

MAKES 12 Marshmallow Muffin Cupcakes

- Preheat the oven to 180°C (160° fan) / 350F / gas 4 and line a deep 12-hole cupcake tin with paper cases.
- Beat the egg in a jug with the oil and milk until well mixed.
- Mix the flour, baking powder, sugar and half the marshmallows in a bowl, then pour in the egg mixture and stir just enough to combine.
- Spoon the mixture into the cases, then bake in the oven for 20 – 25 minutes.
- Test with a wooden toothpick, if it comes out clean, the cakes are done.
- Transfer the cakes to a wire rack and leave to cool completely before topping with the rest of the marshmallows.

PREPARATION TIME 20 MINUTES

COOKING TIME 20 – 25 MINUTES

INGREDIENTS

1 large egg
125 ml / 4 ½ fl. oz / ½ cup sunflower oil
125 ml / 4 ½ fl. oz / ½ cup milk
375 g / 13 oz / 2 ½ cups self-raising flour, sifted
1 tsp baking powder
200 g / 7 oz / ¾ cup caster (superfine) sugar
150 g / 5 ½ oz / 2 ½ cups mini marshmallows

Chocolate Marshmallow Muffin Cupcakes

787

- Add 2 tbsp of cocoa powder to the cake mixture and top the cakes with chocolate buttercream before decorating with the marshmallows.

788

MAKES 12 Almond and Dulce de Leche Cupcakes

- Preheat the oven to 190°C (170° fan) / 375F / gas 5 and line a 12-hole cupcake tin with thick paper cases.
- Combine the flour, sugar, butter, eggs, ground almonds and almond extract in a bowl and whisk together for 2 minutes or until smooth.
- Divide the mixture between the cases, then transfer the tin to the oven and bake for 15 – 20 minutes.
- Test with a wooden toothpick, if it comes out clean, the cakes are done.
- Transfer the cakes to a wire rack and leave to cool completely.
- Spoon the dulce de leche into a piping bag fitted with a star nozzle and pipe a squiggle on top of each cake.
- Scatter over the almonds and dust lightly with icing sugar.

PREPARATION TIME 20 MINUTES

COOKING TIME 15 - 20 MINUTES

INGREDIENTS

110 g / 4 oz / ⅔ cup self-raising flour, sifted
110 g / 4 oz / ½ cup light brown sugar
110 g / 4 oz / ½ cup butter, softened
2 large eggs
2 tbsp ground almonds
½ tsp almond extract
450 g / 1 lb jar of dulce de leche
2 tbsp flaked (slivered) almonds, toasted
icing (confectioners') sugar for dusting

Hazelnut and Dulce de Leche Cupcakes

789

- Replace the ground almonds with 50 g of chopped hazelnuts and top the dulce de leche with whole hazelnuts (cob nuts).

790

MAKES 12

Smoked Mackerel and Lemon Cupcakes

PREPARATION TIME 15 MINUTES

COOKING TIME 20 – 25 MINUTES

INGREDIENTS

2 large eggs
125 ml / 4 ½ oz / ½ cup sunflower oil
175 ml / 6 oz / ⅔ cup Greek yoghurt
100 g / 3 ½ oz / 1 cup Parmesan, grated
225 g / 8 oz / 1 ½ cups plain (all purpose) flour
2 tsp baking powder
½ tsp bicarbonate of (baking) soda
½ tsp salt
1 lemon, zest finely grated
100 g / 3 ½ oz smoked mackerel, chopped

TO DECORATE:
300 g / 10 ½ oz / 1 ⅓ cups cream cheese
12 thick slices of smoked mackerel
12 sprigs of dill
3 lemon slices, quartered

- Preheat the oven to 180°C (160° fan) / 350F / gas 4 and line a 12-hole cupcake tin with paper cases.
- Beat the egg in a jug with the oil, yoghurt and Parmesan until well mixed.
- Mix the flour, raising agents, salt, lemon zest and smoked mackerel in a bowl, then pour in the egg mixture and stir just enough to combine.
- Divide the mixture between the paper cases, then bake in the oven for 20 – 25 minutes.
- Test with a wooden toothpick, if it comes out clean, the cakes are done.
- Transfer the cakes to a wire rack and leave to cool completely.
- Spoon the cream cheese onto the cakes and top each one with a slice of smoked mackerel, a sprig of dill and a piece of lemon.

Smoked Eel and Dill Cupcakes

791

- Replace the smoked mackerel with smoked eel and add 3 tbsp of chopped dill to the cake mixture.

792

MAKES 12

Black Forest Cupcakes

PREPARATION TIME 30 MINUTES

COOKING TIME 15 - 20 MINUTES

INGREDIENTS

110 g / 4 oz / ⅔ cup self-raising flour, sifted
2 tbsp unsweetened cocoa powder
110 g / 4 oz / ½ cup caster (superfine) sugar
110 g / 4 oz / ½ cup butter, softened
2 large eggs
1 tsp almond extract
200 g / 7 oz / ⅔ cup black cherry jam (jelly)

TO DECORATE:
200 ml / 7 fl. oz / ¾ cup double (heavy) cream
12 maraschino cherries
2 tbsp milk chocolate flakes

- Preheat the oven to 190°C (170° fan) / 375F / gas 5 and line a 12-hole cupcake tin with thick paper cases.
- Combine the flour, cocoa, sugar, butter, eggs and almond extract in a bowl and whisk together for 2 minutes or until smooth.
- Divide half the mixture between the cases and add a big spoonful of jam to each one.
- Top with the rest of the cake mixture, then transfer the tin to the oven and bake for 15 – 20 minutes.
- Transfer the cakes to a wire rack and leave to cool completely.
- Whisk the cream until it holds its shape, then spoon it into a piping bag fitted with a large star nozzle and pipe a rosette on top of each cake.
- Add a maraschino cherry to each one and sprinkle with chocolate flakes.

Chocolate and Raspberry Jam Cupcakes

793

- Replace the cherry jam with raspberry jam and top each one with a fresh raspberry.

794

MAKES 12

Chocolate and Melon Cream Cupcakes

- Preheat the oven to 190°C (170° fan) / 375F / gas 5 and line a 12-hole cupcake tin with paper cases.
- Sieve the flour, bicarbonate of soda and cocoa powder together into a bowl.
- Put the golden syrup, butter and brown sugar in a small saucepan and boil gently for 2 minutes, stirring to dissolve the sugar.
- Pour the butter and sugar mixture onto the flour with the eggs, milk and midori, then fold together until smooth.
- Divide the mixture between the cases, then transfer the tin to the oven and bake for 20 – 25 minutes.
- Transfer the cakes to a wire rack and leave to cool.
- Whip the cream with the icing sugar until it holds its shape, then spoon it into a piping bag.
- Pipe a swirl of cream onto the cakes then top each one with a chunk of melon and sprinkles.

PREPARATION TIME 30 MINUTES

COOKING TIME 20 – 25 MINUTES

INGREDIENTS

250 g / 9 oz / 1 ¾ cups self-raising flour
1 tsp bicarbonate of (baking) soda
2 tbsp unsweetened cocoa powder
200 g / 8 ½ oz / ½ cup golden syrup
125 g / 4 ½ oz / ½ cup butter
125 g / 4 ½ oz / ¾ cup dark brown sugar
2 large eggs, beaten
250 ml / 9 fl. oz / 1 cup milk
2 tbsp Midori liqueur

TO DECORATE:
250 ml / 9 fl. oz / 1 cup double (heavy) cream
2 tbsp icing (confectioners') sugar
12 chunks of melon
sugar cake sprinkles

Orange and Melon Cream Cupcakes

795

- Omit the cocoa powder and add the grated zest of an orange to the cake mixture.

796

MAKES 18

Smoked Salmon and Caviar Cupcakes

- Preheat the oven to 180°C (160° fan) / 350F / gas 4 and line a 12-hole cupcake tin with paper cases.
- Beat the egg in a jug with the oil, yoghurt and Parmesan until well mixed.
- Mix the flour, raising agents, salt, lemon zest and smoked salmon in a bowl, then pour in the egg mixture and stir just enough to combine.
- Divide the mixture between the paper cases, then bake in the oven for 20 – 25 minutes.
- Test with a wooden toothpick, if it comes out clean, the cakes are done.
- Transfer the cakes to a wire rack and leave to cool completely.
- Spoon the cream cheese into a piping bag, fitted with a large star nozzle, and pipe a swirl on top of each cake.
- Top each one with 1 tsp of caviar and garnish with the smoked salmon and dill.

PREPARATION TIME 15 MINUTES

COOKING TIME 20 – 25 MINUTES

INGREDIENTS

2 large eggs
125 ml / 4 ½ oz / ½ cup sunflower oil
175 ml / 6 oz / ⅔ cup Greek yoghurt
100 g / 3 ½ oz / 1 cup Parmesan, grated
225 g / 8 oz / 1 ½ cups plain (all purpose) flour
2 tsp baking powder
½ tsp bicarbonate of (baking) soda
½ tsp salt
1 lemon, zest finely grated
100 g / 3 ½ oz smoked salmon, chopped

TO DECORATE:
300 g / 10 ½ oz / 1 ⅓ cups cream cheese
4 tbsp caviar
6 slices smoked salmon, halved
12 sprigs of dill

Smoked Salmon Cupcakes with Salmon Roe

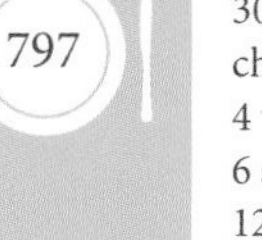

- Replace the caviar with salmon roe.

798

MAKES 12

Orange and Glacé Cherry Muffin Cupcakes

PREPARATION TIME 25 MINUTES

COOKING TIME 20 – 25 MINUTES

INGREDIENTS

1 large egg
1 orange, zest finely grated
125 ml / 4 ½ fl. oz / ½ cup sunflower oil
125 ml / 4 ½ fl. oz / ½ cup milk
375 g / 13 oz / 2 ½ cups self-raising flour, sifted
1 tsp baking powder
200 g / 7 oz / ¾ cup caster (superfine) sugar
75 g / 2 ½ oz / ⅓ cup glacé cherries, chopped

TO DECORATE:
200 g / 7 oz / 2 cups icing (confectioners') sugar
2 – 3 tsp orange juice
6 glacé cherries, chopped

- Preheat the oven to 180°C (160° fan) / 350F / gas 4 and line a 12-hole cupcake tin with thick paper cases.
- Beat the egg in a jug with the orange zest, oil and milk until well mixed.
- Mix the flour, baking powder and sugar in a bowl, then pour in the egg mixture and chopped cherries and stir just enough to combine.
- Divide the mixture between the cases, then bake in the oven for 20 – 25 minutes.
- Test with a wooden toothpick, if it comes out clean, the cakes are done.
- Transfer the cakes to a wire rack and leave to cool completely.
- Sift the icing sugar into a bowl and add just enough orange juice to make a thick, spreadable icing.
- Spoon the icing onto the cakes and sprinkle over the chopped cherries.

Orange and Angelica Muffin Cupcakes

799

- Replace the cherries with chopped glacé angelica.

800

MAKES 12

Spring Cupcakes

PREPARATION TIME 1 HOUR

COOKING TIME 15 - 20 MINUTES

INGREDIENTS

110 g / 4 oz / ⅔ cup self-raising flour, sifted
110 g / 4 oz / ½ cup caster (superfine) sugar
110 g / 4 oz / ½ cup butter, softened
2 large eggs
2 tbsp elderflower cordial

TO DECORATE:
200 g / 7 oz ready to roll fondant icing
icing (confectioners') sugar for dusting
a few drops of yellow food colouring

- Preheat the oven to 190°C (170° fan) / 375F / gas 5 and line a 12-hole cupcake tin with paper cases.
- Combine the flour, sugar, butter, eggs and elderflower cordial in a bowl and whisk together for 2 minutes.
- Divide the mixture between the cases, then transfer the tin to the oven and bake for 15 – 20 minutes.
- Transfer the cakes to a wire rack and leave to cool.
- Reserve a quarter of the fondant icing then dust the work surface lightly with icing sugar and roll out the rest. Cut out 12 circles the same diameter as the top of the cupcakes, wet the backs and stick one to the top of each cake.
- Cut some flower and shamrock shapes out of the off-cuts and attach to the cakes with a dab of water.
- Colour the reserved icing yellow to make the flower centres, then knead together any yellow and white icing off-cuts to make a swirled effect for the hearts.

Elderflower and Lemon Cupcakes

801

- Add the grated zest of a lemon to the cake mixture.

802

MAKES 12

Pistachio Buttercream Cupcakes

Almond Buttercream Cupcakes

803

- Use chopped almonds in place of the pistachios, and top each cake with a whole blanched almond.

Brazil Nut Buttercream Cupcakes

804

- Use chopped Brazil nuts instead of the pistachios and top each cake with a whole Brazil nut.

PREPARATION TIME 30 MINUTES

COOKING TIME COOKING TIME: 15 - 20 MINUTES

INGREDIENTS

110 g / 4 oz / ⅔ cup self-raising flour, sifted
110 g / 4 oz / ½ cup caster (superfine) sugar
110 g / 4 oz / ½ cup butter, softened
2 large eggs
½ tsp almond extract
100 g / 3 ½ oz / ⅔ cup pistachio nuts, chopped

TO DECORATE:
100 g / 3 ½ oz / ½ cup butter, softened
200 g / 7 oz / 2 cups icing (confectioners') sugar
½ tsp almond extract
2 tbsp ground pistachios

- Preheat the oven to 190°C (170° fan) / 375F / gas 5 and line a 12-hole cupcake tin with paper cases.
- Combine the flour, sugar, butter, eggs, almond extract and chopped pistachios in a bowl and whisk together for 2 minutes or until smooth.
- Divide the mixture between the cases, then transfer the tin to the oven and bake for 15 – 20 minutes.
- Test with a wooden toothpick, if it comes out clean, the cakes are done.
- Transfer the cakes to a wire rack and leave to cool completely.
- Beat the butter until smooth, then gradually whisk in the icing sugar and almond extract.
- Spoon the mixture into a piping bag, fitted with a large star nozzle, and pipe a rosette on top of each cake. Sprinkle with the ground pistachios.

805

MAKES 12

Lemon and Poppy Seed Muffin Cupcakes

PREPARATION TIME 35 MINUTES

COOKING TIME 20 – 25 MINUTES

INGREDIENTS

1 large egg
1 lemon, zest finely grated
125 ml / 4 ½ fl. oz / ½ cup sunflower oil
125 ml / 4 ½ fl. oz / ½ cup milk
375 g / 13 oz / 2 ½ cups self-raising flour, sifted
1 tsp baking powder
200 g / 7 oz / ¾ cup caster (superfine) sugar

TO DECORATE:
300 ml / 10 ½ fl. oz / 1 ¼ cups double (heavy) cream
2 tbsp icing (confectioners') sugar
1 tbsp lemon juice
3 tbsp poppy seeds
12 lemon slices

- Preheat the oven to 180°C (160° fan) / 350F / gas 4 and line a 12-hole cupcake tin with paper cases.
- Beat the egg in a jug with the lemon zest, oil and milk until well mixed.
- Mix the flour, baking powder and sugar in a bowl, then pour in the egg mixture and stir just enough to combine.
- Spoon the mixture into the cases, then bake in the oven for 20 – 25 minutes.
- Transfer the cakes to a wire rack and leave to cool completely.
- Whip the cream with the icing sugar and lemon juice until it holds its shape, then spoon it onto the cakes and sprinkle with half of the poppy seeds.
- Top each cake with a lemon slice and sprinkle over the rest of the poppy seeds.

806

Orange and Poppy Seed Muffin Cupcakes

- Replace the lemon juice and zest with orange juice and zest. Top the cakes with fresh orange slices.

807

MAKES 12

Glacé-Iced Physalis Cupcakes

PREPARATION TIME 30 MINUTES

COOKING TIME 15 - 20 MINUTES

INGREDIENTS

110 g / 4 oz / ⅔ cup self-raising flour, sifted
110 g / 4 oz / ½ cup caster (superfine) sugar
110 g / 4 oz / ½ cup butter, softened
2 large eggs
1 tsp vanilla extract

TO DECORATE:
200 g / 7 oz / 2 cups icing (confectioners') sugar
12 physalis

- Preheat the oven to 190°C (170° fan) / 375F / gas 5 and line a 12-hole cupcake tin with paper cases.
- Combine the flour, sugar, butter, eggs and vanilla in a bowl and whisk together for 2 minutes or until smooth.
- Divide the mixture between the cases, then transfer the tin to the oven and bake for 15 – 20 minutes.
- Test with a wooden toothpick, if it comes out clean, the cakes are done.
- Transfer the cakes to a wire rack and leave to cool completely.
- Sieve the icing sugar into a bowl and add just enough water to make a thick, pourable icing.
- Spoon the icing onto the cakes and decorate with the physalis.

808

Physalis and Lemon Cupcakes

- Add the grated zest of a lemon to the cake mixture and use lemon juice instead of water to make the icing.

809

MAKES 12

Kiwi and Lemon Cream Muffin Cupcakes

- Preheat the oven to 180°C (160° fan) / 350F / gas 4 and line a 12-hole cupcake tin with paper cases.
- Beat the egg in a jug with the lemon zest, oil and milk until well mixed.
- Mix the flour, baking powder and sugar in a bowl, then pour in the egg mixture and chopped kiwi and stir just enough to combine.
- Spoon the mixture into the cases, then bake in the oven for 20 – 25 minutes.
- Transfer the cakes to a wire rack and leave to cool completely.
- Whip the cream with the icing sugar and lemon juice until it holds its shape, then spoon it into a piping bag fitted with a large star nozzle.
- Pipe a big swirl on top of the cakes and decorate each one with 2 slices of kiwi and some chocolate flakes.

PREPARATION TIME 35 MINUTES

COOKING TIME 20 – 25 MINUTES

INGREDIENTS

1 large egg
1 lemon, zest finely grated
125 ml / 4 ½ fl. oz / ½ cup sunflower oil
125 ml / 4 ½ fl. oz / ½ cup milk
375 g / 13 oz / 2 ½ cups self-raising flour, sifted
1 tsp baking powder
200 g / 7 oz / ¾ cup caster (superfine) sugar
1 kiwi, peeled and finely chopped

TO DECORATE:
300 ml / 10 ½ fl. oz / 1 ¼ cups double (heavy) cream
2 tbsp icing (confectioners') sugar
1 tbsp lemon juice
2 kiwi fruit, peeled and sliced
chocolate curls to decorate

Kiwi and Lime Muffin Cupcakes

810

- Replace the lemon juice and zest with lime juice and zest.

811

MAKES 18

Parmesan and Walnut Cupcakes

- Preheat the oven to 180°C (160° fan) / 350F / gas 4 and line a 12-hole cupcake tin with paper cases.
- Beat the egg in a jug with the oil, yoghurt and Parmesan until well mixed.
- Mix the flour, raising agents, salt and walnuts in a bowl, then pour in the egg mixture and stir just enough to combine.
- Divide the mixture between the paper cases, then bake in the oven for 20 – 25 minutes.
- Test with a wooden toothpick, if it comes out clean, the cakes are done.
- While the cupcakes are cooling, mix the cream cheese with the walnuts and grated Parmesan.
- Spoon the mixture on top of the cupcakes and garnish each one with a Parmesan shaving.

PREPARATION TIME 15 MINUTES

COOKING TIME 20 – 25 MINUTES

INGREDIENTS

2 large eggs
125 ml / 4 ½ oz / ½ cup sunflower oil
175 ml / 6 oz / ⅔ cup Greek yoghurt
100 g / 3 ½ oz / 1 cup Parmesan, grated
225 g / 8 oz / 1 ½ cups plain (all purpose) flour
2 tsp baking powder
½ tsp bicarbonate of (baking) soda
½ tsp salt
50 g / 1 ¾ oz / ½ cup walnuts, chopped

TO DECORATE:
75 g / 2 ½ oz / ⅓ cup cream cheese
50 g / 1 ¾ oz / ½ cup walnuts, finely chopped
2 tbsp Parmesan, finely grated
Parmesan shavings to garnish

Roquefort and Walnut Cupcakes

812

- Replace the Parmesan in the cake mixture and topping with crumbled Roquefort.

813

MAKES 12

Red and Green Buttercream Cupcakes

PREPARATION TIME 30 MINUTES

COOKING TIME 15 - 20 MINUTES

INGREDIENTS

110 g / 4 oz / ⅔ cup self-raising flour, sifted
110 g / 4 oz / ½ cup caster (superfine) sugar
110 g / 4 oz / ½ cup butter, softened
2 large eggs
½ tsp vanilla extract

TO DECORATE:
100 g / 3 ½ oz / ½ cup butter, softened
200 g / 7 oz / 2 cups icing (confectioners') sugar
1 tsp red food colouring
1 tsp green food colouring

- Preheat the oven to 190°C (170° fan) / 375F / gas 5 and line a 12-hole cupcake tin with paper cases.
- Combine the flour, sugar, butter, eggs and vanilla extract in a bowl and whisk together for 2 minutes or until smooth.
- Divide the mixture between the cases, then transfer the tin to the oven and bake for 15 – 20 minutes.
- Test with a wooden toothpick, if it comes out clean, the cakes are done.
- Transfer the cakes to a wire rack and leave to cool completely.
- Beat the butter until smooth, then gradually whisk in the icing sugar.
- Divide the buttercream between 2 bowls and colour one red and one green.
- Spoon each icing into a piping bag and pipe alternate colours in rings on top of the cakes.

Chocolate Red and Green Cupcakes

814

- Add 2 tbsp of cocoa powder to the cake mixture.

Strawberry and Apple Cupcakes

815

- Add ½ a chopped, peeled apple and 6 chopped strawberries to the cake mixture.

816

MAKES 12 Kiwi Cream Muffin Cupcakes

- Preheat the oven to 180°C (160° fan) / 350F / gas 4 and line a 12-hole cupcake tin with paper cases.
- Beat the egg in a jug with the lemon zest, oil and milk until well mixed.
- Mix the flour, baking powder and sugar in a bowl, then pour in the egg mixture and chopped kiwi and stir just enough to combine.
- Spoon the mixture into the cases, then bake in the oven for 20 – 25 minutes.
- Transfer the cakes to a wire rack and leave to cool completely.
- Whip the cream with the icing sugar until it holds its shape, then spoon it into a piping bag fitted with a large star nozzle.
- Pipe a big swirl on top of the cakes and decorate each one with 2 slices of kiwi.

PREPARATION TIME 35 MINUTES

COOKING TIME 20 – 25 MINUTES

INGREDIENTS

1 large egg
1 lemon, zest finely grated
125 ml / 4 ½ fl. oz / ½ cup sunflower oil
125 ml / 4 ½ fl. oz / ½ cup milk
375 g / 13 oz / 2 ½ cups self-raising flour, sifted
1 tsp baking powder
200 g / 7 oz / ¾ cup caster (superfine) sugar
1 kiwi, peeled and finely chopped

TO DECORATE:
300 ml / 10 ½ fl. oz / 1 ¼ cups double (heavy) cream
2 tbsp icing (confectioners') sugar
2 kiwi fruit, peeled and sliced

Kiwi and Strawberry Muffin Cupcakes

817

- Add 75 g of chopped strawberries to the cake mixture and top each cake with a slice of kiwi and half a strawberry.

818

MAKES 12 Carrot and Cinnamon Cream Cupcakes

- Preheat the oven to 190°C (170° fan) / 375F / gas 5 and line a 12-hole cupcake tin with thick paper cases.
- Whisk the sugar, eggs and oil together for 3 minutes.
- Fold in the flour, baking powder and ground cinnamon, followed by the grated carrots.
- Divide the mixture between the paper cases, then transfer the tin to the oven and bake for 20 - 25 minutes.
- Test with a wooden toothpick, if it comes out clean, the cakes are done.
- Transfer the cakes to a wire rack and leave to cool completely.
- Whisk the cream with the icing sugar until it holds its shape, then spoon it into a piping bag fitted with a large star nozzle.
- Pipe a big swirl on top of each cake and sprinkle with cinnamon.

PREPARATION TIME 35 MINUTES

COOKING TIME 20 – 25 MINUTES

INGREDIENTS

175 g / 6 oz / 1 cup soft brown sugar
2 large eggs
150 ml / 5 fl. oz / ⅔ cup sunflower oil
175 g / 6 oz / 1 ¼ cups wholemeal flour
3 tsp baking powder
2 tsp ground cinnamon
200 g / 7 oz / 1 ⅔ cups carrots, peeled and coarsely grated

TO DECORATE:
300 ml / 10 ½ fl. oz / 1 ¼ cups double (heavy) cream
2 tbsp icing (confectioners') sugar
1 tsp ground cinnamon

Carrot and Clove Cream Cupcakes

819

- Replace the cinnamon with half the amount of ground cloves.

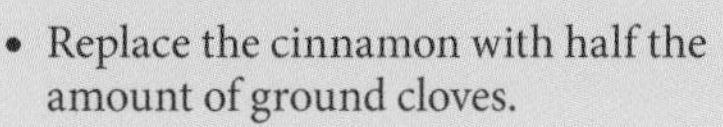

820

MAKES 12

Hot Dog Cupcakes

PREPARATION TIME 15 MINUTES

COOKING TIME 20 – 25 MINUTES

INGREDIENTS

2 tbsp olive oil
2 onions, quartered and sliced
2 large eggs
125 ml / 4 ½ oz / ½ cup sunflower oil
175 ml / 6 oz / ⅔ cup Greek yoghurt
100 g / 3 ½ oz / 1 cup Parmesan, grated
225 g / 8 oz / 1 ½ cups plain (all purpose) flour
2 tsp baking powder
½ tsp bicarbonate of (baking) soda
½ tsp salt
36 mini frankfurters

TO DECORATE:
ketchup and American mustard

- Preheat the oven to 180°C (160° fan) / 350F / gas 4 and oil a 12-hole silicone cupcake mould.
- Heat the olive oil in a frying pan and fry the onion over a low heat for 10 minutes or until nicely caramelised.
- Beat the egg in a jug with the oil, yoghurt, Parmesan and fried onions until well mixed.
- Mix the flour, raising agents and salt in a bowl, then pour in the egg mixture and stir just enough to combine.
- Spoon the mixture into the mould and insert 3 frankfurters into each cup, then bake in the oven for 20 – 25 minutes.
- Test with a wooden toothpick, if it comes out clean, the cakes are done.
- Top the cupcakes with ketchup and mustard and serve warm from the oven.

Chili Dog Cupcakes

821

- Top each cupcake with a spoonful of chilli con carne and a squiggle of mustard.

822

MAKES 12

Glacé-Iced Amaretti Cupcakes

PREPARATION TIME 30 MINUTES

COOKING TIME 15 - 20 MINUTES

INGREDIENTS

110 g / 4 oz / ⅔ cup self-raising flour, sifted
110 g / 4 oz / ½ cup caster (superfine) sugar
110 g / 4 oz / ½ cup butter, softened
2 large eggs
2 tbsp amaretto liqueur

TO DECORATE:
200 g / 7 oz / 2 cups icing (confectioners') sugar
a few drops of almond extract
48 amaretti biscuits

- Preheat the oven to 190°C (170° fan) / 375F / gas 5 and line a 12-hole cupcake tin with paper cases.
- Combine the flour, sugar, butter, eggs and amaretto in a bowl and whisk together for 2 minutes or until smooth.
- Divide the mixture between the cases, then transfer the tin to the oven and bake for 15 – 20 minutes.
- Test with a wooden toothpick, if it comes out clean, the cakes are done.
- Transfer the cakes to a wire rack and leave to cool completely.
- Sieve the icing sugar into a bowl and add the almond extract with just enough water to make a thick, spreadable icing.
- Spoon the icing onto the cakes and top each one with 4 amaretti biscuits.

Orange and Amaretti Cupcakes

823

- Add the finely grated zest of an orange to the cake mixture and use orange juice instead of water to make the icing.

824

MAKES 12

Passion Fruit Cream Cupcakes

- Preheat the oven to 190°C (170° fan) / 375F / gas 5 and line a 12-hole cupcake tin with paper cases.
- Combine the flour, sugar, butter, eggs and passion fruit syrup in a bowl and whisk together for 2 minutes or until smooth.
- Divide the mixture between the cases and bake for 15 – 20 minutes.
- Test with a wooden toothpick, if it comes out clean, the cakes are done.
- Transfer the cakes to a wire rack and leave to cool completely.
- Whip the cream with the icing sugar until it holds its shape.
- Spoon the mixture into a piping bag, fitted with a large star nozzle, and pipe a swirl of cream on top of each cake. Scoop the pulp and seeds out of a passion fruit half onto each cupcake.

PREPARATION TIME 30 MINUTES

COOKING TIME 15 - 20 MINUTES

INGREDIENTS

110 g / 4 oz / ⅔ cup self-raising flour, sifted
110 g / 4 oz / ½ cup caster (superfine) sugar
110 g / 4 oz / ½ cup butter, softened
2 large eggs
1 tbsp passion fruit syrup

TO DECORATE:
300 ml / 10 ½ fl. oz / 1 ¼ cups double (heavy) cream
2 tbsp icing (confectioners') sugar
6 passion fruit, halved

Passion Fruit and Kiwi Cream Cupcakes

825

- Top each cupcake with a slice of kiwi after spooning over the passion fruit.

826

MAKES 12

Chocolate Peppermint Cupcakes

- Preheat the oven to 190°C (170° fan) / 375F / gas 5 and line a 12-hole cupcake tin with paper cases.
- Combine the flour, sugar, butter, eggs, cocoa powder and peppermint extract in a bowl and whisk together for 2 minutes or until smooth.
- Divide the mixture between the cases, then transfer the tin to the oven and bake for 15 – 20 minutes.
- Test with a wooden toothpick, if it comes out clean, the cakes are done.
- Transfer the cakes to a wire rack and leave to cool completely.
- Beat the butter until smooth, then gradually whisk in the icing sugar, peppermint extract and food colouring.
- Stir in the grated chocolate then ice the cupcakes, swirling it with the back of the spoon.

PREPARATION TIME 30 MINUTES

COOKING TIME 15 - 20 MINUTES

INGREDIENTS

110 g / 4 oz / ⅔ cup self-raising flour, sifted
110 g / 4 oz / ½ cup caster (superfine) sugar
110 g / 4 oz / ½ cup butter, softened
2 large eggs
2 tbsp unsweetened cocoa powder
a few drops of peppermint extract

TO DECORATE:
100 g / 3 ½ oz / ½ cup butter, softened
200 g / 7 oz / 2 cups icing (confectioners') sugar
a few drops of peppermint extract
a few drops of green food colouring
50 g / 1 ¾ oz dark chocolate (minimum 60 % cocoa solids), finely grated

After Eight Cupcakes

827

- Top each cupcake with an After Eight mint.

828

Almond-Scented Buttercream Cupcakes

MAKES 12

PREPARATION TIME 30 MINUTES

COOKING TIME 15 - 20 MINUTES

INGREDIENTS

110 g / 4 oz / ⅔ cup self-raising flour, sifted
110 g / 4 oz / ½ cup caster (superfine) sugar
110 g / 4 oz / ½ cup butter, softened
2 large eggs
1 tsp almond extract

TO DECORATE:
100 g / 3 ½ oz / ½ cup butter, softened
200 g / 7 oz / 2 cups icing (confectioners') sugar
1 tsp almond extract
a few drops of pink food colouring
sugar hearts to decorate

- Preheat the oven to 190°C (170° fan) / 375F / gas 5 and line a 12-hole cupcake tin with paper cases.
- Combine the flour, sugar, butter, eggs and almond extract in a bowl and whisk together for 2 minutes or until smooth.
- Divide the mixture between the cases, then transfer the tin to the oven and bake for 15 – 20 minutes.
- Test with a wooden toothpick, if it comes out clean, the cakes are done.
- Transfer the cakes to a wire rack and leave to cool completely.
- Beat the butter until smooth, then gradually whisk in the icing sugar and almond extract.
- Spoon the mixture into a piping bag, fitted with a large star nozzle, and pipe a swirl of icing on top of each cake, then top with the sugar hearts.

829

Elderflower-Scented Buttercream Cupcakes

- Replace the almond extract in the cake mixture and icing with double the amount of elderflower cordial.

830

Vanilla Cupcakes with Pineapple Buttercrea

MAKES 12

PREPARATION TIME 30 MINUTES

COOKING TIME 15 - 20 MINUTES

INGREDIENTS

110 g / 4 oz / ⅔ cup self-raising flour, sifted
110 g / 4 oz / ½ cup caster (superfine) sugar
110 g / 4 oz / ½ cup butter, softened
2 large eggs
1 tsp vanilla extract

TO DECORATE:
100 g / 3 ½ oz / ½ cup butter, softened
200 g / 7 oz / 2 cups icing (confectioners') sugar
2 tbsp pineapple syrup
12 wedges fresh pineapple

- Preheat the oven to 190°C (170° fan) / 375F / gas 5 and line a 12-hole cupcake tin with paper cases.
- Combine the flour, sugar, butter, eggs and vanilla extract in a bowl and whisk together for 2 minutes or until smooth.
- Divide the mixture between the cases and bake for 15 – 20 minutes.
- Test with a wooden toothpick, if it comes out clean, the cakes are done.
- Transfer the cakes to a wire rack and leave to cool completely.
- Beat the butter until smooth, then gradually whisk in the icing sugar and pineapple syrup.
- Spoon the mixture into a piping bag, fitted with a large star nozzle, and pipe a swirl of icing on top of each cake. Top with the pineapple wedges

831

Vanilla Cupcakes with Passion Fruit Buttercream

- Replace the pineapple syrup with passion fruit syrup. Top each cake with 1 tsp of passion fruit seeds and pulp.

832

MAKES 12

Almond Cupcakes with Rolled Icing

Hazelnut Cupcakes with Rolled Icing

833

- Use ground hazelnuts (cob nuts) instead of the ground almonds and replace the almond extract with 1 tbsp of hazelnut syrup.

Pistachio Cupcakes with Rolled Icing

834

- Use ground pistachios instead of the ground almonds.

PREPARATION TIME 1 HOUR

COOKING TIME 15 - 20 MINUTES

INGREDIENTS

110 g / 4 oz / ⅔ cup self-raising flour, sifted
110 g / 4 oz / ½ cup caster (superfine) sugar
110 g / 4 oz / ½ cup butter, softened
2 large eggs
2 tbsp ground almonds
½ tsp almond extract

TO DECORATE:
icing (confectioners') sugar for dusting
200 g / 7 oz ready to roll fondant icing
yellow and green food colouring
pink sugar pearls to decorate

- Preheat the oven to 190°C (170° fan) / 375F / gas 5 and line a 12-hole cupcake tin with paper cases.
- Combine the flour, sugar, butter, eggs, ground almonds and almond essence in a bowl and whisk together for 2 minutes or until smooth.
- Divide the mixture between the cases, then transfer the tin to the oven and bake for 15 – 20 minutes.
- Test with a wooden toothpick, if it comes out clean, the cakes are done.
- Transfer the cakes to a wire rack and leave to cool completely.
- Dust the work surface lightly with icing sugar and roll out ¾ of the icing.
- Cut out 12 circles the same diameter as the top of the cakes then wet the backs and stick them to the top of the cakes.
- Colour some of the reserved icing yellow and some green, then roll it out and cut out shapes to make 12 cameras.
- Attach the shapes to the cakes with a dab of water then decorate with the sugar pearls.

835

Lemon and Caviar Cupcakes

MAKES 12

PREPARATION TIME 15 MINUTES

COOKING TIME 20 – 25 MINUTES

INGREDIENTS

2 large eggs
125 ml / 4 ½ oz / ½ cup sunflower oil
175 ml / 6 oz / ⅔ cup Greek yoghurt
100 g / 3 ½ oz / 1 cup Parmesan, grated
225 g / 8 oz / 1 ½ cups plain (all purpose) flour
2 tsp baking powder
½ tsp bicarbonate of (baking) soda
½ tsp salt
1 lemon, zest finely grated

TO DECORATE:

300 g / 10 ½ oz / 1 ⅓ cups cream cheese
4 tbsp caviar
12 sprigs of dill
3 lemon slices, quartered

- Preheat the oven to 180°C (160° fan) / 350F / gas 4 and line a 12-hole cupcake tin with paper cases.
- Beat the egg in a jug with the oil, yoghurt and Parmesan until well mixed.
- Mix the flour, raising agents, salt and lemon zest in a bowl, then pour in the egg mixture and stir just enough to combine.
- Divide the mixture between the paper cases, then bake in the oven for 20 – 25 minutes.
- Test with a wooden toothpick, if it comes out clean, the cakes are done.
- Transfer the cakes to a wire rack and leave to cool completely.
- Spoon the cream cheese onto the cakes and top each one with 1 tsp of caviar, a sprig of dill and a piece of lemon.

Crab and Caviar Cupcakes

836

- Add 100 g of brown crab meat to the cake mixture and top each cake with a heaped teaspoon of white crab meat before adding the caviar.

837

Prawn Cocktail Cupcakes

MAKES 12

PREPARATION TIME 15 MINUTES

COOKING TIME 20 – 25 MINUTES

INGREDIENTS

2 large eggs
125 ml / 4 ½ oz / ½ cup sunflower oil
175 ml / 6 oz / ⅔ cup Greek yoghurt
100 g / 3 ½ oz / 1 cup Parmesan, grated
225 g / 8 oz / 1 ½ cups plain (all purpose) flour
2 tsp baking powder
½ tsp bicarbonate of (baking) soda
½ tsp salt
½ tsp smoked paprika
½ tsp mustard powder
100 g / 3 ½ oz raw king prawns, peeled and roughly chopped
200 ml / 7 fl. oz / ¾ cup double (heavy) cream
200 ml / 7 fl. oz / ¾ cup mayonnaise
100 g / 3 ½ oz cooked prawns (shrimps), peeled
3 slices of lemon, quartered
12 sprigs of dill

- Preheat the oven to 180°C (160° fan) / 350F / gas 4 and line a 12-hole cupcake tin with paper cases.
- Beat the egg in a jug with the oil, yoghurt and Parmesan until well mixed.
- Mix the flour, raising agents, salt, paprika, mustard and prawns in a bowl, then pour in the egg mixture and stir just enough to combine.
- Divide the mixture between the paper cases, then bake in the oven for 20 – 25 minutes.
- Transfer the cakes to a wire rack and leave to cool completely.
- Whip the cream until it holds its shape, then fold in the mayonnaise.
- Dollop the mixture onto the cakes and top with the prawns. Garnish each one with a quarter of a slice of lemon and a sprig of dill.

Avocado and Prawn Cupcakes

838

- Replace the cream and mayonnaise topping with the flesh of 2 ripe avocados that have been blended to a puree with the juice of a lime and a large pinch of salt.

839

MAKES 12

Pansy Cream Cheese Cupcakes

- Preheat the oven to 190°C (170° fan) / 375F / gas 5 and line a 12-hole cupcake tin with paper cases.
- Combine the flour, sugar, butter, eggs and vanilla extract in a bowl and whisk together for 2 minutes or until smooth.
- Divide the mixture between the cases, then transfer the tin to the oven and bake for 15 – 20 minutes.
- Transfer the cakes to a wire rack and leave to cool completely.
- Beat the cream cheese and butter together until light and fluffy then beat in the icing sugar a quarter at a time.
- Add the vanilla extract then whip the mixture for 2 minutes or until smooth and light.
- Spoon the icing onto the cakes and top each one with a fresh pansy flower.

PREPARATION TIME 30 MINUTES

COOKING TIME 15 - 20 MINUTES

INGREDIENTS

110 g / 4 oz / ⅔ cup self-raising flour, sifted
110 g / 4 oz / ½ cup caster (superfine) sugar
110 g / 4 oz / ½ cup butter, softened
2 large eggs
1 tsp vanilla extract

TO DECORATE:
110 g / 4 oz / ½ cup cream cheese
55 g / 2 oz / ¼ cup butter, softened
110 g / 4 oz / 1 cup icing (confectioners') sugar
1 tsp vanilla extract
12 fresh pansy flowers

Poppy Cream Cheese Cupcakes

840

- Add 1 tbsp of poppy seeds to the cake mixture and decorate each cake with a fresh poppy petal.

841

MAKES 12

Spiced Blackberry Buttercream Cupcakes

- Preheat the oven to 190°C (170° fan) / 375F / gas 5 and line a 12-hole cupcake tin with paper cases.
- Combine the flour, sugar, butter, eggs and ginger in a bowl and whisk together for 2 minutes or until smooth.
- Divide the mixture between the cases and bake for 15 – 20 minutes.
- Test with a wooden toothpick, if it comes out clean, the cakes are done.
- Transfer the cakes to a wire rack and leave to cool completely.
- Beat the butter until smooth, then gradually whisk in the icing sugar, blackberry syrup and mixed spice.
- Spoon the mixture into a piping bag, fitted with a large star nozzle, and pipe a swirl of icing on top of each cake.
- Top the cakes with the sugar paste holly leaves.

PREPARATION TIME 30 MINUTES

COOKING TIME 15 - 20 MINUTES

INGREDIENTS

110 g / 4 oz / ⅔ cup self-raising flour, sifted
110 g / 4 oz / ½ cup caster (superfine) sugar
110 g / 4 oz / ½ cup butter, softened
2 large eggs
1 tsp ground ginger

TO DECORATE:
100 g / 3 ½ oz / ½ cup butter, softened
200 g / 7 oz / 2 cups icing (confectioners') sugar
2 tbsp blackberry syrup
½ tsp mixed spice
sugar paste holly leaves to decorate

Spiced Raspberry Buttercream Cupcakes

842

- Use Raspberry syrup in place of the blackberry syrup and top with fresh raspberries and a sprinkle of mixed spice.

843

MAKES 12

Chocolate Piglet Cupcakes

Strawberry Piglet Cupcakes

844

- Replace the cocoa powder with strawberry syrup and add 50 g of chopped dried strawberries to the cake mixture.

Vanilla Piglet Cupcakes

845

- Replace the cocoa powder with 1 tsp of vanilla extract.

PREPARATION TIME 30 MINUTES

COOKING TIME 15 - 20 MINUTES

INGREDIENTS

110 g / 4 oz / ⅔ cup self-raising flour, sifted
110 g / 4 oz / ½ cup caster (superfine) sugar
110 g / 4 oz / ½ cup butter, softened
2 large eggs
2 tbsp unsweetened cocoa powder

TO DECORATE:
100 g / 3 ½ oz / ½ cup butter, softened
200 g / 7 oz / 2 cups icing (confectioners') sugar
a few drops of pink food colouring
a drop of black food colouring

- Preheat the oven to 190°C (170° fan) / 375F / gas 5 and line a 12-hole cupcake tin with paper cases.
- Combine the flour, sugar, butter, eggs and cocoa in a bowl and whisk together for 2 minutes or until smooth.
- Divide the mixture between the cases, then transfer the tin to the oven and bake for 15 – 20 minutes.
- Test with a wooden toothpick, if it comes out clean, the cakes are done.
- Transfer the cakes to a wire rack and leave to cool completely.
- Beat the butter until smooth, then gradually whisk in the icing sugar.
- Stir in a few drops of pink food colouring, then spoon half the icing into a piping bag, fitted with a small plain nozzle.
- Colour the remaining icing a darker shade of pink and spread it on top of the cupcakes.
- Pipe on the ears, nose, snout and tail of the pigs, then dip a cocktail stick in the black food colouring and add the features.

846

MAKES 12

Fig and Orange Cream Cheese Cupcakes

- Preheat the oven to 190°C (170° fan) / 375F / gas 5 and line a 12-hole cupcake tin with paper cases.
- Combine the flour, sugar, butter, eggs and orange zest in a bowl and whisk together for 2 minutes or until smooth.
- Divide the mixture between the cases, then transfer the tin to the oven and bake for 15 – 20 minutes.
- Transfer the cakes to a wire rack and leave to cool.
- Beat the cream cheese and butter together until light and fluffy then beat in the icing sugar a quarter at a time.
- Add the orange juice then whip the mixture for 2 minutes or until smooth and light.
- Spoon the icing into a piping bag fitted with a star nozzle and pipe a swirl onto the cakes, then top each one with a fresh fig quarter.

PREPARATION TIME 30 MINUTES

COOKING TIME 15 - 20 MINUTES

INGREDIENTS

110 g / 4 oz / ⅔ cup self-raising flour, sifted
110 g / 4 oz / ½ cup caster (superfine) sugar
110 g / 4 oz / ½ cup butter, softened
2 large eggs
1 orange, zest finely grated

TO DECORATE:

110 g / 4 oz / ½ cup cream cheese
55 g / 2 oz / ¼ cup butter, softened
110 g / 4 oz / 1 cup icing (confectioners') sugar
1 tbsp orange juice
3 fresh figs, quartered

Fig and Lemon Cream Cheese Cupcakes

847

- Replace the orange juice and zest with lemon juice and zest.

848

MAKES 12

Blueberry and Rose Buttercream Cupcakes

- Preheat the oven to 190°C (170° fan) / 375F / gas 5 and line a 12-hole cupcake tin with paper cases.
- Combine the flour, sugar, butter, eggs and rose water in a bowl and whisk together for 2 minutes or until smooth.
- Divide the mixture between the cases, then bake for 15 – 20 minutes.
- Test with a wooden toothpick, if it comes out clean, the cakes are done.
- Transfer the cakes to a wire rack and leave to cool completely.
- Beat the butter until smooth, then gradually whisk in the icing sugar, blueberry syrup and rose water.
- Spoon the mixture into a piping bag, fitted with a large star nozzle, and pipe a swirl of icing on top of each cake.
- Decorate the cakes with the roses and sugar pearls.

PREPARATION TIME 30 MINUTES

COOKING TIME 15 - 20 MINUTES

INGREDIENTS

110 g / 4 oz / ⅔ cup self-raising flour, sifted
110 g / 4 oz / ½ cup caster (superfine) sugar
110 g / 4 oz / ½ cup butter, softened
2 large eggs
1 tbsp rose water

TO DECORATE:

100 g / 3 ½ oz / ½ cup butter, softened
200 g / 7 oz / 2 cups icing (confectioners') sugar
2 tbsp blueberry syrup
1 tsp rose water
12 sugar paste roses
purple sugar pearls

Blueberry and Orange Flower Buttercream Cupcakes

849

- Replace the rose water with orange flower water.

850

MAKES 12

Sammy Snake Cupcakes

PREPARATION TIME 30 MINUTES

COOKING TIME 15 - 20 MINUTES

INGREDIENTS

110 g / 4 oz / 2/3 cup self-raising flour, sifted
110 g / 4 oz / ½ cup caster (superfine) sugar
110 g / 4 oz / ½ cup butter, softened
2 large eggs
2 tbsp ground almonds
1 tsp vanilla extract
To decorate:
100 g / 3 ½ oz / ½ cup butter, softened
200 g / 7 oz / 2 cups icing (confectioners') sugar
1 tsp vanilla extract
24 coloured sugar pearls

- Preheat the oven to 190°C (170° fan) / 375F / gas 5 and line a 12-hole cupcake tin with paper cases.
- Combine the cake ingredients in a bowl and whisk together for 2 minutes or until smooth.
- Divide the mixture between the cases and bake for 15 – 20 minutes.
- Test with a wooden toothpick, if it comes out clean, the cakes are done.
- Transfer the cakes to a wire rack and leave to cool.
- Beat the butter until smooth, then gradually whisk in the icing sugar and vanilla extract.
- Spoon the mixture into a piping bag, fitted with a large plain nozzle, and pipe a swirl of icing on top of each cake, looping the outer edge back over the centre.
- Add a pair of sugar pearl eyes to each snake.

851

Almond Snake Cupcakes

- When mixing the buttercream replace the vanilla essence with almond essence.

852

MAKES 12

Gluten Free Butterfly Cupcakes

PREPARATION TIME 15 MINUTES

COOKING TIME 20 MINUTES

INGREDIENTS

110 g / 4 oz / 2/3 cup gluten-free self-raising flour, sifted
110 g / 4 oz / ½ cup caster (superfine) sugar
110 g / 4 oz / ½ cup butter, softened
2 large eggs
1 tsp vanilla extract

To decorate:
100 g / 3 ½ oz / ½ cup butter, softened
200 g / 7 oz / 2 cups icing (confectioners') sugar
2 tbsp apricot syrup
12 sugar paste butterflies

- Preheat the oven to 190°C (170° fan) / 375F / gas 5 and line a 12-hole cupcake tin with paper cases.
- Combine the cake ingredients in a bowl and whisk together for 2 minutes or until smooth.
- Divide the mixture between the cases and bake for 15 – 20 minutes.
- Test with a wooden toothpick, if it comes out clean, the cakes are done.
- Transfer the cakes to a wire rack and leave to cool.
- Beat the butter until smooth, then gradually whisk in the icing sugar and apricot syrup.
- Spoon the mixture into a piping bag, fitted with a large star nozzle, and pipe a swirl of icing on top of each cake before topping with the butterflies.

853

Gluten Free Strawberry Cupcakes

- Top each cupcake with a halved strawberry and a sprig of mint instead of a butterfly.

854

MAKES 12

Sweetie Heart Cupcakes

- Preheat the oven to 190°C (170° fan) / 375F / gas 5 and line a 12-hole cupcake tin with silicone cases.
- Combine the flour, sugar, butter, eggs, rose water and pink food colouring in a bowl and whisk together for 2 minutes or until smooth.
- Divide the mixture between the cases, then transfer the tin to the oven and bake for 15 – 20 minutes.
- Transfer the cakes to a wire rack and leave to cool.
- Sieve the icing sugar into a bowl and add just enough water to make a thick, pourable icing, then spoon it on top of the cakes.
- Knead some food colouring into the fondant icing, then roll it out and cut out a small heart shape for the top of each cake.
- Decorate the cakes with your choice of small sweets and edible metallic balls.

PREPARATION TIME 40 MINUTES

COOKING TIME 15 - 20 MINUTES

INGREDIENTS

110 g / 4 oz / ⅔ cup self-raising flour, sifted
110 g / 4 oz / ½ cup caster (superfine) sugar
110 g / 4 oz / ½ cup butter, softened
2 large eggs
1 tbsp rose water
a few drops of pink food colouring

TO DECORATE:
200 g / 7 oz / 2 cups icing (confectioners') sugar
a few drops of pink or red food colouring
50 g / 1 ¾ oz ready to roll fondant icing
small sweets and edible metallic balls to decorate

Cuddle Cupcakes

855

- Double the amount of fondant icing and cut out 24 arm shapes. Lay 2 arms across the top of each iced cake.

856

MAKES 12

Miss Piggy Cupcakes

- Preheat the oven to 190°C (170° fan) / 375F / gas 5 and line a 12-hole cupcake tin with paper cases.
- Combine the cake ingredients and whisk together until smooth.
- Divide the mixture between the cases and bake for 15 – 20 minutes.
- Test with a wooden toothpick, if it comes out clean, the cakes are done.
- Transfer the cakes to a wire rack and leave to cool.
- Beat the butter until smooth, then gradually whisk in the icing sugar and strawberry syrup.
- Spread three quarters of the icing over the cakes, then use the rest to pipe on the tails.
- Position the pig face cake toppers on top.

PREPARATION TIME 30 MINUTES

COOKING TIME 15 - 20 MINUTES

INGREDIENTS

110 g / 4 oz / 2/3 cup self-raising flour, sifted
110 g / 4 oz / ½ cup caster (superfine) sugar
110 g / 4 oz / ½ cup butter, softened
2 large eggs
75 g / 2 ½ oz strawberries, chopped

To decorate:
100 g / 3 ½ oz / ½ cup butter, softened
200 g / 7 oz / 2 cups icing (confectioners') sugar
2 tbsp strawberry syrup
12 pig face cake toppers

Pink Puppy Cupcakes

857

- Replace the pig candies with white chocolate puppy dog candies or any other novelty animal candies.

858

MAKES 10

Funky Toadstool Cupcakes

PREPARATION TIME 30 MINUTES

COOKING TIME 15-20 MINUTES

INGREDIENTS

110 g / 4 oz / 2/3 cup self-raising flour, sifted
110 g / 4 oz / ½ cup caster (superfine) sugar
110 g / 4 oz / ½ cup butter, softened
2 large eggs
2 tbsp unsweetened cocoa powder

To decorate:
100 g / 3 ½ oz / ½ cup butter, softened
200 g / 7 oz / 2 cups icing (confectioners') sugar
1 tsp vanilla extract
12 sugar paste toadstools

- Preheat the oven to 190°C (170° fan) / 375F / gas 5 and line a 12-hole cupcake tin with paper cases.
- Combine the cake ingredients and whisk together until smooth.
- Divide the mixture between the cases and bake for 15 – 20 minutes.
- Test with a wooden toothpick, if it comes out clean, the cakes are done.
- Transfer the cakes to a wire rack and leave to cool.
- Beat the butter until smooth, then gradually whisk in the icing sugar and vanilla extract.
- Pipe the buttercream onto the cakes and top each one with a toadstool.

Boozy Toadstool Cupcakes

859

- Replace the Baileys with Tia Maria when mixing the buttercream.

860

MAKES 6

Love Hearts Cupcakes

PREPARATION TIME 20 MINUTES

COOKING TIME 35 MINUTES

INGREDIENTS

110 g / 4 oz / 2/3 cup self-raising flour, sifted
110 g / 4 oz / ½ cup caster (superfine) sugar
110 g / 4 oz / ½ cup butter, softened
2 large eggs
1 tsp vanilla extract

To decorate:
100 g / 3 ½ oz / ½ cup butter, softened
200 g / 7 oz / 2 cups icing (confectioners') sugar
1 tsp vanilla extract
12 Love Heart sweets

- Preheat the oven to 190°C (170° fan) / 375F / gas 5 and line a 12-hole cupcake tin with paper cases.
- Combine the cake ingredients in a bowl and whisk together for 2 minutes or until smooth.
- Divide the mixture between the cases and bake for 15 – 20 minutes.
- Test with a wooden toothpick, if it comes out clean, the cakes are done.
- Transfer the cakes to a wire rack and leave to cool.
- Beat the butter until smooth, then gradually whisk in the icing sugar and vanilla extract.
- Spoon the icing into a piping bag fitted with a large star nozzle and pipe a rosette on top of each cake before topping with the Love Heart sweets.

Chocolate Flake Cupcakes

861

- Replace the love heart sweets with a short length of chocolate flake for a more decadent cupcake.

862

MAKES 12

Sweetheart Cupcakes

Chocolate Sweetheart Cupcakes

863

- Add 2 tbsp of cocoa powder to the cake mixture before whisking.

Strawberry Sweetheart Cupcakes

864

- Replace the raspberry jam with strawberry jam.

PREPARATION TIME 40 MINUTES

COOKING TIME 15 - 20 MINUTES

INGREDIENTS

110 g / 4 oz / ⅔ cup self-raising flour, sifted
110 g / 4 oz / ½ cup caster (superfine) sugar
110 g / 4 oz / ½ cup butter, softened
2 large eggs
150 g / 5 ½ oz / ½ cup raspberry jam (jelly)

TO DECORATE:
200 g / 7 oz / 2 cups icing (confectioners') sugar
12 strawberry flavour heart-shaped sweets

- Preheat the oven to 190°C (170° fan) / 375F / gas 5 and line a 12-hole cupcake tin with heart-shaped silicone cases.
- Combine the flour, sugar, butter and eggs in a bowl and whisk together for 2 minutes or until smooth.
- Divide half the mixture between the cases, then add a spoonful of raspberry jam to each one.
- Top with the rest of the cake mixture then transfer the tin to the oven and bake for 15 – 20 minutes.
- Test with a wooden toothpick, if it comes out clean, the cakes are done.
- Transfer the cakes to a wire rack and leave to cool completely.
- Sieve the icing sugar into a bowl and add just enough water to make a thick, pourable icing, then spoon it on top of the cakes.
- Top each cake with a heart-shaped sweet.

865

MAKES 12

Chocolate Teardrop Cupcakes

PREPARATION TIME 30 MINUTES

COOKING TIME 15-20 MINUTES

INGREDIENTS

110 g / 4 oz / 2/3 cup self-raising flour, sifted
110 g / 4 oz / ½ cup caster (superfine) sugar
110 g / 4 oz / ½ cup butter, softened
2 large eggs
2 tbsp unsweetened cocoa powder

To decorate:
200 ml / 7 fl. oz / 3/4 cup double cream
200 g / 7 oz dark chocolate, minimum 60% cocoa solids, chopped
edible glitter

- Preheat the oven to 190°C (170° fan) / 375F / gas 5 and line a 12-hole cupcake tin with paper cases.
- Combine the cake ingredients and whisk together for 2 minutes or until smooth.
- Divide the mixture between the cases and bake for 15 – 20 minutes.
- Test with a wooden toothpick, if it comes out clean, the cakes are done.
- Transfer the cakes to a wire rack and leave to cool.
- Heat the cream until it starts to simmer, then pour it over the chopped chocolate and stir until smooth.
- Leave to cool to room temperature, then chill until thick enough to pipe.
- Spread a thin layer of ganache over the cakes then pipe teardrop shapes on top before sprinkling with glitter.

866

MAKES 12

Sweet Treats Cupcakes

PREPARATION TIME 30 MINUTES

COOKING TIME 15-18 MINUTES

INGREDIENTS

110 g / 4 oz / ⅔ cup self-raising flour, sifted
110 g / 4 oz / ½ cup margarine, softened
110 g / 4 oz / ½ cup caster (superfine) sugar
1 tsp vanilla extract
2 large eggs, a pinch of salt

TO DECORATE
200 g / 7 oz / 1 cup butter, softened
400 g / 14 oz / 4 cups icing (confectioners') sugar
1 tsp vanilla extract
Dolly Mixtures, white chocolate buttons and Jelly Tots to decorate

- Preheat the oven to 180°C (160° fan) / 350F / gas 4.
- Line a 12-hole cupcake tin with 12 cupcake cases.
- Beat together all the ingredients for the batter in a mixing bowl for 2 minutes until smooth and creamy.
- Divide evenly between the paper cases before rapping the tin on a work surface to help settle the batter.
- Bake for 15-18 minutes until risen; test with a wooden toothpick, if it comes out clean, the cakes are done.
- Remove to a wire rack to cool as you prepare the buttercream.
- Beat the softened butter for 2 minutes until creamy and pale.
- Add the icing sugar and vanilla extract and beat well until smooth.
- Spoon into a piping bag fitted with a star-shaped nozzle and pipe stars of buttercream on top of the cupcakes.
- Garnish with the Dolly Mixture, white chocolate buttons and Jelly Tots.

867

MAKES 24

Mini Muesli Muffin Cupcakes

- Preheat the oven to 180°C (160° fan) / 350F / gas 4 and line a 24-hole mini cupcake tin with paper cases.
- Beat the egg in a jug with the oil and milk until well mixed.
- Mix the flour, baking powder and sugar in a bowl, then pour in the egg mixture, and 2 thirds of the muesli and stir just enough to combine.
- Divide the mixture between the cases and sprinkle with the rest of the muesli, then bake for 20 – 25 minutes.
- Test with a wooden toothpick, if it comes out clean, the cakes are done.
- Transfer the cakes to a wire rack and leave to cool completely.

PREPARATION TIME 25 MINUTES

COOKING TIME 20 – 25 MINUTES

INGREDIENTS

1 large egg
125 ml / 4 ½ fl. oz / ½ cup sunflower oil
125 ml / 4 ½ fl. oz / ½ cup milk
375 g / 13 oz / 2 ½ cups self-raising flour, sifted
1 tsp baking powder
200 g / 7 oz / ¾ cup caster (superfine) sugar
75 g / 2 ½ oz / 1 cup muesli

868

Buttercream for Cupcakes

MAKES ENOUGH TO ICE 12 CUPCAKES

PREPARATION TIME 5 MINUTES

INGREDIENTS

100 g / 3 ½ oz / ½ cup butter, softened
200 g / 7 oz / 2 cups icing (confectioners') sugar
1 tsp vanilla extract

- Beat the butter until smooth, then gradually whisk in the icing sugar and vanilla extract.
- Pipe or spread the icing onto your cooled cakes.

869

Easter Basket Cupcakes

MAKES 12

PREPARATION TIME 1 HOUR 10 MINUTES

COOKING TIME 15 - 20 MINUTES

INGREDIENTS

110 g / 4 oz / ⅔ cup self-raising flour, sifted
110 g / 4 oz / ½ cup caster (superfine) sugar
110 g / 4 oz / ½ cup butter, softened
2 large eggs
1 tsp vanilla extract

TO DECORATE:
100 g / 3 ½ oz / ½ cup butter, softened
200 g / 7 oz / 2 cups icing (confectioners') sugar
1 tbsp unsweetened cocoa powder
72 chocolate mini eggs

- Preheat the oven to 190°C (170° fan) / 375F / gas 5 and line a 12-hole cupcake tin with paper cases.
- Combine the flour, sugar, butter, eggs and vanilla extract in a bowl and whisk together for 2 minutes or until smooth. Divide the mixture between the cases, then transfer the tin to the oven and bake for 15 – 20 minutes.
- Test with a wooden toothpick, if it comes out clean, the cakes are done. Transfer the cakes to a wire rack and leave to cool completely.
- Beat the butter until smooth, then add the icing sugar and cocoa powder to the bowl.
- Beat the mixture with a wooden spoon to make a smooth chocolate buttercream.
- Spoon the mixture into a piping bag, fitted with a large basket weave nozzle and pipe an undulating ring of icing on top of each cake.
- Arrange 6 chocolate mini eggs on top of each cake.

870

MAKES 12

Getting Piggy Cupcakes

PREPARATION TIME 30 MINUTES

COOKING TIME 15-20 MINUTES

INGREDIENTS

110 g / 4 oz / 2/3 cup self-raising flour, sifted
110 g / 4 oz / ½ cup caster (superfine) sugar
110 g / 4 oz / ½ cup butter, softened
2 large eggs
75 g / 2 ½ oz strawberries, chopped

To decorate:
100 g / 3 ½ oz / ½ cup butter, softened
200 g / 7 oz / 2 cups icing (confectioners') sugar
2 tbsp strawberry syrup
12 strawberry bonbons
12 pig face cake toppers

- Preheat the oven to 190°C (170° fan) / 375F / gas 5 and line a 12-hole cupcake tin with paper cases.
- Combine the cake ingredients and whisk together until smooth.
- Divide the mixture between the cases and bake for 15 – 20 minutes.
- Test with a wooden toothpick, if it comes out clean, the cakes are done.
- Transfer the cakes to a wire rack and leave to cool.
- Beat the butter until smooth, then gradually whisk in the icing sugar and strawberry syrup.
- Spread three quarters of the icing over the cakes, then position the bonbons and cake toppers on top.
- Use the rest of the icing to pipe on the trotters and tails.

Raspberry Pig Cupcakes

871

- Puree a small handful of raspberries and add to the buttercream before using.

872

MAKES 12

Blueberry Blues Cupcakes

PREPARATION TIME 30 MINUTES

COOKING TIME 15-18 MINUTES

INGREDIENTS

110 g / 4 oz / ⅔ cup self-raising flour, sifted
110 g / 4 oz / ½ cup margarine, softened
110 g / 4 oz / ½ cup caster (superfine) sugar
1 tsp vanilla extract
2 large eggs
a pinch of salt

TO DECORATE
200 g / 7 oz / 1 cup butter, softened
400 g / 14 oz / 4 cups icing (confectioners') sugar
a few drops of blue food colouring
150 g / 5 ½ oz / 1 ½ cups blueberries

- Preheat the oven to 180°C (160° fan) / 350F / gas 4.
- Line a 12-hole cupcake tin with 12 cupcake cases.
- Beat together all the ingredients for the batter in a mixing bowl for 2 minutes until smooth and creamy.
- Divide evenly between the paper cases before rapping the tin on a work surface to help settle the batter.
- Bake for 15-18 minutes until risen. Transfer the cakes to a wire rack and leave to cool.
- Beat the butter with the icing sugar and food colouring until smooth.
- Set aside half of the buttercream and spread the rest over the cakes.
- Pipe a ring of teardrops round the outside of each cake and fill the centres with blueberries.

Black and Blue Cupcakes

873

- Substitute the blueberries for blackberries.

874

Chocolate Holly Cupcakes

MAKES 12

- Preheat the oven to 190°C (170° fan) / 375F / gas 5 and line a 12-hole cupcake tin with paper cases.
- Combine the flour, sugar, butter, eggs and cocoa in a bowl and whisk together for 2 minutes or until smooth.
- Divide the mixture between the cases, then transfer the tin to the oven and bake for 15 – 20 minutes.
- Transfer the cakes to a wire rack and leave to cool completely.
- Sieve the icing sugar into a bowl and add just enough water to make a thick, spreadable icing.
- Divide the fondant icing in half and colour one piece green and the other red. Roll out the green icing and cut out 24 holly leaves then roll the red icing into small balls to make the berries.
- Top the cakes with the white glacé icing and arrange the holly leaves and berries on top.

PREPARATION TIME 30 MINUTES

COOKING TIME 15 - 20 MINUTES

INGREDIENTS

110 g / 4 oz / ⅔ cup self-raising flour, sifted
110 g / 4 oz / ½ cup caster (superfine) sugar
110 g / 4 oz / ½ cup butter, softened
2 large eggs
2 tbsp unsweetened cocoa powder

TO DECORATE:
200 g / 7 oz / 2 cups icing (confectioners') sugar
150 g / 5 ½ oz ready to roll fondant icing
a few drops of red and green food colouring

Chocolate Rudolph Cupcakes

875

- Colour the fondant icing brown and make 12 Rudolph faces for the top of the cakes. Make the noses from halved glacé cherries and use halved pretzels for the antlers.

876

Blueberry Smile Cupcakes

MAKES 12

- Preheat the oven to 180°C (160° fan) / 350F / gas 4.
- Line a 12-hole cupcake tin with 12 cupcake cases.
- Beat together all the ingredients for the batter in a mixing bowl for 2 minutes until smooth and creamy.
- Divide evenly between the paper cases before rapping the tin on a work surface to help settle the batter.
- Bake for 15-18 minutes until risen; test with a wooden toothpick, if it comes out clean, the cakes are done.
- Transfer the cakes to a wire rack and leave to cool.
- Beat the butter with the icing sugar, lemon juice and food colouring until smooth then spread it over the cakes.
- Add 2 blueberry eyes to each cake and draw a mouth on with a toothpick.

PREPARATION TIME 30 MINUTES

COOKING TIME 15-18 MINUTES

INGREDIENTS

110 g / 4 oz / ⅔ cup self-raising flour, sifted
110 g / 4 oz / ½ cup margarine, softened
110 g / 4 oz / ½ cup caster (superfine) sugar
1 tsp vanilla extract
2 large eggs
a pinch of salt

TO DECORATE
200 g / 7 oz / 1 cup butter, softened
400 g / 14 oz / 4 cups icing (confectioners') sugar
1 tbsp lemon juice
a few drops of blue food colouring
24 blueberries

Raspberry Smile Cupcakes

877

- Substitute the blueberries for raspberries.

878

MAKES 12

Pretzel Mania Cupcakes

PREPARATION TIME 30 MINUTES

COOKING TIME 15-20 MINUTES

INGREDIENTS

110 g / 4 oz / 2/3 cup self-raising flour, sifted
110 g / 4 oz / ½ cup caster (superfine) sugar
110 g / 4 oz / ½ cup butter, softened
2 large eggs
1 tsp vanilla extract

To decorate:
100 g / 3 ½ oz / ½ cup butter, softened
200 g / 7 oz / 2 cups icing (confectioners') sugar
1 tsp vanilla extract
12 pretzel biscuits

- Preheat the oven to 190°C (170° fan) / 375F / gas 5 and line a 12-hole cupcake tin with paper cases.
- Combine the cake ingredients in a bowl and whisk together for 2 minutes or until smooth.
- Divide the mixture between the cases and bake for 15 – 20 minutes.
- Test with a wooden toothpick, if it comes out clean, the cakes are done.
- Transfer the cakes to a wire rack and leave to cool.
- Beat the butter until smooth, then gradually whisk in the icing sugar and vanilla extract.
- Spoon the icing into a piping bag fitted with a large star nozzle and pipe a rosette on top of each cake before topping with the pretzels.

879

Coffee Pretzel Mania Cupcakes

- Add 1 tsp of instant espresso powder to the cake mixture

880

Peanut Butter Pretzel Cupcakes

- Add 3 tbsp of peanut butter to the cake mixture and 2 tbsp of peanut butter to the buttercream.

881

MAKES 12

Orange Jelly Ring Cupcakes

- Preheat the oven to 190°C (170° fan) / 375F / gas 5 and line a 12-hole cupcake tin with paper cases.
- Combine the cake ingredients and whisk together until smooth.
- Divide the mixture between the cases and bake for 15 – 20 minutes.
- Transfer the cakes to a wire rack and leave to cool.
- Beat the butter with the icing sugar and orange flower water until smooth.
- Pipe the icing onto the cakes and garnish each one with jelly beans and a jelly ring on top.

PREPARATION TIME 30 MINUTES

COOKING TIME 15-18 MINUTES

INGREDIENTS

110 g / 4 oz / ⅔ cup self-raising flour, sifted
110 g / 4 oz / ½ cup margarine, softened
110 g / 4 oz / ½ cup caster (superfine) sugar
1 tsp orange flower water
2 large eggs
a pinch of salt

TO DECORATE
200 g / 7 oz / 1 cup butter, softened
400 g / 14 oz / 4 cups icing (confectioners') sugar
1 tsp orange flower water
36 orange jelly beans
12 orange jelly rings

Honey Orange Cupcakes

882

- Substitute the icing sugar in the buttercream for honey.

883

MAKES 12

Red and Green Christmas Cupcakes

- Preheat the oven to 190°C (170° fan) / 375F / gas 5 and line a 12-hole cupcake tin with paper cases.
- Combine the flour, sugar, butter, eggs and vanilla extract in a bowl and whisk together for 2 minutes or until smooth.
- Divide the mixture between the cases, then transfer the tin to the oven and bake for 15 – 20 minutes.
- Test with a wooden toothpick, if it comes out clean, the cakes are done.
- Transfer the cakes to a wire rack and leave to cool completely.
- Sieve the icing sugar and divide between 2 bowls. Stir the food colouring to each one, adding a few drops of water if necessary to make a thick, spreadable icing.
- Spoon the icing onto the cakes and spread out with the back of the spoon. Top each cake with a Christmas cake topper and decorate with small sweets.

PREPARATION TIME 30 MINUTES

COOKING TIME 15 - 20 MINUTES

INGREDIENTS

110 g / 4 oz / ⅔ cup self-raising flour, sifted
110 g / 4 oz / ½ cup caster (superfine) sugar
110 g / 4 oz / ½ cup butter, softened
2 large eggs
½ tsp vanilla extract

TO DECORATE:
200 g / 7 oz / 2 cups icing (confectioners') sugar
1 tsp red food colouring
1 tsp green food colouring
small sweets and Christmas cake toppers to decorate

Blue and Yellow Easter Cupcakes

884

- Colour the icing blue and yellow instead and top each cake with a chocolate mini egg and coordinating sweets.

885

Blueberry Heart Buttercream Cupcakes

MAKES 12

PREPARATION TIME 30 MINUTES

COOKING TIME 15 - 20 MINUTES

INGREDIENTS

110 g / 4 oz / ⅔ cup self-raising flour, sifted
110 g / 4 oz / ½ cup caster (superfine) sugar
110 g / 4 oz / ½ cup butter, softened
2 large eggs
150 g / 5 ½ oz / ½ cup blueberry jam (jelly)

TO DECORATE:
100 g / 3 ½ oz / ½ cup butter, softened
200 g / 7 oz / 2 cups icing (confectioners') sugar
2 tbsp blueberry syrup
a few drops of blue food colouring

- Preheat the oven to 190°C (170° fan) / 375F / gas 5 and oil a 12-hole heart-shaped silicone cupcake mould.
- Combine the flour, sugar, butter and eggs in a bowl and whisk together for 2 minutes or until smooth.
- Divide half the mixture between the moulds then add a spoonful of blueberry jam to each one.
- Divide the rest of the cake mixture between the moulds and bake for 15 – 20 minutes.
- Test with a wooden toothpick, if it comes out clean, the cakes are done.
- Transfer the cakes to a wire rack and leave to cool completely.
- Beat the butter until smooth, then gradually whisk in the icing sugar and blueberry syrup. To intensify the colour, stir in a few drops of blue food colouring.
- Spread the buttercream over the top and sides of the cakes with a palette knife.

886

Cherry Heart Buttercream Cupcakes

- Replace the blueberry jam and syrup with cherry jam and syrup and colour the icing red.

887

Smartie Circus Cupcakes

MAKES 12

PREPARATION TIME 10 MINUTES

COOKING TIME 20 MINUTES

INGREDIENTS

110 g / 4 oz / ⅔ cup self-raising flour, sifted
110 g / 4 oz / ½ cup margarine, softened
110 g / 4 oz / ½ cup caster (superfine) sugar
1 tsp vanilla extract
2 large eggs
a pinch of salt

TO DECORATE
200 g / 7 oz / 1 cup butter, softened
400 g / 14 oz / 4 cups icing (confectioners') sugar
1 tsp vanilla extract
Smarties and sugar strands to decorate

- Preheat the oven to 190°C (170° fan) / 375F / gas 5 and line a 12-hole cupcake tin with paper cases.
- Combine the cake ingredients and whisk together until smooth.
- Divide the mixture between the cases and bake for 15 – 20 minutes.
- Transfer the cakes to a wire rack and leave to cool.
- Beat the butter with the icing sugar and vanilla extract until smooth.
- Spread a thin layer of icing onto the cakes, then pipe the rest on top.
- Decorate the cakes with Smarties and a sprinkle of sugar strands.

Crushed Malteser Cupcakes

888

- Crush some maltesers and sprinkle on top of the cupcakes instead of using Smarties.

889

MAKES 12 Kiwi Cupcakes

- Preheat the oven to 190°C (170° fan) / 375F / gas 5 and line a 12-hole cupcake tin with paper cases.
- Combine the cake ingredients and whisk together until smooth.
- Divide the mixture between the cases and bake for 15 – 20 minutes.
- Transfer the cakes to a wire rack and leave to cool.
- Beat the butter with the icing sugar and food colouring until smooth.
- Pipe a double ring of icing round the edge of each cake using a petal nozzle and top with the kiwi slices.

PREPARATION TIME 30 MINUTES

COOKING TIME 15-18 MINUTES

INGREDIENTS

110 g / 4 oz / ⅔ cup self-raising flour, sifted
110 g / 4 oz / ½ cup margarine, softened
110 g / 4 oz / ½ cup caster (superfine) sugar
1 tsp vanilla extract
2 large eggs
a pinch of salt

TO DECORATE
200 g / 7 oz / 1 cup butter, softened
400 g / 14 oz / 4 cups icing (confectioners') sugar
a few drops of green food colouring
12 kiwi slices

Grape Cupcakes

890

- Substitute the kiwi fruit for sliced seedless green grapes.

891

MAKES 12 Lollipop Cupcakes

- Preheat the oven to 190°C (170° fan) / 375F / gas 5 and line a 12-hole cupcake tin with paper cases.
- Combine the cake ingredients and whisk together until smooth.
- Divide the mixture between the cases and bake for 15 – 20 minutes.
- Transfer the cakes to a wire rack and leave to cool.
- Beat the butter with the icing sugar and cocoa powder until smooth.
- Pipe a swirl of buttercream onto the cakes and top each one with a lollipop and some jelly beans.

PREPARATION TIME 30 MINUTES

COOKING TIME 15-18 MINUTES

110 g / 4 oz / ⅔ cup self-raising flour, sifted
110 g / 4 oz / ½ cup margarine, softened
110 g / 4 oz / ½ cup caster (superfine) sugar
55 g / 2 oz / ⅓ cup cocoa powder
55 ml / 2 fl. oz / ¼ cup whole milk
2 large eggs
a pinch of salt

TO DECORATE
100 g / 7 oz / 1 cup butter, softened
400 g / 14 oz / 4 cups icing (confectioners') sugar
1 tbsp cocoa powder
2 tbsp milk
12 lollipops
jelly beans to decorate

Chocolate Marshmallow Cupcakes

892

- Substitute the jelly beans and lollipops for mini marshmallows.

893

Chocolate Mint Sweetie Cupcakes

MAKES 12

PREPARATION TIME 30 MINUTES

COOKING TIME 15-18 MINUTES

INGREDIENTS

FOR THE BATTER

110 g / 4 oz / ⅔ cup self-raising flour, sifted
110 g / 4 oz / ½ cup margarine, softened
110 g / 4 oz / ½ cup caster (superfine) sugar
55 g / 2 oz / ⅓ cup cocoa powder
55 ml / 2 fl. oz / ¼ cup whole milk
2 large eggs
a pinch of salt

TO DECORATE

200 g / 7 oz / 1 cup butter, softened
400 g / 14 oz / 4 cups icing (confectioners') sugar
1 tsp peppermint extract
a few drops of green food colouring
12 wrapped mints

- Preheat the oven to 190°C (170° fan) / 375F / gas 5 and line a 12-hole cupcake tin with paper cases.
- Combine the cake ingredients and whisk together until smooth.
- Divide the mixture between the cases and bake for 15 – 20 minutes.
- Transfer the cakes to a wire rack and leave to cool.
- Beat the butter with the icing sugar, peppermint extract and food colouring until smooth.
- Pipe the icing onto the cakes and garnish each one with a mint.

Chocolate Softmint Cupcakes

894

- Substitute the wrapped mint on top for a softmint and a dusting of cocoa powder.

895

Chocolate Cola Bottle Cupcakes

MAKES 12

PREPARATION TIME 10 MINUTES

COOKING TIME 20 MINUTES

INGREDIENTS

110 g / 4 oz / ⅔ cup self-raising flour, sifted
110 g / 4 oz / ½ cup margarine, softened
110 g / 4 oz / ½ cup caster (superfine) sugar
55 g / 2 oz / ⅓ cup cocoa powder
55 ml / 2 fl. oz / ¼ cup whole milk
2 large eggs, a pinch of salt

TO DECORATE

200 g / 7 oz / 1 cup butter, softened
400 g / 14 oz / 4 cups icing (confectioners') sugar
2 tbsp cocoa powder
1 tbsp milk
12 cola bottle sweets
12 straws

- Preheat the oven to 190°C (170° fan) / 375F / gas 5 and line a 12-hole cupcake tin with paper cases.
- Combine the cake ingredients and whisk together until smooth.
- Divide the mixture between the cases and bake for 15 – 20 minutes.
- Transfer the cakes to a wire rack and leave to cool.
- Beat the butter with the icing sugar until smooth and set a quarter of the mixture aside.
- Whisk the cocoa powder and milk into the rest and pipe it onto the cakes.
- Pipe a small star of the plain buttercream on top then garnish with the cola bottles and straws.

Cherry Cola Cupcakes

896

- Substitute the cola bottles for cherry cola bottles and a cocktail cherry on top.

897

MAKES 12

Easter Buttercream Cupcakes

Leftover Easter Egg Cupcakes

898

- Replace the chocolate chips and marzipan with 100 g of finely chopped leftover Easter egg chocolate. Ice the cakes with 100 g of melted Easter egg chocolate.

Crème Egg Cupcakes

899

- Top each cupcake with 2 mini crème eggs.

PREPARATION TIME 30 MINUTES

COOKING TIME 15 - 20 MINUTES

INGREDIENTS

110 g / 4 oz / ⅔ cup self-raising flour, sifted
110 g / 4 oz / ½ cup caster (superfine) sugar
110 g / 4 oz / ½ cup butter, softened
2 large eggs
½ tsp vanilla extract
50 g / 1 ¾ oz / ⅓ cup milk chocolate chips
75 g / 2 ½ oz marzipan, cut into small cubes

TO DECORATE:
100 g / 3 ½ oz / ½ cup butter, softened
200 g / 7 oz / 2 cups icing (confectioners') sugar
food colouring of your choice
Easter novelties to decorate

- Preheat the oven to 190°C (170° fan) / 375F / gas 5 and line a 12-hole cupcake tin with paper cases.
- Combine the flour, sugar, butter, eggs and vanilla extract in a bowl and whisk together for 2 minutes or until smooth.
- Fold in the chocolate chips and marzipan then divide the mixture between the cases and bake for 15 – 20 minutes.
- Test with a wooden toothpick, if it comes out clean, the cakes are done.
- Transfer the cakes to a wire rack and leave to cool completely.
- Beat the butter until smooth, then gradually whisk in the icing sugar and any food colouring of your choice.
- Spread the icing on top of the cakes and decorate with Easter novelties.

900

MAKES 12

Glacé-Iced Red Velvet Cupcakes

PREPARATION TIME 30 MINUTES

COOKING TIME 15 - 20 MINUTES

INGREDIENTS

110 g / 4 oz / ⅔ cup self-raising flour, sifted
110 g / 4 oz / ½ cup caster (superfine) sugar
110 g / 4 oz / ½ cup butter, softened
2 large eggs
1 tsp vanilla extract
1 tbsp red food colouring

TO DECORATE:
200 g / 7 oz / 2 cups icing (confectioners') sugar
12 red heart-shaped sweets

- Preheat the oven to 190°C (170° fan) / 375F / gas 5 and line a 12-hole cupcake tin with foil cases.
- Combine the flour, sugar, butter, eggs, vanilla extract and food colouring in a bowl and whisk together for 2 minutes or until smooth.
- Divide the mixture between the cases, then transfer the tin to the oven and bake for 15 – 20 minutes.
- Test with a wooden toothpick, if it comes out clean, the cakes are done.
- Transfer the cakes to a wire rack and leave to cool completely.
- Sieve the icing sugar into a bowl and add just enough water to make a thick pourable icing.
- Spoon the icing on top of the cakes so that it comes level with the top of the case, then top each cake with a heart-shaped sweet.

901

Chocolate Glacé-Iced Red Velvet Cupcakes

- Sieve 2 tbsp of cocoa powder with the icing sugar before adding the water.

902

MAKES 12

Mint Cookie Cupcakes

PREPARATION TIME 30 MINUTES

COOKING TIME 15-18 MINUTES

INGREDIENTS

FOR THE BATTER
110 g / 4 oz / ⅔ cup self-raising flour, sifted
110 g / 4 oz / ½ cup margarine, softened
110 g / 4 oz / ½ cup caster (superfine) sugar
55 g / 2 oz / ⅓ cup cocoa powder
55 ml / 2 fl. oz / ¼ cup whole milk
2 large eggs
a pinch of salt

TO DECORATE
200 g / 7 oz / 1 cup butter, softened
400 g / 14 oz / 4 cups icing (confectioners') sugar
1 tsp peppermint extract
a few drops of green food colouring
6 bourbon biscuits, chopped

- Preheat the oven to 190°C (170° fan) / 375F / gas 5 and line a 12-hole cupcake tin with paper cases.
- Combine the cake ingredients and whisk together until smooth.
- Divide the mixture between the cases and bake for 15 – 20 minutes.
- Transfer the cakes to a wire rack and leave to cool.
- Beat the butter with the icing sugar, peppermint extract and food colouring until smooth.
- Spread the icing onto the cakes and top with the chopped biscuits.

903

Coconut, Mint and Bourbon Cupcakes

- Garnish the cupcakes with a sprinkle of desiccated coconut on top before serving.

904

Chocolate Kiwi Mud Cupcakes

MAKES 12

- Preheat the oven to 190°C (170° fan) / 375F / gas 5 and line a 12-hole cupcake tin with paper cases.
- Combine the cake ingredients and whisk together until smooth.
- Divide the mixture between the cases and bake for 15 – 20 minutes.
- Transfer the cakes to a wire rack and leave to cool.
- Beat the butter with the icing sugar, cocoa and milk until smooth then pipe it onto the cakes.
- Sprinkle with cocoa powder, then arrange the chopped kiwi round the outside and garnish with a chocolate shape.

PREPARATION TIME 30 MINUTES

COOKING TIME 15-18 MINUTES

INGREDIENTS

110 g / 4 oz / ⅔ cup self-raising flour, sifted
110 g / 4 oz / ½ cup margarine, softened
110 g / 4 oz / ½ cup caster (superfine) sugar
55 g / 2 oz / ⅓ cup cocoa powder
55 ml / 2 fl. oz / ¼ cup whole milk
2 large eggs, a pinch of salt
To decorate
200 g / 7 oz / 1 cup butter, softened
400 g / 14 oz / 4 cups icing (confectioners') sugar
2 tbsp cocoa powder, plus extra for dusting
1 tbsp milk
3 kiwi fruit, peeled and chopped
12 chocolate shapes

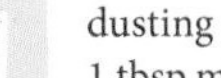

Chocolate and Pretzel Kiwi Cupcakes

905

- Substitute the chocolate shape garnish with salted pretzels.

906

Orange Swirl Cupcakes

MAKES 12

- Preheat the oven to 190°C (170° fan) / 375F / gas 5 and line a 12-hole cupcake tin with paper cases.
- Combine the cake ingredients and whisk together until smooth.
- Divide the mixture between the cases and bake for 15 – 20 minutes.
- Transfer the cakes to a wire rack and leave to cool.
- Beat the butter with the icing sugar, orange flower water and food colouring until smooth.
- Pipe the icing onto the cakes and garnish each one with a physalis and a sprinkle of orange zest.

PREPARATION TIME 30 MINUTES

COOKING TIME 15-18 MINUTES

INGREDIENTS

FOR THE BATTER
110 g / 4 oz / ⅔ cup self-raising flour, sifted
110 g / 4 oz / ½ cup margarine, softened
110 g / 4 oz / ½ cup caster (superfine) sugar
1 tsp orange flower water
2 large eggs
a pinch of salt

TO DECORATE
200 g / 7 oz / 1 cup butter, softened
400 g / 14 oz / 4 cups icing (confectioners') sugar
1 tsp orange flower water
a few drops of orange food colouring
12 physalis
1 orange, zest finely pared

Lime and Ginger Cupcakes

907

- Substitute the kiwi fruit garnish for a piece of crystallised ginger on top of the cupcakes.

908

MAKES 12

Jammy Dodger Cupcakes

Crushed Digestive Cupcakes

909

- Substitute the Jammy Dodgers for crushed Digestive biscuits.

Strawberry Liquorice Cupcakes

910

- Omit the jammy dodgers and double the quantity of belts to cover the whole surface of the cupcakes.

PREPARATION TIME 30 MINUTES

COOKING TIME 15-18 MINUTES

INGREDIENTS

110 g / 4 oz / ⅔ cup self-raising flour, sifted
110 g / 4 oz / ½ cup margarine, softened
110 g / 4 oz / ½ cup caster (superfine) sugar
1 tsp vanilla extract
2 large eggs
a pinch of salt

TO DECORATE

200 g / 7 oz / 1 cup butter, softened
400 g / 14 oz / 4 cups icing (confectioners') sugar
1 tsp vanilla extract
12 strawberry belts, halved lengthways and cut into 3 cm strips
12 jammy dodger biscuits

- Preheat the oven to 190°C (170° fan) / 375F / gas 5 and line a 12-hole cupcake tin with paper cases.
- Combine the cake ingredients and whisk together until smooth.
- Divide the mixture between the cases and bake for 15 – 20 minutes.
- Transfer the cakes to a wire rack and leave to cool.
- Beat the butter with the icing sugar and vanilla extract until smooth then spread it onto the cakes.
- Fold over each piece of strawberry belt and press the loops into the icing round the edge of the cakes.
- Top each cake with a jammy dodger.

911

MAKES 12

Chocolate and Ginger Brownie Cupcakes

- Preheat the oven to 160°C (140° fan) / 325F / gas 3 and oil 12 small bucket tins.
- Melt the chocolate, cocoa and butter together in a saucepan, then leave to cool a little.
- Whisk the sugar and eggs together with an electric whisk for 3 minutes or until very light and creamy.
- Pour in the chocolate mixture and sieve over the flour and ginger, then fold everything together until evenly mixed.
- Divide the mixture between the tins and bake for 30 – 35 minutes or until they are just set in the centre.
- Serve warm or leave to cool on a wire rack.

PREPARATION TIME 25 MINUTES

COOKING TIME 30 – 35 MINUTES

INGREDIENTS

100 g / 3 ½ oz milk chocolate chopped
75 g / 2 ½ oz / ¾ cup unsweetened cocoa powder, sifted
225 g / 8 oz / 1 cup butter
450 g / 1 lb / 2 ½ cups light brown sugar
4 large eggs
100 g / 3 ½ oz / ⅔ cup self-raising flour
2 tsp ground ginger

Chocolate and Cinnamon Brownie Cupcakes

912

- Replace the ground ginger with ground cinnamon.

913

MAKES 18

Choco-Orange Cinnamon Cupcakes

- Preheat the oven to 190°C (170° fan) / 375F / gas 5 and line a 12-hole cupcake tin with paper cases.
- Combine the cake ingredients and whisk together until smooth.
- Divide the mixture between the cases and bake for 15 – 20 minutes.
- Transfer the cakes to a wire rack and leave to cool.
- Beat the butter with the icing sugar and orange flower water until smooth. Use half of it to pipe a mound of icing onto the centre of each cake and sprinkle with cinnamon.
- Colour the rest of the icing orange and pipe a row of teardrops round the outside and a small mound on top, then garnish with the buttons and flowers.

PREPARATION TIME 30 MINUTES

COOKING TIME 15-18 MINUTES

INGREDIENTS

110 g / 4 oz / ⅔ cup self-raising flour, sifted
110 g / 4 oz / ½ cup margarine
110 g / 4 oz / ½ cup caster (superfine) sugar
30 g / 1 oz / 2 tbsp cocoa powder
30 ml / 1 fl. oz / 2 tbsp whole milk
1 tsp orange flower water
2 large eggs, a pinch of salt
TO DECORATE
200 g / 7 oz / 1 cup butter, softened
400 g / 14 oz / 4 cups icing (confectioners') sugar
1 tsp orange flower water
1 tsp ground cinnamon
a few drops of orange food colouring
12 chocolate buttons
12 chocolate flowers

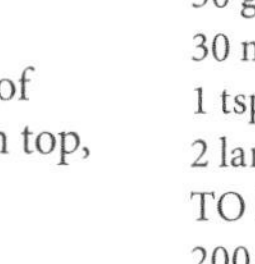

Orange, Chocolate and Vanilla Cupcakes

914

- Omit the cocoa powder and milk from the cupcake batter, replacing the orange flower water with vanilla extract.

915

MAKES 12

Pink Guitar Cupcakes

PREPARATION TIME 10 MINUTES

COOKING TIME 20 MINUTES

INGREDIENTS

110 g / 4 oz / 2/3 cup self-raising flour, sifted
110 g / 4 oz / ½ cup caster (superfine) sugar
110 g / 4 oz / ½ cup butter, softened
2 large eggs
75 g / 2 ½ oz strawberries, chopped

To decorate:
200 g / 7 oz ready to roll fondant icing
12 pink guitar cake toppers
candy necklace beads to decorate

- Preheat the oven to 190°C (170° fan) / 375F / gas 5.
- Line a 12-hole cupcake tin with foil cases.
- Combine the cake ingredients and whisk together for 2 minutes.
- Divide the mixture between the cases and bake for 15 – 20 minutes.
- Transfer the cakes to a wire rack and leave to cool.
- Roll out the icing and cut out 12 circles with a fluted cookie cutter.
- Wet the backs and stick them to the cakes, then top with the cake toppers and candy beads.

916

Jelly Tot Fondant Cupcakes

- Substitute the candy beads for raspberry Jelly Tots.

917

MAKES 12

Chocolate and Sesame Cupcakes

PREPARATION TIME 15 MINUTES

COOKING TIME 15 - 20 MINUTES

INGREDIENTS

110 g / 4 oz / ⅔ cup self-raising flour, sifted
110 g / 4 oz / ½ cup caster (superfine) sugar
110 g / 4 oz / ½ cup butter, softened
2 large eggs
2 tbsp unsweetened cocoa powder
1 tbsp sesame oil
2 tbsp sesame seeds

- Preheat the oven to 190°C (170° fan) / 375F / gas 5 and oil 12 non-stick dariole moulds.
- Combine the flour, sugar, butter, eggs, cocoa and sesame oil in a bowl and whisk together for 2 minutes or until smooth.
- Divide the mixture between the moulds and sprinkle with sesame seeds, then bake for 15 – 20 minutes.
- Test with a wooden toothpick, if it comes out clean, the cakes are done.
- Transfer the cakes to a wire rack and leave to cool completely.

918

Chocolate and Sesame Brittle Cupcakes

- Add 75 g of roughly chopped sesame brittle to the cake mixture. Ice the cakes with chocolate ganache and top each one with a piece of sesame brittle.

919

MAKES 18

Minty Heart Cupcakes

- Preheat the oven to 190°C (170° fan) / 375F / gas 5 and line a 12-hole cupcake tin with paper cases.
- Combine the cake ingredients and whisk together until smooth.
- Divide the mixture between the cases and bake for 15 – 20 minutes.
- Transfer the cakes to a wire rack and leave to cool.
- Beat the butter with the icing sugar, peppermint extract and food colouring until smooth.
- Pipe the icing onto the cakes and top each one with a heart and a sprig of mint.

PREPARATION TIME 30 MINUTES

COOKING TIME 15-18 MINUTES

INGREDIENTS

FOR THE BATTER

110 g / 4 oz / ⅔ cup self-raising flour, sifted
110 g / 4 oz / ½ cup margarine, softened
110 g / 4 oz / ½ cup caster (superfine) sugar
1 tsp vanilla extract
2 large eggs
a pinch of salt

TO DECORATE

200 g / 7 oz / 1 cup butter, softened
400 g / 14 oz / 4 cups icing (confectioners') sugar
1 tsp peppermint extract
a few drops of green food colouring
12 jelly sweet hearts
12 mint sprigs

920

Mint and White Chocolate Cupcakes

- Substitute the jelly hearts with grated white chocolate.

921

MAKES 12

Afternoon Tea Cupcakes

- Preheat the oven to 190°C (170° fan) / 375F / gas 5 and line a 12-hole cupcake tin with paper cases.
- Combine the flour, sugar, butter, eggs and vanilla extract in a bowl and whisk for 2 minutes or until smooth. Divide the mixture between the cases, then transfer the tin to the oven and bake for 15 – 20 minutes.
- Transfer the cakes to a wire rack and leave to cool.
- Beat the butter until smooth, then gradually whisk in the icing sugar and vanilla extract. Spread half of the buttercream on top of the cakes, levelling the top.
- Colour fondant icing red and roll out on.
- Use a teapot-shaped cookie cutter to cut out 12 teapots.
- Carefully transfer the teapots to the top of the cakes.
- Spoon the rest of the buttercream into a piping bag fitted with a small plain nozzle and pipe the outline onto each teapot.
- Pipe dots onto the teapots to decorate.

PREPARATION TIME 1 HOUR 15 MINUTES

COOKING TIME 15 - 20 MINUTES

INGREDIENTS

110 g / 4 oz / ⅔ cup self-raising flour, sifted
110 g / 4 oz / ½ cup caster (superfine) sugar
110 g / 4 oz / ½ cup butter, softened
2 large eggs
1 tsp vanilla extract

TO DECORATE:

100 g / 3 ½ oz / ½ cup butter, softened
200 g / 7 oz / 2 cups icing (confectioners') sugar
½ tsp vanilla extract
200 g / 7 oz ready to roll fondant icing
red food colouring

922

Coffee Pot Cupcakes

- Flavour the cake mixture with 2 tsp of instant espresso powder and use a coffee pot shaped cookie cutter to make the decoration.

923

MAKES 12

Animal Print Cupcakes

PREPARATION TIME 1 HOUR

COOKING TIME 15 - 20 MINUTES

INGREDIENTS

110 g / 4 oz / ⅔ cup self-raising flour, sifted
110 g / 4 oz / ½ cup caster (superfine) sugar
110 g / 4 oz / ½ cup butter, softened
2 large eggs
1 tsp vanilla extract

TO DECORATE:
100 g / 3 ½ oz / ½ cup butter, softened
200 g / 7 oz / 2 cups icing (confectioners') sugar
½ tsp vanilla extract
200 g / 7 oz ready to roll fondant icing
black food

- Preheat the oven to 190°C (170° fan) / 375F / gas 5 and line a 12-hole cupcake tin with paper cases.
- Combine the flour, sugar, butter, eggs and vanilla extract in a bowl and whisk for 2 minutes or until smooth. Divide the mixture between the cases, then transfer the tin to the oven and bake for 15 – 20 minutes.
- Transfer the cakes to a wire rack and leave to cool.
- Beat the butter until smooth, then gradually whisk in the icing sugar and vanilla extract. Spread the buttercream on top of the cakes, levelling the top.
- Dust the work surface lightly with icing sugar and roll out the fondant icing.
- Use a cookie cutter the same diameter as the top of the cakes to cut out 12 circles. Attach an icing circle to the top of each cake.
- Thin some black food dye with a few drops of water.
- Use a fine paint brush to paint black stripes.

Tiger Print Cupcakes

924

- Colour the fondant icing orange before rolling it out and topping the cakes. Paint on the black lines as before.

925

MAKES 12

Gingerbread Man Cupcakes

PREPARATION TIME 1 HOUR 10 MINUTES

COOKING TIME 15 - 20 MINUTES

INGREDIENTS

110 g / 4 oz / ⅔ cup self-raising flour, sifted
110 g / 4 oz / ½ cup caster (superfine) sugar
110 g / 4 oz / ½ cup butter, softened
2 large eggs
1 lemon, juiced and zest finely grated

TO DECORATE:
100 g / 3 ½ oz / ½ cup butter, softened
200 g / 7 oz / 2 cups icing (confectioners') sugar
½ lemon, juiced and zest finely grated
yellow, brown and red food colouring
110 g / 4 oz ready to roll fondant icing

- Preheat the oven to 190°C (170° fan) / 375F / gas 5 and line a 12-hole cupcake tin with paper cases.
- Combine the flour, sugar, butter, eggs and lemon juice and zest and whisk for 2 minutes. Divide the mixture between the cases, then bake for 15 – 20 minutes.
- Transfer the cakes to a wire rack and leave to cool.
- Beat the butter then gradually whisk in the icing sugar, lemon juice, zest and drops of yellow food dye.
- Spoon the mixture into a piping bag and pipe a swirl of buttercream on top of each cake.
- Colour the fondant icing brown and roll it out on a surface lightly dusted with icing sugar.
- Cut out 12 gingerbread men.
- Use the end of a round piping nozzle to make the imprint of buttons down their chests.
- Paint on their shoes with some brown food colouring.
- Add the facial features with a plain piping nozzle, pressing an angle to make a semi-circle for the mouth.
- Paint on some gloves using red food colouring. Transfer each gingerbread man to the top of a cake.

926

MAKES 12

Fruit, Nut and Marzipan Cupcakes

Ginger and Marzipan Cupcakes

927

- Replace the mixed spice with ground ginger and add ½ tsp almond essence. Top the marzipan layer with sliced stem ginger.

Dundee Cupcakes

928

- Omit the marzipan layer and decorate as before.

Fruit and Nut Honey Cupcakes

929

- Drizzle a little runny honey over the cupcakes before serving.

PREPARATION TIME 30 MINUTES

COOKING TIME 20 – 25 MINUTES

INGREDIENTS

250 g / 9 oz / 1 ¾ cups self-raising flour
1 tsp bicarbonate of (baking) soda
2 tsp mixed spice
200 g / 8 ½ oz / ½ cup golden syrup
125 g / 4 ½ oz / ½ cup butter
125 g / 4 ½ oz / ¾ cup dark brown sugar
2 large eggs, beaten
250 ml / 9 fl. oz / 1 cup milk
50 g / 1 ¾ oz / ½ cup pistachio nuts, chopped
50 g / 1 ¾ oz / ½ cup sultanas
200 g / 7 oz marzipan
50 g / 1 ¾ oz / ½ cup macadamia nuts
50 g / 1 ¾ oz / ½ cup slivered pistachio nuts
50 g / 1 ¾ oz / ½ cup glacé cherries, halved
4 tbsp runny honey

- Preheat the oven to 190°C (170° fan) / 375F / gas 5 and line a 12-hole cupcake tin with paper cases.
- Sieve the flour, bicarbonate of soda and mixed spice together into a bowl.
- Put the golden syrup, butter and brown sugar in a small saucepan and boil gently for 2 minutes, stirring to dissolve the sugar.
- Pour the butter and sugar mixture onto the flour with the eggs and milk, then fold it all together with the pistachios and sultanas until smooth.
- Divide the mixture between the cases, then transfer the tin to the oven and bake for 20 – 25 minutes.
- Test with a wooden toothpick, if it comes out clean, the cakes are done.
- Transfer the cakes to a wire rack and leave to cool completely.
- Divide the marzipan into 12 balls. Flatten them with your fingers then wet the backs and stick them to the top of the cupcakes.
- Arrange the nuts and cherries on top, then glaze with the honey.

930

MAKES 12

Festive Cupcakes

PREPARATION TIME 15 MINUTES
COOKING TIME 15 - 20 MINUTES
MACERATING TIME 3 HOURS

INGREDIENTS

3 tbsp brandy
50 g / 1 ¾ oz / ¼ cup sultanas
50 g / 1 ¾ oz / ¼ cup mixed peel
50 g / 1 ¾ oz / ¼ cup glacé cherries, chopped
110 g / 4 oz / ⅔ cup self-raising flour, sifted
110 g / 4 oz / ½ cup caster (superfine) sugar
110 g / 4 oz / ½ cup butter, softened
2 large eggs

TO DECORATE:
300 g / 10 ½ oz / 3 cups royal icing powder
a few drops of red and green food colouring
sugar paste holly leaves and berries to decorate

- Pour the brandy over the sultanas, mixed peel and cherries and leave to macerate for 3 hours or overnight.
- Preheat the oven to 190°C (170° fan) / 375F / gas 5 and line a 12-hole cupcake tin with foil cases.
- Combine the flour, sugar, butter and eggs in a bowl and whisk together for 2 minutes or until smooth.
- Whisk in the fruit and brandy mixture then divide between the cases and bake for 15 – 20 minutes.
- Transfer the cakes to a wire rack and leave to cool.
- Whisk the royal icing powder with 50 ml of cold water for 5 minutes with an electric whisk until smooth.
- Spread half of the icing over the cakes and divide the rest into 2 bowls. Colour one red and one green, then spoon them into piping bags.
- Pipe alternate coloured lines round the cakes and top each one with sugar paste holly leaves and berries.

Brandy Butter Cupcakes

931

- Top the cakes with brandy butter instead of the royal icing.

932

MAKES 12

Sheep Cupcakes

PREPARATION TIME 1 HOUR 30 MINUTES
COOKING TIME 15 - 20 MINUTES

INGREDIENTS

110 g / 4 oz / ⅔ cup self-raising flour, sifted
110 g / 4 oz / ½ cup caster (superfine) sugar
110 g / 4 oz / ½ cup butter, softened
2 large eggs
2 tbsp unsweetened cocoa powder

TO DECORATE:
100 g / 3 ½ oz / ½ cup butter, softened
200 g / 7 oz / 2 cups icing (confectioners') sugar
½ tsp vanilla extract
green food colouring
300 g / 10 ½ oz ready to roll fondant icing
pink and blue food colouring
150 g / 5 ½ oz mini marshmallows

- Preheat the oven to 190°C (170° fan) / 375F / gas 5 and line a 12-hole cupcake tin with paper cases.
- Combine the flour, sugar, butter, eggs and cocoa powder and whisk for 2 minutes. Divide the mixture between the cases, then bake for 15 – 20 minutes.
- Transfer the cakes to a wire rack and leave to cool.
- Beat the butter until smooth, then gradually whisk in the icing sugar and vanilla extract.
- Colour the buttercream pale green and spread half of it over the surface of the cakes.
- Spoon the rest into a piping bag and pipe a ring of teardrops round the edge of each cake.
- Colour 1 third of the fondant icing pale pink. Shape it into 12 quail's egg shapes and 48 pea-sized balls.
- Flatten 24 of the pea-sized balls and pinch one end together to make the ears.
- Use a little of the white icing to make circles for the eyes. Paint the pupils in with blue food colouring. Use a scalpel to score in the mouth details.
- Make 2 indentations in each head and insert the ears.
- Shape the white icing into 12 bodies and attach a head and 2 front feet to each one with a little water.
- Cut the mini marshmallows in half with scissors.
- Use the sticky side of the marshmallows to attach to the sheep, then transfer to the top of a cake.

933

MAKES 12

Chocolate Candy Cane Cupcakes

- Preheat the oven to 190°C (170° fan) / 375F / gas 5 and line a 12-hole cupcake tin with paper cases.
- Combine the cake ingredients and whisk until smooth.
- Divide the mixture between the cases and bake for 15 – 20 minutes.
- Transfer the cakes to a wire rack and leave to cool.
- Beat the butter with the icing sugar and cocoa powder then pipe it in a spiral on top of the cakes
- Roll the red and white fondant into 2 long sausages, then twist them together and cut into 12 canes.
- Roll out the green icing and cut out 24 tiny holly leaves, then add a cane and 2 leaves to the top of each cake.

PREPARATION TIME 1 HOUR 10 MINUTES

COOKING TIME 15 - 20 MINUTES

INGREDIENTS

110 g / 4 oz / ⅔ cup self-raising flour, sifted
110 g / 4 oz / ½ cup caster (superfine) sugar
110 g / 4 oz / ½ cup butter, softened
2 large eggs
2 tbsp unsweetened cocoa powder

TO DECORATE:
100 g / 3 ½ oz / ½ cup butter, softened
200 g / 7 oz / 2 cups icing (confectioners') sugar
1 tbsp unsweetened cocoa powder
100 g / 3 ½ oz red ready to roll fondant icing
100 g / 3 ½ oz white ready to roll fondant icing
30 g / 1 oz green ready to roll fondant icing

934

MAKES 12

Nautical Cupcakes

- Preheat the oven to 190°C (170° fan) / 375F / gas 5 and line a 12-hole cupcake tin with paper cases.
- Combine the cake ingredients and whisk until smooth.
- Divide the mixture between the cases and bake for 15 – 20 minutes.
- Transfer the cakes to a wire rack and leave to cool.
- Roll out the blue fondant and cut out 12 circles the same diameter of the cakes with a fluted cookie cutter. Wet the backs and attach to the cakes.
- Roll out the red and white fondant and cut out the boat, sail and mast; attaching to the cake with a dab of water.
- Position the mini polos as the lifebuoys.

PREPARATION TIME 1 HOUR 30 MINUTES

COOKING TIME 15 - 20 MINUTES

INGREDIENTS

110 g / 4 oz / ⅔ cup self-raising flour, sifted
110 g / 4 oz / ½ cup caster (superfine) sugar
110 g / 4 oz / ½ cup butter, softened
2 large eggs
1 lemon, juiced and zest finely grated

TO DECORATE:
200 g / 7 oz blue ready to roll fondant icing
100 g / 3 ½ oz red ready to roll fondant icing
30 g / 1 oz white ready to roll fondant icing
24 mini polo mints

935

Jolly Rodger Cupcakes

- Use black fondant icing for the background and cut a white skull and cross bones for each cake out of white icing.

936

MAKES 12

Hedgehog Cupcakes

PREPARATION TIME 1 HOUR 30 MINUTES

COOKING TIME 15 - 20 MINUTES

INGREDIENTS

110 g / 4 oz / ⅔ cup self-raising flour, sifted
110 g / 4 oz / ½ cup caster (superfine) sugar
110 g / 4 oz / ½ cup butter, softened
2 large eggs
2 tbsp unsweetened cocoa powder

TO DECORATE:
100 g / 3 ½ oz / ½ cup butter, softened
200 g / 7 oz / 2 cups icing (confectioners') sugar
½ tsp vanilla extract
100 g / 3 ½ oz brown ready to roll fondant icing
30 g / 1 oz white ready to roll fondant icing
30 g / 1 oz green ready to roll fondant icing

- Preheat the oven to 190°C (170° fan) / 375F / gas 5 and line a 12-hole cupcake tin with paper cases.
- Combine the cake ingredients and whisk until smooth.
- Divide the mixture between the cases and bake for 15 – 20 minutes.
- Transfer the cakes to a wire rack and leave to cool.
- Beat the butter with the icing sugar and brown food colouring then pipe it on top of the cakes
- Shape ¾ of the brown fondant into 12 ovals then use a pair of scissors to snip the surface into spikes.
- Use the rest of the brown fondant to make the faces and the white fondant to make the eyes.
- Make 12 leaves from the green fondant and assemble the hedgehogs on top of the cakes.

Hen Cupcakes

937

- Shape and snip the dark brown icing as before. Shape 12 balls to make the hens' heads and model beaks and combs out of yellow and red fondant icing.

Pinecone Cupcakes

938

- Snip the brown fondant as before, but omit the faces and eyes.

939

MAKES 12

White Chocolate Raspberry Cupcakes

- Preheat the oven to 190°C (170° fan) / 375F / gas 5 and line a 12-hole cupcake tin with paper cases.
- Combine the flour, sugar, butter, eggs and vanilla extract in a bowl and whisk for 2 minutes or until smooth. Divide the mixture between the cases, then transfer the tin to the oven and bake for 15 – 20 minutes.
- Transfer the cakes to a wire rack and leave to cool.
- Beat the butter until smooth, then gradually whisk in the icing sugar and vanilla extract.
- Swirl through half of the raspberry jam.
- Spread the buttercream onto the cakes.
- Make an indent in the top of the icing with a teaspoon.
- Press 8 white chocolate buttons into the icing round the edge of each cake.
- Fill the indentation in the icing with the rest of the raspberry jam and top each one with 3 raspberries.

PREPARATION TIME 1 HOUR

COOKING TIME 15 - 20 MINUTES

INGREDIENTS

110 g / 4 oz / ⅔ cup self-raising flour, sifted
110 g / 4 oz / ½ cup caster (superfine) sugar
110 g / 4 oz / ½ cup butter, softened
2 large eggs
1 tsp vanilla extract

TO DECORATE:
100 g / 3 ½ oz / ½ cup butter, softened
200 g / 7 oz / 2 cups icing (confectioners') sugar
4 tbsp raspberry jam (jelly)
96 white chocolate buttons
36 raspberries

940

White Chocolate Blueberry Cupcakes

- Use blueberry jam in place of the raspberry jam and use fresh blueberries instead of the raspberries.

941

MAKES 12

Colours Cupcakes

- Preheat the oven to 190°C (170° fan) / 375F / gas 5 and line a 12-hole cupcake tin with paper cases.
- Combine the cake ingredients and whisk until smooth.
- Divide the mixture between the cases and bake for 15 – 20 minutes.
- Transfer the cakes to a wire rack and leave to cool.
- Roll out the white fondant and cut out 12 circles the same diameter of the cakes. Wet the backs and attach to the cakes.
- Roll out the coloured icings and use a 2 cm plunger cutter to cut out circles, then a 1 cm plunger cutter to cut out off-set centres.
- Use a dab of water to attach the rings and cut-out centres to the top of the cakes.

PREPARATION TIME 1 HOUR 30 MINUTES

COOKING TIME 15 - 20 MINUTES

INGREDIENTS

110 g / 4 oz / ⅔ cup self-raising flour, sifted
110 g / 4 oz / ½ cup caster (superfine) sugar
110 g / 4 oz / ½ cup butter, softened
2 large eggs
1 lemon, juiced and zest finely grated

TO DECORATE:
200 g / 7 oz white ready to roll fondant icing
30 g / 1 oz orange ready to roll fondant icing
30 g / 1 oz blue ready to roll fondant icing
30 g / 1 oz pink ready to roll fondant icing
30 g / 1 oz purple ready to roll fondant icing

942

Peacock Feather Cupcakes

- Use the method above to make icing peacock feathers with a blue centre, gold ring and brown background. Use scissors to feather the edge of the brown icing.

943

MAKES 12

Baby Boots Cupcakes

PREPARATION TIME 1 HOUR 15 MINUTES

COOKING TIME 15 - 20 MINUTES

INGREDIENTS

110 g / 4 oz / ⅔ cup self-raising flour, sifted
110 g / 4 oz / ½ cup caster (superfine) sugar
110 g / 4 oz / ½ cup butter, softened
2 large eggs
1 tsp vanilla extract

TO DECORATE:
400 g / 14 oz ready to roll fondant icing
blue food colouring
icing (confectioners') sugar for dusting
12 sugar flowers

- Preheat the oven to 190°C (170° fan) / 375F / gas 5 and line a 12-hole cupcake tin with paper cases.
- Combine the cake ingredients and whisk until smooth.
- Divide the mixture between the cases and bake for 15 – 20 minutes.
- Transfer the cakes to a wire rack and leave to cool.
- Colour half of the fondant icing bright blue then roll out and cut out 12 circles the same diameter of the cakes. Wet the backs and attach to the cakes.
- Colour the rest of the fondant pale blue and model it into 12 baby boots.
- Attach a boot to each cake with a dab of water and press a sugar flower into the sides.

944

MAKES 12

Green Ribbon Cupcakes

PREPARATION TIME 1 HOUR 30 MINUTES

COOKING TIME 15 - 20 MINUTES

SETTING TIME OVERNIGHT

INGREDIENTS

10 g / 4 oz / ⅔ cup self-raising flour, sifted
110 g / 4 oz / ½ cup caster (superfine) sugar
110 g / 4 oz / ½ cup butter, softened
2 large eggs
2 tbsp unsweetened cocoa powder

TO DECORATE:
100 g / 3 ½ oz ready to roll fondant icing
green food colouring
100 g / 3 ½ oz / ½ cup butter, softened
200 g / 7 oz / 2 cups icing (confectioners') sugar
½ tsp vanilla extract
green sugar sprinkles

- Preheat the oven to 190°C (170° fan) / 375F / gas 5 and line a 12-hole cupcake tin with paper cases.
- Combine the cake ingredients and whisk until smooth.
- Divide the mixture between the cases and bake for 15 – 20 minutes.
- Transfer the cakes to a wire rack and leave to cool.
- Roll out the fondant icing and cut it into long strips. Wrap them round a wooden dowel and leave to harden overnight.
- Beat the butter with the icing sugar, vanilla extract and food colouring and spread half of it over the cakes.
- Pipe the rest into a row of teardrops round the edge, then fill the centre with green sugar sprinkles and the icing ribbons.

Yellow Ribbon Cupcakes

945

- Colour the fondant icing and butter icing yellow.

946

MAKES 12

Pink Champagne Cupcakes

- Preheat the oven to 190°C (170° fan) / 375F / gas 5. line a cupcake tin with 12 paper cases.
- Combine the flour, sugar, butter, eggs and vanilla extract and whisk for 2 minutes. Divide between the cases, then bake for 15 – 20 minutes.
- Transfer the cakes to a wire rack and leave to cool.
- Reserve some icing for the labels and colour the rest pink. Shape the pink icing into 12 bottle shapes.
- Roll out the white icing until very thin.
- Cut out 12 labels and attach them to the bottles.
- Roll the off-cuts into 12 small corks and attach each one.
- Beat the butter until smooth, then gradually whisk in the icing sugar and vanilla extract.
- Spoon the mixture into a piping bag and pipe 2 rosettes of buttercream on top of each other on each cake.
- Press a champagne bottle into the top of each cake.

PREPARATION TIME 10 MINUTES

COOKING TIME 15 - 20 MINUTES

INGREDIENTS

110 g / 4 oz / ⅔ cup self-raising flour, sifted
110 g / 4 oz / ½ cup caster (superfine) sugar
110 g / 4 oz / ½ cup butter, softened
2 large eggs
1 tsp vanilla extract

TO DECORATE:
100 g / 3 ½ oz / ½ cup butter, softened
200 g / 7 oz / 2 cups icing (confectioners') sugar
½ tsp vanilla extract
110 g / 4 oz ready to roll fondant icing
pink food colouring

Beer Bottle Cupcakes

947

- Colour the icing dark green or brown instead of pink and shape it into 12 beer bottles.

948

MAKES 12

Patchwork Cupcakes

- Preheat the oven to 190°C (170° fan) / 375F / gas 5. Line a cupcake tin with 12 paper cases.
- Combine the flour, sugar, butter, eggs and vanilla extract and whisk for 2 minutes. Divide between the cases, then bake for 15 – 20 minutes.
- Beat the butter then whisk in the icing sugar and vanilla extract. Spread on top of the cakes.
- Dust the work surface with icing sugar and roll out half of the fondant icing.
- Divide the remaining icing into 4 pieces and dye 1 light blue, 1 dark blue, 1 red and one pink.
- Roll out the icings and cut each one into squares. Cut into quarters.
- Brush the white fondant sheet with water and arrange the squares on top in a patchwork pattern.
- Cut out 12 circles. Attach a patchwork circle to the top of each cake.

PREPARATION TIME 1 HOUR 15 MINUTES

COOKING TIME 15 - 20 MINUTES

INGREDIENTS

110 g / 4 oz / ⅔ cup self-raising flour, sifted
110 g / 4 oz / ½ cup caster (superfine) sugar
110 g / 4 oz / ½ cup butter, softened
2 large eggs
1 tsp vanilla extract

TO DECORATE:
100 g / 3 ½ oz / ½ cup butter, softened
200 g / 7 oz / 2 cups icing (confectioners') sugar
½ tsp vanilla extract
200 g / 7 oz ready to roll fondant icing
red, blue and pink food dye

Harlequin Cupcakes

949

- Cut the coloured icing into diamonds and fit together as before. Pipe lines of black royal icing to mark the edges of the colours.

950

MAKES 12

Filigree Swirl Cupcakes

PREPARATION TIME 1 HOUR 10 MINUTES

COOKING TIME 15 - 20 MINUTES

INGREDIENTS

110 g / 4 oz / ⅔ cup self-raising flour, sifted
110 g / 4 oz / ½ cup caster (superfine) sugar
110 g / 4 oz / ½ cup butter, softened
2 large eggs
1 tsp vanilla extract

TO DECORATE:
100 g / 3 ½ oz / ½ cup butter, softened
200 g / 7 oz / 2 cups icing (confectioners') sugar
½ tsp vanilla extract
200 g / 7 oz purple ready to roll fondant icing

- Preheat the oven to 190°C (170° fan) / 375F / gas 5 and line a 12-hole cupcake tin with paper cases.
- Combine the cake ingredients and whisk until smooth.
- Divide the mixture between the cases and bake for 15 – 20 minut
- Transfer the cakes to a wire rack and leave to cool.
- Beat the butter with the icing sugar and vanilla extract and sprea it onto the cakes.
- Roll out the fondant icing and cut out 12 circles the same diamete as the cakes. Wet the backs and attach to the cakes.
- Put the off-cuts in a bowl and add enough warm water to make a pipable icing, then pipe filigree swirls over the surface of the cake

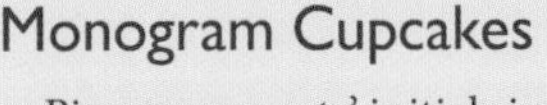

Monogram Cupcakes

951

- Pipe your guests' initials in elegant script on top of the cakes instead of the filigree swirls.

952

MAKES 12

Polka Dot Cupcakes

PREPARATION TIME 1 HOUR 15 MINUTES

COOKING TIME 15 - 20 MINUTES

INGREDIENTS

110 g / 4 oz / ⅔ cup self-raising flour, sifted
110 g / 4 oz / ½ cup caster (superfine) sugar
110 g / 4 oz / ½ cup butter, softened
2 large eggs
1 tsp vanilla extract

TO DECORATE:
100 g / 3 ½ oz / ½ cup butter, softened
200 g / 7 oz / 2 cups icing (confectioners') sugar
½ tsp vanilla extract
100 g / 3 ½ oz pink ready to roll fondant icing
100 g / 3 ½ oz purple ready to roll fondant icing

- Preheat the oven to 190°C (170° fan) / 375F / gas 5 and line a 12-hole cupcake tin with paper cases.
- Combine the cake ingredients and whisk until smooth.
- Divide the mixture between the cases and bake for 15 – 20 minutes.
- Transfer the cakes to a wire rack and leave to cool.
- Beat the butter with the icing sugar and vanilla extract and pipe a swirl onto each cake.
- Roll out the coloured fondants and cut out 1.5 cm circles, then stick them to the buttercream.

Fondant Hearts Cupcakes

953

- Use a heart-shaped plunger cutter to cut out small hearts instead of polka dots.

954

MAKES 18

Black and White Cupcakes

Checkerboard Cupcakes

955

- Cut the white icing and black icing into squares and alternate them on top of the cakes in a checkerboard pattern.

Black and White Spiral Cupcakes

956

- Make the black icing into a long thin sausage and curl it round into a spiral on top of each cake.

PREPARATION TIME 1 HOUR

COOKING TIME 15 - 20 MINUTES

INGREDIENTS

110 g / 4 oz / ⅔ cup self-raising flour, sifted
110 g / 4 oz / ½ cup caster (superfine) sugar
110 g / 4 oz / ½ cup butter, softened
2 large eggs
1 tsp vanilla extract

TO DECORATE:
100 g / 3 ½ oz / ½ cup butter, softened
200 g / 7 oz / 2 cups icing (confectioners') sugar
½ tsp vanilla extract
200 g / 7 oz ready to roll fondant icing
black food colouring

- Preheat the oven to 190°C (170° fan) / 375F / gas 5. Line a cupcake tin with 12 paper cases.
- Combine the flour, sugar, butter, eggs and vanilla extract in a bowl and whisk for 2 minutes. Divide between the cases, then bake in the oven for 15 – 20 minutes.
- Transfer the cakes to a wire rack and leave to cool completely.
- Beat the butter until smooth, then whisk in the icing sugar and vanilla extract. Spread the buttercream on top of the cakes.
- Dust the surface with icing sugar and roll out two thirds of the icing. Cut out 12 circles, and attach one to the top of each cake.
- Dye the remaining icing black, divide in half and roll out into 2 strips. Slice one piece into 5 mm slices. Cut out 5 mm circles from the other piece with a small plunger cutter.
- Lay 4 strips of black icing across the top of each cake, securing with water.
- Cut off the over-hanging icing. Add a row of black dots between 2 of the strips, securing with water.

957

MAKES 12

Chocolate Decadence Cupcakes

PREPARATION TIME 1 HOUR 10 MINUTES

COOKING TIME 15 - 20 MINUTES

INGREDIENTS

110 g / 4 oz / ⅔ cup self-raising flour, sifted
110 g / 4 oz / ½ cup caster (superfine) sugar
110 g / 4 oz / ½ cup butter, softened
2 large eggs
2 tbsp unsweetened cocoa powder

TO DECORATE:
100 g / 3 ½ oz / ½ cup butter, softened
200 g / 7 oz / 2 cups icing (confectioners') sugar
1 tbsp unsweetened cocoa powder
100 g / 3 ½ oz dark chocolate, melted
48 Maltesers
48 chocolate buttons

- Preheat the oven to 190°C (170° fan) / 375F / gas 5. Line a cupcake tin with 12 paper cases.
- Combine the flour, sugar, butter, eggs and cocoa powder and whisk for 2 minutes. Divide between the cases, then bake for 15 – 20 minutes. Leave to cool.
- Beat the butter, then gradually whisk in the icing sugar and cocoa powder.
- Spoon a quarter of the buttercream into a bowl and set aside. Fold the chocolate into the rest of the buttercream.
- Spoon the dark chocolate buttercream into a piping bag and pipe a swirl of buttercream on top of each cake.
- Spoon the reserved paler buttercream into a piping bag fitted with a large star nozzle and pipe a rosette on top of each dark chocolate swirl.
- Arrange 4 Maltesers on top of each cake.
- Slide a chocolate button between each Malteser.

Chocolate Orange Decadence Cupcakes

958

- Add the grated zest of an orange to the cake mixture and buttercream.

959

MAKES 12

Sweeties Cupcakes

PREPARATION TIME 1 HOUR

COOKING TIME 15 - 20 MINUTES

INGREDIENTS

110 g / 4 oz / ⅔ cup self-raising flour, sifted
110 g / 4 oz / ½ cup caster (superfine) sugar
110 g / 4 oz / ½ cup butter, softened
2 large eggs
1 tsp vanilla extract

TO DECORATE:
100 g / 3 ½ oz / ½ cup butter, softened
200 g / 7 oz / 2 cups icing (confectioners') sugar
½ tsp vanilla extract
12 packets of Palma Violets
36 strawberry jelly sweets

- Preheat the oven to 190°C (170° fan) / 375F / gas 5 and line a 12-hole cupcake tin with paper cases.
- Combine the flour, sugar, butter, eggs and vanilla extract and whisk together for 2 minutes. Divide the mixture between the cases, then transfer the tin to the oven and bake for 15 – 20 minutes.
- Transfer the cakes to a wire rack and leave to cool.
- Beat the butter until smooth, then gradually whisk in the icing sugar and vanilla extract.
- Spoon the mixture into a piping bag, fitted with a large star nozzle and use 2 thirds of the buttercream to pipe a rosette on top of each cake.
- Open the packets of Palma Violets and press them round the outside of the buttercream rosette.
- Pipe the remaining buttercream into a rosette on top of each cake.
- Top each cake with 3 strawberry jelly sweets.

Jelly Baby Cupcakes

960

- Top the buttercream with jelly babies instead of the Palma Violets and strawberry sweets.

961

MAKES 12

Handbag Cupcakes

- Preheat the oven to 190°C (170° fan) / 375F / gas 5. Line a cupcake tin with 12 paper cases.
- Combine the flour, sugar, butter, eggs and cocoa powder and whisk for 2 minutes. Divide between the cases, then bake in the oven for 15 – 20 minutes. Leave to cool.
- Beat the butter then whisk in the icing sugar and cocoa.
- Pipe the buttercream onto the cakes.
- Reserve a small piece of icing and dye the rest red.
- Shape into 12 cubes. Flatten half of each cube. Cut the flattened side into a curve. Fold the flattened curve back over to form the flap of the bag.
- Roll out the reserved white icing and cut into strips. Attach a strip along the edge of the bag flap. Cut out 12 tiny white clasps and attach them to the bags.
- Shape the red icing off-cuts into 12 handbag straps, then attach to the bags with water. Sit the handbags in the centre of the cakes.

Satchel Cupcakes

962

- Use the method above to sculpt 12 school satchels out of brown icing.

PREPARATION TIME 1 HOUR 10 MINUTES

COOKING TIME 15 - 20 MINUTES

INGREDIENTS

110 g / 4 oz / ⅔ cup self-raising flour, sifted
110 g / 4 oz / ½ cup caster (superfine) sugar
110 g / 4 oz / ½ cup butter, softened
2 large eggs
2 tbsp unsweetened cocoa powder

TO DECORATE:
100 g / 3 ½ oz / ½ cup butter, softened
200 g / 7 oz / 2 cups icing (confectioners') sugar
1 tbsp unsweetened cocoa powder
200 g / 7 oz ready to roll fondant icing
red food colouring

963

MAKES 12

Birdcage Cupcakes

- Preheat the oven to 190°C (170° fan) / 375F / gas 5 and line a 12-hole cupcake tin with paper cases.
- Combine the cake ingredients and whisk until smooth.
- Divide the mixture between the cases and bake for 15 – 20 minutes.
- Transfer the cakes to a wire rack and leave to cool.
- Beat the butter with the icing sugar and vanilla extract and spread ¾ of it over the cakes.
- Reserve a quarter of the fondant icing and colour the rest pale pink.
- Roll it out and cut out 12 circles the same diameter as the cakes, then wet the backs and attach to the cakes.
- Colour the remaining buttercream brown and pipe a birdcage on top of each cake.
- Attach the flowers and doves to the cage while the icing is still wet.

Dog Basket Cupcakes

964

- Use the brown buttercream to pipe a dog basket on top of each cake and use a mould to model a small dog's face to look out the top of each one.

PREPARATION TIME 1 HOUR 15 MINUTES

COOKING TIME 15 - 20 MINUTES

INGREDIENTS

110 g / 4 oz / ⅔ cup self-raising flour, sifted
110 g / 4 oz / ½ cup caster (superfine) sugar
110 g / 4 oz / ½ cup butter, softened
2 large eggs
1 tsp vanilla extract

TO DECORATE:
100 g / 3 ½ oz / ½ cup butter, softened
200 g / 7 oz / 2 cups icing (confectioners') sugar
½ tsp vanilla extract
200 g / 7 oz ready to roll fondant icing
pink and brown food colouring
12 small sugar flowers
12 sugar doves

965

MAKES 12

Crown Cupcakes

PREPARATION TIME 1 HOUR 10 MINUTES

COOKING TIME 15 - 20 MINUTES

INGREDIENTS

110 g / 4 oz / ⅔ cup self-raising flour, sifted
110 g / 4 oz / ½ cup caster (superfine) sugar
110 g / 4 oz / ½ cup butter, softened
2 large eggs
1 lemon, juiced and zest finely grated

TO DECORATE:
100 g / 3 ½ oz / ½ cup butter, softened
200 g / 7 oz / 2 cups icing (confectioners') sugar
½ lemon, juiced and zest finely grated
yellow food colouring
400 g / 7 oz ready to roll fondant icing
edible silver balls

- Preheat the oven to 190°C (170° fan) / 375F / gas 5 and line a 12-hole cupcake tin with paper cases.
- Combine the flour, sugar, butter, eggs and lemon juice and zest in a bowl and whisk together for 2 minutes or until smooth. Divide the mixture between the cases, then transfer the tin to the oven and bake for 15 – 20 minutes.
- Transfer the cakes to a wire rack and leave to cool.
- Beat the butter until smooth, then gradually whisk in the icing sugar, lemon juice and zest and a few drops of yellow food colouring.
- Spoon the mixture into a piping bag and pipe a swirl of buttercream on top of each cake.
- Colour the fondant icing yellow and roll it out on a work surface that has been lightly dusted with icing sugar.
- Cut it into 12 ribbons 2.5 cm thick, then cut a zigzag into one edge with a sharp knife.
- Make a dent below the centre of each pint with a small ball tool.
- Paint a little edible flower glue into each indentation.
- Press a silver ball into each indentation and wait for a few minutes for the glue to work.
- Fold each strip round to form a crown and press them lightly into the top of the buttercream to hold the shape.

Tiara Cupcakes

966

- Colour the fondant icing silver and cut it into tiara shapes. Decorate with multi-coloured silver ball jewels.

Baseball Cap Cupcakes

967

- Use blue and yellow fondant icing to model 12 baseball caps to top the cakes with.

968

MAKES 12

Beach Shoes Cupcakes

- Preheat the oven to 190°C (170° fan) / 375F / gas 5 and line a 12-hole cupcake tin with paper cases.
- Combine the flour, sugar, butter, eggs and cocoa powder in a bowl and whisk together for 2 minutes or until smooth. Divide between the cases, then bake for 15 – 20 minutes.
- Transfer the cakes to a wire rack and leave to cool.
- Top each cake with a thick layer of brown sugar 'sand' and make ripples.
- Reserve 1 quarter of the fondant icing and dye the rest red.
- Press a small amount of the white icing into the strap details inside a silicone flip-flop mould, making sure the top is flush with the design.
- Press a ball of red icing into each of the mould's indents and press down firmly to flatten.
- Turn the mould upside down and peel it away to reveal the icing flip-flops. Position 2 flip flops on top of each cake.

PREPARATION TIME 1 HOUR 10 MINUTES

COOKING TIME 15 - 20 MINUTES

INGREDIENTS

110 g / 4 oz / ⅔ cup self-raising flour, sifted
110 g / 4 oz / ½ cup caster (superfine) sugar
110 g / 4 oz / ½ cup butter, softened
2 large eggs
2 tbsp unsweetened cocoa powder

TO DECORATE:
110 g / 4 oz / ½ cup light brown sugar
110 g / 4 oz ready to roll fondant icing
red food colouring

Beach Cupcakes

969

- Omit the icing flip flops. Colour some royal icing blue and cover half of the top of each cake with an icing wave. Insert a paper umbrella into the 'sand' of each cupcake.

970

MAKES 12

Ladybird Cupcakes

- Preheat the oven to 190°C (170° fan) / 375F / gas 5. Line a cupcake tin with 12 paper cases.
- Combine the flour, sugar, butter, eggs and vanilla extract and whisk for 2 minutes. Divide between the cases, then bake for 15 – 20 minutes. Transfer to a wire rack and leave to cool.
- Beat the butter, then whisk in the icing sugar and vanilla extract. Spread buttercream on top of the cakes.
- Dust a surface with icing sugar. Dye two thirds of the fondant icing red and roll it out.
- Cut out 12 circles and attach one to the top of each cake.
- Reserve a small piece of white fondant icing for the eyes then dye the rest black.
- Roll out the black icing and cut part of it into 12 thin strips. Lay one strip down the centre of each cake – secure with water.
- Cut 12 small circles from the black icing and cut one edge off. Attach to the cakes to make the ladybirds' heads.
- Cut out 48 small circles to make the spots. Attach 4 spots to each ladybird.
- Roll out the reserved white icing and cut out 24 small circles for the eyes. Paint on the blue pupils with the food pen, then attach eyes to the cake.

PREPARATION TIME 1 HOUR 15 MINUTES

COOKING TIME 15 - 20 MINUTES

INGREDIENTS

110 g / 4 oz / ⅔ cup self-raising flour, sifted
110 g / 4 oz / ½ cup caster (superfine) sugar
110 g / 4 oz / ½ cup butter, softened
2 large eggs
1 tsp vanilla extract

TO DECORATE:
100 g / 3 ½ oz / ½ cup butter, softened
200 g / 7 oz / 2 cups icing (confectioners') sugar
½ tsp vanilla extract
200 g / 7 oz ready to roll fondant icing
red and black food colouring
blue food colour pen

971

Pearls Cupcakes

MAKES 12

PREPARATION TIME 1 HOUR 30 MINUTES

COOKING TIME 15 - 20 MINUTES

INGREDIENTS

110 g / 4 oz / ⅔ cup self-raising flour, sifted
110 g / 4 oz / ½ cup caster (superfine) sugar
110 g / 4 oz / ½ cup butter, softened
2 large eggs
1 lemon, juiced and zest finely grated

TO DECORATE:
400 g / 14 oz ready to roll fondant icing
ivory food colouring
icing (confectioners') sugar for dusting
pearlescent dusting powder

- Preheat the oven to 190°C (170° fan) / 375F / gas 5. Line a cupcake tin with 12 paper cases.
- Combine the flour, sugar, butter, eggs and lemon juice and zest and whisk for 2 minutes. Divide between the cases, then bake for 15 – 20 minutes. Leave to cool.
- Dust a surface with icing sugar and roll out two thirds of the fondant icing. Use a scalloped edge cutter to cut out 12 circles. Attach one circle to the top of each cake with water and reserve the off-cuts.
- Dye the rest of the icing ivory and roll it out. Use a smaller scalloped edge cutter to cut out 12 circles and attach each one to the top of a cake.
- Roll the white icing off-cuts into a 5 mm diameter sausage and cut into 5 mm lengths. Roll each piece into a ball and coat in pearlescent powder.
- Brush the rim of the ivory icing circles with water. Place pearls where the icing is wet. Add a pearl to the centre of each cake.

972

Black Pearl Cupcakes

- Make the pearls out of black icing before rolling in the pearlescent dusting powder.

973

Candles Cupcakes

MAKES 12

PREPARATION TIME 1 HOUR

COOKING TIME 15 - 20 MINUTES

INGREDIENTS

110 g / 4 oz / ⅔ cup self-raising flour, sifted
110 g / 4 oz / ½ cup caster (superfine) sugar
110 g / 4 oz / ½ cup butter, softened
2 large eggs
1 tsp vanilla extract

TO DECORATE:
100 g / 3 ½ oz / ½ cup butter, softened
200 g / 7 oz / 2 cups icing (confectioners') sugar
½ tsp vanilla extract
edible pink glitter
96 birthday candles
96 candle holders

- Preheat the oven to 190°C (170° fan) / 375F / gas 5 and line a 12-hole cupcake tin with paper cases.
- Combine the flour, sugar, butter, eggs and vanilla extract in a bowl and whisk together for 2 minutes or until smooth. Divide the mixture between the cases, then transfer the tin to the oven and bake for 15 – 20 minutes.
- Transfer the cakes to a wire rack and leave to cool.
- Beat the butter until smooth, then gradually whisk in the icing sugar and vanilla extract.
- Spoon the icing into a piping bag.
- Pipe 8 rosettes of icing on top of each cake.
- Use a dry paint brush to sprinkle a little pink edible glitter over the top of each cake.
- Insert each candle into a candle holder.
- Stick a candle in the top of each icing rosette and light them just before serving.

974

Sparklers Cupcakes

- Use 12 indoor cake sparklers in place of the candles.

975

MAKES 18

Butterfly Cupcakes

Dragonfly Cupcakes

976

- Cut out 12 dragonfly shapes and use blue and green pearlescent dusts to make the paint.

Tiger Moth Cupcakes

977

- Paint the fondant butterflies to look like a tiger moth.

PREPARATION TIME 1 HOUR 10 MINUTES

COOKING TIME 15 - 20 MINUTES

SETTING TIME OVERNIGHT

INGREDIENTS

110 g / 4 oz / ⅔ cup self-raising flour, sifted
110 g / 4 oz / ½ cup caster (superfine) sugar
110 g / 4 oz / ½ cup butter, softened
2 large eggs
2 tbsp unsweetened cocoa powder

TO DECORATE:
110 g / 4 oz ready to roll fondant icing
orange food colouring powder
100 g / 3 ½ oz / ½ cup butter, softened
200 g / 7 oz / 2 cups icing (confectioners') sugar
½ tsp vanilla extract

- Preheat the oven to 190°C (170° fan) / 375F / gas 5 and line a 12-hole cupcake tin with paper cases.
- Combine the flour, sugar, butter, eggs and cocoa powder in a bowl and whisk for 2 minutes or until smooth. Divide the mixture between the cases, then transfer the tin to the oven and bake for 15 – 20 minutes.
- Transfer the cakes to a wire rack and leave to cool.
- Roll out the fondant icing and cut out 12 butterfly shapes.
- Fold a piece of card in half to make a 'v' shape and lay the butterflies down the centre. Leave to set and harden overnight.
- Put a little orange food colouring powder in a plastic tray and add a few drops of water to make a paint.
- Paint the edge of the wings and the body onto the butterflies then add a spot to each wing.
- Beat the butter until smooth, then gradually whisk in the icing sugar, vanilla extract and a little of the orange food colouring powder.
- Spoon the mixture into a piping bag, fitted with a large star nozzle. Starting in the centre, pipe the icing on in a spiral, keeping the piping bag completely vertical to produce a rose effect.
- Press a butterfly onto the side of each one.

978

MAKES 12

Fondant Cherry Cupcakes

PREPARATION TIME 1 HOUR 10 MINUTES

COOKING TIME 15 - 20 MINUTES

INGREDIENTS

110 g / 4 oz / ⅔ cup self-raising flour, sifted
110 g / 4 oz / ½ cup caster (superfine) sugar
110 g / 4 oz / ½ cup butter, softened
2 large eggs
2 tbsp unsweetened cocoa powder

TO DECORATE:
100 g / 3 ½ oz / ½ cup butter, softened
200 g / 7 oz / 2 cups icing (confectioners') sugar
½ tsp vanilla extract
110 g / 4 oz ready to roll fondant icing
red and green food colouring

- Preheat the oven to 190°C (170° fan) / 375F / gas 5 and line a 12-hole cupcake tin with paper cases.
- Combine the flour, sugar, butter, eggs and cocoa powder in a bowl and whisk together for 2 minutes or until smooth. Divide the mixture between the cases, then transfer the tin to the oven and bake for 15 – 20 minutes.
- Test with a wooden toothpick, if it comes out clean, the cakes are done. Transfer the cakes to a wire rack and leave to cool completely.
- Beat the butter until smooth, then gradually whisk in the icing sugar and vanilla extract.
- Spoon the mixture into a piping bag, fitted with a large star nozzle and pipe a swirl of buttercream on top of each cake.
- Colour three quarters of the fondant icing red and roll it into 12 balls.
- Make an indentation in the top of each one with a veining tool.
- Colour the rest of the icing green and roll it into a long thin sausage.
- Cut the green icing into 12 cherry stalks.
- Sit a cherry on top of each cake and attach the stalks with a dab of water.

979

MAKES 12

Key Cupcakes

PREPARATION TIME 1 HOUR

COOKING TIME 15 - 20 MINUTES

INGREDIENTS

110 g / 4 oz / ⅔ cup self-raising flour, sifted
110 g / 4 oz / ½ cup caster (superfine) sugar
110 g / 4 oz / ½ cup butter, softened
2 large eggs
1 tsp vanilla extract

TO DECORATE:
200 g / 7 oz ready to roll fondant icing
purple food colouring
100 g / 3 ½ oz ready to pipe royal icing

- Preheat the oven to 190°C (170° fan) / 375F / gas 5 and line a 12-hole cupcake tin with paper cases.
- Combine the flour, sugar, butter, eggs and vanilla extract in a bowl and whisk together for 2 minutes or until smooth. Divide the mixture between the cases, then transfer the tin to the oven and bake for 15 – 20 minutes.
- Test with a wooden toothpick, if it comes out clean, the cakes are done. Transfer the cakes to a wire rack and leave to cool completely.
- Colour the fondant icing purple with the food colouring. Dust the work surface lightly with icing sugar and roll out the purple icing.
- Use a cookie cutter the same diameter as the top of the cakes to cut out 12 circles.
- Attach an icing circle to the top of each cake with a dab of water.
- Spoon the royal icing into a piping bag fitted with a small plain nozzle.
- Pipe a key on top of each cake: start with a circle to make the handle, followed by a straight line for the shaft.
- Pipe on the teeth of the key.
- Finish the cakes by piping a ring of dots around the outer edge.

980

MAKES 12

Silver Snowflake Cupcakes

- Preheat the oven to 190°C (170° fan) / 375F / gas 5 and line a 12-hole cupcake tin with paper cases.
- Combine the cake ingredients and whisk until smooth.
- Divide the mixture between the cases and bake for 15 – 20 minutes.
- Transfer the cakes to a wire rack and leave to cool.
- Pipe a swirl of buttercream onto each cake and top with the snowflakes and silver balls.

PREPARATION TIME 1 HOUR 10 MINUTES

COOKING TIME 15 - 20 MINUTES

INGREDIENTS

110 g / 4 oz / 2/3 cup self-raising flour, sifted
110 g / 4 oz / ½ cup caster (superfine) sugar
110 g / 4 oz / ½ cup butter, softened
2 large eggs
1 tsp vanilla extract
300 g / 10 ½ oz / 2 cups buttercream
icing snowflakes and silver balls to decorate

981

White Choc Easter Cupcakes

MAKES 12

PREPARATION TIME 1 HOUR

COOKING TIME 15 - 20 MINUTES

INGREDIENTS

110 g / 4 oz / 2/3 cup self-raising flour, sifted
110 g / 4 oz / ½ cup caster sugar
110 g / 4 oz / ½ cup butter, softened
2 large eggs
1 tsp vanilla extract
75 g / 2 ½ oz white chocolate, roughly chopped

TO DECORATE:
100 g / 3 ½ oz / ½ cup butter
200 g / 7 oz / 2 cups icing (confectioners') sugar
4 tbsp white chocolate, melted
purple and white sugar sprinkles
36 chocolate mini eggs

- Preheat the oven to 190°C (170° fan) / 375F / gas 5 and line a 12-hole cupcake tin with paper cases.
- Combine the flour, sugar, butter, eggs and vanilla extract in a bowl and whisk together for 2 minutes or until smooth. Fold in the chocolate chunks then divide the mixture between the cases and bake for 15 – 20 minutes.
- Test with a wooden toothpick, if it comes out clean, the cakes are done. Transfer the cakes to a wire rack and leave to cool completely.
- Beat the butter until smooth, then gradually whisk in the icing sugar and melted chocolate.
- Spoon the buttercream into a piping bag fitted with a large star nozzle and pipe a swirl onto each cake.
- Sprinkle the cakes with purple and white sugar sprinkles and top each one with 3 mini eggs.

982

Vintage Rose Cupcakes

MAKES 12

PREPARATION TIME 1 HOUR

COOKING TIME 15 - 20 MINUTES

INGREDIENTS

110 g / 4 oz / ⅔ cup self-raising flour, sifted
110 g / 4 oz / ½ cup caster (superfine) sugar
110 g / 4 oz / ½ cup butter, softened
2 large eggs
2 tbsp unsweetened cocoa powder

TO DECORATE:
200 g / 7 oz ready to roll fondant icing
blue pearlescent dusting powder

- Preheat the oven to 190°C (170° fan) / 375F / gas 5. Line a cupcake tin with 12 paper cases.
- Combine the flour, sugar, butter, eggs and cocoa in a bowl and whisk for 2 minutes. Divide between the cases, then transfer to the oven and bake for 15 – 20 minutes.
- Transfer the cakes to a wire rack and leave to cool completely.
- Dust the work surface lightly with icing sugar and roll out the icing.
- Dust a rose-shaped embossing tool with icing sugar.
- Press the embossing tool into the surface of the icing, being careful not to cut all the way through.
- Repeat until the surface of the icing is filled with roses.
- Use a cookie cutter the same diameter as the top of the cakes to cut out 12 circles.
- Using a dry paint brush, work a little blue pearlescent dusting powder into the embossed lines.
- Attach an icing circle to the top of each cake, using a dab of water to secure.

983

MAKES 12

Christmas Tree Cupcakes

PREPARATION TIME 1 HOUR 15 MINUTES

COOKING TIME 15 - 20 MINUTES

INGREDIENTS

110 g / 4 oz / ⅔ cup self-raising flour, sifted
110 g / 4 oz / ½ cup caster (superfine) sugar
110 g / 4 oz / ½ cup butter, softened
2 large eggs
1 tsp vanilla extract

TO DECORATE:
100 g / 3 ½ oz / ½ cup butter, softened
200 g / 7 oz / 2 cups icing (confectioners') sugar
½ tsp vanilla extract
orange and red food colouring
200 g / 7 oz green ready to roll fondant icing
coloured sugar balls to decorate

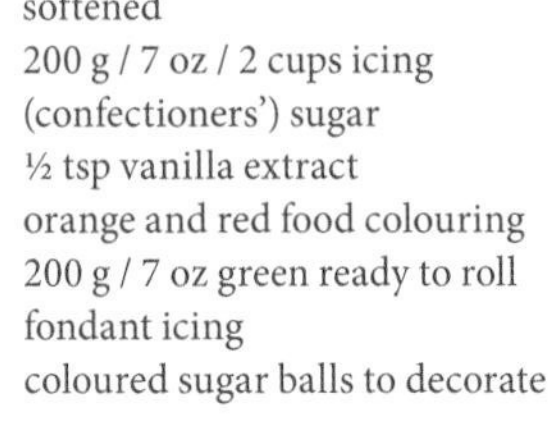

- Preheat the oven to 190°C (170° fan) / 375F / gas 5 and line a 12-hole cupcake tin with paper cases.
- Combine the cake ingredients and whisk until smooth.
- Divide the mixture between the cases and bake for 15 – 20 minutes.
- Transfer the cakes to a wire rack and leave to cool.
- Beat the butter with the icing sugar, vanilla extract and orange food colouring.
- Swirl through a few drops of red food colouring, then pipe the buttercream onto the cakes.
- Shape the green fondant into 12 cones and snip the branches into the sides with scissors.
- Use a dab of water to attach coloured sugar balls to make the baubles and sit a tree on top of each cake.

Pinecone Cupcakes

984

- Use the scissor sniping method to make pinecones out of brown fondant icing.

985

MAKES 12

Halloween Cupcakes

PREPARATION TIME 1 HOUR 20 MINUTES

COOKING TIME 15 - 20 MINUTES

INGREDIENTS

110 g / 4 oz / ⅔ cup self-raising flour, sifted
110 g / 4 oz / ½ cup caster (superfine) sugar
110 g / 4 oz / ½ cup butter, softened
2 large eggs
1 lemon, juiced and zest finely grated

TO DECORATE:
200 g / 7 oz ready to roll fondant icing
orange and green food colouring
100 g / 3 ½ oz / ½ cup butter, softened
200 g / 7 oz / 2 cups icing (confectioners') sugar
1 tbsp lemon juice
½ tsp ground cinnamon

- Preheat the oven to 190°C (170° fan) / 375F / gas 5. Line a cupcake tin with 12 paper cases.
- Combine the flour, sugar, butter, eggs and lemon juice and zest and whisk for 2 minutes. Divide between the cases, then bake for 15 – 20 minutes. Leave to cool.
- Reserve some icing for the stalks and dye the rest orange.
- Divide the orange fondant icing into 12 pieces and roll into balls. Score each ball into segments. Use a ball tool to make a dip in the top.
- Dye the fondant icing green and roll into 12 cones. Attach the stalks to the pumpkins with water.
- Beat the butter, then whisk in the sugar and lemon juice.
- Spoon half the mixture into a piping bag, and pipe a mound onto each cake. Sprinkle with cinnamon.
- Dye the rest of the buttercream orange and spoon it into a piping bag. Pipe a ring of teardrops round the outside of the plain buttercream, then pop a pumpkin on top.

Halloween Lantern Cupcakes

986

- Cut eyes and mouths out of black fondant icing and attach them to the pumpkins with a dab of water.

987

Nutty Cupcakes

MAKES 12

- Preheat the oven to 190°C (170° fan) / 375F / gas 5 and line a 12-hole cupcake tin with paper cases.
- Combine the flour, sugar, butter, eggs and vanilla extract in a bowl and together for 2 minutes or until smooth. Divide the mixture between the cases, then transfer the tin to the oven and bake for 15 – 20 minutes.
- Transfer the cakes to a wire rack and leave to cool.
- Beat the butter until smooth, then whisk in the icing sugar and vanilla extract.
- Spoon the mixture into a piping bag, fitted with a large plain nozzle and pipe mound onto each cake.
- Reserve 96 almonds and finely chop the rest.
- Dip the cakes in the chopped almonds so that they stick to the buttercream.
- Stick 8 whole blanched almonds around the edge of the buttercream like the petals of a flower.

Chocolate Nutty Cupcakes

988

- Add 2 tbsp of cocoa powder to the cake mixture and 1 tbsp of cocoa to the buttercream when you add the icing sugar.

PREPARATION TIME 1 HOUR 10 MINUTES

COOKING TIME 15 - 20 MINUTES

INGREDIENTS

110 g / 4 oz / ⅔ cup self-raising flour, sifted
110 g / 4 oz / ½ cup caster (superfine) sugar
110 g / 4 oz / ½ cup butter, softened
2 large eggs
1 tsp vanilla extract

TO DECORATE:
100 g / 3 ½ oz / ½ cup butter, softened
200 g / 7 oz / 2 cups icing (confectioners') sugar
½ tsp vanilla extract
200 g / 7 oz / 1 ½ cups blanched almonds

989

Rainbow Cupcakes

MAKES 12

- Preheat the oven to 190°C (170° fan) / 375F / gas 5. Line a cupcake tin with 12 paper cases.
- Combine the flour, sugar, butter, eggs and vanilla extract and whisk for 2 minutes. Divide between the cases, then transfer to the oven and bake for 15 – 20 minutes. Leave to cool.
- Beat the butter until smooth, then gradually whisk in the icing sugar and vanilla extract. Spread the buttercream on top of the cakes.
- Divide the fondant icing into 6 pieces and colour each piece a different colour.
- Pack the first colour into a sugar shaper gun and extrude a plain rope of fondant.
- Repeat with the other colours to make the ropes, then stick together with a little water. Trim the ends.
- Cut the rainbow sheet into 12 rounds. Transfer each round carefully to the top of a cake.

Braided Cupcakes

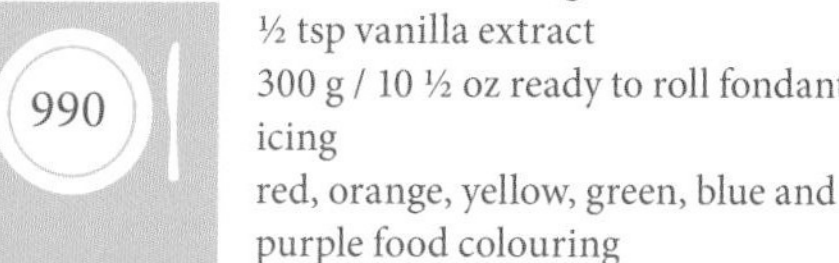

990

- Braid the fondant ropes together before arranging on top of the cupcakes.

PREPARATION TIME 1 HOUR 15 MINUTES

COOKING TIME 15 - 20 MINUTES

INGREDIENTS

110 g / 4 oz / ⅔ cup self-raising flour, sifted
110 g / 4 oz / ½ cup caster (superfine) sugar
110 g / 4 oz / ½ cup butter, softened
2 large eggs
1 tsp vanilla extract

TO DECORATE:
100 g / 3 ½ oz / ½ cup butter, softened
200 g / 7 oz / 2 cups icing (confectioners') sugar
½ tsp vanilla extract
300 g / 10 ½ oz ready to roll fondant icing
red, orange, yellow, green, blue and purple food colouring

991

Graduation Cupcakes

MAKES 12

PREPARATION TIME 1 HOUR 30 MINUTES

COOKING TIME 15 - 20 MINUTES

SETTING TIME OVERNIGHT

INGREDIENTS

110 g / 4 oz / ⅔ cup self-raising flour, sifted
110 g / 4 oz / ½ cup caster (superfine) sugar
110 g / 4 oz / ½ cup butter, softened
2 large eggs
2 tbsp unsweetened cocoa powder

TO DECORATE:
100 g / 3 ½ oz ready to roll fondant icing
purple and pink food colouring
100 g / 3 ½ oz / ½ cup butter, softened
200 g / 7 oz / 2 cups icing (confectioners') sugar
½ tsp vanilla extract
purple sugar sprinkles

- Preheat the oven to 190°C (170° fan) / 375F / gas 5. Line a cupcake tin with 12 paper cases.
- Combine the flour, sugar, butter, eggs and cocoa powder and whisk for 2 minutes. Divide between the cases, then bake for 15 – 20 minutes. Leave to cool.
- Dust a surface with icing sugar and roll out 2 thirds of the fondant icing. Cut into 12 squares.
- Roll each square around the handle of a paint brush to make scrolls, leave to set overnight.
- Reserve a small piece of the remaining fondant icing and dye the rest purple. Cut into 12 thin ribbons and cut a 'v' out of each end.
- Wrap each ribbon around one of the icing scrolls, securing with a dab of water.
- Dye the reserved icing pink and roll it out, then cut out 12 small discs and attach to the ribbons as seals.
- Beat the butter, then whisk in the icing sugar and vanilla extract.
- Dye the mix purple then spread half of it over the cakes and sprinkle with sugar sprinkles.
- Spoon the rest of the buttercream into a piping bag and pipe a ring of rosettes round the edge of each cake. Position the fondant scrolls in the centre of the cakes.

992

Mortar Board Cupcakes

- Colour the fondant icing black and mould it into the shape of 12 mortarboard graduation hats.

993

21st Birthday Cupcakes

- Cut the fondant icing into the number "21" for the top of the cakes.

994

Ring Cupcakes

- Cut the icing into the shape of two rings for engagement celebrations..

995

MAKES 12

Lemon Meringue Cupcakes

- Preheat the oven to 190°C (170° fan) / 375F / gas 5 and line a 12-hole cupcake tin with paper cases.
- Combine the flour, sugar, butter, eggs and lemon juice and zest in a bowl and whisk for 2 minutes or until smooth. Divide the mixture between the cases, then transfer the tin to the oven and bake for 15 – 20 minutes.
- Transfer the cakes to a wire rack and leave to cool.
- Use an apple corer to remove the centre of each cupcake.
- Fill the cavity in each cupcake with a heaped teaspoon of lemon curd.
- Spoon the marshmallow fluff into a piping bag and cover the surface of the cakes with small teardrops.
- Use a fork to rough up the top, making sure there are no gaps.
- Use a blowtorch to toast the marshmallow topping then top each one with a wedge of lemon.

PREPARATION TIME 1 HOUR 10 MINUTES

COOKING TIME 15 - 20 MINUTES

INGREDIENTS

110 g / 4 oz / ⅔ cup self-raising flour, sifted
110 g / 4 oz / ½ cup caster (superfine) sugar
110 g / 4 oz / ½ cup butter, softened
2 large eggs
1 lemon, juiced and zest finely grated

TO DECORATE:
100 g / 3 ½ oz / ½ cup lemon curd
200 g / 7 oz / 2 cups marshmallow fluff
1 lemon, cut into 12 wedges

996

Baked Alaska Cupcakes

- Replace the lemon curd with a small scoop of ice cream then top with the marshmallow fluff and toast as before. Serve immediately.

997

MAKES 12

Pink Bow Cupcakes

- Preheat the oven to 190°C (170° fan) / 375F / gas 5 and line a 12-hole cupcake tin with paper cases.
- Combine the cake ingredients and whisk until smooth.
- Divide the mixture between the cases and bake for 15 – 20 minutes.
- Transfer the cakes to a wire rack and leave to cool.
- Beat the butter with the icing sugar and vanilla extract, then spread it onto the cakes.
- Roll out 2 thirds of the pink icing and cut out 12 circles the same diameter as the cakes. Attach to the cakes with a dab of water.
- Use the rest of the pink icing to make 12 bows and attach to the cakes with an extra ball of pink icing.
- Top with the sugar flowers.

PREPARATION TIME 1 HOUR 30 MINUTES

COOKING TIME 15 - 20 MINUTES

INGREDIENTS

110 g / 4 oz / ⅔ cup self-raising flour, sifted
110 g / 4 oz / ½ cup caster (superfine) sugar
110 g / 4 oz / ½ cup butter, softened
2 large eggs
1 tsp vanilla extract

TO DECORATE:
100 g / 3 ½ oz / ½ cup butter, softened
200 g / 7 oz / 2 cups icing (confectioners') sugar
½ tsp vanilla extract
200 g / 7 oz pink ready to roll fondant icing
12 sugar flowers

998

MAKES 12

Birthday Number Cupcakes

PREPARATION TIME 1 HOUR 10 MINUTES

COOKING TIME 15 - 20 MINUTES

INGREDIENTS

110 g / 4 oz / ⅔ cup self-raising flour, sifted
110 g / 4 oz / ½ cup caster (superfine) sugar
110 g / 4 oz / ½ cup butter, softened
2 large eggs
1 lemon, juiced and zest finely grated

TO DECORATE:
400 g / 14 oz ready to roll fondant icing
blue food colouring
icing (confectioners') sugar for dusting

- Preheat the oven to 190°C (170° fan) / 375F / gas 5. Line a cupcake tin with 12 paper cases.
- Combine the flour, sugar, butter, eggs and lemon juice and zest in a bowl and whisk for 2 minutes. Divide between the cases, then transfer to the oven and bake for 15 – 20 minutes. Leave to cool.
- Dye half of the fondant icing blue. Dust the work surface with icing sugar and roll out the blue icing. Cut out 12 circles, then attach to the cakes with water.
- Roll out the white fondant icing until 2 mm thick. Use a flower-shaped cutter to cut out 12 flowers. Attach a flower to the top of each cake with a dab of water.
- Briefly knead the blue icing off-cuts and roll them out until 4 mm thick. Use a number-shaped cutter to cut out 12 numbers.
- Brush the back of each number with water, then attach one to the centre of each flower.

Alphabet Cupcakes

999

- Use letter-shaped cutters to cut out a different letter for the top of each cake.

1000

MAKES 12

Blue Baby Feet Cupcakes

PREPARATION TIME 1 HOUR 10 MINUTES

COOKING TIME 15 - 20 MINUTES

INGREDIENTS

110 g / 4 oz / ⅔ cup self-raising flour, sifted
110 g / 4 oz / ½ cup caster (superfine) sugar
110 g / 4 oz / ½ cup butter, softened
2 large eggs
1 lemon, juiced and zest finely grated

TO DECORATE:
400 g / 14 oz ready to roll fondant icing
blue and pink food colouring
icing (confectioners') sugar for dusting

- Preheat the oven to 190°C (170° fan) / 375F / gas 5. Line a cupcake tin with 12 paper cases.
- Combine the flour, sugar, butter, eggs and lemon juice and zest and whisk for 2 minutes. Divide between the cases, then bake for 15 – 20 minutes. Leave to cool.
- Dye two thirds of the fondant icing blue. Dust a surface with icing sugar and roll out the blue icing. Cut out 12 circles then attach them to the cakes with water.
- Chop the remaining white fondant icing and place in a bowl. Work in warm water a few drops at a time until you have a thick icing.
- Add a tiny amount of pink food dye to turn the icing flesh coloured.
- Spoon half of the icing into a piping bag fitted with a flat nozzle and pipe 2 feet onto each cake.
- Spoon the rest of the icing into a piping bag and pipe on toes.

Pink Baby Feet Cupcakes

1001

- Colour the background icing pink instead of blue.

1002

MAKES 12

Owl Cupcakes

Canary Cupcakes

1003

- Use yellow icing instead of red icing and omit the ears to make canary cupcakes.

Budgie Cupcakes

1004

- Use yellow and blue icing to make budgies for the top of the cakes.

PREPARATION TIME 1 HOUR 30 MINUTES

COOKING TIME 15 - 20 MINUTES

INGREDIENTS

110 g / 4 oz / ⅔ cup self-raising flour, sifted
110 g / 4 oz / ½ cup caster (superfine) sugar
110 g / 4 oz / ½ cup butter, softened
2 large eggs
1 lemon, juiced and zest finely grated

TO DECORATE:
400 g / 14 oz ready to roll fondant icing
blue, brown, red, purple and yellow food colouring
icing (confectioners') sugar for dusting

- Preheat the oven to 190°C (170° fan) / 375F / gas 5. Line a cupcake tin with 12 paper cases.
- Combine the flour, sugar, butter, eggs and lemon juice and zest and whisk for 2 minutes. Divide between the cases, then bake for 15 – 20 minutes. Leave to cool.
- Dye half of the icing pale blue. Dust a surface with icing sugar and roll out the blue icing. Cut out 12 circles then attach them to the top of the cakes.
- Divide the rest of the icing into 3 pieces. Dye one brown and one red. Divide the remaining piece in half and dye one yellow and the other purple.
- Roll out the brown icing and cut into 12 branches. Attach the branches to the cakes.
- Roll out the red icing and cut out 12 circles 5 cm in diameter. Cut the top off each circle and attach them to the cakes with the flat edge at the top.
- Cut 24 triangles out of the red trimmings to make the ears. Roll out the yellow icing and cut out 12 pairs of eyes. Use the purple icing to make circles for the pupils.
- Knead the yellow and red off-cuts together to make orange icing for the beaks and cut out 12 small triangles.
- Cut out 12 flowers from the purple icing, then cut them in half and use for the feet.
- Attach the extras to the cake with water.
- Use the edge of a star cutter to emboss the feather detail on the owls' bodies.

Shooting Star Cupcakes

MAKES 12

PREPARATION TIME 1 HOUR 30 MINUTES

COOKING TIME 15 - 20 MINUTES

INGREDIENTS

110 g / 4 oz / ⅔ cup self-raising flour, sifted
110 g / 4 oz / ½ cup caster (superfine) sugar
110 g / 4 oz / ½ cup butter, softened
2 large eggs
1 tsp vanilla extract

TO DECORATE:
100 g / 3 ½ oz / ½ cup butter, softened
200 g / 7 oz / 2 cups icing (confectioners') sugar
½ tsp vanilla extract
200 g / 7 oz ready to roll fondant icing
pink food colouring
48 floral wires

- Preheat the oven to 190°C (170° fan) / 375F / gas 5. Line a cupcake tin with 12 paper cases.
- Combine the flour, sugar, butter, eggs and vanilla extract and whisk for 2 minutes. Divide between the cases, then bake for 15 – 20 minutes. Leave to cool.
- Beat the butter then whisk in the icing sugar and vanilla. Spread the buttercream on top of the cakes.
- Reserve a third of the fondant icing for the stars and dye the rest pink. Roll out the pink icing and cut out 12 circles with a fluted cookie cutter.
- Roll out the white icing. Cut out 60 medium sized stars and stick one star in the centre of each cake.
- Use a small star plunger cutter to cut out 12 tiny stars for each cake and attach them round the outside of the cupcakes as before.
- Thread each star onto a piece of floral wire.
- Insert 4 wires into each cake and fan them out.

Seagull Cupcakes

1006

- Use a seagull shaped cutter and thread them onto wires as before. Colour the background icing blue instead of pink and omit the stars.

1007

Pink Flower Cupcakes

MAKES 12

PREPARATION TIME 1 HOUR 30 MINUTES

COOKING TIME 15 - 20 MINUTES

INGREDIENTS

110 g / 4 oz / ⅔ cup self-raising flour, sifted
110 g / 4 oz / ½ cup caster (superfine) sugar
110 g / 4 oz / ½ cup butter, softened
2 large eggs
1 tsp vanilla extract

TO DECORATE:
200 g / 7 oz pink ready to roll fondant icing
pink food colour pen
100 g / 3 ½ oz / ½ cup butter, softened
200 g / 7 oz / 2 cups icing (confectioners') sugar
½ tsp vanilla extract

- Preheat the oven to 190°C (170° fan) / 375F / gas 5 and line a 12-hole cupcake tin with paper cases.
- Combine the cake ingredients and whisk until smooth.
- Divide the mixture between the cases and bake for 15 – 20 minutes.
- Transfer the cakes to a wire rack and leave to cool.
- Roll out the fondant and cut out 12 large and 12 medium flowers, shaping the petals with a ball tool.
- Reroll the off-cuts and cut out 12 round centres for the flowers, then use the pink food colour pen to draw in the stamens.
- Ad enough warm water to the icing off-cuts to make a pipable icing.
- Colour half of it darker pink and pipe round the edge of the big flowers, adding a dot in the centres. Attach a medium flower to the centre of each large flower then pipe in the edges with the pale icing.
- Add the flower centres and pipe the ends on the stamens.
- Beat the butter with the icing sugar and vanilla extract, then pipe it onto the cakes and add a flower to each.

1008

MAKES 12

Dove Cupcakes

- Preheat the oven to 190°C (170° fan) / 375F / gas 5. Line a cupcake tin with 12 paper cases.
- Combine the flour, sugar, butter, eggs and vanilla extract and whisk for 2 minutes. Divide between the cases, then bake for 15 – 20 minutes. Leave to cool.
- Beat the butter, then whisk in the icing sugar and vanilla. Spread the buttercream on top of the cakes.
- Roll out three quarters of the fondant icing.
- Use a cookie cutter the same diameter as the top of the cakes to cut out 12 circles.
- Attach an icing circle to the top of each cake. Colour the rest of the icing a pale ivory colour.
- Dust the dove-shaped mould with icing sugar. Press a ball of icing into the mould.
- Turn out the dove onto the surface and repeat to make 12.
- Attach a dove to each cake with a dab of water.

PREPARATION TIME 1 HOUR

COOKING TIME 15 - 20 MINUTES

INGREDIENTS

110 g / 4 oz / ⅔ cup self-raising flour, sifted
110 g / 4 oz / ½ cup caster (superfine) sugar
110 g / 4 oz / ½ cup butter, softened
2 large eggs
1 tsp vanilla extract

TO DECORATE:
100 g / 3 ½ oz / ½ cup butter, softened
200 g / 7 oz / 2 cups icing (confectioners') sugar
½ tsp vanilla extract
200 g / 7 oz ready to roll fondant icing
ivory food colouring

Horseshoe Cupcakes

1009

- Colour the icing silver instead of ivory and use a horseshoe shaped mould to make the cake toppers.

1010

MAKES 12

Presents Cupcakes

- Preheat the oven to 190°C (170° fan) / 375F / gas 5. Line a cupcake tin with 12 paper cases.
- Combine the flour, sugar, butter, eggs and vanilla extract and whisk for 2 minutes. Divide between the cases, then bake for 15 – 20 minutes. Leave to cool.
- Beat the butter until smooth, then gradually whisk in the icing sugar and vanilla extract.
- Spoon the buttercream into a piping bag and pipe a swirl onto each cake.
- Reserve a small amount of icing and dye the rest pink. Roll into 12 balls.
- Make them into cubes. Smooth and sharpen the edges.
- Roll out the reserved white icing and cut it into thin ribbons. Paint a cross on top of each cube with water. Lay 2 fondant ribbons across each box and smooth down the sides. Trim off the ends.
- Make 12 tiny bows from the remaining ribbons. Attach the bows to the top of the presents.
- Roll some of the pink icing off-cuts into 12 tiny balls and use as the centres of the bows.
- Position a present on each cupcake.

PREPARATION TIME 1 HOUR 15 MINUTES

COOKING TIME 15 - 20 MINUTES

INGREDIENTS

110 g / 4 oz / ⅔ cup self-raising flour, sifted
110 g / 4 oz / ½ cup caster (superfine) sugar
110 g / 4 oz / ½ cup butter, softened
2 large eggs
1 tsp vanilla extract

TO DECORATE:
100 g / 3 ½ oz / ½ cup butter, softened
200 g / 7 oz / 2 cups icing (confectioners') sugar
½ tsp vanilla extract
300 g / 9 oz ready to roll fondant icing
pink food colouring

1011

MAKES 12

Red Velvet Heart Flower Cupcakes

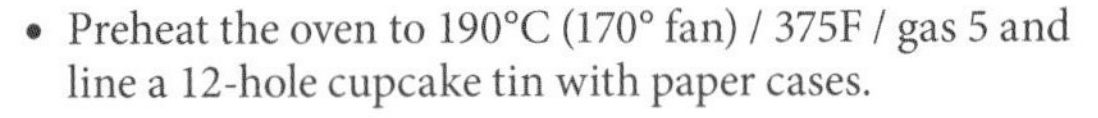

PREPARATION TIME 30 MINUTES

COOKING TIME 15 - 20 MINUTES

INGREDIENTS

110 g / 4 oz / ⅔ cup self-raising flour, sifted
110 g / 4 oz / ½ cup caster (superfine) sugar
110 g / 4 oz / ½ cup butter, softened
2 large eggs
1 tsp ground cinnamon
1 tbsp red food colouring

TO DECORATE:
110 g / 4 oz / ½ cup cream cheese
55 g / 2 oz / ¼ cup butter, softened
110 g / 4 oz / 1 cup icing (confectioners') sugar
1 tsp vanilla extract
150 g / 5 ½ oz ready to roll fondant icing
red food colouring
edible glitter

- Preheat the oven to 190°C (170° fan) / 375F / gas 5 and line a 12-hole cupcake tin with paper cases.
- Combine the flour, sugar, butter, eggs, cinnamon and food colouring in a bowl and whisk together for 2 minutes or until smooth. Divide the mixture between the cases, then transfer the tin to the oven and bake for 15 – 20 minutes.
- Test with a wooden toothpick, if it comes out clean, the cakes are done. Transfer the cakes to a wire rack and leave to cool completely.
- Beat the cream cheese and butter together until light and fluffy then beat in the icing sugar a quarter at a time. Add the vanilla extract then whip the mixture for 2 minutes or until smooth and light.
- Spoon the icing into a piping bag, fitted with a large plain nozzle, and pipe some icing on top of each cake.
- Colour the fondant icing red and roll it out on a work surface that has been lightly dusted with icing sugar.
- Use a heart-shaped cutter to cut out 60 hearts and attach 5 hearts to the top of each cake like the petals of a flower.
- Cut out 12 small circles of icing and attach one to the centre of each cake.
- Use a small dry cake brush to apply a little edible glitter to the top of each cake.

Blue Velvet Cupcakes

1012

- Replace the red food colouring with blue food colouring in the cake mixture and to colour the fondant icing.

Green Emerald Cupcakes

1013

- Use green food colouring to colour the cake mixture and fondant icing.

Pink Velvet Cupcakes

1014

- Use half of the amount of red dye to make a pink colour.

1015

MAKES 12

Football Cupcakes

- Preheat the oven to 190°C (170° fan) / 375F / gas 5. Line a cupcake tin with 12 paper cases.
- Combine the flour, sugar, butter, eggs and vanilla extract and whisk for 2 minutes. Divide between the cases, then bake for 15 minutes. Leave to cool.
- Beat the butter then whisk in the icing sugar and vanilla. Spread the buttercream on top of the cakes.
- Dust the work surface lightly with icing sugar and roll out two thirds of the fondant icing.
- Use a cutter the same diameter as the top of the cakes to cut out 12 circles. Attach to the top of each cake.
- Colour the icing black and roll it out into a large rectangle. Cut out 36 circles with a 3 cm diameter cutter.
- Cut the circles into pentagons, reserve the trimmings.
- Cut the trimmings into thin strips and use them to emphasise the white hexagons in between.

PREPARATION TIME 1 HOUR

COOKING TIME 15 - 20 MINUTES

INGREDIENTS

110 g / 4 oz / ⅔ cup self-raising flour, sifted
110 g / 4 oz / ½ cup caster (superfine) sugar
110 g / 4 oz / ½ cup butter, softened
2 large eggs
1 tsp vanilla extract

TO DECORATE:
100 g / 3 ½ oz / ½ cup butter, softened
200 g / 7 oz / 2 cups icing (confectioners') sugar
½ tsp vanilla extract
200 g / 7 oz ready to roll fondant icing
black food colouring

1016

Cricket Ball Cupcakes

- Colour the fondant icing red and pipe the stitching on with white royal icing.

1017

MAKES 12

Engagement Ring Cupcakes

- Preheat the oven to 190°C (170° fan) / 375F / gas 5 and line a 12-hole cupcake tin with paper cases.
- Combine the flour, sugar, butter, eggs and cocoa powder in a bowl and whisk for 2 minutes or until smooth. Divide the mixture between the cases, then transfer the tin to the oven and bake for 15 – 20 minutes.
- Beat the butter then whisk in the icing sugar and vanilla.
- Spoon the mixture into a piping bag, fitted with a large star nozzle and pipe a swirl on top of each cake.
- Roll out the fondant icing until 4 mm thick and cut out 12 circles with a 2 cm diameter plunger cutter.
- Cut out the centres with a 1.5 cm plunger cutter and leave to harden overnight.
- Attach a pink sugar ball 'jewel' to the top of each icing ring with a dab of water, then transfer to the cakes.

PREPARATION TIME 1 HOUR 10 MINUTES

COOKING TIME 15 - 20 MINUTES

SETTING TIME OVERNIGHT

INGREDIENTS

110 g / 4 oz / ⅔ cup self-raising flour, sifted
110 g / 4 oz / ½ cup caster (superfine) sugar
110 g / 4 oz / ½ cup butter, softened
2 large eggs
2 tbsp unsweetened cocoa powder

TO DECORATE:
100 g / 3 ½ oz / ½ cup butter, softened
200 g / 7 oz / 2 cups icing (confectioners') sugar
½ tsp vanilla extract
100 g / 3 ½ oz ready to roll fondant icing
12 pink sugar balls

1018

Wedding Ring Cupcakes

- After the rings have hardened, spray them with edible gold paint and leave to dry before topping the cakes.

1019

MAKES 12

Cookie Monster Cupcakes

PREPARATION TIME 1 HOUR 15 MINUTES

COOKING TIME 15 - 20 MINUTES

INGREDIENTS

110 g / 4 oz / ⅔ cup self-raising flour, sifted
110 g / 4 oz / ½ cup caster (superfine) sugar
110 g / 4 oz / ½ cup butter, softened
2 large eggs
1 tsp vanilla extract

TO DECORATE:
250 g / 9 oz ready to pipe royal icing
12 cookies
100 g / 3 ½ oz ready to roll fondant icing
red and purple food colouring

- Preheat the oven to 190°C (170° fan) / 375F / gas 5. Line a cupcake tin with 12 paper cases.
- Combine the flour, sugar, butter, eggs and vanilla extract and whisk for 2 minutes. Divide between the cases, then bake for 15 – 20 minutes. Leave to cool.
- Use a third of the royal icing to attach a cookie to the top of each cake.
- Use some fondant icing to make 12 pairs of eyes and attach them to the cookies.
- Dye a piece of fondant icing purple for the pupils.
- Dye the remaining fondant red and roll it out. Cut out 12 mouth shapes and attach them to the cookies.
- Use the icing off-cuts to make the tongues and attach.
- Dye the remaining royal icing red and spoon it into a piping bag fitted with a grass piping nozzle.
- Pipe a mane of hair around each cookie.

Lion Cupcakes

1020

- Use the same method to pipe a brown mane onto lion faces that have been modelled out of yellow fondant icing.

MAKES 12

Camper Van Cupcakes

PREPARATION TIME 1 HOUR 30 MINUTES

COOKING TIME 15 - 20 MINUTES

INGREDIENTS

110 g / 4 oz / ⅔ cup self-raising flour, sifted
110 g / 4 oz / ½ cup caster (superfine) sugar
110 g / 4 oz / ½ cup butter, softened
2 large eggs
1 lemon, juiced and zest finely grated

TO DECORATE:
400 g / 14 oz ready to roll fondant icing
blue, orange, yellow, red and black food colouring
icing (confectioners') sugar for dusting

- Preheat the oven to 190°C (170° fan) / 375F / gas 5. Line a cupcake tin with 12 paper cases.
- Combine the flour, sugar, butter, eggs and lemon juice and zest and whisk for 2 minutes. Divide between the cases, then bake for 15 – 20 minutes. Leave to cool.
- Dye half of the fondant icing blue. Dust a surface with icing sugar and roll out the blue icing. Cut out 12 circles then attach them to the cakes with water.
- Make a template for the camper van out of strong card.
- Dye half of the remaining icing orange and roll it out then use the template to cut out 12 van shapes. Roll out the white icing and cut out 12 more van shapes.
- Stack the white shapes on top of the orange shapes and cut a 'v' through each.
- Assemble the vans on top of the cakes, attaching with water.
- Cut small circles out of the orange icing off-cuts and attach them to the cakes with water.
- Dye half of the white icing off-cuts yellow and make the headlights and indicators.
- Knead the remaining white off-cuts with the blue off-cuts to make a pale blue icing, then cut out and attach the windows and number plate.
- Add some red food dye to the remaining orange off-cuts then cut out and attach a bumper to each van.
- The tires can be painted directly onto the cakes using a little black food dye.

1022

MAKES 24

Spinach and Bacon Cupcakes

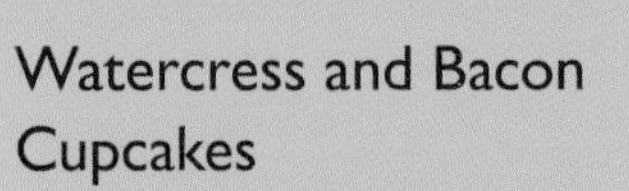

Watercress and Bacon Cupcakes

1023

- Replace the spinach with finely chopped watercress.

Spinach and Mushroom Cupcakes

1024

- Replace the bacon with 50 g of sliced button mushrooms.

Spinach and Onion Cupcakes

1025

- Replace the bacon with finely diced onion.

PREPARATION TIME 25 MINUTES

COOKING TIME 15 – 20 MINUTES

INGREDIENTS

6 rashers of smoked streaky bacon
2 large eggs
120 ml / 4 fl. oz / ½ cup sunflower oil
180 ml / 6 fl. oz / ¾ cup Greek yoghurt
110 g / 4 oz / 1 cup Parmesan, grated
a handful of spinach leaves, finely shredded
225 g / 8 oz / 1 ½ cups plain (all purpose) flour
2 tsp baking powder
½ tsp bicarbonate of (baking) soda
½ tsp salt

- Preheat the oven to 180°C (160° fan) / 350F / gas 4 and line 2 x 12-hole cupcake tins with silicone cases.
- Grill the bacon for 3 minutes on each side or until crisp, then slice it very thinly.
- Beat the egg in a jug with the oil, yoghurt, Parmesan, spinach and half the bacon until well mixed.
- Mix the flour, raising agents and salt in a bowl, then pour in the egg mixture and stir just enough to combine.
- Divide the mixture between the moulds, then bake in the oven for 15 – 20 minutes.
- Test with a wooden toothpick, if it comes out clean, the cakes are done.
- Sprinkle the cakes with the rest of the bacon and serve warm or at room temperature.

Index

21st Birthday Cupcakes 288

After Eight Cupcakes 241
Afternoon Tea Cupcakes 267
Almond and Apricot Muffin Cupcakes 73
Almond and Chocolate Mini Cupcakes 40
Almond and Dulce de Leche Cupcakes 231
Almond and White Chocolate Cupcakes 209
Almond Bakewell Cupcakes 48
Almond Buttercream Cupcakes 235
Almond Cupcakes with Blackcurrant Buttercream 110
Almond Cupcakes with Rolled Icing 243
Almond Muffin Cupcakes 73
Almond Snake Cupcakes 248
Almond-Scented Buttercream Cupcakes 242
Alphabet Cupcakes 290
Angelica Star Cupcakes 21
Animal Print Cupcakes 268
Apple Crumble Muffin Cupcakes 11
Apple Cupcakes 211
Apple Cupcakes with Rolled Icing 108
Apple Snow Cupcakes 211
Apple Vanilla Rose 162
Apricot and Coconut Cupcakes 83
Apricot and Pistachio Cupcakes 38
Apricot Buttercream Cupcakes 185
Apricot Cupcakes 51
Apricot Heart Cupcakes 117
Apricot Jam Cupcakes 83
Apricot Jam-filled Cupcakes 168
Apricot Rose and Pearl Cupcakes 120
Avocado and Prawn Cupcakes 244

Baby Boots Cupcakes 274
Baby Shower Cupcakes 176
Bacon and Egg Chocolate Cupcakes 228
Baileys and Chocolate Cupcakes 92
Baileys Buttercream Cupcakes 205
Baked Alaska Cupcakes 289
Banana and Cardamom Cupcakes 43
Banana and Cinnamon Cupcakes 75
Banana and Ginger Cupcakes 43
Banana and Lime Cupcakes 25
Banana and Mango Cupcakes 25
Banana and Poppy Seed Cupcakes 75
Banana Cupcakes 25
Banana Heart Cupcakes 117
Banoffee Cupcakes 8
Banoffee Pie Cupcakes 102
Baseball Cap Cupcakes 280
Bastille Day Cupcakes 204
Beach Cupcakes 281
Beach Shoes Cupcakes 281
Beer Bottle Cupcakes 275
Birdcage Cupcakes 279
Birthday Blues Cupcakes 160
Birthday Number Cupcakes 290
Birthday Sparkler Cupcakes 160
Black and Blue Cupcakes 254
Black and Orange Flower Cupcakes 112
Black and White Cupcakes 277
Black and White Spiral Cupcakes 277
Black Forest Cupcakes 232
Black Pearl Cupcakes 107
Blackberry and Apple Muffin Cupcakes 60
Blackberry and Cardamom Muffin Cupcakes 65
Blackberry and Cinnamon Muffin Cupcakes 65
Blackberry and Clove Muffin Cupcakes 65
Blackberry and Lemon Cupcakes 224
Blackberry and Orange Cupcakes 224
Blackberry Muffin Cupcakes 60
Blackberry Truffle Cupcakes 178
Blackcurrant and Apple Cupcakes 35
Blackcurrant Buttercream Cupcakes 110
Blackcurrant Cupcakes 35
Blackcurrant Sweetie Cupcakes 19
Blackcurrant Syrup Cream Cheese Cupcakes 220
Blue and Yellow Easter Cupcakes 257
Blue Baby Feet Cupcakes 290
Blue Butterfly Cupcakes 113
Blue Pearl Cupcakes 72
Blue Suede Cupcakes 119
Blue Velvet Cupcakes 294
Blueberry Almond Cream Cupcakes 87
Blueberry and Chocolate Cakes 183
Blueberry and Fig Muffin Cupcakes 44
Blueberry and Lemon Cupcakes 67
Blueberry and Orange Flower Buttercream Cupcakes 247
Blueberry and Redcurrant Cupcakes 124
Blueberry and Rose Buttercream Cupcakes 247
Blueberry Blues Cupcakes 254
Blueberry Buttercream Chocolate Curl Cupcakes 212
Blueberry Cinnamon Cupcakes 179
Blueberry Dream Cupcakes 87
Blueberry Heart Buttercream Cupcakes 258
Blueberry Smile Cupcakes 255
Blueberry Syrup Cream Cheese Cupcakes 147
Blueberry Vanilla Cupcakes 96
Blueberry, Hazelnut and Lemon Cupcakes 213
Blueberry, Hazelnut and Orange Cupcakes 213
Blue-Iced Lemon Cupcakes 73
Bonfire Cupcakes 200
Boozy Toadstool Cupcakes 250
Braided Cupcakes 287
Brandy Butter Cupcakes 270
Brazil Nut Buttercream Cupcakes 235
Bubble Gum Cream Cheese Cupcakes 147
Budgie Cupcakes 291
Bundt Cupcakes 59
Buttercream for Cupcakes 253
Butterfly Cupcakes 283

Camper Van Cupcakes 296
Canary Cupcakes 291
Candied Fruit Cupcakes 156
Candied Lemon Cream Cheese Cupcakes 24
Candied Orange Cream Cheese Cupcakes 24
Candles Cupcakes 282
Cappuccino Cupcakes 34
Caramel Cupcakes 8
Cardamom and Orange Flower Cupcakes 177
Cardamom and Rose Water Cupcakes 149
Carrot and Cinnamon Cream Cupcakes 239
Carrot and Clove Cream Cupcakes 239
Carrot and Lemon Cupcakes 30
Carrot and Milk Chocolate Cupcakes 161
Champagne and Roses Cupcakes 106
Champagne Truffle Cupcakes 119
Chantilly Cream for Cupcakes 61
Checkerboard Cupcakes 277
Cherry and Chestnut Cream Cupcakes 18
Cherry Bakewell Cupcakes 48
Cherry Cola Cupcakes 260
Cherry Heart Buttercream Cupcakes 258
Cherry Syrup Cream Cheese Cupcakes 220
Chestnut and Chocolate
Chestnut Cream Cupcakes 216
Chestnut Muffin Cupcakes 30
Chili Dog Cupcakes 240
Chilli Chocolate Brownie Cupcakes 57
Choc-chip Cream Cheese Muffin Cupcakes 190
Chocolate Almond Buttercream Cupcakes 159
Chocolate and Almond Mini Cupcakes 20
Chocolate and Amaretto Cream Cheese Cupcakes 46
Chocolate and Banana Cupcakes 17
Chocolate and Blackcurrant Cupcakes 49
Chocolate and Blueberry Buttercream Cupcakes 172
Chocolate and Blueberry Cupcakes 212
Chocolate and Cinnamon Brownie Cupcakes 265
Chocolate and Coffee Cupcakes 121

Chocolate and Crystallised Rose Petal Cupcakes 143
Chocolate and Ginger Brownie Cupcakes 265
Chocolate and Grenadine Cupcakes 49
Chocolate and Hazelnut Mini Cupcakes 70
Chocolate and Honey Cream Cupcakes 134
Chocolate and Melon Cream Cupcakes 233
Chocolate and Nutty Cream Cheese Cupcakes 46
Chocolate and Orange Cream Cupcakes 134
Chocolate and Orange Cupcakes 33
Chocolate and Pear Muffin Cupcakes 9
Chocolate and Pecan Buttercream Cupcakes 20
Chocolate and Pistachio Mini Muffin Cupcakes 20
Chocolate and Pretzel Kiwi Cupcakes 263
Chocolate and Pumpkin Seed Cupcakes 171
Chocolate and Raspberry Jam Cupcakes 232
Chocolate and Sesame Brittle Cupcakes 266
Chocolate and Sesame Cupcakes 266
Chocolate and Strawberry Muffin Cupcakes 9
Chocolate and Toffee Cupcakes 146
Chocolate and Walnut Mini Cupcakes 40
Chocolate and Watermelon Cupcakes 138
Chocolate and Blueberry Cream Cupcakes 138
Chocolate Baby Shower Cupcakes 132
Chocolate Brownie Cupcakes 58
Chocolate Brownie Cupcakes with Chantilly 77
Chocolate Butterfly Cupcakes 71
Chocolate Butterfly Cupcakes 90
Chocolate Button Cupcakes 41
Chocolate Buttons Cupcakes 184
Chocolate Candy Cane Cupcakes 271
Chocolate Cherry Brownie Cupcakes 57
Chocolate Chilli Cream Cheese Cupcakes 64
Chocolate Chip and Chestnut Cream Cupcakes 216
Chocolate Chip Buttercream Cupcakes 29
Chocolate Chip Cream Cupcakes 82
Chocolate Chip Vermicelli Cupcakes 192
Chocolate Christmas Buttercream Cupcakes 217
Chocolate Chunk Muffin Cupcakes 42
Chocolate Cigarillo Cupcakes 81
Chocolate Cinnamon Cream Cupcakes 82
Chocolate Cola Bottle Cupcakes 260
Chocolate Cookies and Cream Cupcakes 98
Chocolate Cookies Cupcakes 85
Chocolate Cream Cupcakes 134
Chocolate Cream Raspberry Cupcakes 82
Chocolate Crispy Cupcakes 148
Chocolate Cross Cupcakes 208
Chocolate Cupcakes with Buttercream 155
Chocolate Cupcakes with Cinnamon Buttercream 121
Chocolate Cupcakes with Coffee Cream 200
Chocolate Cupcakes with Lavender Buttercream 118
Chocolate Cupcakes with Orange Buttercream 155
Chocolate Cupcakes with Rose Buttercream 118
Chocolate Decadence Cupcakes 278
Chocolate Flag Cupcakes 94
Chocolate Flake Cupcakes 250
Chocolate Fondant Cupcakes 199
Chocolate Glace-Iced Lemon Cupcakes 22
Chocolate Glacé-Iced Red Velvet Cupcakes 262
Chocolate Greengage Cupcakes 17
Chocolate Heart Cupcakes 167
Chocolate Holly Cupcakes 255
Chocolate Kiwi Mud Cupcakes 263
Chocolate Lime Cupcakes 101
Chocolate Lime Drizzle Cupcakes 101
Chocolate Malteser Buttercream Cupcakes 66
Chocolate Malteser Cupcakes 66
Chocolate Marshmallow Cupcakes 259
Chocolate Marshmallow Dreams 68
Chocolate Marshmallow Muffin Cupcakes 231
Chocolate Minstrel Cupcakes 93
Chocolate Mint Cigarillo Cupcakes 81
Chocolate Mint Dream Cupcakes 194
Chocolate Mint Sweetie Cupcakes 260
Chocolate Mirabelle Cupcakes 17
Chocolate Muffin Cupcakes 13
Chocolate Muffin Cupcakes with
Strawberry Buttercream 155
Chocolate Nutty Cupcakes 287
Chocolate Orange Brownie Cream Cupcakes 77
Chocolate Orange Chunk Muffin Cupcakes 42
Chocolate Orange Decadence Cupcakes 278
Chocolate Orange Marbled Cupcakes 14
Chocolate Orange Muffin Cupcakes 13
Chocolate Orange Syrup Cupcakes 114
Chocolate Orange Vermicelli Cupcakes 192
Chocolate Peanut Cupcakes 15
Chocolate Pearl Cupcakes 127
Chocolate Peppermint Cupcakes 241
Chocolate Piglet Cupcakes 246
Chocolate Pistachios Cupcakes 169
Chocolate Rainbow Cupcakes 15
Chocolate Raspberry Cupcakes 172
Chocolate Red and Green Cupcakes 238
Chocolate Reese's Cupcakes 15
Chocolate Rudolph Cupcakes 255
Chocolate Rum Cupcakes 99
Chocolate Smarties Cream Cheese Cupcakes 41
Chocolate Smarties Cupcakes 15
Chocolate Softmint Cupcakes 260
Chocolate Star Cupcakes 167
Chocolate Strawberry Cupcakes 172
Chocolate Sweetheart Cupcakes 251
Chocolate Syrup Cream Cupcakes 113
Chocolate Syrup Cream Cupcakes 141
Chocolate Teardrop Cupcakes 252
Chocolate Truffle Cupcakes 119
Chocolate Vanilla Dreams 161
Chocolate Vermicelli Cupcakes 158
Chocolate Vermicelli Cupcakes 192
Chocolate, Almond and Mint Buttercream Cupcakes 139
Chocolate, Almond and Rose Buttercream Cupcakes 139
Chocolate, Honey and Pecan Cupcakes 207
Chocolate, Maple and Pecan Buttercream Cupcakes 207
Chocolate, Orange and Pecan Buttercream Cupcakes 20
Chocolate, Orange and Raspberry Muffin Cupcakes 154
Chocolate, Orange and Strawberry Cupcakes 154
Chocolate, Raspberry and Kiwi Cupcakes 197
Chocolate, Toffee and Banana Cupcakes 146
Chocolate-Chip Muffin Cupcakes 12
Chocolate-glazed Apricot and Lavender Cupcakes 163
Chocolate-Glazed Brownie Cupcakes 57
Chocolate-Glazed Chocolate Cupcakes 37
Chocolate-Glazed Coffee Cupcakes 40
Chocolate-Glazed Lavender Cupcakes 163
Chocolate-Glazed Mocha Cupcakes 40
Chocolate-Glazed Orange Cupcakes 37
Chocolate-Glazed Raspberry and Lavender Cupcakes 163
Choco-Latte Cupcakes 71
Choco-Orange Cinnamon Cupcakes 265
Choco-Vanilla Teaser Cupcakes 79
Christmas Buttercream Cupcakes 214
Christmas Tree Cupcakes 286
Chunk Muffin Cupcakes 30
Cigarillo and Smartie Cupcakes 194
Cinnamon Baby Shower Cupcakes 176
Cinnamon Cherry Buttercream Cupcakes 214
Cinnamon Cupcakes with Chocolate Buttercream 37
Cinnamon Rose Cupcakes 173
Citrus Glacé Icing for Cupcakes 193
Classic Strawberry Sprinkles Cupcakes 159
Cocoa, Mint and Raspberry Cupcakes 194
Coconut and Blueberry Star Cupcakes 109
Coconut and Ginger Buttercream Cupcakes 125
Coconut and Lemon Cream Cupcakes 188
Coconut and Lime Buttercream Cupcakes 217
Coconut and Mint Buttercream Cupcakes 125
Coconut and Orange Buttercream Cupcakes 23
Coconut and Orange Cream Cupcakes 188
Coconut and Pineapple Buttercream Cupcakes 217

Index

Coconut and Pineapple Pearl Cupcakes 114
Coconut Buttercream Cupcakes 23
Coconut Cupcakes with Rolled Icing 124
Coconut Moon and Star Cupcakes 227
Coconut Pearl Cupcakes 114
Coconut Rum Cupcakes 89
Coconut Rum Cupcakes 99
Coconut Star Cupcakes 109
Coconut, Mint and Bourbon Cupcakes 262
Coffee and Orange Flower Cupcakes 177
Coffee and Rose Water Cupcakes 149
Coffee and Toffee Cupcakes 146
Coffee and Vanilla Cupcakes 93
Coffee and White Chocolate Cupcakes 91
Coffee Cupcakes with Meringue Icing 35
Coffee Muffin Cupcakes 13
Coffee Pot Cupcakes 267
Coffee Pretzel Mania Cupcakes 256
Coffee Ruffle Cupcakes 175
Coffee Syrup Cream Cupcakes 147
Coffee Truffle Cupcakes 90
Coffee Walnut Cupcakes 87
Colourful Flower Cupcakes 110
Colourful Rose Cupcakes 110
Colours Cupcakes 273
Coming Up Roses Cupcakes 173
Cookie Monster Cupcakes 296
Courgette and Lemon Cupcakes 30
Crab and Caviar Cupcakes 244
Cream and Berry Cupcakes 197
Cream Cheese Frosting for Cupcakes 130
Cream Cheese Purple Cupcakes 95
Crème de Cacao Cupcakes 33
Crème Egg Cupcakes 261
Cricket Ball Cupcakes 295
Crimson Raspberry Cupcakes 100
Crown Cupcakes 280
Crushed Almond and Chocolate Cupcakes 90
Crushed Digestive Cupcakes 264
Crushed Malteser Cupcakes 258
Crystallised Ginger Cupcakes 189
Crystallised Rose Petal Cupcakes 143
Crystallised Violet Cupcakes 143
Cuddle Cupcakes 249
Cute Kitten Cupcakes 209

Dairy and Gluten-Free Party Cupcakes 187
Dairy-Free Buttercream for Cupcakes 173
Dairy-Free Chocolate and Rose Water Cupcakes 136
Dairy-Free Chocolate Buttercream for Cupcakes 173
Dairy-Free Chocolate Cupcakes 136
Dairy-Free Cupcakes 137
Dairy-Free Party Cupcakes 187
Dark and White Chocolate Cupcakes 128
Dark Chocolate Champagne Cupcakes 86
Dark Chocolate Chip Cupcakes 169
Dark Chocolate Delight Cupcakes 86
Dark Chocolate Dream Cupcakes 78
Date and Rum Cupcakes 89
Date and Walnut Cupcakes 49
Digestive Biscuit Cupcakes 98
Dog Basket Cupcakes 279
Double Chocolate and Banana Cupcakes 17
Double Chocolate and Mint Cupcakes 190
Double Chocolate Muffin Cupcakes 67
Double Chocolate Pearl Cupcakes 127
Double Chocolate Pillow Cupcakes 166
Double Chocolate Syrup Cupcakes 141
Double Mint Cupcakes 81
Double Peanut Butter Mini Cupcakes 55
Double Shot Cupcakes 91
Double Strawberry Muffin Cupcakes 139
Dove Cupcakes 293
Dragonfly Cupcakes 283
Dried Apricot and Almond Cupcakes 60
Dried Apricot Buttercream Cupcakes 185
Dried Cranberry and Almond Cupcakes 103
Dried Cranberry and Almond Cupcakes 52
Dried Fruit-Topped Cupcakes 53
Dried Sour Cherry and Almond Cupcakes 52
Dulce de Leche Cupcakes 23
Dundee Cupcakes 269

Earl Grey Cupcakes 69
Easter Basket Cupcakes 253
Easter Buttercream Cupcakes 261
Egg and Ketchup Cupcakes 219
Egg and Soldiers Cupcakes 219
Elderflower and Lemon Cupcakes 234
Elderflower Cupcakes 131
Elderflower Cupcakes 186
Elderflower-Scented Buttercream Cupcakes 242
E-Motions Cupcakes 206
Engagement Ring Cupcakes 295
Eton Mess Cupcakes 174

Fatless Cupcakes 61
Fennel and Coffee Syrup Cupcakes 147
Festive Cupcakes 270
Fig and Orange Cream Cheese Cupcakes 247
Fig and Lemon Cream Cheese Cupcakes 247
Filigree Swirl Cupcakes 276
Flower Garland Cupcakes 10
Flower Spiral Cupcakes 10
Flower Water Glacé Icing for Cupcakes 193
Flower-Iced Blueberry Cupcakes 179
Flower-Iced Raspberry Cupcakes 179
Flower-Iced Vanilla Cupcakes 151
Plain-Iced Vanilla Cupcakes 151
Fondant Cherry Cupcakes 284
Fondant Fancy Cupcakes 199
Fondant Flower Cupcakes 186
Fondant Heart Cupcakes 223
Fondant Hearts Cupcakes 276
Fondant Rose Cupcakes 183
Fondant Roses for Cupcakes 131
Fondant-Iced Cupcakes 199
Football Cupcakes 295
Forest Fruits Buttercream Cupcakes 145
Forest Fruits Buttercream Cupcakes 204
Forget-me-not Cupcakes 186
Framboise Cupcakes 177
Framboise Drizzle Cupcakes 80
French Fries and Ketchup Cupcakes 219
Fresh Apricot and Almond Cupcakes 60
Fresh Forest Fruits Buttercream Cupcakes 145
Frosted Chocolate Muffin Cupcakes 138
Frosted Double Chocolate Muffin Cupcakes 138
Fruit and Cream Cupcakes 182
Fruit and Nut Honey Cupcakes 269
Fruit Jelly Cupcakes 223
Fruit, Nut and Marzipan Cupcakes 269
Fruity Easter Buttercream Cupcakes 205
Funky Toadstool Cupcakes 250

Gel-Iced Mini Cupcakes 131
Getting Piggy Cupcakes 254
Giant Chocolate Cupcake 132
Giant Spotted Cupcake 132
Ginger and Lemon Cream Cheese Cupcakes 196
Ginger and Lime Cupcakes 15
Ginger and Marzipan Cupcakes 269
Ginger and Orange Cupcakes 99
Ginger Beer Cupcakes 218
Ginger Birthday Cupcakes 160
Ginger Cheesecake Cupcakes 196
Ginger Cream Cheese Cupcakes 196
Ginger Cream Cupcakes 99
Ginger Nut Cupcakes 221
Ginger Nut Cupcakes 76

Gingerbread Man Cupcakes 268
Glace Cherry Star Cupcakes 21
Glace Icing for Cupcakes 85
Glace-Iced Almond Mini Cupcakes 66
Glacé-Iced Amaretti Cupcakes 240
Glace-Iced Apple Muffin Cupcakes 148
Glacé-Iced Christmas Spice Cupcakes 221
Glacé-Iced Dairy-Free Cupcakes 162
Glace-Iced Gluten-Free Cupcakes 112
Glace-Iced Honey Cupcakes 135
Glace-Iced Lemon and Ginger Cupcakes 45
Glace-Iced Lemon Cupcakes 22
Glacé-Iced Lemon Dairy-Free Cupcakes 162
Glace-Iced Lemon Gluten-Free Cupcakes 112
Glace-Iced Lime and Ginger Cupcakes 45
Glace-Iced Muesli Muffin Cupcakes 150
Glace-Iced Oat Muffin Cupcakes 150
Glace-Iced Orange and Ginger Cupcakes 45
Glace-Iced Pear Muffin Cupcakes 148
Glace-Iced Pecan Cupcakes 41
Glacé-Iced Physalis Cupcakes 236
Glace-Iced Pistachio Mini Cupcakes 66
Glace-Iced Plain Cupcakes 50
Glacé-Iced Red Velvet Cupcakes 262
Glacé-Iced Rose Petal Cupcakes 189
Glace-Iced Vanilla Cupcakes 50
Glacé-Iced Violet Cupcakes 189
Glace-Iced Walnut Cupcakes 41
Glazed Fresh Cherry Mini Cupcakes 76
Glazed Preserved Cherry Mini Cupcakes 76
Glitter Magic Cupcakes 78
Gluten- and Dairy-Free Chocolate Cupcakes 55
Gluten Free Butterfly Cupcakes 248
Gluten-Free Chocolate Cupcakes 55
Gluten-Free Cupcakes 137
Gluten-Free Strawberry Cupcakes 248
Gold Nugget Buttercream Cupcakes 29
Gooseberry Curd Cupcakes 153
Gooseberry Jam Muffin Cupcakes 62
Graduation Cupcakes 288
Grape Cupcakes 259
Grapefruit and Gin Cream Cupcakes 170
Grapefruit and Gin Cream Cupcakes 171
Grapefruit and Lime Buttercream Cupcakes 126
Grapefruit Curd Cupcakes 27
Grated Chocolate and Vanilla Cupcakes 94
Greek Yoghurt Cupcakes 180
Green Emerald Cupcakes 294
Green Ribbon Cupcakes 274
Green Rose Cupcakes 115
Green Sugar Cupcakes 79
Greengage Jam Muffin Cupcakes 62
Grenadine Cream Cheese Cupcakes 156
Grenadine, Orange and Raspberry Cupcakes 144
Grenadine, Orange Chocolate Cupcakes 144

Half and Half Buttercream Cupcakes 230
Half and Half Cream Cupcakes 230
Half and Half Cupcakes 230
Halloween Cupcakes 286
Halloween Lantern Cupcakes 286
Handbag Cupcakes 279
Harlequin Cupcakes 275
Hazelnut and Dulce de Leche Cupcakes 231
Hazelnut Cream Cupcakes 140
Hazelnut Cupcakes with Rolled Icing 243
Hazelnut Latte Cupcakes 91
Heart Cream Cupcakes 228
Hedgehog Cupcakes 272
Hen Cupcakes 272
Hibiscus Cupcakes 151
Honey Buttercream Cupcakes 100
Honey Cream Cheese Cupcakes 135
Honey Nut Chocolate Cupcakes 144
Honey Nut Cupcakes 144
Honey Orange Cupcakes 257
Horlicks Cupcakes 70
Horseshoe Cupcakes 293
Hot Chocolate and Almond Cupcakes 44
Hot Chocolate Powder Cupcakes 34
Hot Dog Cupcakes 240
Hot Orange and Almond Cupcakes 44
Hot Toddy Mini Muffin Cupcakes 43
Hot Toddy Muffin Cupcakes 43
Humbug Cupcakes 187

Ice Cream Sundae Chocolate Cupcakes 229
Ice Mint Rose Cupcakes 8
Iced Mini Almond Muffin Cupcakes 47
Independence Day Cupcakes 204
Indigo Sugar Cupcakes 95
Irresistible Dark Chocolate Cupcakes 169

Jaffa Cake Cupcakes 215
Jammy Dodger Cupcakes 264
Jasmine Cupcakes 69
Jelly Baby Cupcakes 223
Jelly Baby Cupcakes 278
Jelly Mint Cupcakes 187
Jelly Tot Fondant Cupcakes 266
Jelly Tot Temptation Cupcakes 141
Jolly Rodger Cupcakes 271
Jubilee Cupcakes 205

Key Cupcakes 284
Kiwi and Ginger Cupcakes 97
Kiwi and Lemon Cream Muffin Cupcakes 237
Kiwi and Lime Cupcakes 97
Kiwi and Lime Muffin Cupcakes 237
Kiwi and Strawberry Muffin Cupcakes 239
Kiwi Cream Muffin Cupcakes 239
Kiwi Cupcakes 259
Knickerbocker Glory Cupcakes 229

Ladybird Cupcakes 281
Latte Butterfly Cupcakes 180
Lavender and Lemon Cupcakes 185
Lavender Buttercream Cupcakes 177
Lavender Buttercream Cupcakes 222
Lavender Cream Cheese Cupcakes 213
Lavender Pillow Cupcakes 185
Layered Flower Cupcakes 121
Leftover Easter Egg Cupcakes 261
Lemon and Blue Sweetie Cupcakes 18
Lemon and Caviar Cupcakes 244
Lemon and Lime Buttercream Cupcakes 126
Lemon and Lime Cupcakes 12
Lemon and Poppy Seed Muffin Cupcakes 236
Lemon and Poppy Seed Star Cupcakes 84
Lemon Baby Shower Cupcakes 132
Lemon Bonbon Cupcakes 31
Lemon Buttercream Cupcakes 207
Lemon Buttercream Star Cupcakes 218
Lemon Butterfly Cupcakes 180
Lemon Cream Cheese Cupcakes 26
Lemon Cupcakes with Rolled Icing 124
Lemon Curd Cream for Cupcakes 61
Lemon Curd-Iced Lemon Cupcakes 22
Lemon Drop Cupcakes 167
Lemon Fondant Flower Cupcakes 152
Lemon Jelly Bean Cupcakes 18
Lemon Meringue Cupcakes 289
Lemon Moon and Star Cupcakes 227
Lemon Muffin Cupcakes 63
Lemon Party Cupcakes 123
Lemon Pink Cupcakes 157
Dolly Mixture Daydream Cupcakes 158
Lemon Sorbet Cupcakes 122
Lemon, Lime and Chocolate Cupcakes 150
Lemon, Lime and Ginger Cupcakes 150

Index

Lemon, Lime and Orange Cupcakes 12
Lime and Chocolate Chip Cupcakes 101
Lime and Dulce de Leche Cupcakes 23
Lime and Ginger Cupcakes 263
Lime and Ginger Cupcakes 97
Lime and Ginger Jelly Bean Cupcakes 102
Lime and Mandarin Cupcakes 198
Lime and Mint Buttercream Cupcakes 215
Lime and Orange Buttercream Cupcakes 126
Lime and Rice Flour Muffin Cupcakes 56
Lime Buttercream Cupcakes 215
Lime Curd Cupcakes 27
Lime Fondant Flower Cupcakes 152
Lime Green Sugar Cupcakes 103
Lime Marmalade Cream Cupcakes 75
Limoncello Cupcakes 208
Lion Cupcakes 296
Liquorice Frosted Carrot Cupcakes 229
Liquorice Frosted Parsnip Cupcakes 229
Loganberry Dream Cupcakes 170
Lollipop Cupcakes 259
Love Hearts Cupcakes 250
Low-Fat Chocolate Cupcakes 61

Macchiato Cupcakes 93
Magenta Sprinkle Cupcakes 181
Malteser Mint Cupcakes 188
Mandarin Dream Cupcakes 198
Maple Pecan Cupcakes 198
Marmalade Bakewell Cupcakes 48
Marmalade Cream Cupcakes 75
Marsala Sultana Mini Cupcakes 53
Marshmallow and Orange Cupcakes 68
Marshmallow Muffin Cupcakes 231
Marzipan and Christmas Spice Cupcakes 221
Marzipan Butterfly Cupcakes 136
Marzipan Duck Cupcakes 136
Melting Centre Chocolate Cupcakes 52
Melting Centre Chocolate Orange Cupcakes 52
Milk and White Chocolate Cupcakes 128
Mini Almond Muffin Cupcakes 47
Mini Chestnut Cream Cupcakes 225
Chocolate Frosted Almond Cupcakes 226
Mini Chocolate and Blackberry Cupcakes 74
Mini Chocolate and Raspberry Cream Cupcakes 74
Mini Coconut Buttercream Cupcakes 69
Mini Coconut Cupcakes 69
Mini Maroons Glacé Cupcakes 225
Mini Muesli Muffin Cupcakes 253
Mini No-Bake Lemon Cheesecakes 50
Mini No-Bake Pomegranate Cheesecakes 50
Mini Orange and Blackberry Cream Cupcakes 74
Mini Peanut Butter Muffin Cupcakes 55
Mini Raisin Muffin Cupcakes 38
Mini Vanilla Muffin Cupcakes 38
Mini Wholemeal Cupcakes 39
Mini Wholemeal Raisin Cupcakes 39
Mint and Bailey's Cupcakes 193
Mint and Grated Chocolate Cupcakes 191
Mint and White Chocolate Cupcakes 267
Mint Choc Brownie Cream Cupcakes 77
Mint Chocolate Cross Cupcakes 208
Mint Cookie Cupcakes 262
Mint Julep Cupcakes 193
Mint Truffle Cupcakes 190
Minty Heart Cupcakes 267
Miss Piggy Cupcakes 249
Mocha Cupcakes 130
Mocha Cupcakes 175
Mochaccino Cupcakes 92
Molten Centre Chocolate Cherry Cupcakes 51
Molten Centre Chocolate Marmalade Cupcakes 51
Molten Centre White Chocolate and
Monogram Cupcakes 276
Mortar Board Cupcakes 288

Nautical Cupcakes 271
Nectarine Cupcakes 103
Neon Sprinkle Cupcakes 181
Nutella Layer Cupcakes 47
Nut-Topped Cupcakes 53
Nutty Cupcakes 287
Nutty Cupcakes with Glace Icing 28

Oat and Cream Cheese Cupcakes 46
Oat and Honey Cream Cheese Cupcakes 46
Oat and Honey Cream Cupcakes 220
Oat and Honey Muffin Cupcakes 224
Chilli Cream Cupcakes 225
Oat Cupcakes with Choc-Chip Buttercream 27
Oat Cupcakes with Granola Buttercream 27
Oat Muffin Cupcakes 224
Oaty Cream Cupcakes 220
Orange and Amaretti Cupcakes 240
Orange and Angelica Muffin Cupcakes 234
Orange and Chestnut Cream Cupcakes 18
Orange and Chestnut Cream Cupcakes 18
Orange and Chilli Cream Cupcakes 225
Orange and Cranberry Muffin Cupcakes 26
Orange and Glacé Cherry Muffin Cupcakes 234
Orange and Melon Cream Cupcakes 233
Orange and Nutella Layer Cupcakes 47
Orange and Nutella Mini Cupcakes 70
Orange and Nutella Mini Cupcakes 70
Orange and Physalis Cupcakes 100
Orange and Poppy Seed Muffin Cupcakes 236
Orange and Strawberry Muffin Cupcakes 142
Orange and Sultana Muffin Cupcakes 26
Orange and Violet Cupcakes 32
Orange Blossom Cupcakes 201
Orange Buttercream Cupcakes 207
Orange Cream Cheese Cupcakes 26
Orange Cream Cheese Muffin Cupcakes 190
Orange Drop Cupcakes 167
Orange Flower Cream Cupcakes 212
Orange Flower Cupcakes 112
Orange Flower Water Cupcakes 208
Orange Jelly Ring Cupcakes 257
Orange Jelly Sweet Cupcakes 31
Orange Muffin Cupcakes 63
Orange Party Cupcakes 123
Orange Sweetie Cupcakes 19
Orange Swirl Cupcakes 263
Orange, Chocolate and Vanilla Cupcakes 265
Oreo Cookie Cupcakes 215
Owl Cupcakes 291

Pansy Cream Cheese 245
Parmesan and Walnut Cupcakes 237
Parsnip and Chocolate Cream Cupcakes 161
Passion Fruit and Kiwi Cream Cupcakes 241
Passion Fruit Cream Cupcakes 241
Pasta and Peas Chocolate Cupcakes 228
Patchwork Cupcakes 275
Peach Syrup Cream Cheese Cupcakes 116
Peacock Feather Cupcakes 273
Peanut and Lime Buttercream Cupcakes 191
Peanut Brittle Cupcakes 98
Peanut Buttercream Cupcakes 191
Peanut Cupcakes 58
Peanut Popcorn Cupcakes 142
Peanut Truffle Cupcakes 198
Pear and Banana Blue Pearl Cupcakes 72
Pearls Cupcakes 282
Black Pearl Cupcakes 282
Peppermint Butterfly Cupcakes 113
Peppermint Cream Cheese Cupcakes 36
Peppermint Crisp Cupcakes 81
Peppermint Moon and Star Cupcakes 227
Peppermint Rose Cupcakes 8

Peppermint Sugar Cupcakes 191
Physalis and Lemon Cupcakes 236
Pillow Cupcakes 166
Pinecone Cupcakes 272
Pinecone Cupcakes 286
Pink and White Flag Cupcakes 94
Pink Baby Feet Cupcakes 290
Pink Bow Cupcakes 289
Pink Butterfly Cupcakes 171
Pink Champagne Cupcakes 275
Pink Crown Raspberry Cupcakes 80
Pink Flower Cupcakes 292
Pink Glitter Magic Cupcakes 78
Pink Grapefruit Cream Cupcakes 170
Pink Guitar Cupcakes 266
Pink Party Cupcakes 123
Pink Puppy Cupcakes 249
Pink Rose Cupcakes 100
Pink Velvet Cupcakes 294
Pink-Iced Orange Cupcakes 73
Pistachio and Rose Water Cupcakes 149
Pistachio and White Chocolate Cupcakes 209
Pistachio Buttercream Cupcakes 235
Pistachio Cream Cupcakes 140
Pistachio Cupcakes with Rolled Icing 243
Playing Card Cupcakes 223
Polka Dot Cupcakes 276
Pomegranate and Date Cupcakes 153
Pomegranate and Pistachio Cupcakes 216
Pomegranate Cream Cheese Cupcakes 153
Popcorn Cupcakes 142
Poppy Cream Cheese Cupcakes 245
Poppy Seed Cream Cheese Cupcakes 54
Prawn Cocktail Cupcakes 244
Presents Cupcakes 293
Pretty Flower Cupcakes 121
Pretzel Mania Cupcakes 256
Prune and Hazelnut Cupcakes 38
Prune and Orange Cupcakes 210
Prune and Walnut Cupcakes 49
Prune Cupcakes 210
Pumpkin and Cinnamon Cupcakes 165
Pumpkin and Clove Cream Cheese Cupcakes 165
Puppy Love Cupcakes 209
Purple Coconut Cupcakes 176

Rainbow Cupcakes 287
Rainbow Nut Muffin Cupcakes 16
Rainbow Raisin Muffin Cupcakes 16
Rainbow Sprinkle Muffin Cupcakes 16
Raspberry and Fig Muffin Cupcakes 44
Raspberry and Ginger Cupcakes 11
Raspberry and Lemon Cupcakes 67
Raspberry and Lime Cupcakes 14
Raspberry and Orange Cream Cheese Cupcakes 9
Raspberry and Redcurrant Cupcakes 124
Raspberry and Violet Buttercream Cupcakes 154
Raspberry Buttercream Cupcakes 154
Raspberry Butterfly Cupcakes 171
Raspberry Cream Cheese Cupcakes 9
Raspberry Curd Cupcakes 153
Raspberry Dream Cupcakes 170
Raspberry Greek Yoghurt Cupcakes 180
Raspberry Jelly Tot Cupcakes 92
Raspberry Mess Cupcakes 174
Raspberry Muffin Cupcakes 56
Raspberry Pig Cupcakes 254
Raspberry Rose and Pearl Cupcakes 120
Raspberry Rose Cream Cheese Cupcakes 122
Raspberry Smile Cupcakes 255
Raspberry Sorbet Cupcakes 122
Raspberry Sprinkles 159
Raspberry Surprise Cupcakes 164
Raspberry Syrup Cream Cheese Cupcakes 128
Raspberry Tot Temptation 141
Raspberry Truffle Cupcakes 178
Raspberry Violet Cream Cheese Cupcakes 122
Raspberry Yoghurt Cupcakes 96
Red and Blue Cupcakes 179
Red and Green Buttercream Cupcakes 238
Red and Green Christmas Cupcakes 257
Red Sugar Cupcakes 79
Red Velvet Cupcakes 119
Red Velvet Heart Flower Cupcakes 294
Red Wine Gum Cupcakes 92
Red, White and Blue Cupcakes 96
Redcurrant and Ginger Cupcakes 11
Redcurrant and Pistachio Cupcakes 216
Redcurrant Truffle Cupcakes 80
Rhubarb Crumble Muffin Cupcakes 11
Rhubarb Jam Muffin Cupcakes 62
Rhubarb Rose Cupcakes 162
Rhubarb Syrup Cream Cheese Cupcakes 116
Rice Flour Muffin Cupcakes 56
Rich Chocolate Cream Cupcakes 135
Ring Cupcakes 288
Rocky Road Muffin Cupcakes 145
Rocky Road Topped Muffin Cupcakes 145
Root Beer Cupcakes 218
Roquefort and Walnut Cupcakes 237
Rose and Pearl Cupcakes 107
Rose Cream Cheese Cupcakes 213
Rose Cupcakes 106
Rum and Raisin Mini Cupcakes 53
Rusk Cupcakes 76

Sammy Snake Cupcakes 248
Satchel Cupcakes 279
Seagull Cupcakes 292
Sesame Cream Cheese Cupcakes 54
Sheep Cupcakes 270
Shooting Star Cupcakes 292
Silver Nugget Buttercream Cupcakes 29
Silver Snowflake Cupcakes 285
Simple Chocolate Cupcakes 21
Simple Double Chocolate Cupcakes 21
Simple Iced Wedding Muffin Cupcakes142
Simple Vanilla Cupcakes 33
Smartie Circus Cupcakes 258
Smartie Truffle Cupcakes 194
Smarties Buttercream Cupcakes 184
Smiley Cupcakes 206
Smoked Eel and Dill Cupcakes 232
Smoked Mackerel and Lemon Cupcakes 232
Smoked Salmon and Caviar Cupcakes 233
Smoked Salmon Cupcakes with Salmon Roe 233
Softmint and Cocoa Cupcakes 188
Sour Cream and Raspberry Cupcakes 95
Sour Cream Cupcakes 95
Sparklers Cupcakes 282
Speculoos Cupcakes 221
Spiced Apple Cupcakes 211
Spiced Blackberry Buttercream Cupcakes 245
Spiced Blueberry Buttercream Cupcakes 214
Spiced Cherry Buttercream Cupcakes 217
Spiced Fondant Flower Cupcakes 152
Spiced Gluten-Free Cupcakes 137
Spiced Mini Wholemeal Cupcakes 39
Spiced Raspberry Buttercream Cupcakes 245
Spiced Wholemeal Baby Shower Cupcakes 133
Spinach and Bacon Cupcakes 297
Spinach and Mushroom Cupcakes 297
Spinach and Onion Cupcakes 297
Spotty Chocolate Buttercream Cupcakes 29
Spring Cupcakes 234
Squidgy Chocolate Mini Cupcakes 63
Squidgy Chocolate Orange Mini Cupcakes 72
Squidgy Milk Chocolate Mini Cupcakes 72
Squidgy White Chocolate Mini Cupcakes 63
St Clements Cupcakes 201

Index

St George's Day Cupcakes 205
St Patrick's Day Cupcakes 226
St Patrick's Day Cupcakes 226
Star Cream Cupcakes 228
Strawberry and Apple Cupcakes 238
Strawberry and Lime Cupcakes 14
Strawberry and Orange Buttercream 127
Strawberry and Orange Cupcakes 118
Strawberry and Rose Cupcakes 159
Strawberry and Vanilla Cupcakes 118
Strawberry Buttercream Heart Cupcakes 218
Strawberry Cream Cheese Cupcakes 159
Strawberry Cupcakes 59
Strawberry Cupcakes with Rolled Icing 108
Strawberry Cupcakes with Vanilla Buttercream 111
Strawberry Frosted Muffin Cupcakes 139
Strawberry Glace-Iced Lemon Muffin Cupcakes 107
Strawberry Glace-Iced Orange Cupcakes 107
Strawberry Heart Chocolate Cupcakes 182
Strawberry Heart Cupcakes 117
Strawberry Jam Cupcakes 83
Strawberry Jam Frosted Cupcakes 84
Strawberry Jam Lattice Cupcakes 106
Strawberry Jam Spiral Cupcakes 106
Strawberry Jam-filled Cupcakes 168
Strawberry Liquorice Cupcakes 264
Strawberry Piglet Cupcakes 246
Strawberry Ripple Cupcakes 157
Strawberry Rose and Pearl Cupcakes 120
Strawberry Surprise Cupcakes 164
Strawberry Sweetheart Cupcakes 251
Strawberry Sweetie Cupcakes 19
Strawberry Syrup Cream Cheese Cupcakes 128
Sugar Rose Cupcakes 201
Sugared Blueberry Cupcakes 174
Sugared Redcurrant Cupcakes 174
Sultana Cupcakes with Glace Icing 28
Summer Fruit Crème Fraiche Cupcakes 85
Sunflower Seed Cream Cheese Cupcakes 54
Sunshine Cupcakes 206
Sweet Dreams Cupcakes 68
Sweet Tooth Cupcakes 158
Sweet Treats Cupcakes 252
Sweetheart Cupcakes 251
Sweetie Heart Cupcakes 249
Sweeties Cupcakes 278

Tayberry Truffle Cupcakes 178
Thunder and Lightning Cupcakes 168
Tiara Cupcakes 280
Tiger Moth Cupcakes 283
Tiger Print Cupcakes 268
Treacle Cream Cheese Cupcakes 168
Triple Chocolate Chunk Cupcakes 113
Triple Chocolate Cream Cupcakes 135
Triple Chocolate Cupcakes 165
Triple Chocolate Muffin Cupcakes 67
Two Chocolate Butterfly Cupcakes 90
Two Chocolate Cupcakes 166

Vanilla & Blackberry Buttercream Cupcakes 115
Vanilla and Chocolate Cigarillo Cupcakes 175
Vanilla and Strawberry Cupcakes 127
Vanilla Chocolate Cupcakes 165
Vanilla Cream Cheese Cupcakes 36
Vanilla Cream Raspberry Cupcakes 82
Vanilla Cupcakes with Butterscotch Buttercream 133
Vanilla Cupcakes with Chocolate Ganache 34
Vanilla Cupcakes with Chocolate Topping 37
Vanilla Cupcakes with Cinnamon Buttercream 116
Vanilla Cupcakes with Coffee Buttercream 116
Vanilla Cupcakes with Glace Icing 28
Vanilla Cupcakes with Grenadine Buttercream 115
Vanilla Cupcakes with Meringue Icing 35
Vanilla Cupcakes with Passion Fruit Buttercream 242
Vanilla Cupcakes with Peach Buttercream 133
Vanilla Cupcakes with Pineapple Buttercream 242
Vanilla Cupcakes with Raspberry Buttercream 204
Vanilla Cupcakes with Rolled Icing 108
Vanilla Cupcakes with Vanilla Buttercream 111
Vanilla Cupcakes with White Chocolate Ganache 34
Vanilla Goat's Curd Cupcakes 36
Vanilla Ice Cream Cupcakes 111
Vanilla Piglet Cupcakes 246
Vanilla Pod Cupcakes 109
Vanilla Rose Cupcakes 109
Vanilla Sprinkles Cupcakes 161
Very Blackberry Cupcakes 88
Very Blueberry Cupcakes 88
Very Raspberry Cupcakes 88
Violet and Cinnamon Cupcakes 129
Violet and Clementine Buttercream Cupcakes 222
Violet and Ginger Cupcakes 129
Violet and Lemon Cream Cheese Cupcakes 64
Violet and Lemon Cupcakes 129
Violet and Orange Cream Cheese Cupcakes 64
Violet and Orange Cream Cheese Cupcakes 64
Violet Buttercream Cupcakes 222
Violet Cream Cupcakes 212
Violet Garland Cupcakes 10
Violet Lemon Jelly Bean Cupcakes 184
Violet Meringue Cupcakes 184
Violet Sprinkle Cupcakes 181
Violet Tip Cupcakes 176

Walnut Cream Cupcakes 140
Walnut Whip Cupcakes 87
Watercress and Bacon Cupcakes 297
Wedding Ring Cupcakes 295
White Almond Cupcakes 183
White and Dark Marbled Muffin Cupcakes 14
White and Milk Chocolate Cupcakes 71
White Choc Chip Dream Cupcakes 78
White Choc Easter Cupcakes 285
Vintage Rose Cupcakes 285
White Choc Raspberry Drizzle Cupcakes 96
White Choc Raspberry Liquorice Cupcake 89
White Chocolate and Black Liquorice Cupcakes 89
White Chocolate and Orange Cream
Cheese Cupcakes 210
White Chocolate and Orange Puddle Cupcakes 24
White Chocolate Blueberry Cupcakes 273
White Chocolate Champagne Cupcakes 86
White Chocolate Chip Muffin Cupcakes 12
White Chocolate Chip Sprinkle Cupcakes 125
White Chocolate Chunk Muffin Cupcakes 42
White Chocolate Cream Cheese Cupcakes 210
White Chocolate Crispy Cupcakes 148
White Chocolate Cupcakes 197
White Chocolate Cupcakes 59
White Chocolate Delight Cupcakes 86
White Chocolate Frosted Almond Cupcakes 226
White Chocolate Lemon Muffin Cupcakes 195
White Chocolate Muffin Cupcakes 195
White Chocolate Orange Muffin Cupcakes 195
White Chocolate Puddle Cupcakes 24
White Chocolate Raspberry Cupcakes 273
White Chocolate Sprinkle Cupcakes 125
White Chocolate-Topped Cupcakes 197
White Rose Cupcakes 115
White Rose Cupcakes 151
White-Choc Coffee Cupcakes 93
Wholemeal Baby Shower Cupcakes 133
Wholemeal Chocolate Chunk Muffin Cupcakes 164
Wholemeal Chocolate Muffin Cupcakes 164
Wholemeal Raspberry Muffin Cupcakes 56
Wine Gum Cupcakes 31

Yellow Ribbon Cupcakes 274